THE —
AMERICAN POLITICAL SYSTEM

★ An Owner's Manual ★

JOSEPH A. MELUSKY
SAINT FRANCIS COLLEGE (PA)

Mc Graw Hill

Boston   Burr Ridge, IL   Dubuque, IA   Madison, WI   New York   San Francisco   St. Louis
Bangkok   Bogotá   Caracas   Lisbon   London   Madrid
Mexico City   Milan   New Delhi   Seoul   Singapore   Sydney   Taipei   Toronto

McGraw-Hill Higher Education

A Division of The **McGraw-Hill** Companies

THE AMERICAN POLITICAL SYSTEM: AN OWNER'S MANUAL

This book is printed on acid-free paper.

1 2 3 4 5 6 7 8 9 0 DOC/DOC 0 9 8 7 6 5 4 3 2 1 0

ISBN 0-697-39592-8

Editorial director: *Jane E. Vaicunas*
Sponsoring editor: *Monica Eckman*
Developmental editor: *Hannah Glover*
Senior marketing manager: *Suzanne Daghlian*
Editing associate: *Joyce Watters*
Senior production supervisor: *Sandra Hahn*
Designer: *Gino Cieslik*
Photo research coordinator: *John C. Leland*
Supplement coordinator: *Tammy Juran*
Compositor: *Shepherd, Inc.*
Typeface: *10/12 Slimbach Book*
Printer: *R. R. Donnelley & Sons Company/Crawfordsville, IN*

Cover design: *Gino Cieslik*
Interior design: *Kay Fulton*
Cover illustrator: *Kirk Caldwell*
Photo research: *Toni Michaels Picture Research and Editing*

Library of Congress Cataloging-in-Publication Data

Melusky, Joseph Anthony.
    The American political system : an owner's manual / Joseph
Melusky.—1st ed.
    p.   cm.
    Includes index.
    ISBN 0-697-39592-8
    1. United States—Politics and government.   I. Title.
JK274.M525   2000
320.473—dc21   99-29137
                                                          CIP

www.mhhe.com

To my children, Michael and Jessica,

to my wife, Marie,

to my mom, Eleanor,

and to the memory of my dad, George

Acknowledgements

First, I want to acknowledge my students, whose questions and comments over the years have helped shape this project. Thanks to Linda A. Kline at Saint Francis College for her secretarial assistance.

I also want to express my appreciation to all the reviewers who took the time to read drafts of this work and to offer suggestions. Their recommendations were invaluable.

Dr. John David Rausch, Jr.	West Texas A&M University
Dr. Tom Caiazzo	Collin Community College
Professor Peter Howse	American River College
Professor John Buckley	Orange Coast College
Professor William J. Zogby	Mowhawk Valley Community College
Dr. Paul D. Davis	Truckee Meadows Community College
Professor Jim Mayes	Florida Community College – Jacksonville
Dr. William E. Kelly	Auburn University
Dr. Stephen Snow	Wagner College
Dr. Robert Spitzer	SUNY Cortland
Dr. Herbert E. Gooch III	California Lutheran University
Dr. John Cavanaugh	University of South Carolina
Dr. Carl E. Mecham	SUNY Oneonta
Dr. Kennith G. Hunter	University of Tennessee at Chattanooga
Dr. Ted Rueter	University of Texas at Brownsville
Dr. John S. Robey	Texas Southmost College

Thanks also go to Scott Spoolman, an editor who initially saw promise in this book, and to all the people at McGraw-Hill who worked to make this book a success, including Suzanne Daghlian and Lyn Uhl. Thanks to Toni Michaels for her help in obtaining photos. I would also like to extend my gratitude to the Project Manager, Joyce Watters, Designer, Gino Cieshik and Cover Artist, Kirk Caldwell, who each contributed to the production of the final product. Special thanks are due Hannah Glover, whose attention to detail and editorial assistance were crucial. Finally, thanks to my editor, Monica Eckman for her encouragement and guidance. Her personal commitment to this project made me feel that I was working on something important.

Joseph A. Melusky

Contents

part 1 The Political System

part 2 **Popular Control—
The Accountability of Leaders
to the People**

part 3 Governmental Institutions

7 Congress   150

Conclusions 258

Appendix 266

Endnotes 314

Index 363

Warranty Message

Congratulations on being a citizen/owner of the American political system! Your system is covered by a lifetime warranty. However, some routine maintenance is required.

•• Never leave this system unattended. Pay attention to the actions of the public officials who operate the political machinery on your behalf.

•• This system requires close supervision. Provide public officials with instructions, notify them of your displeasure, and take corrective measures on election day and at other times if necessary.

•• Never use this system while drowsy or while under the influence of drugs or alcohol.

•• Use this system only for its intended purposes as described in this manual. Please read this manual carefully for information about how this system operates and how it was designed to operate.

•• This system is a democratic one. It will not operate properly if you "unplug" it through neglect. (To paraphrase Benjamin Franklin, "It's a [democracy], if you can keep it.")

**Failure to read the owner's manual
will result in less-than-satisfactory performance.**

**FAILURE TO SUPPLY ROUTINE MAINTENANCE
WILL VOID THE WARRANTY.**

Introduction: The Citizen as Sovereign

Democracy is commonly defined as "government by the people." The Preamble to the United States Constitution begins with the words, "We the people of the United States . . . " Yet **direct** democracy is not feasible in a country as large as the United States. "The people" do not directly participate in their own governance. It is physically impossible for everyone to participate in governmental decision making.[1] An **indirect** democracy or a **"republic"** remains a possibility.

It is fair to say that political elites, not the mass public, operate all political systems. As Harold Lasswell said, "Government is always government by the few."[2] This condition does not render democracy impossible: "[A] society may be democratic and express itself through a small leadership. The key question turns on **accountability**."[3] This book examines ways in which the masses hold political leaders accountable and influence them. In the process we will consider the accuracy of describing the American political system as a "democratic" one.

Elected officials and civil servants. Congresspeople and presidents. Judges and bureaucrats. They do not own the American political system; the American people do. That is to say, *you* do. Public officials work for you. You can retain their services, or you can fire them. You are the ultimate source of all legitimate political authority. In short you are sovereign.

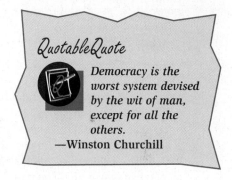

QuotableQuote

Democracy is the worst system devised by the wit of man, except for all the others.
—**Winston Churchill**

QuotableQuote

Government is too big and important to be left to the politicians.
—**Chester Bowles**

Sovereignty refers to "autonomous, absolute political and military power embodied in a ruler or governmental body."[4] **Popular sovereignty** is a keystone principle in democratic thought. It means that in a democracy, "absolute power" comes from the *people* who permit public officials to operate the machinery of government on their behalf. These sovereign people reserve the right to remove control from public officials who disappoint them. In other words, such officials remain accountable to the public.

About This Book

The subtitle of this book reflects its emphasis on popular sovereignty and citizenship. If you own an automobile and expect it to operate properly, you should familiarize yourself with the owner's manual. You should understand how the car works and how to maintain it. Of course, you do not have to do all the work yourself. You can hire a mechanic to service your vehicle. But you should know about maintenance schedules, what it means when your oil light goes on, and when to take the car into a service station. If you fail in these responsibilities, you will not have that car for long. Similarly, citizens should learn about their political system. They should pay attention, notice, and take action when "warning lights" go on. This brief book is designed to function as an owner's manual. With any luck, it will be shorter—and more comprehensible—than the owner's manuals accompanying some automobiles.[5]

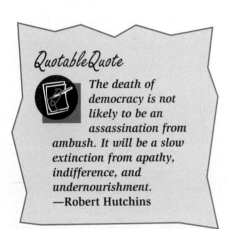

QuotableQuote

The death of democracy is not likely to be an assassination from ambush. It will be a slow extinction from apathy, indifference, and undernourishment.
—Robert Hutchins

I hope that this book avoids either a liberal or conservative slant. Reach your own conclusions; don't adopt mine. The book does have a bias, however. Its premise is that the people should take an interest in political affairs, should keep an eye on public officials, and should participate in their own governance. This premise does not mean that citizens should be unquestioning cheerleaders for the political system. Skepticism is healthy. It does not make any difference to me whether you favor Democrats or Republicans or whether you take liberal or conservative positions on the issues. It matters to all of us, however, that you participate in your own fashion.

In addition to its emphasis on popular sovereignty, this book has several distinctive features. First, the political system is large and potentially confusing. To avoid becoming lost, we need a map. The **systems framework** serves this purpose and is used to organize much of our information. It highlights ways in which parts of the system relate to other parts; ways in which the American political system relates to other political systems; and ways in which the political system relates to economic, social, and other kinds of systems.

Second, this book argues that the rules of the political game are not neutral. They encourage certain outcomes and inhibit others. Rules do not determine all political behavior, but they do matter. If you want to play any game effectively, you should understand the rules. The same is true of the game of politics and its citizen-players. Do not become overly reliant on lawyers and other experts to read the rules for you. We're talking about politics here, not neurosurgery. You certainly can handle this.

Third, this book emphasizes the **theoretical, historical,** and **constitutional underpinnings** of the American political system. Why? You are not merely studying current events. Awareness of some of the early controversies and debates that forged this political system can help you place contemporary issues into a broader context. Why does the government act so slowly? Why do we have to pay taxes? Why don't we do more to fight terrorists? Why do we have so many laws? These questions are not new. Earlier generations grappled with them, and future ones will face them too. Experiences and ideas from our past can frame and illuminate our discussions today.

Fourth, the book is irreverent.[6] It draws heavily from **popular culture** to explain political developments and concepts. Examples are drawn from movies, television, sports, music, comedy, the headlines, and elsewhere. If an anecdote can assist in illustrating a point, I will use it even if its relationship to political science

QuotableQuote

What are lawyers really? To me a lawyer is basically the person that knows the rules of the country. We're all throwing the dice, playing the game, moving our pieces around the board, but if there's a problem, the lawyer is the only person that has actually read the inside of the top of the box.
—**Jerry Seinfeld**

is not immediately apparent. Some of my examples of governmental foul-ups may seem cynical. That is not my intention. My criticisms of political actors are not mean-spirited. I confess to several biases. I have faith in the good sense and common decency of the American people. I also believe that most public officials are dedicated, well-intentioned, and motivated by a desire to serve the public, popular opinion to the contrary notwithstanding. Sometimes we get lazy and pay less attention to political affairs than we should. Sometimes public officials take shortcuts, do selfish things they think they can get away with, and make poor decisions. Sometimes programs that look good on paper fall apart when we try to put them into practice. Pretending that our system is perfect is not wise. There is nothing cynical about acknowledging shortcomings on the part of the system, public officials, and citizens. We have to recognize problems before we can do anything about them. And when we hear that a state road crew paved over a deer instead of moving it, maybe we should just shake our heads and laugh.

Fifth, the book features **"Something to Think About"** boxes. Here I will step back, tap you on the shoulder, direct you to a headline or some other point of interest, and ask you to give it some thought. **"Quotable Quotes"** are sprinkled liberally throughout the text. Quotes are included if they are relevant, insightful, and/or amusing. Key terms and actors are highlighted in **boldface** print.

Sixth, the book includes an appendix that contains some important **documents** and carefully edited selections from the *Federalist Papers*. Exposure to such **primary source materials** gives you a chance to form your own opinions without relying exclusively on some textbook author to tell you "what the framers really meant."[7]

Finally, this book is designed to provide students in introductory American government courses with a brief, readable, and solid text. It provides nuts-and-bolts information in a straightforward fashion. I hope it will be regarded as a teaching and learning book that students will be comfortable reading and instructors will be confident assigning; it is not meant to be a glossy reference book that sits on students' shelves until the end-of-semester used-book sales.

A Note to Students

This course is the first political science course for many of you. In most cases it will be your only political science course. Your instructor knows this too. That is precisely why this course is so important and why I hope this book helps you to make sense of the political system.

You will notice that I sometimes write in the first and second person instead of the more customary third person. Why? I am attempting to engage you in a "conversation" by way of the printed page. You will also notice that my treatment of the subject matter is occasionally, to use that word again, irreverent. I hope you will pardon these informalities. If departing from stylistic conventions on occasion helps us to communicate more effectively, let's do it. There is no regulation in *The Professional Political Scientist's Handbook* that requires political conversations to be stilted and starched.[8]

A Note to Instructors

I tried to develop a book that is brief, readable, and solid. I wanted the book to be brief so you could supplement the text with outside readings of your own choosing without making the reading load too burdensome for students. I wanted it to be readable so students would read it (obviously), understand it, and even enjoy it. I wanted it to be solid so you could be confident that your students would gain a sound conceptual foundation from the book. These three objectives necessitated some trade-offs.

My efforts to make the book readable and accessible led to the book's informal tone and to assorted simplifications. My "systems lite" approach to systems analysis is just one of the more obvious examples.[9] I have tried to keep things relatively simple without making them simplistic.

My attempts to make the book simultaneously brief and solid led to some difficult choices. For example, you will notice the absence of a full chapter on public policy. Although I included "minichapter" for the convenience of instructors who cover this topic in class, I did not include a policy case study. Such case studies can become dated rather quickly, and many instructors prefer to select their own cases anyway. Further, I sometimes consolidated much material into a single chapter. In such cases I relied heavily on extended content endnotes to amplify the text. Brevity is important, but so is accuracy. I leave it to you to decide how much emphasis to place on such elaborations.

Ancillary Package

Please visit the Internet site devoted to this book, which offers up-to-date and current information, exercises, simulations, a photo gallery, video clips, and an historical speech archive and further resources for students and professors alike, at www.mhhe.com/melusky. For instructors, there is also a print version of the IM available (007-229307-1) and the McGraw-Hill American Government Video Library series, created by Baker-Losco Multimedia to enhance course lectures and presentations.

THE
AMERICAN POLITICAL SYSTEM

The Political System

About This Section

This section introduces the American political system. Later sections provide more detailed "operating instructions" on how the political system works.

chapter 1 — Politics, the Political System, and You

Presents several definitions of "politics" and explains why we call our political machinery a "system." It also describes **your** role in a democratic political system and offers some reasons why you should take an active interest in political affairs.

chapter 2 — Foundations of the American Political System

Provides some history and theory to help you place more contemporary political developments into their proper context. The chapter discusses the influence of social contract theorists on the founders of the American political system. It demonstrates that many of the issues they debated hundreds of years ago— security versus liberty and equality versus freedom, to cite a few—continue to challenge us today. The chapter considers the debate over the writing and ratification of the Constitution and suggests why it came out the way that it did.

chapter 3 — Constitutional Rights and Liberties

Points out that our Constitution is relatively brief, was written more than two hundred years ago, and remains viable because many of its provisions are so open-ended that they can be reinterpreted as times change. The chapter then "walks" through various power-granting and power-limiting provisions to illustrate this point.

part

1

Politics, the Political System, and You

Why Study Politics?

It has been said that the American educational system is in trouble, that it is failing to prepare students for life after college. Students are criticized for preferring easy courses offered at convenient times. Compared to their counterparts in other nations, American college graduates have little understanding of the sciences, arts, humanities, mathematics, politics, and world affairs. Their communication skills are deteriorating.

Their sense of their own history is slight. All in all, they are poorly prepared for the demands of citizenship.

Recent college freshmen are less interested in political issues and affairs than any previous entering classes. UCLA's Higher Education Research Institute conducts an annual freshman survey. The thirty-third annual survey, taken in 1998, revealed that students' commitment to "keeping up with political affairs" as an important life goal dropped to an all-time low of 25.9 percent. This result compares to a record high of 57.8 percent in 1966. As recently as 1990, political awareness was important to 42.4 percent of freshmen. Reacting to a previous survey, Alexander Astin, then the project's director and a professor at UCLA's Graduate School of Education and Information Studies said, "[t]his continuing erosion of students' political interest and engagement should be a red flag to all of us who believe in the democratic process."[1]

You may or may not be alarmed by any of the above observations. Let's consider for a few moments why you *should* take an interest in political affairs.

First of all, there is a dream at stake here, a dream that envisions the use of information about the past and present to predict and even shape the future. It involves developing the ability to predict the likely consequences of competing policy proposals. The new Speaker of the House announces a sweeping agenda to reform welfare; curb entitlement programs; limit taxes; abolish some government departments and agencies; ease regulations on businesses, nursing homes, livestock grazing, and endangered species; and a host of additional proposals designed to reduce the budget deficit and produce economic prosperity. The Senate majority leader has mixed feelings about the proposals. Conservative radio talk show personalities enthusiastically endorse the Speaker's plans. The president calls a press conference and claims that enactment of the Speaker's agenda would be calamitous for the nation. Health care spokespersons worry aloud about young and elderly Americans receiving inadequate care. Environmental groups protest the proposals. Large city newspapers editorialize that inner-city residents will grow desperate and angry as they deal with benefit cuts.

What is an American citizen to do? How can we evaluate these widely—even wildly—varying predictions sensibly? Who is right? How can we expend our limited resources efficiently and compassionately? How can we achieve desirable outcomes? Why should we care about and study politics? We study politics to acquire information that we can use to solve problems and achieve goals. We study politics not simply to acquire knowledge for its own sake, but to gain knowledge needed to improve the human condition. Admiral Rickover once predicted that "we're going to blow ourselves up." We study politics to prevent this prophecy from coming true.

Any other reasons? Try this one. The American political system may be seriously flawed. Gridlock. Scandals. A spiraling national

QuotableQuote

It is simply untrue that all our institutions are evil, that all adults are unsympathetic, that all politicians are mere opportunists, that all aspects of university life are corrupt. Having discovered an illness, it's not terribly useful to prescribe death as a cure.
—George McGovern

debt. Negative advertising. Rising campaign costs. Low voter turnout. The list goes on. However, you cannot be intelligently critical of the political system until you understand how the system was designed to operate and the goals it was designed to accomplish. Uninformed cynicism is easy, personally comforting, and counterproductive; informed skepticism is useful, productive, and democratic.

Some writers who view the masses in a negative light see political apathy, inactivism, and withdrawal as *good* things in that they contribute to the stability of the system. Perhaps you have heard the story about the pollster who asked this question: "In your opinion, is the biggest problem facing this country ignorance or apathy?" The respondent replied, "I don't know, and I don't care." Those who criticize the capabilities of American citizens agree that most people know little about politics. And for precisely that reason, the same critics maintain that it is fortunate that most people do not *care* much about politics. If they did care more, they would *disrupt* the system with their ignorance. As such, the argument continues, the viability of American democracy depends on the vigilance of educated elites and the continued apathy of the mass public.

Is this the picture that comes into your mind when you think about a "democratic" system? The classical theorists believed that ideal democratic citizens were not ignorantly supportive of their government. Rather, the ideal citizenry consisted of informed and active skeptics who forced public officials to account for their actions. The "best" ideas and policies were expected to emerge from a dynamic clash of informed opposing opinions. Democracy requires an informed public. The democratic citizen has **responsibilities** as well as rights. If you think that a democratic political system is worth having, then it is your responsibility to pay attention and participate.

QuotableQuote

A silent majority and government by the people are incompatible.
—Tom Hayden

Thomas Jefferson thought the nation should invest heavily in its educational system because democracy depends on informed and active citizens. He saw education as the means for preparing citizens for democratic participation.

> I know of no safe depository of the ultimate powers of the society but the people themselves. . . . If we think them not enlightened enough to exercise their control with a wholesome discretion, the remedy is not to take it from them, but to inform their discretion by education.[2]

Perhaps even more familiar, and just as relevant, is his comment, "If a nation expects to be ignorant and free . . . it expects what never was and never will be."[3]

James Madison also thought that it was important for citizens to take an active interest in political affairs. In his words, "Knowledge will forever govern ignorance and a people that mean to be their own governors must arm themselves with the power that knowledge brings."[4]

A more recent report from the Carnegie Foundation for the Advancement of Teaching said that

> The most critical demand is to restore to higher education its original purpose of preparing graduates for a life of involved and committed citizenship. . . . If there

is a crisis in education in the United States today, it is less that test scores have declined than it is that we have failed to provide the education for citizenship which is still the most significant responsibility of the nation's schools and colleges. . . . This nation began with a conviction at once deceptively simple and profound, that for democracy to work, education is essential. . . . The advancement of civic learning, therefore, must become higher education's most central goal.[5]

Writing about campus discourse on curricular reform and the democratic purposes of general education, David Hiley observed:

No matter how successful we are at designing a curriculum, developing course descriptions, implementing changes, reallocating resources, reforming pedagogy, and assessing outcomes, if we cannot prepare students who can participate meaningfully in democratic deliberation about important issues, and if we cannot do so in ways that preserve the democratic institutions that make our activity possible, we will have failed.[6]

In the same issue of the Association of American Colleges and Universities' publication, *Liberal Education,* Bruce Jennings, James Lindemann Naelson, and Erik Parens said that "[i]f democratic institutions are to work, they require citizens who are reflective and self conscious about their civic responsibilities."[7]

Any other reasons to pay attention to politics? The concept of **anticipated reactions** comes to mind. If people are attentive and informed, elected officials must watch their step. They know that if they anger voters, they will be punished for their offenses. The problem is that people are not as universally attentive and informed as they would be in some utopian democratic state. Many citizens are bored by political activities. Public inattentiveness gives politicians freedom to wheel and deal without close scrutiny. But public officials know that if they do something extremely unpopular or scandalous, voters might wake up and remove them from office. As such officials try to **anticipate** how voters would **react** if they found out what the public officials did. In this way, even though most constituents may not be paying close attention, elected officials still have an incentive to be careful. The point is that the more attentive you are, the more control you have over your elected representatives.

QuotableQuote

The price of liberty is eternal vigilance.
—John Stuart Mill

Another argument? Consider this. People sometimes tell me that they are "not interested in politics." When I get over my initial shock, I tell them that although they might have no subjective interest in politics, they do have a very real objective stake in the political system.

What is your stake? Imagine you are sitting at home minding your own business. You are taking a break from doing some reading for your favorite course (no doubt, that would be political science) and watching a rerun of a really good episode of *Friends.* You are at peace with the universe. There is a knock at your door. You try to ignore it, but the knocking grows more persistent. You reluctantly turn off the television and make your way to the door. Standing there is a middle-aged, white man wearing a navy blue suit, a white shirt, and a red tie. You hope he will go away. He looks you in the eye, firmly shakes your hand, and begins to speak. He says, "Hi. I'm your neighbor. I have the authority to take away 28 percent of all the money you earn this year. I can ration your gasoline. I can see to it that a new exit ramp from the turnpike runs right through your front yard. I can take away your student loan and your federal work study job. I can send you halfway around the world, put you in a uniform, place a weapon in your hands, and make you use it against some people you have never even heard of. Just thought I would stop by and introduce myself. See you around." He leaves. You are speechless. Do you still have no interest in this man? Are you wondering who he really is? You just met your congressman. Whether you find him interesting or not, you do have an objective interest or stake in his actions. He and other public officials at various levels of the government can affect you in direct and profound ways.

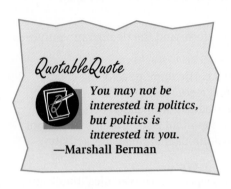

QuotableQuote

You may not be interested in politics, but politics is interested in you.
—**Marshall Berman**

Anything else? Consider an undergraduate who enjoys following politics, who is thinking about majoring in political science, but who is worried about job prospects. What can you **do** with a degree in political science? If you major in accounting, you can become an accountant. If you major in nursing, you can become a nurse. If you major in engineering, you can become an engineer. But if you major in political science, do you have to get a Ph.D. and become a political scientist (exciting though that prospect may seem)? Not necessarily. Some people say that political science does not train students for specific jobs in the same way that some other majors more obviously do; instead, it educates them for many jobs. This flexibility is not something to dismiss lightly in a time when career counselors are predicting that today's college graduates will change jobs—and even careers—far more frequently than their predecessors did. Students develop analytical reasoning, critical thinking, written and verbal communication skills, and other abilities that employers in assorted fields value. Double majors, minors, and internships combined with a solid background in political science can lead to jobs with interest groups and international organizations and to careers in law, government, journalism, teaching, management, and other fields that value the skills possessed by liberal arts graduates. In short, the study of politics is not an ivory tower enterprise to be pursued only by the independently wealthy.

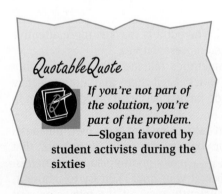

QuotableQuote

If you're not part of the solution, you're part of the problem.
—**Slogan favored by student activists during the sixties**

Still not convinced that you have a reason to study politics? Permit me to invoke ancient wisdom. The ancient Greeks coined the word **idiot** to refer to one who took no interest in the affairs of his or her state. Feel free to call your politically apathetic friends and associates idiots without fear of physical reprisal, provided that you quickly explain that you are using the term in its classical Greek sense.

What's "Politics"?

The American **political** system involves more than governmental institutions. It includes Congress, the president, courts, and other governmental bodies to be sure, but it also includes political parties, voters, interest groups, demonstrators, and the like. The term *politics* is often defined by reference to government and the machinery of the state. A broader definition, however, would better suit our present purposes. We are not saying that a broad definition of politics is correct and a narrow definition is incorrect; we are saying that a broad definition will be more useful to us than a narrow one would be.

Let's play a word association game. What words come to your mind when you hear the word *politics*?

- Some of you will think of government (Congress, the president, courts, governors, state legislatures, school boards, borough councils).
- Some of you will think about laws and public policy.
- Some of you will think of values and concepts (liberty, equality, democracy).
- Some of you will think of elections, voting, campaigns, parties, and interest groups.
- Some of you will think about conflict and attempts to resolve conflicts.
- Some of you will think about attempts to define and pursue the "common good."
- Some of you will think of corruption.
- Some of you will think about so-called office politics.

The list of word associations will be long. And none of these associations will be wrong. However, we are seeking a definition that is broad or general enough to account for all these ideas and even more.

If we defined politics exclusively in terms of **governmental institutions,** the definition would account for the actions of Congress, the president, and the courts, but it would be too narrow to apply to the actions of nongovernmental actors. Most people would agree that voters and lobbyists engage in political activities, but are not members of governmental bodies. Alternative definitions of politics include the following:

- Aristotle saw politics as the striving for "the good life" by a society or a community.[8]
- Vernon Van Dyke defined politics as a "struggle among actors pursuing conflicting desires on public issues."[9]
- Robert Dahl said that political systems are persistent patterns of human relationships that involve "power, rule, or authority."[10]
- E. C. Banfield defined politics as "the activity by which an issue is agitated or settled."[11]
- Harold Lasswell said that political acts determine "who gets what, when, and how."[12]

There are many more definitions, and different political scientists have their own favorites. If you examine the preceding definitions, however, you will notice that they encompass more than government. They are sufficiently general to include persuasion, negotiation, bargaining, compromise, argument, consensus building, force, and other activities as disagreements about public policies are worked out.

Political commentator and humorist P. J. O'Rourke says that politics exists only because different people are interested in and want different things:

> If the effect of government were always the same on everyone and if no one stood to lose or gain anything from government except what his fellows did, there would be little need for debate and no need for coalitions, parties or intrigue. Indeed, when some great national item appears on the governmental agenda, something that involves every person in the country—World War II or the interstate highway system—government turns apolitical (at least until the defense and paving contracts begin to be handed out).[13]

Let's look more closely at a related definition supplied by **David Easton.** Easton saw politics resulting in "the authoritative allocation of values for a society."[14] Valued resources, benefits, and obligations are authoritatively distributed in a society. Valued resources are in limited supply, and people desire and compete for them. Political decisions determine winners and losers. Resources include things like clean water and air, jobs, weapons systems, schools, hospitals, and roads. Conflicts arise concerning whether society should place a higher value on jobs and highways on one hand or on environmental protection on the other. A decision that the government will spend more money on defense may mean that less money will be available for education, health care, mass transit, agriculture, unemployment benefits, and deficit reduction. Or it may mean that tax increases will be necessary to support a new defense buildup. Benefits in the form of defense industry jobs and enhanced weaponry capabilities are distributed, while benefits in other areas are withheld. Simultaneously, obligations are distributed in "authoritative" fashion as citizens can be forced to pay taxes or to comply with a new draft-registration law. Some interest groups pressured policy makers for new defense programs and won; others pressured policy makers for different decisions and lost. Partial victories and partial defeats are also possible. Some voters will support these new policies and will vote to reelect the policy makers responsible for them. Others will oppose these policies and their sponsors. Easton's definition is broad enough to account for such a wide array of behavior.

The definition is even broader than it initially appears.

- If a labor union calls for a strike, the decision is "political" in that workers are obliged to leave the workplace to walk picket lines. Manufacturing firms are obliged to do without their regular workforce, and consumers have to make do without certain products or services—all because the union is seeking improved benefits for its members.
- When OPEC sets production quotas and fixes prices, these decisions are political in that they determine how much gasoline will be available (the benefit) and what we will have to pay for it (the obligation).
- When a student is required to take a certain course (the obligation) to qualify for graduation (the benefit), political aspects of the decision are apparent.

In short, this broad definition lets us account for widely varied behavior and recognize it as political. Remember "office politics"? Easton's definition covers it, too.

A Map of the Political System

The American political system is big, it is complex, and it affects us. Policy decisions dealing with war, peace, and transnational economic affairs have a national and even global impact. Some policy decisions have a direct and personal effect on us. Think about decisions dealing with inspections of our local fast-food restaurants, the cost of postage stamps, and the kinds of warning labels that are attached to children's bicycle helmets. We need a way to guide ourselves through the American political system's terrain. Without guidance we can feel as lost as a driver trying to navigate an unfamiliar road without a map.

The **systems model**[15] is a map that can help us to sift through political information and recognize how one part of the political system relates to other parts and how the political system as a whole relates to other systems. We will not consider here all of the complexities and debates surrounding systems theory as an analytical framework for political analysis.[16] Rather, we will rely on the systems approach only to the extent to which it helps us organize and make sense out of a large, otherwise confusing mass of political information.

Map reading is an acquired skill. It takes some practice, but it is worth the effort in the long run. People who can read maps feel more confident and better oriented in unfamiliar surroundings. Similarly, some of the terminology associated with systems analysis seems daunting at first glance. With practice will come familiarity. You will find that the underlying concepts are not that difficult to understand once you learn the vocabulary.

A **system** has several characteristics. First, it has different parts or **units.** We can distinguish or differentiate one part from another. This process is called **differentiation.** Second, the different parts interact to perform certain functions. They function together as parts of a team. This process is called **integration.** The removal of one part will directly affect the performance of the rest of the system. The differentiated units are integrated.

A **function** is the result or consequence of a system's activities. These results can be intended or unintended. The goal of a school system is to educate children. We would hope that a given school functions to accomplish this goal. In fact, however, a substandard school system may function to dampen the enthusiasm of students. Either way, the results are the "functions."

Next we encounter the **boundaries** of a system: Which units are parts of this system, and which units are not? To answer this question, we must determine whether or not a given unit contributes to the performance of the system's functions. Imagine that you are trying to figure out which bodily organs are parts of the circulatory system and which organs are outside the boundaries of the circulatory system. You could reason as follows: The circulatory system functions to circulate oxygenated blood throughout the body. Body parts that contribute to the circulation of blood would be parts of the circulatory system. The heart, veins, and arteries contribute to the circulation of blood and would, therefore, be parts of the circulatory system. The earlobes, nose, hair, and fingernails are parts of the body, but since they do not help circulate blood, they are not parts of the circulatory system. What about the boundaries of the political system? Recall Easton's

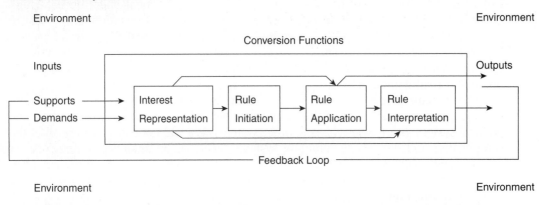

Figure 1.1

The Political System.

Environment   Environment

Conversion Functions

Inputs   Outputs

| Supports | → | Interest Representation | → | Rule Initiation | → | Rule Application | → | Rule Interpretation |

Feedback Loop

Environment   Environment

definition of politics and the making of authoritative public policy decisions. Those actors and groups of actors who contribute to the making of such policy decisions are parts of the political system. Those actors who are not involved in the making of such policy decisions are outside the boundaries of the political system.

A **subsystem** also has differentiation and integration as different parts interact to perform functions. However, the functions of subsystems are more specialized than those of the political system at large. The political system functions to make authoritative public policy decisions, but the judicial subsystem functions to make authoritative **judicial** decisions.

These are some of the characteristics of a political system. The next question is How do things work? The political system is not a static entity, carved in stone and forever unchanging. Rather, the system is **dynamic;** there is a continual interchange between the political system and its **environment.** In the process neither remains the same. The respiratory system affects—and is affected by—the circulatory system. If an illness impairs the functioning of the respiratory system, the ability of the circulatory system to circulate oxygenated blood will likewise be impaired. Similarly, the political system affects—and is affected by—the social system and the economic system. Suppose that policy makers reduce spending on social welfare programs in order to reduce the budget deficit and stimulate the economy. In the process, systems would interact, affect one another, and change.

Figure 1.1 helps illustrate some of these concepts.

Inputs are channeled into the political system. Through a series of steps, these inputs are **converted** into authoritative **policy outputs.** In turn, there is a response to these policy decisions, and this response **feeds back** and influences new inputs. The policy-making processes, then, continue in ongoing, cyclical fashion.

Look more closely at these elements. Inputs, in the form of supports or demands, flow into the political system. **Supports** are given to the system as a whole and to the

On March 12, 1996, the National Basketball Association (NBA) indefinitely suspended without pay then–Denver Nuggets guard, Mahmoud Abdul-Rauf, who refused to stand during the playing of the U.S. and Canadian national anthems before games. Abdul-Rauf was suspended for violating an NBA rule requiring players "to stand and line up in a dignified posture" during the anthem. Abdul-Rauf, a converted Moslem who had changed his name from Chris Jackson, said that he viewed the American flag as a "symbol of oppression, of tyranny" and that honoring it would violate Moslem teachings.

Some critics of the suspension claimed that it violated Abdul-Rauf's freedom of expression and religion. Others said that Islamic teaching did not forbid expressions of national allegiance.

Abdul-Rauf's suspension was lifted on March 14 as he agreed to stand for the national anthem, but he said that he would use those moments to pray "for those who are suffering."

regime, or the constitutional rules of the game that govern how conflicts are settled and how decisions are put into effect. A system tries to build up as much support as possible to ensure its survival during difficult times. If a system relies primarily on coercion to suppress dissatisfaction, only limited resources will be left to provide the very services that people seek in exchange for their support. Support can be expressed in various ways. When people pay taxes, obey laws, salute the flag, and stand during the national anthem, they are expressing support. When people vote, they are expressing support for some favored candidate in particular and for the electoral processes in general. When people feel loyal or patriotic, they are emotionally supportive, even though these feelings may presently be unexpressed.

Demands are actions that people want government to take or reject. Individuals and groups may demand new policies or that existing ones be modified or abolished. Demonstrations, petitions, letter-writing campaigns, and interest-group activities are examples of ways in which people express demands. Instead of standing during the national anthem, a dissatisfied party may remain seated. Instead of saluting the flag, a protestor may burn an American flag as a symbolic expression of political displeasure. Voting can be regarded as a demand for new policies and/or policy makers.

Inputs can come from international sources as well as domestic ones. When Iraq invaded Kuwait in 1990 and attempted to seize territory and oil reserves, the Iraqi political system made strong demands on its neighbor. The United States and other members of the international community responded with Operations Desert Shield and

Denver Nuggets guard Mahmoud Abdul-Rauf stands with his teammates and prays during the national anthem before a game with the Chicago Bulls on March 15, 1996. Abdul-Rauf saying that the U.S. flag was a symbol of "oppression and tryanny" was suspended three days earlier for sitting down during the national anthem.

© AP/Wide World Photos.

Desert Storm. In this way the international community supported Kuwait and demanded Iraq's withdrawal.

Inputs are then converted into policy outputs. The four **conversion functions** are shown in Figure 1.1.

1. **Interest representation** occurs when voters, interest groups, demonstrators, political parties, candidates, unions, reporters, and others who articulate what different actors want bring those interests into the system.

2. **Rule initiation** occurs when policy makers devise new rules or change existing policies in response to such interests. Such responses are general in nature.

3. **Rule application** occurs when agency bureaucrats take a general policy and apply it to specific cases and circumstances.

4. **Rule interpretation** occurs when there are conflicts about the meaning of some rule, the intent of the policy makers, the manner in which it is being applied, or the policy makers' authority to make this rule in the first place. Often courts are called upon to settle such disputes.

As a result of these activities, an authoritative policy **output** emerges. Imagine that a group of citizens wants the national government to ensure adequate health care at reasonable rates. The individuals form an interest group and begin publicizing their views. A political party responds favorably, and its presidential candidate promises to pursue this issue if elected. The candidate wins. The president appoints a national health care task force. The president's spouse assumes a leadership role. Amid controversy and media scrutiny, the task force develops a set of proposals. The president submits these proposals to Congress. Members of the president's party respond favorably. An intense lobbying campaign by forces on both sides of the issue ensues, the president personally attempts to persuade congresspeople to support his plan, and a modified version of the plan is approved. The program includes tax increases to pay for it and a new national health care agency to administer it. It survives a series of legal challenges and goes into effect. Some citizens now feel more medically secure. They respond by supporting the president and others responsible for the new program. Others fear that the program will be inefficient and too expensive. They think that another national bureaucratic agency is a bad idea. They prefer to see health care handled at the state level or through private insurance providers. Hospitals claim that they are understaffed to meet increasing demands for medical services. People on this side of the issue respond by opposing the new health care program and demanding changes.

The system will monitor such positive and negative feedback, make ongoing adjustments, and perform several **system-maintenance functions** in an attempt to ensure its own survival. There are three such system-maintenance functions:

1. The political system engages in **conflict resolution.** It is subjected to competing demands from different parties who are seeking different resources from a scarce supply. Somehow the system must resolve such conflicts peaceably so that all interested parties are at least willing to live with the results. The American political system features frequent bargaining and compromising. You may not get everything you desire, but at least you may come away with something and will accept the outcome.

2. The system **generates support** for itself and its policies. The American political system is a relatively "open" one and permits diverse parties to "have their say." The expectation is that even disappointed actors will remain supportive of a system that lets them be heard.

3. The system **creates legitimacy** through socialization and educational processes designed to reinforce attachments of people to the nation. The system relies heavily on traditions, rituals, and symbols. Think about all of the ceremony and pageantry that accompany presidential inaugurations. If a new president simply and quietly moved into the White House in the dead of night while the former president exited, the transition would seem disconcerting and it would be much more difficult for citizens to accept the new president as "legitimate."

A final note on **political culture** is in order. Different political systems exist in different political cultures. There are different ways to make demands on a political system. Cultural context determines what demands are legitimate and how they should be expressed.

- Against the backdrop of the political culture of the United States, **legitimate** and **conventional** ways of making demands include voting, interest-group participation, political party activities, and letter-writing campaigns.
- Still legitimate but **less conventional** ways of making demands include demonstrations, strikes, protests, and boycotts.
- **Illegitimate** ways of making demands include riots, letter bombs, terrorism, hostage taking, blackmail, bribery, and assassination.

Bribery is an accepted practice in some cultures. Assassination is more common in some systems than it is in others. But the political culture of the United States determines what it means to make demands on the political system in "appropriate" ways.

That is our map. It should help us stay on course as we navigate through the American political system. To that end Figure 1.2 summarizes the functions that major political institutions or structures perform and offers an assessment of the relative importance of these institutions in the performance of different functions.

Figure 1.2

Functions That Political Structures Perform.

Functions	Structures

Functions   **Structures**

Interest Representation
Directly Important: Political Parties, Interest Groups
Generally Important: President, Congress
Occasionally Important: Bureaucratic Agencies, Courts
Usually Unimportant: None

Rule Initiation
Directly Important: Congress
Generally Important: President, Bureaucratic Agencies
Occasionally Important: Courts
Usually Unimportant: Political Parties, Interest Groups

Rule Application
Directly Important: Bureaucratic Agencies
Generally Important: President, Congress
Occasionally Important: None
Usually Unimportant: Political Parties, Interest Groups, Courts

Rule Interpretation
Directly Important: Courts
Generally Important: None
Occasionally Important: President, Congress, Bureaucratic Agencies
Usually Unimportant: Political Parties, Interest Groups

Conflict Resolution
Directly Important: Congress, Courts
Generally Important: President, Bureaucratic Agencies, Political Parties
Occasionally Important: Interest Groups
Usually Unimportant: None

Generating Support
Directly Important: Political Parties, Interest Groups, President, Congress, Bureaucratic Agencies, Courts
Generally Important: None
Occasionally Important: None
Usually Unimportant: None

Creating Legitimacy
Directly Important: Courts
Generally Important: President, Congress
Occasionally Important: Bureaucratic Agencies
Usually Unimportant: Political Parties, Interest Groups

Key Terms

responsibilities   6
Thomas Jefferson   6
James Madison   6
anticipated reactions   7
anticipate   7

react   7
do   8
idiot   8
political   9

chapter 2

Foundations of the American Political System

Some Theory: The Social Contract

Fear is a powerful motivator. Fear is solitary, and fear is shared. Fear is a social adhesive that bonds individuals into communities. You may be afraid to be alone, to have no friends, no family, no relationships. You may be afraid of war, crime, and economic collapse. Maybe you are afraid that no one will hire you, respect you, like you, and love you. Perhaps you are afraid that a terrorist will destroy your commuter train, office building, or airplane. Or

On February 26, 1993, terrorists exploded a massive bomb in a garage below the World Trade Center in New York City, killing six people. More than one thousand people were treated for injuries. Structural damage was extensive. It was the deadliest bombing in the United States since eleven people were killed by an explosion at New York's La Guardia airport in December 1975.

On April 19, 1995, the bombing of a federal office building in Oklahoma resulted in many deaths. Included among the fatalities were children who were in a day care facility in the building.

On April 3, 1996, federal agents raided a remote Montana cabin and took into custody a former university professor suspected of being the serial bomber known as the Unabomber. Theodore Kaczynski eventually admitted responsibility for bombing incidents spanning seventeen years in which three men had been killed and twenty-three other people were wounded. By pleading guilty on January 22, 1998, the antitechnology terrorist avoided the possibility of execution. He said he wanted to avoid being portrayed in court as a madman. Kaczynski was sentenced to prison for life.

On May 20, 1996, a bomb exploded in a Walker Plaza building in Laredo, Texas, which housed an FBI field office.

On June 25, 1996, a terrorist truck bombing of an apartment building at a United States Air Force complex in Saudi Arabia killed 19 soldiers and injured 270 others.

On July 27, 1996, a pipe bomb exploded at the crowded Olympic Centennial Park in Atlanta. Two people were killed and more than 110 injuries were reported.

On July 24, 1998, a gunman fatally shot two police officers just inside an entrance to the U.S. Capitol. In a radio address House Speaker Newt Gingrich (R-GA) asked Americans to join him praying, "Please help this country to learn to live with its freedom."

On August 7, 1998, twin bombings occurred at United States embassies in Nairobi, Kenya, and Dar es Salaam, Tanzania. The attacks killed at least 247 people, including twelve Americans. More than five thousand people were injured.

In the wake of these and other related events, public officials examine the need for tighter security. Outraged citizens generally support such measures, accepting guards, metal detectors, scanners, and security cameras as contemporary facts of life at airports, government buildings, and other public places.

The desire for safety is natural. But how much liberty are you willing to trade for security? The social contract theorists grappled with this question. So did the framers of the Constitution. So do we.

Ruins of the Alfred P. Murrah Building in Oklahoma City that was the target of a terrorist attack on April 19, 1995.

© AP/Wide World Photos.

you are afraid that some faceless adversary will release a canister of poison gas in the subway. Things happen. You read the papers. You watch the news. What will you do?

The framers of the United States Constitution were influenced by the writings of "social contract" theorists. In general terms these theorists believed that men and women once lived in a **state of nature** where they were selfish, competitive, and insecure. Conflicts were common. These natural men and women were capable of reason. To live more secure lives, they drafted a **social contract** in which they agreed to enter into civil society. They established a government and gave it the power to make laws that limited individual liberty. This government was designed to promote security, and its authority came from the **consent** of the governed. Civil men and women retained some of their **natural rights** against the government. If the government violated these rights, the contract would likewise be violated and the people could withdraw their consent. In this way social contract theorists explained the origins of governmental authority and challenged the idea that rulers ruled by divine right.

Thomas Hobbes

Thomas Hobbes (1588–1679) was a prominent social contract theorist. He argued that there was no sense of community or common purpose in the state of nature; people were

JEFF STAHLER reprinted by permission of Newspapers Enterprise Association.

unconnected and alone. Natural men and women were exclusively self-interested, concerned only with satisfying their own desires. Hobbes's state of nature was a place of absolute liberty. An individual had an absolute right to everything, including the right to kill others. As such, Hobbesian natural men and women were in constant fear for their very lives. No one could feel safe or secure:

Airport security gate.

© Rob Nelson/Stock Boston.

> [D]uring the time men live without a common power to keep them all in awe, they are in that condition which is called war . . . of every man against every man. . . . In such
condition . . . the life of man [is] solitary, poor, nasty, brutish, and short.[1]

Hobbes believed that natural men and women were capable of using reason to alleviate their perpetual fear and anxiety. All shared the basic natural right of self-preservation. On this basis Hobbes argued that men and women drafted a social contract through which they created an artificial entity—a "state"—to help them achieve at least this minimal objective. So they agreed to create a tremendously powerful state—a **Leviathan**—to protect them from one another by keeping them all in awe. In the process, they exchanged the extreme liberty of the state of nature for the **security** of civil society. Civil men and women retained one right: **the right to life.** Because the state was created

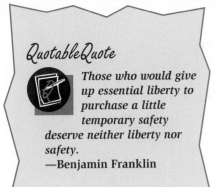
to protect the lives of the contractors, the contract would be violated if the state failed to protect their lives and consent could be withdrawn.

Hobbes's defense of a powerful state stemmed from his vision of the state of nature as a place of *extreme* conflict and *intolerable* insecurity. He reasoned that the contractors were so desperate for security that they were willing to sacrifice almost all of their natural rights to the Leviathan they created.

John Locke

Another social contract theorist, **John Locke** (1632–1704), had a major influence on the American Revolution.[2] Like Hobbes, Locke used the state of nature as a starting point in analyzing the origins and limits of governmental power. Unlike Hobbes, whose state of nature resembled a perilous jungle, Locke presented a relatively more optimistic view of the natural state.

Locke saw natural men and women as relatively free and equal, but all possessed God-given natural rights. All were required to respect God's natural laws. Such an early shared agreement about basic values was absent from Hobbes's state of nature. Locke saw natural men and women as interconnected members of a primitive community who were capable of treating one another with some degree of empathy and respect.

But Locke's natural men and women were still primarily motivated by self-interest. When several desired the same end, conflict inevitably followed. It was not always clear to competing parties, who were blinded by self-interest, how natural laws applied to their immediate dispute. They needed an impartial third party to adjudicate and resolve their conflicts peacefully. What could be done?

Locke's natural men and women formed a social contract in which they exchanged *some* of their natural freedom for increased security and convenience. They established a state and authorized it to draft laws and resolve disputes. But they insisted on keeping some of their natural rights even after entering civil society. They retained the **rights to life, liberty,** and **property.** Broad areas of individual conduct remained beyond the control of the state. If the state violated the contract by abridging such rights, popular consent could be withdrawn.

Hobbes's state of nature was a place of extreme peril and intolerable insecurity. His contractors were so desperate to live more secure lives that they relinquished almost all of

their natural rights when entering civil society. They retained only the right to life. By contrast, Locke's state of nature was relatively less perilous, and his contractors were less desperate. For this reason, Locke's contractors kept more of their rights against their more limited state. In short, grounds for revolution were more numerous and varied in a civil society inspired by Locke's views than in one inspired by those of Hobbes.

A **social contract** is an agreement among people to grant certain powers to a government while specifying

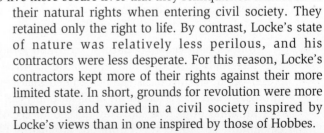

that certain rights will be retained and protected against governmental encroachment. The scope of the rights retained is a function of the degree of peril present in the state of nature. The more perilous the state of nature, the fewer are the rights retained (see Hobbes). The less perilous the state of nature, the more numerous are the rights retained (see Locke).

Finally, government authority is based on the consent of the governed, and this consent can be withdrawn if citizens conclude that the government violated the contract by infringing upon protected rights. The people are sovereign and the source of all authority.

Some History: An American Social Contract?

What does social contract theory have to do with the American political system? The United States Constitution is a social contract in the sense that it **grants powers** to a government and **limits** it by describing rights retained by individuals. Colonial America, however, was not a state of nature. The colonists were already British subjects. A social contract already existed with the king. Over time, the colonists felt that the king had broken the contract by violating their rights. They withdrew their consent and fought a war for independence. Following the war a new central government was established through the Articles of Confederation. This document can be regarded as a second American social contract. It eventually proved to be inadequate and was replaced by a new Constitution—a third social contract, if you will. Let's take a closer look.

Several factors contributed to the development of a **sense of independence** on the part of the colonists:

- A desire for religious independence brought some colonists to America in the first place. They had a desire for independence upon arrival.
- Land was plentiful. Relatively speaking, ownership was widely distributed. Unlike Europe, there was no feudal structure. By using the land, individuals had opportunities to achieve economic success, which contributed to a sense of self-sufficiency or independence.
- Distance from England encouraged independence because it was difficult for the king's royal governors to keep him abreast of all significant colonial developments. In the language of systems analysis, England's failure to **monitor feedback** adequately and its failure to make appropriate adjustments contributed to its eventual inability to **maintain** itself intact. In more colloquial terms, we might say that the king lacked good "street ears."
  - Specific actions like the Stamp Act of 1765 served as catalysts.

England saw the Stamp Act as a way to raise revenue to defray the expenses incurred in defending the colonies during the French and Indian Wars. Colonists objected not only to the level of the tax, but on principle as well. They claimed that they had a natural right to genuine representation before they could be taxed and that such representation was denied to them. The tax was repealed. Other taxes met opposition. A tax on tea led to a tea boycott followed by the Boston Tea Party in 1773 when tea was taken from ships and dumped into the Boston Harbor. Tensions continued to mount.

The Declaration of Independence

The Continental Congress approved a Resolution of Independence on July 2, 1776, a dramatic "demand" upon the British political system. Thomas Jefferson was charged with

The Liberty Bell.

© Rick Smolan/Stock Boston.

drafting a formal **Declaration of Independence** that would justify the American Revolution to the world. A final draft was approved on July 4, 1776. The document combined a theory of governmental authority with a list of specific grievances against King George III.

Jefferson's writing had a distinctively **Lockean flavor.** In the opening passages he invoked natural law in support of the claim that the king had violated the colonists' rights. Like Locke, Jefferson argued that

- All men are created equal.
- They enjoy certain natural rights (including rights to life, liberty, and "the pursuit of happiness").
- They create governments to defend these rights.
- Governmental authority rests on the consent of the governed.
- Consent can be withdrawn if the government becomes destructive of those rights.

Jefferson followed these principles with a twenty-seven paragraph bill of particulars in which he detailed ways in which the king had violated the colonists' rights. The war for independence soon followed.

The Articles of Confederation

The Second Continental Congress assembled in 1775 as a provisional government to direct action against the British. To establish a central government, delegates to that Congress formed a committee, chaired by Pennsylvania's John Dickinson, to draft articles of confederation and submit them to the states in 1777. In March 1781, after all thirteen states had ratified the articles, a formal and authorized government assumed powers. This government lasted until 1789.

The **Articles of Confederation** created a national government with very limited powers. With the memory of British rule still fresh, the new nation was reluctant to establish another powerful central government. Further, **state**-level governance was already familiar. Such considerations affected the shape of the Articles of Confederation:

- The Articles did not provide for an independent chief executive officer or president. To do so, some feared, would risk creating an American king.
- The Articles did not provide for a national court system.
- The Articles established Congress in which each state would have a single vote. But this Congress was given limited powers.

Congress had the power to declare war, enter into treaties, and establish and control the armed forces. But Congress could not compel states to respect treaties, nor could it draft soldiers. Consequently, congressional power to conduct foreign relations was questionable. Further, Congress could not regulate interstate and foreign commerce. It could neither collect taxes directly from the people nor compel states to pay a share of governmental costs. Instead, Congress relied on states to collect and forward funds to meet national expenses. Complaints were soon heard that the Articles of Confederation were too weak and required revision:

- Some were dissatisfied because Congress was unable to construct stable trade agreements with foreign nations.
- Some were dissatisfied because states sometimes used their taxing powers to the advantage of in-state businesses and to the disadvantage of out-of-state businesses trying to conduct commercial transactions across state lines.
- Some were dissatisfied because Congress could not draft troops to provide adequate protection against Indian raids, piracy, and so on.
- Some were dissatisfied because Congress was unable to enact retaliatory trade tariffs which might have induced England to relax trade and shipping restrictions imposed against the United States.

Independence Hall, Philadelphia, PA.

© *Joseph Nettis/Tony Stone Images.*

Such dissatisfactions fueled growing sentiment that the Articles of Confederation should be revised to establish a stronger national government.

Criticisms of the Articles of Confederation intensified in the mid-1780s. In September 1786 delegates from five states met in **Annapolis** to discuss the situation. The small turnout disappointed nationalists in attendance. They persuaded Congress to support a second meeting in Philadelphia "to render the constitution of the Federal Government adequate to the exigencies of the Union." Congress announced that the convention would be held in May 1787 for "the sole and express purpose of revising the Articles of Confederation."

In the meantime a group of impoverished farmers led by **Daniel Shays** rebelled against high taxes, high interest rates, and mortgage foreclosures in Massachusetts. State militiamen put down the rebellion before United States troops were able to arrive on the scene. These developments led some delegates to participate in the **Philadelphia Convention** in order to strengthen the national government. Fifty-five delegates from twelve states attended. They actually exceeded their charge and drafted a new constitution.

Compromises at the Constitutional Convention

Despite similarities in their backgrounds, the delegates represented diverse areas and interests. Their disagreements were varied and, frequently, severe. Large-state delegates clashed with those from small states. Nationalists clashed with proponents of states' rights. Numerous **compromises** were necessary to draft the new charter:

- One compromise produced a **bicameral legislature.** Each state received two seats in the Senate, but seats in the House of Representatives reflected population differences. Representatives were **elected** through a direct popular vote, but in light of some doubts about the capabilities of the general electorate, senators were selected by state legislators. The delegates permitted states to set their own **suffrage requirements.** Subsequently, the vote was widely denied to women, blacks, and others.
- Another disagreement about **population counts** resulted in the **three-fifths compromise.** It was decided that for purposes both of apportioning House seats and taxation, slaves would be counted as three-fifths of all other persons.
- Unable to reach an agreement on **slavery,** the delegates decided that Congress could not halt the importation of new slaves before 1808.

It is apparent that the delegates sometimes compromised ideals and principles in their attempts to resolve their differences and draft a new constitution.

Conflicting Ideals

Conflicts and compromises remain common to the American political system and many of these tensions involve "democratic principles." For example, Americans value both **freedom** and **security.** But how much freedom are we willing to give up in return for security? This question is a central conflict that the social contract theorists faced. Hobbes's contractors placed a higher value on security than Locke's did. Locke's contractors were not as willing to sacrifice freedoms. This tension remains unresolved today.

The American people simultaneously value **freedom** and **equality.** The Declaration of Independence proclaims that all men are created equal, but there is no guarantee that they would *stay* equal. Individuals also have freedom to achieve their potential, they are free to work hard, and they are free to become successful. In the process they can become unequal. Successful individuals are also free to pass on the fruits of their achievements to their heirs, who can use such inheritances as a head start in building their own fortunes. After several generations descendants of successful individuals are not "born equal" to people of less distinguished ancestry. Is equality at birth a reality when one person's ancestors were wealthy and another's were slaves?

But what about a society in which people are promised **equal opportunities,** as distinct from actual equality? It is illogical to say that we want people to be both free and equal. If they are free, they will not remain equal. It is not illogical, however, to say that we want people to be free and to have equal opportunities to achieve success. Yet even this more modest

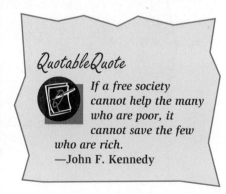

QuotableQuote

If a free society cannot help the many who are poor, it cannot save the few who are rich.
—**John F. Kennedy**

On May 20, 1996, at the Pittsburgh, Pennsylvania, office of the Department of Veterans Affairs (VA), a disabled veteran, upset with results of a hearing about money he owed the VA, used a homemade gun to shoot an assistant finance officer in the face. The gun, a four-inch metal tube with a twelve-gauge shotgun shell and a firing mechanism, was small enough to fit in his pants pocket. The shooting raised questions about public safety in a building where security had been tightened only two months earlier. The assailant had arrived in a VA van that drove directly into the parking garage of the building, bypassing metal detectors at the street entrance. Security officers changed their procedures immediately after the shooting and began making all visitors pass through metal detectors.

On May 20, 1995, President Clinton cited security concerns in ordering Pennsylvania Avenue closed to vehicle traffic in the wake of the bombing of a federal building in Oklahoma City. The president said that the only significant change would be on traffic patterns in Washington, D.C. Senator Rod Grams (R-MN), disagreed:

> By barricading a symbol of democracy that dates back nearly to the birth of this nation, we've surrendered to fear. . . . [T]he words "secure the blessings of liberty" must ring awfully hollow when [school children] visit the White House and find this symbol of liberty blocked by barricades. . . . [R]eturning Pennsylvania Avenue to the way it was before May 20, 1995, would be the greatest tribute to democracy we could offer. We all need to stop, catch our breath and put aside fear. If we don't, where will it stop? Already the drastic security measures undertaken on Pennsylvania Avenue have set a precedent and have been mirrored on Capitol Hill. How much of Washington are we going to rope off before the public begins thinking we simply don't want them here? . . . We must not allow fear to claim the victory. Dismantle the barricades, Mr. President, and may the souls of the patriots who founded this nation in freedom's name take pity on us if we don't."[3]

Multiple-victim rampages in schools, like the April 20, 1999 attack at Littleton, Colorado's Columbine High School that left fifteen dead, have heightened public sensitivity to school violence. Parental supervision is critical, but what can schools do to curb violence? Counseling programs. Visitor registration. Teachers in hallways. Mesh book bags. Dress codes. School uniforms. Drug testing. Armed security guards. Bomb-sniffing dogs. Night-vision cameras for campus parking lots. Metal detectors. Tighter gun control laws. The school-safety industry, which barely existed a few years ago, has become a major part of the United States security business. Texas-based Garrett Metal Detectors has seen sales to schools grow from almost nothing into the largest share of the company's business—surpassing orders for airports, prisons, and courts.

Although the impulse to "crack down" is understandable, again we must ask ourselves how much liberty we are willing to exchange for security. For the record, Columbine High School had an armed guard. And one week before the massacre, Columbine High held a staff crisis training session as part of the school district's effort to update its security. That updated report was due at the end of the school year.

promise is problematic. If Jones is born into poverty and Smith is born into privilege, do they really start life with equal opportunities? Can equal opportunity be provided? Jefferson turned to public education for an answer. If the rich and the poor alike have access to equal educational facilities, then they have equal opportunities to achieve success. Sensible, in theory. But are all school districts equal? Do all parents have the same educational options for their children? Contemporary conflicts about busing to achieve desegregation, tuition voucher programs to provide school choice, and affirmative action reflect

Pedestrians walking on Pennsylvania Avenue in front of the White House. The avenue is barricaded to vehicular traffic.

© Brad Markel/Liaison Agency.

America's ongoing attempts to resolve the tension between freedom and equality.

In a related vein the American people value **equality** and, at the same time, they value **efficiency.** Affirmative action programs. Minority set asides. Programs providing special preferences for victims of past discrimination. Such measures are motivated by

Today the top 1 percent of Americans possess more net wealth than the bottom 90 percent. In 1968 the Kerner Commission on Civil Disorders warned, "Our nation is moving toward two societies, one black, one white—separate and unequal." A thirtieth-anniversary update prepared by the Eisenhower Foundation concluded that "the prophecy has come to pass."[4]

Some evidence? The unemployment rate for young men in inner cities is more than 30 percent; the national rate is less than 5 percent. One in three black men is in prison, on probation, or on parole. States now spend more per year on prisons than on higher education.

A Commerce Department report entitled "Falling through the Net II" was released on July 28, 1998. The report revealed a widening "digital divide" between whites and minorities; compared to blacks and Hispanics, whites were more than twice as likely to own home computers. A racial divide in computer ownership existed even among families earning more than $75,000 per year. Larry Irving, President Clinton's top telecommunications advisor, said:

> If you're telling me that 80 percent of black America is not going to be involved in commerce, the education, the political discourse, the information, the entertainment that the Internet provides . . . then we've got a problem as a nation.

a desire to provide **compensatory justice** today for the victims of earlier injustice. Proponents argue that it is not enough to promise to end discriminatory treatment; it is necessary to take **affirmative** steps to bring disadvantaged parties into a position where they can compete fairly with others. But critics say that it is unfair to provide these benefits at the expense of other people who were not themselves responsible for historical injustices. Affirmative action, they argue, is reverse discrimination, and reverse discrimination is wrong. It also runs counter to the notion that people should be hired, promoted, and rewarded on the basis of **merit** and achievement, not on the basis of being a member of a disadvantaged class. As such, affirmative action programs are criticized for eroding efficiency.

An even deeper tension involves the meaning of democracy itself. *Democracy* is commonly defined as "government by the people" or "government by popular majorities."

But does a democratic majority have an unlimited right to rule? What if the majority is so offended by some segment of the population that it votes to execute these outcasts without trial? In addition to being unfair, unjust, and unwise, this decision is also undemocratic. Why? In a **constitutional democracy,** individuals and minorities have certain rights that must be respected no matter how unpopular these people become. In a constitutional democracy, **majority rule** must be weighed against **minority rights.** Sometimes the interests of the majority conflict with the interests of the minority, and striking an acceptable balance is not always easy.

QuotableQuote

A free society is one where it is safe to be unpopular.
—Adlai Stevenson

Ratifying the Constitution: Popular Consent

In his "Notes on the Last Day of the Constitutional Convention,"[5] Madison described the fears of some delegates that they had drafted an imperfect document.

- **Benjamin Franklin** said that he had reservations about some provisions, but as a fallible man, he recognized that he might eventually change his mind. In any event he hoped that the Constitution would be approved "heartily and unanimously."
- **Alexander Hamilton** also hoped for unanimous approval and predicted that rejection of the Constitution would mean anarchy.
- Pennsylvania's **Gouverneur Morris,** writer of the Preamble and a key figure on the Committee on Style, expressed reservations but signed. Like Hamilton, Morris saw the choice as one between "national government" and "general anarchy."
- Governor **Edmund Randolph** of Virginia did not sign. In the event that the Constitution was not ratified, leadership would be needed to cope with resulting chaos and confusion. He feared that his authority to deal with such a crisis would be undermined if he signed the Constitution. In effect, he abstained.
- **Elbridge Gerry,** governor of Massachusetts, refused to sign. He expected the Constitution to meet resistance and thought that sending the Constitution out for a yes or no vote would magnify disagreements. He would have preferred proposing the Constitution in a less conflict-inviting way.
- **George Mason** of Virginia refused to sign because he thought the Constitution gave too much power to the national government.

All the delegates except Mr. Randolph, Mr. Gerry, and Mr. Mason signed the Constitution. While the last members were signing, Benjamin Franklin looked toward the back of the presiding officer's chair on which was painted a rising sun. He observed that painters found it difficult to distinguish a rising sun from a setting sun. During deliberations, he remarked, he often studied this painting and wondered whether it was rising or setting. As the Constitution neared approval, Franklin said, "[N]ow at length I have the happiness to know that it is a rising and not a setting sun."[6]

Article 7 of the proposed Constitution specified that it would go into effect when nine states **ratified** it. The framers of the Constitution, seeking speedy approval, sent it to single-chambered, specially elected state ratifying conventions. Such conventions seemed more likely to ratify than existing state legislatures, which in most cases would have required approval by two chambers. Approval by popularly elected conventions was also consistent with the framers' desire to ground the Constitution in the authority of the people.[7]

The Federalists and the Anti-Federalists

Opponents of the Constitution, the **Anti-Federalists,** were concerned that the Constitution gave too much power to the national government at the expense of the states.

- They worried that elites in the form of a kinglike president and an aristocratic Senate would grab power from the people.
- They complained that individual rights were not adequately protected and argued for the inclusion of a written Bill of Rights.
- They made their arguments through newspapers, pamphlets, and public meetings.

Despite some well-founded objections, however, the Anti-Federalists failed to provide an alternative plan of their own.[8]

Supporters of the Constitution—the **Federalists**—were men of prestige and political experience, points that counted heavily at the time. The Federalists defended the Constitution in a series of eighty-five letters to New York newspapers published between October 27, 1787, and May 28, 1788. The letters were brought out in book form as *The Federalist* in June of 1788. Writing under the pseudonym **Publius,** Alexander Hamilton contributed fifty-one letters, James Madison contributed twenty-nine, and John Jay wrote five. The Federalists argued that

- Rejection of the Constitution would create a power vacuum and a return to the impotent Articles of Confederation.
- The Constitution would provide energetic government while respecting the different interests of states and preserving individual liberties.
- The Constitution would provide for popular participation and would protect the rights of minorities.[9]

Delaware was the first state to ratify, doing so on December 7, 1787. On June 21, 1788, New Hampshire became the ninth state to ratify. Virginia and New York had not yet ratified, however. Their inclusion in the Union was important for commercial, cultural, and political reasons. The Virginia state ratification convention took place in Richmond in June of 1788. George Mason and Patrick Henry led the Anti-Federalist forces. Unlike Mason, Henry did not participate in the Philadelphia Convention because, as he put it, he "smelt a rat."[10] Madison defended the new Constitution and prevailed. On June 25, 1788, the Virginia convention ratified the Constitution by a vote of eighty-nine to seventy-nine.

The Virginia convention nearly ended in a duel between Patrick Henry and Governor Edmund Randolph. Randolph had refused to sign the Constitution in Philadelphia, but he supported it during Virginia debates. Henry suggested that Randolph had accepted bribes in exchange for his support. Randolph had also received a letter from Governor George Clinton of New York suggesting that if Virginia would hold out against ratification, New York would do likewise. The letter could have forged an alliance leading both states to reject the Constitution. Randolph kept the letter to himself until Virginia ratified.

The New York ratifying convention met in Poughkeepsie in June and July 1788. Anti-Federalists outnumbered Federalists, but the leadership of Alexander Hamilton and John Jay carried the day. New York, by a vote of thirty to twenty-seven, ratified the Constitution on July 26, 1788.

Eventually, North Carolina and Rhode Island joined the Union. Rhode Island did so only after Congress threatened to sever relations with the state and to treat it as a foreign nation.[11]

James Madison's "Blueprint" for a Political System

James Madison is regarded as the architect of the American political system. *The Federalist*, Numbers 10 and 51, can be viewed as his blueprints. He tried to design a popularly based political system that would avoid tyranny by minorities or majorities. He also confronted the fact that prior democratic systems tended to be short-lived as they deteriorated into mob rule. Stability was an important goal. Further, he was particularly concerned with the problem of factions. He feared that citizens pursuing their selfish interests would band together and use their collective strength to deprive minorities of their interests and rights.

Accepting **popular sovereignty** as the basis of the American political system, Madison expected people to participate in their own governance. But Madison worried about the tyrannical use of power:

> The friend of popular governments, never finds himself so much alarmed for their character and fate, as when he contemplates their propensity to [the] dangerous vice [of faction]. . . . The instability, injustice and confusion introduced into the public councils, have, in truth, been the mortal diseases under which popular governments have everywhere perished. . . . Complaints are everywhere heard . . . that our governments are too unstable, that the public good is disregarded in the conflicts of rival parties, and that measures are too often decided, not according to the rules of justice and the rights of the minor party, but by the superior force of an interested and overbearing majority.[12]

Factions

Minority tyranny occurs when an individual or a relatively small group of individuals acquires political power and abuses it. Colonial experiences with the king made

Madison sensitive to such problems. He reasoned that widespread suffrage would enable the people to protect themselves by voting tyrants out of office. Bloodless revolutions could be waged through the ballot box. Madison was not concerned with **unelected** officials who abused their powers or with "private" actors who assume "public" power by virtue of their economic influence over a community. He was more worried about the **majority tyranny** that occurs when like-minded individuals band together in the pursuit of their shared interests and deny the rights and interests of minorities. He defined such groups, or **factions,** as follows:

> [a] number of citizens, whether amounting to a majority or a minority of the whole, who are united and actuated by some common impulse or passion, or of interest adverse to the rights of other citizens, or to the permanent and aggregate interests of the community.[13]

What could be done to prevent factions from destroying America's popular government? What could be done to prevent the people themselves from destroying their own democratic system in their shortsighted pursuit of selfish ends? Madison replied that "[t]here are two methods of curing the mischiefs of faction. The one, by removing its causes; the other, by controlling its effects."[14] Madison added that there are two ways to remove the causes of faction: "The one, by destroying the liberty which is essential to its existence; the other, by giving every citizen the same options, the same passions, and the same interests."[15] He rejected the first remedy as worse than the disease:

> Liberty is to faction what air is to fire, an aliment without which it instantly expires. But it would not be less a folly to abolish liberty, which is essential to political life because it nourishes faction, than it would be to wish the annihilation of air, which is essential to animal life, because it imparts to fire its destructive agency.[16]

He dismissed the second approach—giving every citizen the same interests and passions—as impracticable:

> The latent causes of faction are . . . sown in the nature of man. . . . A zeal for different opinions . . . divided mankind into parties, inflamed them with mutual animosity, and rendered them much more disposed to vex and oppress each other, than to co-operate for their common good. . . . The regulation of these various and interfering interest forms the principle task of modern legislation.[17]

Concluding that the *causes* of factions cannot be removed, Madison tried to control their *effects*. He relied on farsighted representatives, an extended republic, and structural safeguards to deal with the effects of factions. Consider each in turn.

Madison believed that a **pure democracy,** in which citizens assemble and administer the government in person, would be plagued by "the mischief of faction":

THE FAR SIDE   By GARY LARSON

A common passion or interest will, in almost every case, be felt by a majority . . . and there is nothing to check the inducements to sacrifice the weaker party, or an obnoxious individual. Hence it is, that such democracies have ever been spectacles of turbulence and contention; have ever been found incompatible with personal security, or the rights of property; and have, in general, been as short in their lives, as they have been violent in their deaths.[18]

Representatives as Trustees

Instead, Madison proposed an indirect democracy or a **republic.** One point of difference between a democracy and a republic is "the delegation of the government, in the latter, to a small number of citizens elected by the rest."[19] In a republic the people's representatives operate governmental machinery on behalf of the general public. Madison did not think that these representatives should act like instructed delegates, carrying out the wishes of the most vocal citizens. In such a setting the inflamed passions of an angry mob would produce legislation infringing on the rights of minority groups deemed offensive to popular opinion. Representatives should not be immediately responsive to such shortsighted demands. Instead, Madison thought that representatives should act like "trustees" for the public good, basing decisions on their own wisdom and judgment, looking to the *long-term* best interests of the community. They would vote their consciences, not their constituencies. Such an arrangement would

> [R]efine and enlarge the public views by passing them through the medium of a chosen body of citizens, whose wisdom may best discern the true interest of their community, and whose patriotism and love of justice, will be least likely to sacrifice it to temporary or partial considerations. Under such a regulation, it may well happen, that the public voice, pronounced by the representatives of the people, will be more consonant to the public good, than if pronounced by the people themselves.[20]

Ultimately, the Madisonian representative would be accountable to the voters. If after time passed, representatives were unable to convince their constituents to temper their views, the voters could elect new representatives. The Madisonian system responds, but in light of the need for stability, it is designed to respond in **delayed** fashion.

An Extended Republic

Another difference between a democracy and a republic is the "extent of territory, which may be brought within the compass of republican than of democratic government."[21] Direct democracy is feasible only on a small scale. But there, passions and prejudices can become inflamed and spread rapidly, and the majority can more easily "execute their plans of oppression."[22] On the other hand, in an **extended republic,** groups or factions form but there are many groups. For every group there is an opposing group. Plural groups would compete and balance. It is difficult for *any* majority to form, and as a result, the danger of suffering tyranny at the hands of an oppressive majority is minimized. Madison wrote the following words:

Extend the sphere, and you take in a greater variety of parties and interests; you make it less probable that a majority of the whole will have a common motive to invade the rights of other citizens; or if such a common motive exists, it will be more difficult for all who feel it to discover their own strength, and act in unison with each other.[23]

Separation of Powers, Checks and Balances, and Federalism

Madison also built into the Constitution a series of mechanical safeguards to guard against the abuse of concentrated power. The Constitution has three such premises: separation of powers, checks and balances, and federalism.

In *The Federalist,* Number 51, Madison argued that the "preservation of liberty" requires each branch or department of the government to "have a will of its own."[24] Noting that "[a]mbition must be made to counteract ambition," each department should have sufficient power to "resist encroachments of the others."[25] He saw it as "a reflection on human nature, that such devices should be necessary to control the abuses of government."[26] Madison summarized his pessimistic view of human nature as follows:

If men were angels, no government would be necessary. If angels were to govern men, neither external nor internal controls on government would be necessary. In framing a government which is to be administered by men over men, the great difficulty lies in this: you must first enable the government to control the governed; and in the next place oblige it to control itself.[27]

Separation of powers operates on the national level to prevent power from becoming concentrated and abused. A **legal** separation of powers divides labor. Each national department is assigned separate formal duties.

- **Article 1** establishes the United States Congress and gives it legislative responsibilities.
- **Article 2** establishes the presidency of the United States and gives this branch executive and administrative responsibilities.
- **Article 3** establishes United States courts and gives them judicial responsibilities.

In addition, a **political** separation of powers provides different ways to select national officials and varying terms of office.

- **Representatives** serve two-year terms and are elected through a direct popular vote.
- **Senators,** in contrast, serve six-year terms and were selected by state legislatures prior to the ratification of the Seventeenth Amendment.
- **Presidents** serve a maximum of two 4-year terms and are selected through the electoral college.
- **Federal judges** serve life terms, in many cases, and are appointed by the president with the consent of the Senate.

In this way Madison ensured that an agitated electorate could not completely overhaul the national government in a single election. At most, voters could select a new president, 435 representatives, and one-third of the Senate. Federal judges and two-thirds of the members eidi Fleiss, the so-called Hollywood Madam, was convicted in May 1995 for pandering, a state crime. In August of the same year, she was convicted on federal money-laundering and tax-evasion charges. In September, a superior court judge rejected Fleiss's request to merge the two sentences.

Fleiss's conviction followed two separate investigations. In the state case undercover officers solicited prostitutes from Fleiss. In the federal trial prosecutors examined her bank records and proved that she laundered hundreds of thousands of dollars in money made from her prostitution ring.

of the Senate would remain in place and positioned to urge moderation and calm deliberation. This arrangement is another illustration of Madison's **delayed** responsiveness.

These departments were also designed to be functionally interdependent. **Checks and balances** guard against concentration of power. To pass a law, both the House and the Senate must approve. One chamber can check the other. Then the president can sign the bill into law or check Congress by vetoing it. A vetoed bill is returned to Congress, which can override a presidential veto. The bill can later be challenged in a case heard by the United States Supreme Court. The Court could provide an additional check by declaring the law unconstitutional. However, Congress has much power over the federal courts and their appellate jurisdiction. Federal judges are appointed by the president, with senatorial consent, and Congress can impeach these judges. No single department, therefore, operates with complete independence. Checks and balances reflect Madison's efforts to equip departments with the capacity to "resist encroachments" from others. The system of checks and balances is another example of the importance of **conflict** in the American political system.

Federalism is yet another way to protect against concentrated power. "Separation of powers" refers to a division of responsibilities on the **national** level. "Federalism" involves a division of power that moves downward from the national level through the state levels.

- Some powers are granted **exclusively** to the national government. Only the national government can regulate **interstate** commerce, conduct foreign affairs, and make treaties.
- Some powers are granted exclusively to states. Only states can regulate **intrastate** commerce (that is, commercial transactions wholly internal to a state that have no substantial effect on interstate commerce).
- Some powers are shared **concurrently** by state and national governments. We can be taxed by our national, state, and local governments. There are also a federal criminal code, state criminal laws, and local ordinances, all of which prohibit certain actions and prescribe penalties.

The Madisonian political system produces cumbersome structural mechanisms. Power is spread. Power checks power. Responsiveness is delayed. Today many complain about governmental drift, paralysis, deadlock, gridlock, and inefficiency. Why did we not opt for a more efficient and streamlined design? Recall Madison's task. He sought to construct a stable republic that would avoid tyranny. When faced with a choice between efficiency and stability, Madison stressed the latter. The result is a clumsy system that is relatively stable. Stability is not an unqualified good. Inefficiency and delay are frequent by-products. Perhaps recognizing the sources of such frustrations can help render them more tolerable.

Key Terms

Notes

chapter 3

Constitutional Rights and Liberties

A "Living" Constitution

A constitution serves as the supreme law of the land. Statutes inconsistent with its provisions are invalid. Most constitutions provide general frameworks for governments.

- Constitutions establish structures and rules and specify how public officials will be selected.
- Constitutions delegate **powers** to government institutions and actors.
- Constitutions sometimes **limit** such powers by recognizing that individuals retain certain rights.

The United States Constitution was written in 1787. At the time it was highly unusual to draft a written constitution, whereas today few nations lack written constitutions. In such countries the "constitution" consists of laws, judicial decisions, and customs that have not been collected in one single document. Israel and Great Britain are two examples of nations with **unwritten constitutions.**

No constitution in the world has lasted as long as that of the United States.

- Nearly two-thirds of the world's 160 national constitutions have been written or revised since 1970.
- Only fourteen predate World War II.
- More than half of the independent nations of the world have been under more than one constitution since World War II.
- The average nation has had two constitutions since 1945.[1]

Scene at the signing of the U.S. Constitution, September 17, 1787. (Oil on canvas, 1940, by Howard Chandler Christy.)

By contrast, the United States Constitution has been remarkably durable.

The original United States Constitution contained just 4,223 words—the equivalent of about seventeen typewritten, double-spaced pages. Several state constitutions are much longer. The first ten amendments (termed *articles*), known as the Bill of Rights, were added almost immediately, but only seventeen amendments have been added since then. And two of these amendments—the eighteenth, establishing, and the twenty-first, repealing, prohibition respectively—cancel each other. How has this short document remained viable for so long?

The secret to the Constitution's durability is its **language.** Some provisions describe governmental powers; others describe individual rights. But many of these provisions were written in highly general, open-ended fashion. The Constitution

- Guarantees the right to a "speedy trial" by an "impartial jury"
- Prohibits "unreasonable searches and seizures"
- Protects against "cruel and unusual punishments"

What do these and other constitutional phrases actually mean? The framers did not say.

The use of such open-ended language can be traced, in part, to the authors' inability to resolve certain disputes. To cite just one example, because the framers were unable to reach a satisfactory compromise regarding voting rights, they decided to let each state set its own suffrage requirements. However, this ambiguity in diction can also be credited to the framers' foresight. They recognized that they were drafting something far more important than a traffic code. The flexibility of the Constitution's language permits it to evolve with changing times. The framers laid down a series of fundamental concepts and principles but left the precise meaning of their words to the interpretation of future generations. Such constitutional ambiguities are the key to the document's continued relevance and viability, making it a growing, changing, **living constitution.**

Our imprecise Constitution requires interpretation. Courts are often asked to interpret the Constitution in order to apply it to contemporary matters. As judges engage in such **rule interpretations,** they must rely on these factors:

- Precedents
- The actual text of the Constitution
- The assumed intent of the framers

Judges are not free to substitute what they consider wise public policy for decisions made by the elected representatives of the people. The discretion of judges is limited. Still, judging is not a purely mechanical process.

It can be difficult to determine what the framers really intended. Further, even if their intentions could be ascertained, judges cannot ignore more than two hundred years of legal developments since the framers' time. For example, the Fourth Amendment prohibits "unreasonable searches and seizures." What is an "unreasonable" search? Did the framers intend to address wiretapping, infrared telescopes, airplane overflights, and other forms of modern surveillance? Or might one argue that what the framers intended was to protect a sphere of personal privacy from unreasonable governmental intrusions, and technology-enhanced eavesdropping constitutes just such unreasonable intrusions.

If the Constitution were more explicit, fewer disputes about its meaning would arise and it would not make much difference who the judges were, but the document would then require continual revision to account for each technological advance. Even now, open-ended language sometimes allows judges to interpret the same provision distinctly. While some object to this uncertainty, this unique quality allows the Constitution to adapt to change and to continue to live.

We have seen that a social contract both grants powers to a government and limits those powers. The United States Constitution grants powers to a national government and requires the government to protect and respect the individual rights retained by the people. As a living document the Constitution sometimes does these things in vague fashion. Let's take a closer look.

Power-Granting Provisions: The Legislative, Executive, and Judicial Branches

The first three articles established the three departments of the national government.

- **Article 1** provides for a bicameral national legislature—the United States Congress.
- Article 1, Section 8 lists the express powers of Congress.
- Clause 3 of this article gives Congress the power to "**regulate commerce** with foreign nations, and among the several States, and with the Indian tribes."

In this clause the framers were addressing one of the perceived weaknesses of the Articles of Confederation: Congress's inability to regulate interstate commerce. But what did they mean by the term *commerce*? Did it relate only to the shipment of goods and products from state A to state B, or might it include passengers on a ferry boat navigating in waters between New York and New Jersey? The framers did not say, so the Supreme Court was asked to clarify in 1824. In *Gibbons* v. *Ogden*[2] the Court interpreted commerce broadly to include passengers, ferry-boat traffic, and other forms of commercial intercourse. Additionally, although the Constitution permits Congress to regulate interstate commerce (that is, commerce between and among states), the Constitution does not permit Congress to regulate purely *intrastate* commerce (that is, commercial activities wholly internal to a particular state). But what if in-state commercial activities have a substantial effect on nationwide markets? What if commercial practices inside state A make it impossible for out-of-state suppliers to conduct business profitably with businesses inside state A? Can Congress regulate **intrastate** commerce if it has a substantial impact on **interstate** commerce? In a long line of decisions, the Supreme Court eventually provided an affirmative answer.[3]

Clause 8 gives Congress the power to "**promote** the progress of **science** and useful **arts.**" To this end Congress sometimes makes federal money available for scientific research and the performing arts. Applicants for such grants must agree to abide by certain requirements; that is, the money comes with strings attached. While it is reasonable to limit the way in which grant money can be used, at what point do the

In 1986 a documentary entitled "The Africans" was funded, in part, through a grant from the National Endowment for the Humanities (NEH). When NEH officials viewed the finished product, some were dismayed to discover that, among other things, it portrayed Libya's Moammar Quadaffi in a favorable light. Some suggested that the documentary's producers had violated NEH guidelines and that the grant money should be returned. Regardless of what you might think of the documentary itself, at what point do guidelines violate freedom of expression? At what point are guidelines wrong? At what point do guidelines mean that the government is using tax money to make sure that the American people are exposed only to some officially sanctioned version of a story? The framers did not say, and we continue to grapple with such questions today.

In 1998 the Supreme Court upheld a requirement that the National Endowment for the Arts (NEA) consider "decency" in awarding grants.[4] Will this decision stifle artistic and academic freedom?

regulations become overly restrictive? At what point do they impinge upon freedom of inquiry, creative expression, or some other freedom that commands constitutional protection?

Clause 11 gives Congress the power to **declare war.** However, Article 2 provides that the president will serve as commander in chief of the armed forces. If the nation is at war, the president commands the troops. That much is clear. But what if the president wants to deploy troops and Congress has not formally declared war? Can the president take such steps unilaterally? Such questions continue to generate controversy.[5] What about United States military actions in Korea and Vietnam? Congress provided no formal declarations of war. Were they "illegal" wars? Such issues found their way to courts because the framers were not more precise.

Clauses 12 through 16 deal with Congress's power to **raise and regulate an army, navy, and militia.** Here again, the Constitution addresses one of the perceived weaknesses of the Articles of Confederation. But how could Congress go about raising an army? What about a draft? The Thirteenth amendment prohibits involuntary servitude. If you are drafted into the army, by definition, you did not volunteer to serve. The Court has ruled that the amendment was not designed to prohibit a draft.

Today males are required to register for the draft when they become eighteen years of age, but females are not. Does such disparate treatment violate constitutional protections? In *Rostker* v. *Goldberg*[6] the Court held that Congress's decision to authorize the president to require registration of males but not females for possible military service did not constitute gender discrimination in violation of the due process clause of the Fifth Amendment. In his majority opinion Justice Rehnquist observed that Congress considered and rejected registering women in light of combat restrictions on females.[7]

Article 1, Section 8, clause 18 is the **elastic clause.** It gives Congress the power to make "all laws **necessary and proper** for carrying into execution the foregoing powers." The clause grants unwritten powers to Congress. In this way Congress can institute a draft as a necessary and proper way to raise an army. But how do we distinguish a necessary and proper law from an unnecessary and improper one? Must a draft be **absolutely** necessary to raise an army? Or is it enough that Congress thinks it would be useful or convenient to resort to a draft? The framers did not say.

President Washington asked **Thomas Jefferson** and **Alexander Hamilton** for their views on whether Congress had the unwritten power to establish a **national bank.** Jefferson urged a narrow interpretation of the clause, under which Congress could establish a bank only if it were absolutely necessary to do so. Hamilton urged a looser, or broader, interpretation.[8] In a landmark 1819 decision, *McCulloch* v. *Maryland*, Chief Justice Marshall interpreted the elastic clause as providing Congress with broad, unwritten powers, including the power to incorporate a national bank.[9]

Article 2 addresses yet another perceived weakness of the Articles of Confederation by providing for a **president.** The article provides the president with certain express powers.

- The president is named **commander in chief** of the armed forces and actually shares war powers with Congress. Their relationship is not always clear.
- The president has the power to **appoint** various federal officers, but questions sometimes arise concerning the president's power to **remove** such officers.[10]

Section 3 specifies that "he shall take care that the laws be **faithfully executed.**" Consider these questions:

- Do these words do for the president what the elastic clause does for Congress?
- Do they give the president unwritten powers?
- Can a president assume unwritten powers to protect national security, reasoning that only then will it be possible to make sure that laws are faithfully executed?

President Nixon claimed that it was the executive's "privilege" to protect the confidentiality of his conversations with his aides. He argued that presidents need candid advice to execute laws and can get such candor only if they are able to assure their advisors that their conversations with the president will remain confidential. In *United States* v. *Nixon,*[11] the Supreme Court proved receptive to this idea.

Under the Articles of Confederation, there were no **federal courts. Article 3** of the Constitution addresses this perceived weakness with the provisions that "[t]he judicial power of the United States will be vested in one **Supreme Court** and in such **inferior courts** as Congress may from time to time ordain and establish." So there would be a federal court system consisting of a Supreme Court and lower courts. But what would the lower federal courts look like? The framers decided to leave these details to Congress.

Article 3 also specifies that in certain cases the Supreme Court has **original jurisdiction.** In other cases the Court has "**appellate jurisdiction** . . . under such regulations as the Congress shall make." The vast majority of cases heard by the Supreme Court get there on appeal. That is, these cases reach the Supreme Court through routes mapped out by Congress, not by the framers. Even more fundamentally, Article 3 said that the **judicial power** of the United States would extend to cases involving federal questions or federal parties. Question: *What* judicial power? The framers did not specify what these courts could do with the cases they heard. The framers created judicial power but left it undefined.

The remaining original Articles provide the following:

- **Article 4** dealt with intergovernmental relations and federalism.
- **Article 5** provided an amendment mechanism so the Constitution could be updated to meet future developments.
- **Article 6** announced the supremacy of the Constitution to contrary enactments and stated that ratification would require the approval of nine states.

In short, the first several articles of the Constitution granted powers to a national government. In light of ambiguities in the framers' language, however, many of these powers remained open-ended.

Power-Limiting Provisions

A Written Bill of Rights

Brutus and some of his fellow Anti-Federalists argued that a **written bill of rights** should be added to the Constitution. They maintained that if the powers of the federal government are spelled out in writing, limits on the government and the rights of individuals against the state should be spelled out as well. A written statement would make fundamental principles seem more permanent. Subsequent government actions could be judged against these standards. In this way persons who offended the prevailing popular opinion of the moment would be assured of fair treatment. No matter how offensive their views, their fundamental constitutional rights would be respected and protected. The fact that something is popular would not necessarily mean that it was constitutionally permissible. Furthermore, the actions of future elected officials and public figures could be judged against more enduring standards than the public opinion of their day.[12]

Alexander Hamilton contended that a written bill of rights was **unnecessary.** He noted that the Constitution already prohibited *ex post facto* laws and provided for the right of *habeas corpus.* Further, the people did not give up their popular rights and liberties in the Constitution in the first place, and there was no need to try to reclaim what has never been surrendered. He also thought that a written bill of rights would be **dangerous.** The danger was that some might construe this written list of rights as comprehensive. What if an important right was inadvertently omitted from this list? If citizens attempted to assert this unwritten right at some future time, the government might plausibly counter that no such right exists. After all, if the framers had envisioned such a right, it would have been listed.[13]

On balance the Anti-Federalist position proved more persuasive than Hamilton's. The First Congress, drafted a written bill of rights and these first ten amendments to the Constitution were ratified in 1791. An examination of these amendments reveals that just as powers were sometimes vaguely granted, so too were powers limited in an indistinct fashion.

Civil Liberties and Civil Rights

The **First Amendment** provides that, "Congress shall make no law . . . abridging the **freedom of speech.**" There would appear to be no ambiguity whatsoever in these terms. *No law* abridging freedom of speech means "no law." Or does it?

- What about libel?
- What about slander?
- What about perjury?
- What about treason?
- What about obscenity?

The Supreme Court has held that First Amendment protections are not absolute. As Justice Holmes put it in *Schenck* v. *United States,* "[t]he most stringent protection of free speech would not protect a man in falsely shouting fire in a theater, and causing a panic."[14] First Amendment protections depend on the circumstances surrounding the expression in question. Restrictions on words are constitutionally permissible if there is "a clear and present danger that they will bring about substantive evils that Congress has a right to prevent."[15] Following this reasoning, the Court has upheld restrictions against obscenity,[16] fighting words,[17] and other controversial forms of expression.

Something to Think About

The United States soccer team finished dead last in the thirty-two-team field at the 1998 World Cup tournament. American players departed amid acrimony, criticizing their coach, Steve Sampson, for his strategy and lineup changes. Sampson, apparently no fan of the Bill of Rights, remarked, "I don't understand where athletes get this freedom to express themselves. There will be fines imposed."

In his classic book, *On Liberty* (1859), John Stuart Mill argued that neither the government nor majority opinion should be permitted to suppress nonconformist views. On the other hand, some behavior obviously cannot be tolerated. The problem of liberty is to define the legitimate extent of the majority's power over the individual. Mill answered that society is justified in limiting an individual's liberty of action only to protect itself against harm.

Mill placed great value on freedom of expression. He thought that we should hesitate to silence a contrary opinion for three reasons. First, the opinion we seek to suppress may turn out to be true. In his words, "[a]ll silencing of discussion is an assumption of infallibility." Second, the silenced opinion may be in error, yet it might contain an element of truth. Prevailing opinion can be improved through its collision with opposing views. Third, even if the majority view is entirely true, it will be held as mere prejudice or enfeebled dogma unless it is vigorously and earnestly defended against contrary views.

Consider how Mill's "harm principle" can be applied to a debate about the legitimacy of suppressing "hate speech." If one believes that racist, sexist, and other generally offensive statements convey ideas, then they deserve protection. If one believes that when such words are directed against particular individuals they inflict real harm, restrictions are easier to defend. Does your college or university have a speech code? What do you think about this?

Political correctness, or lack thereof, is frequently in the headlines. In 1993 major league baseball's ruling executive council suspended Marge Schott, owner of the Cincinnati Reds, for one year and fined her $25,000. The council announced Schott was being "reprimanded and censured in the strongest terms for her use of racially and ethnically insensitive language." The suspension later was shortened to eight months. In 1996 she was again suspended and agreed to give up control of the Reds through the 1998 season. Schott angered the council after she said in an ESPN interview that Adolph Hitler "was good in the beginning, but then he went too far." She was also quoted in *Sports Illustrated* making remarks critical about Asians and women in the workplace. National League President Leonard Coleman said, "We just cannot condone any type of ethnic insensitivity. We've got to have tolerance, not intolerance." Was Major League Baseball right to suspend Marge Schott?

In 1997 John Calipari, then coach of the New Jersey Nets, called reporter Dan Garcia a "Mexican idiot." Verbal and written apologies followed. So did a $25,000 fine from the NBA—the largest fine ever levied against a coach. Garcia later sued Calipari for "extreme humiliation and emotional distress." Around the same time, Miami Heat radio broadcaster David Halberstam (not the author with the same name) was working the Heat-Warriors game. Attempting to compliment a player who had attended the University of Virginia, Halberstam remarked that the slaves on Thomas Jefferson's plantation "would have made good basketball players." The NBA fined Halberstam $2,500 for his comment. During the 1997 NBA finals between the Chicago Bulls and Utah Jazz, forward Dennis Rodman used expletives and off-color references to describe Utah's Mormon fans. The Anti-Defamation League harshly criticized Rodman for his "vulgar and derogatory" comments. On June 12, 1997, the NBA fined Rodman a record $50,000. League Commissioner David Stern said, ". . . [I]nsensitive or derogatory comments involving race or other classifications are unacceptable in the NBA. Dennis Rodman's comments were exactly the kind of offensive remarks that cannot be tolerated or excused." Was the NBA right to levy fines in these instances?

On March 26, 1998, Green Bay Packer Reggie White, who is black and an ordained minister, spoke before Wisconsin's legislature about his social-work efforts. He observed that blacks are gifted at "celebration and worship," whites "know how to tap into money," Hispanics are good at family structure and "can put twenty or thirty people in one home," and Asians "can turn a television into a watch." When questioned about his use of racial stereotypes, White explained that he was trying to "get people to come together." CBS, which had auditioned White for a job as an NFL analyst, announced that he was no longer in the running for the job.

Cincinnati Reds owner, Marge Schott, and her dog, Schottzie.

© Couponco Worldwide/Liaison Agency.

Dennis Rodman.

© Reuters/Steve Dipaola/Archive Photos.

Sometimes people try to express their political views through **symbolic** gestures. Does the First Amendment protect symbolic forms of expression?

- In *Stromberg* v. *California*,[18] the Supreme Court invalidated the state's anti-red-flag law. The Court held that a peaceful display of a red flag as a sign of opposition to the government is constitutionally protected "speech."
- In *Street* v. *New York*,[19] the Court overturned the conviction of a man who burned an American flag—in violation of a New York law—to protest the shooting of civil rights activist, James Meredith.
- In *Tinker* v. *Des Moines Independent Community School District*,[20] the Court held that school officials acted improperly by suspending students who wore black armbands to signify their opposition to United States involvement in the Vietnam War.
- In *Spence* v. *Washington*,[21] a student violated the state's flag-defacement law by superimposing a peace symbol on an American flag and flying it upside down outside his window. He did this to protest the United States invasion of Cambodia and the shooting of four students by national guardsmen at Kent State University. The Court ruled that his symbolic action was a protected form of expression.

However, the Court has not upheld all forms of symbolic expression. In *United States* v. *O'Brien*,[22] a man publicized his antiwar sentiments by burning his draft card. The Court upheld his conviction for violating a federal law that made it a crime to mutilate draft cards. Writing for the Court, Chief Justice Warren balanced O'Brien's interest in freedom of expression against the government's interest in conducting an efficient and systematic selective service system. Emphasizing the administrative importance of the actual draft cards, Warren concluded that the regulation was justified.

Flag burning continues to generate controversy. Consider the case *Texas* v. *Johnson*.[23] While the Republican National Convention was taking place in Dallas in 1984, Gregory Lee Johnson participated in a political demonstration protesting policies of the Reagan administration and of certain Dallas-based corporations. In front of city hall, Johnson doused an American flag with kerosene and set it on fire. While the flag burned, protestors chanted, "America, the red, white, and blue, we spit on you." Several witnesses testified that they had been seriously offended, but no one was injured or threatened with physical injury. Following the demonstration, a witness collected the flag's remains and buried them in his backyard. Johnson was charged with the desecration of a venerated object in violation of the Texas penal code. He was convicted, sentenced to one year in prison, and fined $2,000. The Court of Appeals for the Fifth District of Texas at Dallas affirmed the conviction. The Court of Criminal Appeals of Texas reversed the lower courts. In a five-to-four vote, the U.S. Supreme Court sided with Johnson.

Protestors burning the American flag.

© D. Sears/Liaison Agency.

Justice Brennan, joined by Justices Marshall, Blackmun, Scalia, and Kennedy, wrote the majority opinion. Brennan noted that the First Amendment protects "expressive conduct" as well as written and spoken words. While a state can prevent "imminent lawless action," Johnson's symbolic expression of dissatisfaction with government policies did not lead to a disturbance of the peace and did not implicate the state's interest in maintaining order. Instead, Johnson's expression was restricted because of the **content** of his message. "If there is a bedrock principle underlying the First Amendment," Brennan observed, "it is that the Government may not prohibit the expression of an idea simply because society finds the idea itself offensive or disagreeable." Toleration of Johnson's criticism reinforces the freedom that the flag represents. Brennan continued, as follows:

> The way to preserve the flag's special role is not to punish those who feel differently about such matters. It is to persuade them that they are wrong. . . . We can imagine no more appropriate response to burning a flag than waving one's own, no better way to counter a flag burner's message than by saluting the flag that burns.

ubsequently, a constitutional amendment was introduced in Congress that would permit the states and the national government to restrict flag burning. The amendment fell short of the two-thirds majority required in both houses. The amendment was reintroduced. One of the individuals who testified at Senate hearings in July 1998 was Tommy Lasorda of the Los Angeles Dodgers. George Washington. Benjamin Franklin. James Madison. Alexander Hamilton. Tommy Lasorda.

The Ku Klux Klan burns crosses to express its views symbolically. Does the First Amendment treat flag burning differently than cross burning? More specifically, does the First Amendment protect the Ku Klux Klan's right to burn a cross at a rally held in the middle of a field? Does the First Amendment protect the Klan's right to burn a cross on the front lawn of a black family's house? Is there a difference between the two circumstances?

Chief Justice Rehnquist, in a dissenting opinion joined by Justices White and O'Connor, emphasized the unique role of the flag and the "profoundly offensive" nature of Johnson's conduct. In a separate dissent Justice Stevens argued that Johnson was prosecuted not for his criticism of government policies but for the *method* he chose to express his views.[24]

The First Amendment also guarantees **freedom of the press.** Although this freedom is important, it is not absolute. For example, a person who has been libeled by statements in print can sue for damages. In *New York Times* v. *Sullivan*,[25] however, the Court held that libel laws cannot be used to "cast a pall of fear and timidity" over the press.[26]

Reporters maintain that their ability to preserve the secrecy of their news sources is essential to a free press. Reporters sometimes argue that courts should give the same respect to reporter-source confidentiality as they do to the lawyer-client relationship. In *Branzburg* v. *Hayes*[27] the Supreme Court refused to recognize such a privilege. The Court ruled that a reporter must testify and reveal the contents of his notebooks to a grand jury.

Sometimes the government attempts to suppress publication of a report. Such a request for **prior restraint** on expression comes to the Court bearing "a heavy presumption against its constitutional validity."[28] Such questions were at issue in *New York Times Co.* v. *United States.*[29] During the Vietnam War, Secretary of Defense Robert McNamara ordered an internal study of how the United States became involved in the conflict. This study was entitled "History of the U.S. Decision-Making Process on Viet Nam Policy." Daniel Ellsberg, a Pentagon employee, gave copies of the study to n 1995 Congress passed the Computer Decency Act, a sprawling telecommunications law that criminalizes certain expressions in the on-line world. If someone "makes available" to minors words or images that a judge finds "indecent," that person can be fined $100,000 and sent to prison. Should writers, publishers, artists, and others be able to speak freely, or should all electronic discourse be limited what is suitable for children? In *Reno* v. *ACLU* (521 U.S.___, 138 L.Ed. 2d 874, 117 S. Ct.___, 1997), the Supreme Court declared the law unconstitutional.

The technological challenges involved as the First Amendment heads into cyberspace are enormous. But the philosophical issues remain no less daunting. What do you think?

the *New York Times* and the *Washington Post.* The *New York Times* began to publish excerpts from these **Pentagon Papers.** The Justice Department obtained injunctions preventing the *Times,* the *Washington Post,* and the *Boston Globe* from publishing additional installments on grounds that such publication would harm national security.

The United States Supreme Court, in a six-to-three vote, lifted the injunctions. Justices Black and Douglas concluded that the government never has the authority to suppress publication. Justice Brennan argued that prior restraint is permissible only when the nation is at war and the government can prevent obstruction of its recruiting services or publication of sailing dates of troop transports and location of troops. During peacetime the government might seek to suppress information that would set in motion "a nuclear holocaust." He was unconvinced that any information in the Pentagon Papers was of this nature. In sum, freedom of the press is not absolute, but it is extensive.

The First Amendment also protects **freedom of religion.** Like freedom of speech and press, religious freedom is not absolute. Courts have upheld laws prohibiting polygamy, the use of hallucinogenics in religious services, and the like. Human sacrifice can be barred. Recall, once again, John Staurt Mill's "harm principle." It is one thing to *believe* what one will; it is another thing to *practice* one's beliefs in a manner that harms others.

Many children in the United States are educated at church-affiliated private schools. If these schools did not exist, there would be a tremendous additional burden on the public school systems of this country. Consider these questions:

- Does the Constitution permit states to assist parochial schools?
- What about bus service?
- What about textbooks?

Something to Think About

onsider parents of a sick child who, for religious reasons, deny the child conventional medical treatment. Instead, they pray for the child's recovery. The child dies. Should the state be able to bring charges against these parents? Unfortunately, this case is not hypothetical. It is relatively common. Courts will consider the child's age and other relevant factors in making decisions, but the state's authority to bring charges is generally upheld.

- What about supplements to help pay teachers' salaries?
- What about tax breaks for parents who send their children to religious schools?
- Are such accommodations fair to other taxpayers?
- What about reciting prayers in public schools?
- Is this practice unfair to children who do not subscribe to "mainstream" religious views?
- Would a moment for silent meditation be an acceptable alternative?
- What about expelling Jehovah's Witnesses from public schools unless they recite the pledge of allegiance, despite the fact that doing so would violate their religious beliefs?
- What if city hall wants to put up a nativity scene as part of a seasonal Christmas display? Might not Jewish residents be offended (not to mention the community's atheists)?

Courts have produced vast amounts of case law on these and related questions.[30] The immediate point is that the First Amendment in application is more complicated than it first appears.

The **Second Amendment** reads "A well regulated Militia, being necessary to the security of a free State, the right of the people to keep and bear Arms, shall not be infringed." Does this amendment absolutely protect the right of individuals to arm themselves, and does it bar the government from attempting to restrict gun ownership? What about the 1993 Brady Bill, which regulates the purchase of handguns? Does this law violate the Second Amendment?

The Second Amendment recalls days when guns were necessary for defense, food, and fur trading. It recalls days when a musket hung over the mantle place, to be taken down when a man was called into militia service. During this period colonies maintained their own militias, which fought alongside British regular soldiers against the French and the Indians. In the 1760s and 1770s, these militia units figured prominently in colonial resistance to British rule. After obtaining independence, many Americans distrusted permanent, standing armies as being too reminiscent of the British forces that had occupied Boston, Lexington, and Concord. These troops had tried to destroy armaments and munitions of colonial militias. The **Third Amendment,** which provides that no soldier shall be quartered in any house in peacetime without the owner's consent also reflected the framers' distrust of permanent standing armies. In many ways, then, the Second Amendment can be seen as the "militia amendment."

A 1792 federal statute defined the militia as consisting of all able-bodied men between the ages of eighteen and forty-five. At the time the government could not afford to supply guns and ammunition, so the law required these men to have their own guns and ammunition. This is the "militia" described by the Second Amendment. A 1903 federal law provided that the "regularly enlisted, organized, and uniformed active militia in the several states shall constitute the organized militia" and will be known as the "National Guard."

In several relevant cases the Supreme Court has held that the Second Amendment protects the **collective right** of the people to arm their militias, not the unlimited right of individual citizens to carry weapons for their own private purposes. The amendment prohibits the national government from infringing on the power of states to arm their well-regulated militias.[31]

The colonists objected to England's use of **general warrants** and **writs of assistance** to search homes for smugglers and others suspected of violating navigation laws. These general warrants and writs of assistance authorized anyone—including private parties—to conduct broad searches without any time constraints.

The **Fourth Amendment** prohibits **"unreasonable searches and seizures."** Further, **warrants** must "particularly describ[e] the place to be searched and the person or things to be seized." Such warrants must be supported by a showing of **probable cause.** Important safeguards, to be sure. But when is a search "unreasonable"? And what is meant by "probable cause"?

Because of such imprecision, courts have often been asked to interpret the Fourth Amendment.

- In *Dumbra* v. *United States,*[32] the Supreme Court said that probable cause entails a "belief that the law was being violated on the premises to be searched" and the facts must be such that "a reasonably discreet and prudent man would be led to believe that there was a commission of the offense charged."
- The Court has also ruled that warrants must be issued by detached and neutral magistrates, not by police officers or government enforcement agents.[33]

If an individual who owns or occupies the place to be searched voluntarily **consents** to the search, no warrant is needed.[34] Searches not accompanied by warrants are generally unreasonable unless they are supported by special circumstances that make a warrantless search necessary. In other words, warrantless searches may be reasonable if they are necessitated by **exigent circumstances.** Examples include searches conducted incident to a lawful arrest, searches of areas in plain view, searches of automobiles, searches conducted as part of a "hot pursuit," searches involving readily destructible evidence, and stop-and-frisk investigations. With the exception of stop-and-frisk "searches," which permit a law enforcement officer acting

Police officer arresting and searching a suspect.

© N. R. Rowan/Stock Boston.

on "reasonable suspicion" to conduct a limited patdown of a suspect's outer garments in search of a weapon,[35] such searches are normally supported by probable cause. That is, the person conducting the search has probable cause to obtain a warrant but, under the circumstances, does not have time to get one. In such cases the warrant requirement is impractical because a suspect might flee or evidence may be destroyed while a law enforcement officer discusses the matter with a magistrate.

What about technological advances? Does the Fourth Amendment apply to **electronic surveillance**? In *Olmstead* v. *United States*,[36] federal prohibition officers had tapped a telephone used by a bootlegger and obtained incriminating evidence against him. The Supreme Court upheld his conviction over his Fourth Amendment objections. The Court found, first, that no physical trespass into his premises took place. As such, there had been no search. Second, he intended to project his voice to distant places when he talked on the phone. Third, no tangible evidence had been seized. In sum, the Court ruled that the Fourth Amendment did not apply to the case.

Things began to change in *Silverman* v. *United States*.[37] Police had driven a spike mike into an air duct in a building wall so they could eavesdrop on conversations inside the building. Distinguishing the case from *Olmstead*, the Court held that physical trespass or a search, had occurred. On this ground the Court ruled that the evidence was inadmissible.

In *Katz* v. *United States*,[38] FBI agents had used an electronic device to obtain evidence that Katz was violating federal communications statutes. Because no physical trespass occurred and nothing tangible was seized, the FBI did not get a warrant. Writing for a seven-to-one majority, Justice Stewart held that the Fourth Amendment protects the privacy of *persons,* not just areas, and its reach should not depend on whether or not there was some physical trespass. In this way *Olmstead* was overruled, and the Fourth Amendment was applied to cases involving electronic surveillance. Is this what the framers intended? Their language was sufficiently open-ended to make such an interpretation plausible.

As electronic mail becomes increasingly common, messages are sometimes encrypted to shield them from prying neighbors, business competitors, and other third parties. On the other hand, law enforcement officials have an interest in monitoring communication between criminals and terrorists. How should these privacy interests and security interests be balanced?

The **Fifth Amendment** prohibits **double jeopardy,** or trying a person twice for the same offense. The amendment also guarantees that in criminal cases, no person will be compelled to testify against her- or himself. This protection against **compulsory**

self-incrimination can be waived, but the waiver must be knowingly and intentionally made. Sometimes testimony is elicited in exchange for a grant of immunity. In language recalling John Locke's views on the social contract, the Fifth Amendment states that no person shall be "deprived of life, liberty, or property without due process of law." It is reassuring to know that our lives, liberty, and property enjoy this security. But here is an important question: What is **due process of law?** The framers did not spell it out. Whatever it is, we are entitled to it. But if we get it, we can be deprived of a great deal.

- Sometimes due process has meant that defendants were entitled to jury trials or attorneys.
- But sometimes courts ruled otherwise.

The **Fifth Amendment** also says that private property shall not be taken for public use without (just compensation). In *Barron* v. *Baltimore*[39] the Supreme Court considered the just compensation clause and the broader issue of the extent to which the Bill of Rights applies against the states. While paving its streets, the City of Baltimore diverted certain streams from their natural courses. As a result, deposits of sand and gravel built up near Barron's wharf, making the water shallow and rendering the wharf useless. Barron claimed that the city's action had taken his private property for public use, in violation of the Fifth Amendment. The amendment makes no mention of state or local action, but Barron maintained that it should be interpreted as restraining the states (and cities) as well as the national government.

In this, his last constitutional decision, Chief Justice John Marshall observed that the question was "of great importance, but not of much difficulty." He agreed that Barron had been denied effective use of his property without just compensation but held that the Fifth Amendment affords protection against the *national* government alone. Had the framers of the Bill of Rights intended them to limit the powers of state governments, Marshall reasoned, "they would have . . . expressed that intention . . . in plain and intelligible language." Because the amendments "contain no expression indicating an intention to apply them to the State government," Marshall concluded that the Fifth Amendment did not protect Barron against the city.[40]

The **Sixth Amendment** provides that, in criminal prosecutions, the accused will enjoy a right to a **speedy trial** by an **impartial jury.** What is a "speedy trial"? an "impartial jury"? Today we embrace the right to a trial before a jury of ones "peers." But what does this mean? How closely must the jurors resemble the defendant in terms of race, age, income, education, and so on?

Lawyers for the prosecution and the defense examine prospective jurors during *voir dire* **proceedings.**

- Both sides get a number of **peremptory challenges,** which can be used to remove jurors whom they think will favor the other side.
- Each side can also have prospective jurors removed for **cause.**
- In high-profile cases lawyers will seek the services of professional jury consultants in an attempt to empanel a jury most likely to decide in their favor.

Jury selection has been raised to a high art. In highly publicized cases it can be difficult to select jurors who have not already heard about the case and formed opinions. It can be difficult to select an impartial jury in a speedy fashion.[41]

O. J. Simpson in court in 1995, trying on one of the leather gloves prosecutors say he wore the night his ex-wife Nicole Brown Simpson and Ron Goldman were murdered.

© AP/Wide World Photos.

The right to a jury trial applies to federal cases. Does this right also apply at the state level? The Supreme Court faced this question in *Duncan* v. *Louisiana*.[42] Duncan, a black youth, was convicted of simple battery, a misdemeanor, and sentenced in Louisiana to sixty days and a $150 fine. His request for a jury trial was denied because the Louisiana constitution provided juries only in capital cases or cases of imprisonment at hard labor. Writing for a seven-to-two majority, Justice White observed that Duncan could have been sentenced for up to two years with a $300 fine. He faced serious jeopardy. White concluded that trial by jury in criminal cases is fundamentally important and applies in state criminal cases which—were they to be tried in federal court—would be covered by the Sixth Amendment's guarantee.[43]

In brief, jury trials are required in state criminal cases, though a jury trial can be waived. If a jury trial is provided at the state level, however, it need not be a twelve-person jury and the verdict does not necessarily have to be unanimous. We know this not because the framers said so, but because over the years judicial decisions have worked out the details.[44]

The Sixth Amendment also guarantees that the accused will have a right to the **assistance of counsel** for his or her defense. In fact, many criminal defendants have gone unrepresented by counsel. For years the right depended on the ability of defendants to pay for their own attorneys. In *Powell* v. *Alabama*[45] the famous Scotsboro Boys case, nine black youths had been charged with the rape of two white girls. The youths were tried by a jury six days after their arrest in an atmosphere of intense public hostility. They were poor, illiterate, away from home, and separated from friends and family. The trial judge appointed all members of the bar to defend them; no single attorney came forward to do so. The jury returned the death penalty. Writing for a seven-to-two majority, Justice Sutherland concluded that the defendants in this state capital case had been unable to receive a fair trial without counsel.

Sutherland used the Fourteenth Amendment's due process clause to extend the right to counsel to the state level. He emphasized the illiteracy of the defendants, the atmosphere of public hostility, and other circumstances surrounding the case in order to limit the scope of his decision. In later noncapital cases, courts sometimes ruled that defendants had received fair trials even though they did not have the assistance of counsel.[46] In capital cases, however, the Court consistently held that defendants required counsel.

Clarence Gideon was arrested in Florida for breaking and entering. He appeared in court without a lawyer. He was indigent and asked the court to appoint counsel to assist him. Gideon's request was refused in light of Florida law, which provided for the appointment of counsel only in capital cases. Gideon was convicted and appealed, claiming his Sixth Amendment right to counsel had been denied. The Supreme Court agreed with him. Writing for a unanimous Court, Justice Black concluded that criminal defendants cannot be assured a fair trial without the assistance of counsel. As a result, the right to counsel was applied to both capital and noncapital criminal cases in state courts. Gideon was retried with a lawyer and acquitted.[47]

During the 1960s the Warren Court expanded the right to counsel and the protection against compulsory self-incrimination. In some ways the Court merged these two complementary rights. Because it is difficult to prove what actually happened during a police interrogation, the presence of counsel is one way to protect against coerced confessions. In *Miranda* v. *Arizona*[48] the Court held that the police must *inform* persons accused of a crime that they need not incriminate themselves and that they have a right to an attorney. Ernesto Miranda was suspected of kidnapping and rape. He was arrested at his home and taken to a police station for questioning without being advised of either his right to remain silent or his right to counsel. After two hours of questioning, he signed a written confession and was then convicted. Writing for a five-to-four majority, Chief Justice Warren found that the confession was inadmissible and that defendants must be informed of their rights.[49]

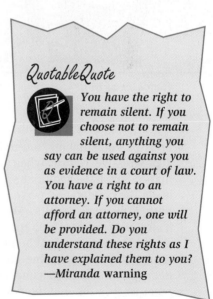

QuotableQuote

You have the right to remain silent. If you choose not to remain silent, anything you say can be used against you as evidence in a court of law. You have a right to an attorney. If you cannot afford an attorney, one will be provided. Do you understand these rights as I have explained them to you?
—*Miranda* **warning**

iranda was retried and again convicted. Following his eventual release, he was playing cards. A fight erupted, and Miranda was stabbed to death. On his person were a number of "Miranda cards." When police arrived on the scene, the arresting officer read one of Miranda's own cards to the suspect arrested for his murder.

SMOKING OR NON?

Florida

"Smoking or Non?"

As Published in Newsweek, April 7, 1997, p. 25.

The **Eighth Amendment** prohibits **excessive bail** and **excessive fines.** What is "excessive"? The framers wisely did not specify a dollar amount, for if they had, periodic constitutional amendments would be necessary to adjust for inflation. Moreover, wealth is relative. What is excessive for one person may be pocket change for another. The Eighth Amendment also prohibits **cruel and unusual punishments.** What does this mean? Does it mean the same thing now as it did during the framers' times? Today most people would probably agree that burning at the stake, drawing and quartering, or breaking someone on the wheel are cruel and unusual punishments, but that was not always the case. The guillotine was hailed as a progressive reform when it was introduced. Previously, an inept or drunken ax man might have required several blows to sever a head. An improper noose could leave the condemned person to suffocate slowly. Electric chairs have malfunctioned with gruesome results. Many states are moving to lethal injections as a more humanitarian method for performing executions. Still, opponents of capital punishment argue that the notion of "humanitarian executions" is a contradiction in terms. Undeniably, some methods are more painful than others. Most recent court decisions have been concerned with whether the punishment fits the crime, or whether it is the one intended by the legislature, when determining whether capital punishment is cruel or unusual.[50]

Opponents of capital punishment sometimes argue that it is flatly prohibited by the Eighth Amendment. Review the text of the Fifth Amendment. How might a supporter of capital punishment use this amendment to argue that the framers of the Constitution accepted the legitimacy the death penalty?

The concept of cruel and unusual punishment is not restricted to capital cases. Under a mandatory sentencing system, a three-time offender might be sentenced to life imprisonment for shoplifting. Recall that Michael Fay, an American citizen who committed an offense in Singapore, was sentenced to be beaten with a cane. While the event took place outside United States jurisdiction, Americans debated whether such forms of punishment are barbaric or justified.

In 1997 Florida's electric chair malfunctioned during an execution, and the condemned prisoner burst into flames. Afterwards, Florida Attorney General Bob Butterworth quipped, "People who wish to commit murder, they better not do it in the state of Florida, because we may have a problem with our electric chair."

On July 15, 1997, Richard Dieter, executive director of the Death Penalty Information Center, announced the results of the center's new study. The report identified sixty-nine people who had been released from death rows since 1973 "after evidence of their innocence emerged." The study concluded that "[t]he current emphasis on faster executions, less resources for the defense and an expansion in the number of death cases mean that the execution of innocent people is inevitable."

Unwritten Rights

The **Ninth Amendment** states that "the enumeration in the Constitution of certain rights shall not be construed to deny or disparage others retained by the people." The Ninth Amendment has great potential significance as a source of **unenumerated rights.** Because most justices have interpreted the amendment in more limited fashion, it has had less actual significance. While the Ninth Amendment supports the idea that the American people enjoy constitutional rights beyond those listed in the written text of the

Constitution, the amendment's open texture provides little guidance for judges attempting to define those rights. Testifying before Congress, **Robert Bork** argued that the Ninth Amendment cannot be used without a full understanding of what it means. For example, if an amendment said "Congress shall make no" and the rest of the sentence was covered by an inkblot, a court can not "make up what might be under the inkblot."[51]

Constitutional Powers and Rights at the State Level

The **Tenth Amendment** states that "powers not delegated to the United States by the Constitution, nor prohibited by it to the States, are reserved to the States respectively, or to the people." This amendment deals with **federalism,** the relationship between national and state governments. It addresses concerns of those who fear that the national government will take away too many powers from the states. The framers acknowledged that the national government was not all powerful and that its powers were only those that had been **delegated** to it. In light of the elastic clause and other provisions giving the national government unwritten powers, however, one can see room for disagreement about the respective powers of the nation and the states.

Until the ratification of the **Fourteenth Amendment,** only state constitutions and state laws protected basic liberties against encroachment by state and local governments. According to *Barron* v. *Baltimore,* the Bill of Rights did not apply directly to state governments. In 1868, however, additional limits were placed on state power.

The Fourteenth Amendment prohibits **states** from denying persons "the privileges and immunities of citizens of the United States" or depriving them of "life, liberty, or property without due process of law." Over the years courts have held that the "liberties" protected against state infringement resemble many of the rights protected in the Bill of Rights against national abridgment. In effect, courts have **nationalized** portions of the Bill of Rights in this way.

- In *Chicago, Burlington and Quincy Railroad Co.* v. *Chicago,*[52] the Supreme Court held that states must supply just compensation to owners when private property is taken for public use. That is, the Court **incorporated** or **absorbed** the Fifth

Amendment's just compensation clause into the Fourteenth Amendment and applied it at the state level.

- In *Twining* v. *New Jersey,*[53] the Court rejected an invitation to apply the Fifth Amendment's self-incrimination provision against states, but the Court acknowledged that *some* rights resembling those in the Bill of Rights were among the *liberties* protected by the Fourteenth Amendment.

A series of subsequent Fourteenth Amendment decisions effectively nationalized the First Amendment, including freedom of speech, press, and religion.[54] In addition, the Fourteenth Amendment has protected many of the rights of the accused against state infringement.[55] Most of the rights in the Bill of Rights now apply to the states as well. For this reason the Fourteenth Amendment can be regarded almost as a second Bill of Rights for the states.

The Fourteenth Amendment also provides that no state shall deny to any person **the equal protection of the laws.** In practice, this provision has not meant that all persons must be treated in exactly the same way. The Fourteenth Amendment sometimes permits states to discriminate. It is not necessary for a state to treat all persons in identical fashion if there are legitimate reasons for treating them differently. For example, states can prevent ten-year-old children from driving cars or consuming alcohol or voting because there are good reasons for doing so. Conversely, a state could not show legitimate reasons for prohibiting Catholics or Republicans or females from engaging in such activities.

In *Plessy* v. *Ferguson*[56] the Supreme Court held that state laws requiring **separate but equal** facilities for blacks and whites did not violate the equal protection clause of the Fourteenth Amendment. In fact, separate facilities provided for blacks were often substandard. Much attention was directed to racially segregated schools. In *Sweatt* v. *Painter*[57] the Supreme Court considered the case of a black student who was denied admission to the University of Texas Law School on racial grounds. Instead, he was directed to a separate law school for blacks in the state. The Court concluded that the black law school was, in fact, inferior to the white law school with respect to library holdings, curriculum, faculty, and alumni attainments. As a result, the Court ordered that the black student be admitted into the University of Texas Law School. The Court did not abandon *Plessy*'s separate but equal principle in this case; instead, it found that the facilities in question were **not equal.** In *Brown* v. *Board of Education of Topeka,*[58] the Court squarely overruled *Plessy*. Writing for a unanimous Court, Chief Justice Warren did not scrutinize black and white schools to compare the relative quality of their facilities. Rather, he

QuotableQuote

To separate [black children] from others of similar age and qualifications solely because of their race generates a feeling of inferiority as to their status in the community that may affect their hearts and minds in a way unlikely ever to be undone. . . . We conclude that in the field of public education the doctrine of "separate but equal" has no place.
—**Chief Justice Earl Warren**

espite this order, many schools remained racially segregated. As a result, courts began to intervene more directly, sometimes ordering local school boards to implement bussing plans to achieve desegregation. Controversy ensued and continues. Affirmative action programs are also designed to even out the playing field by compensating the victims of past injustice for their injuries. All such efforts are rooted in the belief that American citizens deserve equal educational opportunities. What do you think?

White students at Arkansas' North Little Rock High School deny access to six black students on Sept. 9, 1957. Moments later, the black students were shoved down a flight of stairs and onto the sidewalk, where police broke up the altercation.

© *AP/Wide World Photos.*

concluded that separate education facilities are "inherently unequal." The Court ordered that desegregation proceed "with all deliberate speed."

The Constitution grants powers to a government and limits those powers by specifying that individuals will retain certain rights. The framers were frequently imprecise. This imprecision permits the Constitution to remain viable but frequently makes judicial interpretation of constitutional rules necessary.

The United States Constitution is more than two hundred years old. Its history has been long and distinguished. But with technological advances accelerating, with a rising tide of popular discontent with politics and politicians, and with other challenges sure to present themselves as we move into the twenty-first century, is the Constitution still up to the job?

Key Terms

powers 41	Article 1 43	arts 43
limit 41	regulate commerce 43	declare war 44
unwritten constitutions 41	intrastate 43	raise and regulate an army, navy,
language 42	interstate 43	militia 44
living constitution 42	promote 43	elastic clause 45
rule interpretations 42	science 43	necessary and proper 45

*C*onsider the impact of technology on the right to life (abortion, cloning, custody battles over in vitro eggs); the right to die (life support system disputes, living wills, physician-assisted suicide); freedom of speech and press (regulating the Internet); unreasonable searches and seizures (new frontiers in electronic surveillance); cruel and unusual punishment (new methods of capital punishment, televised executions, chemical "castration" for sex offenders); issues concerning government structures and processes (voting by modem and other matters related to "cyberdemocracy," "virtual citizenship," or "the electronic town hall"; free airtime for political candidates; term limits; balanced budget amendments); and so on.

Does the Constitution require dramatic overhaul? Does it require modest revision? Or is it sufficiently adaptable to continue to serve us as it stands into the foreseeable future?

Popular Control—

The Accountability of Leaders to the People

About This Section

This section describes ways in which people influence the government (interest representation). It also describes how people respond to public policy decisions (feedback).

chapter 4
Linking Public Officials to the Public: Public Opinion and Voting

Discusses how inputs (both demands and supports) come into the political system. In a *democratic* system, the accountability of public officials to the public is critical. That is, public opinion must influence public policy. This chapter considers the role and development of public opinion and voter behavior. It addresses two key questions. First, how well-**informed** are American voters? Second, how **active** are American voters?

chapter 5
Collective Links to Public Officials: Parties and Interest Groups

Concentrates on how **groups** of people try to influence public policy. Although there are important differences between parties and interest groups, this chapter addresses both because both types of groups represent collective ways of influencing public policy.

chapter 6
Elections: Presidential and Congressional

Discusses national elections. The role of character in national elections, relevant rules, and recent outcomes are examined.

chapter 4

Linking Public Officials to the Public: Public Opinion and Voting

Inputs into the Political System

Consider the **inputs** side of the political system. Interests are represented and brought into the system. In a democratic political system, the people are sovereign; they are the source of all government authority. Therefore, in a democratic system the people are entitled and expected to participate actively in politics. The people are **participants** in governing and not merely the **subjects** of government. In a large society direct democracy is not feasible. Instead, as James Madison recognized, it is more realistic to establish an **indirect** or **representative democracy,** a **republic.** As Harold Lasswell observed, "Government is always government by the few."[1] Leadership is always exercised by an elite few. The key question for determining whether or not a system is democratic turns on the **accountability** of the leaders to the public. In a democratic system the public must influence public officials, and public opinion must influence public policy.

Public Opinion

Several terms should be defined at the outset. First, an **opinion** is a self-conscious position taken on a specific issue. If I have an opinion, I am aware of it. "The Chicago Bulls won" is simply a statement of fact. "I am pleased that the Bulls won" is an opinion. An **attitude** is a more general tendency or inclination. Attitudes may be unconsciously held. I can have attitudes and remain unaware of them. I might have an antilabor union attitude. I might also have a consciously held opinion that teachers should not be allowed to go out on strike. Finally, for an opinion to become part of **public opinion,** three threshold requirements must be met. First, the issue must have general public importance. You may have an opinion about where you would like to eat dinner this evening, but very few people care. Second, the opinion must be expressed in some way, or it remains a private thought. Third, the person expressing the opinion must be capable of producing some kind of result. Others must at least notice the opinion for it to have any effect.[2] Next question: Where do political attitudes and opinions come from? How are they formed?

Political Socialization

We learn to have different attitudes towards and expectations of the political system as we grow up. We acquire certain values and become familiar with certain traditions that are part of our shared **political culture.** The political culture of a society is transmitted to new members through **political socialization** or **politicization.** *Formal* political socialization involves deliberate efforts by the government, schools, and parents to teach desired values and attitudes. Reading assignments on patriotic themes and required civics courses are examples of formal political socialization. Unintentional *informal* political socialization also occurs. An uncle's efforts to "beat" a traffic ticket or a parent's casual disparaging remarks about another race set examples for children. Children learn by example. Children may learn from parents to fear other races, and this attitude may remain in force in later life. Our unconscious attitudes can affect our later opinions on specific political issues through **selective perception.**

- If we encounter information that seems consistent with our underlying attitudes, we will probably be receptive to it.
- If information runs counter to our underlying attitudes, we may reject it as lacking credibility.

Children's first view of government focuses on individual leaders and casts them as powerful but kindly figures. The president is seen as a strong, benevolent, national father figure. Gradually, children acquire more realistic, sometimes cynical, and more abstract ideas about government institutions and processes. At first the **passive virtues** of citizenship are stressed to children. Obey the law. Respect authority. Later **active virtues** emerge. Good citizens pay attention to politics. They vote. They can influence the government. Of course, the messages conveyed during political socialization are not uniform. Different social, ethnic, and economic groups transmit different political values to their children. Compared to middle-class parents, some working-class parents are more likely to demand obedience and allow less input from children in family decision making. As such their children are less likely to see themselves as influential participants in the political processes.[3]

5th Grade students reciting the Pledge of Allegiance.

© M. Siluk/Image Works.

Political socialization processes are relatively successful in building support among citizens for the nation and its institutions. Opinion surveys reveal that 96 percent of respondents are "proud to be an American." Eighty-nine percent say that they are "very patriotic." Eighty percent say their love of country is "strong" or "extremely strong." Eighty-five percent say that "whatever its faults, the United States still has the best system of government in the world."[4] Many are highly critical of specific political figures, but support for the institutions of government, for political processes, and for the nation seems to be widespread.

Numerous events and actors play a role in political socialization. Our first politically relevant learning takes place in the **family.** In early life the family cares for a child's needs, providing food, shelter, clothing, and protection. A child's attitudes about trust, rules, authority, obedience, and cooperation begin to form in this environment.

- Some families rarely discuss politics and give children little encouragement to be politically active.
- Other families regularly discuss political events around the dinner table, providing a different set of expectations.

Schools are instruments of formal political socialization. They provide basic information about how the political system operates and who major political figures are. Furthermore, schools try to reinforce the attachment of children to the nation by singing patriotic songs, teaching about national monuments and historically significant buildings, and reciting the pledge of allegiance. A prevalence of middle-class values among teachers ensures a reasonable degree of consistency in the message being conveyed to children. Nevertheless, just as there are differences among families, there are differences among school districts and teachers. To cite just one example, teachers disagree about the correctness of including the right to dissent in their definition of democracy.[6]

Peer groups also influence the opinions and attitudes of individuals. Survey respondents report that most of their friends have the same party preferences as they do.[7] Families and friends tend to be fairly homogeneous. Friendship groups naturally form so that individuals with much in common, including their political views, come together. On the other hand, people sometimes tailor their own opinions to conform to the expectations of a relevant peer group and to win acceptance.

The **mass media** also influence political opinions and attitudes. Through the media, vast amounts of political information are easily available. Candidates spend enormous sums of money on media advertising to get their messages out to voters. Numerous commentators criticize the media for oversimplifying issues and for reducing complex issues to sound bites and slogans. The media are chastised for overemphasizing titillating but unimportant matters, for putting that which is salacious ahead of that which is substantive, for "dumbing down" our level of political discourse, and for contributing to the decay of societal values. The line between the news division and the entertainment division of the television networks is becoming increasingly blurred.

- Are news magazines like *60 Minutes, 20/20,* or *Prime Time* news programs or entertainment programs?
- When a congresswoman like Susan Molinari (R-NY) announces her retirement from Congress to take over her own morning talk show, do we become even more confused?
- Do we watch?
- Do you really have to ask?

Significant emotional events can also affect our political attitudes in enduring ways. Many individuals who lived through the Great Depression in the 1930s never

Differences among school districts can be dramatic, as illustrated by a school board decision in Oakland, California, in December 1996 to recognize Black English (or "Ebonics") as a second language. Proponents explained that teachers would be trained to understand Black English so they could translate their students' statements and help them learn standard English. The emphasis would be on translation rather than correction. School board members said their motivation was to improve the performance of black students. Critics called the acceptance of Black English racist and claimed that it created lower standards for black students. Kweisi Mfume, leader of the National Association for the Advancement of Colored People, called the Oakland decision "a cruel joke being played on a number of students who need educational excellence, not educational excuses." Maya Angelou, the poet who read at President Clinton's inauguration in 1993 said, "I'm incensed. The very idea that African-American language is a language separate and apart is very threatening, because it can encourage young men and women not to learn standard English."

Children watching television.

© *Elizabeth Crews/Image Works.*

again trusted banks. When savings and loan institutions collapsed in the 1980s, some of these people shook their heads and said, "I told you so." Many Americans who lived during World War II will never trust Japan, and they view this formidable economic competitor with particular apprehension. People who experienced the Vietnam War and Watergate may never overcome their cynicism towards government. Will those who watched Kenneth Starr's investigation of President Clinton and the president's efforts to stave off impeachment ever learn to trust political leaders?

Finally, **demographic factors** seem to be related to political attitudes and orientations. Catholics; Jews; blacks; and blue-collar, working-class people have

Something to Think About

By the time American children reach the age of five, they have already spent more time watching television than they will spend talking with their fathers during their entire lifetimes.

Consider also the world of tabloid television. A "Talk Summit" was held in New York in November 1995 between daytime talk show producers and social service professionals. Participants discussed shows like the following: "Housewives vs. Strippers" (Richard Bey); "You're Cheating and I Have Proof" (Rickie Lake); "Confronting the Woman Coming on to My Man" and "Mother Who Ran off with Her Daughter's Fiance" (Jenny Jones); "My Mom Is Way Too Sexy" and "You're Too Old to Be Dating a Teen" (Maury Povich); "Get Bigger Breasts—or Else" (Rolanda); "Surprise, I'm Your Secret Lover" (Sally Jessy Raphael); "My Sister Stole My Lover" (Jerry Springer); "Irresponsible Teen Moms" and "Married Men Who Have Relationships with Their Next-Door Neighbors" (Montel Williams). Such shows are on in the morning, afternoon, and early evening when more than 650,000 American children ages two to eleven are watching television. Connecticut Senator Joseph Lieberman says that these shows "make the abnormal normal." A *Newsweek* poll found that nearly two-thirds of the public believe that talk shows decrease the amount of shame attached to abhorrent behavior "by making these people seem like celebrities or victims themselves."[8]

The American Medical Association reported in November 1995 that it surveyed children between the ages of eleven and fourteen and found that most of the boys (76 percent) and girls (56 percent) thought it was sometimes OK to force someone to have sex. The "acceptable" circumstances included the following: if the boy spent a lot of money on the girl (51 percent of the boys and 41 percent of the girls); if a man raped a woman with whom he had a past sexual history (31 percent of the boys and 32 percent of the girls); if the man and woman were married (87 percent of the boys and 79 percent of the girls); if they had been dating more than six months (65 percent of the boys and 47 percent of the girls).[9] Is America's sexual-assault-awareness campaign succeeding?

Although it would be unfair to hold television entirely responsible for cultural pollution, television is undeniably an important socialization instrument.

Table 4.1

Partisan Identification, Gallup Poll, Cross Section, 1996 (percent)

	Republican	Independent	Democrat
Gender			
Men	33	35	32
Women	29	30	40
Age			
18–29	27	40	33
30–49	31	34	35
50–64	35	29	36
65 and over	31	23	46
Race			
White	35	33	32
Black	3	24	73
Education			
No college	26	32	43
College incomplete	33	33	34
College graduate	41	29	30
Postgraduate	34	35	31
Household income			
Under $20,000	19	34	47
$20,000–29,999	27	28	45
$30,000–49,999	34	34	33
$50,000 and over	41	30	29
Ideology			
Conservative	51	25	25
Moderate	23	36	41
Liberal	6	34	59
Region			
East	24	31	45
Midwest	32	34	34
South	32	35	33
West	35	30	35
National	31	33	37

Note: Question: "In politics, as of today, do you consider yourself a Republican, a Democrat, or an Independent?" Percentages are based on the 2,416 total respondents in a general election tracking poll, November 3–4, 1996. Sources: Unpublished data from the Gallup Poll as cited in Harold W. Stanley and Richard G. Niemi, *Vital Statistics on American Politics,* 6th ed. (Congressional Quarterly, 1998), p. 111.

historically been more likely to identify themselves as Democrats rather than as Republicans. Protestants and college-educated, upper-income, white-collar professionals have been more likely to be Republican identifiers. Table 4.1 displays some relevant figures concerning party identification.

There is overlap, to be sure. There are Republican welders and Catholic bankers. Such individuals, however, are subjected to **cross pressures.** Here two (or more) forces act on the individual, one in a Democratic direction and another in a Republican direction. The cross-pressure hypothesis holds that the behavior of individuals under consistent pressure is different from that of individuals under cross pressure. According to this theory

- Individuals subjected to consistent pressure are more likely to vote a straight ticket; make early voting decisions; and have a high interest in politics, high information levels, and consistent attitudes.
- Individuals subjected to cross pressures are more likely to vote split tickets, make late voting decisions, and have a low interest in politics, low information levels, and conflicting attitudes.[10]

Intensity of Preference

America's political culture places a high value on the one person, one vote principle. We believe that all votes should be weighted equally. Accordingly, a woman's vote counts the same as a man's vote. A black person's vote counts the same as a white person's vote. A poor person's vote counts the same as a wealthy person's vote. But the principle also means that an uninformed person's vote counts the same as an informed person's vote. And the vote of a person who cares very little about the issues counts the same as the vote of a person who cares a great deal. In short, the one person, one vote principle does not account for differences in the intensity of our preferences.

Imagine that two referendum questions are put before the voters. On the first question 75 percent of the people vote yes, and they care more about the issue than the no voters do. Here the majority wins by virtue of its greater numbers. And the yes voters should win because of their greater intensity. On the second question the yes position wins by the slimmest of margins: 51 percent to 49 percent. This time, however, the yes voters care little about the matter, whereas the no voters have great intensity. Here the numbers are on the yes side, but the greater intensity is on the no side. Who wins? According to the one person, one vote principle, the majority wins. Period. All votes are counted equally. But in terms of intensity levels, it would be better if the no voters had prevailed.

Does the American political system account for differences in intensity? Yes. Two of James Madison's ideas are directly relevant. First, Madison's **trustee representative** acts on the basis of calm deliberation and enlightened self-interest. It is reasonable for this legislator to resist the wishes of the lukewarm majority and to follow, instead, the minority's more intense instructions. Further, the intense minority has the motivation to mobilize into a **faction** or group. In this form the minority can demonstrate the depth of its commitment and reemphasize it's views to representatives. If the lukewarm majority later becomes concerned about such developments, its own intensity level would increase. These voters could also approach the representative and could, eventually, vote him or her out of office for not responding to them. In this way the system is designed to respond but in **delayed** fashion.[11]

Voting and Voters: How Well-Informed Are Voters?

In an ideal democratic system, voters are well-informed and active. Do American voters match this ideal? Who is the average American voter? According to demographic profiles, in the 1970s she was a thirty-year-old housewife living in suburban Dayton, Ohio, married to a machinist. More recently, she is a thirty-three-year-old mother who attended college, works outside the home part-time, lives in a housing development in the Sunbelt, and is married to the manager of the produce department at the supermarket (that is, he wears a white collar with a blue ring around it). She is of European descent; owns a home, two televisions, and a VCR; has credit-card debt, and drinks low-fat milk. There she is. The average American voter. Question: How well-informed is she?

Mixed Evidence

During the 1950s and 1960s, many observers concluded that American citizens lack political sophistication. Some went so far as to claim that Americans are incapable of making intelligent voting decisions. An ironic implication was that educated elites were seen as protectors of the "democratic creed" against the ill-tempered, ill-informed masses. Put bluntly, this **democratic-elitist** message was that "the masses are asses." But contrary studies began to emerge. In *The Responsible Electorate*, V. O. Key Jr. explained that his book was dedicated to "the perverse and unorthodox argument . . . that voters are not fools."[12] Others noted that in national elections, voters generally reject extremely liberal and extremely conservative candidates, preferring moderates. Successful candidates target these moderate voters and frame their issue positions accordingly. In the process candidates blur differences between themselves. Voters who have trouble identifying differences between candidates, are not necessarily uninformed. In fact, the actual differences may be slight.[13]

Evidence concerning voter information levels remains mixed. Consider some of the following studies:

- There is wide support among the masses for democratic ideals in the abstract, but that support diminishes if the abstract ideal is put into more concrete terms. For example, a respondent agrees that citizens have a right to dissent, but flag burning should be outlawed. Or citizens have a right to circulate petitions but should not be allowed to come to my house asking for my signature on a petition to legalize marijuana.

- Americans do take positions on public policy questions but those positions are not necessarily consistent. **Issue constraint** or issue consistency is not impressive, especially when the relationship between domestic and foreign policy issues is studied.

Many Americans have trouble naming their representatives, senators, and their parties. There is more. During national bicentennial celebrations at Philadelphia's Independence Hall, copies of the Declaration of Independence were circulated, and most people could not identify it. On July 4, 1976, the *New York Daily News* surveyed people in Times Square with the question, What do Americans celebrate on the Fourth of July? Fewer than one in four knew the answer. Children and foreign tourists did best.

- In general, Americans are neither consistently liberal nor consistently conservative on a wide range of issues. An individual may have liberal views on social issues, conservative views on economic policy, and moderate views on international affairs. The more **educated** people are, the more likely they are to hold consistent views. However, **interest** in politics is the most important factor here. People's views become more **consistent** as they become more concerned with issues and more attentive to political leaders.[14]

- Voters often base their decisions on their political experiences. They assess the past performances of the parties and elected officials, keep a running tally of party promises and performances, and decide on the basis of this **retrospective evaluation.** Even though the voter does not know much about the issues in a current campaign, his or her choice has a rational basis over time.[15]

- Others conclude that political awareness has not declined and citizens are sufficiently informed to make meaningful voting choices. However, there are systematic biases in what citizens know based on ethnicity, gender, race, and class.[16]

On the positive side voters' issue positions are sometimes closely related to voting in presidential elections. A study of the 1964 Johnson–Goldwater contest found that only 25 percent of the electorate was "nonrational" or uninformed.[17] Research on the 1972 Nixon–McGovern campaign demonstrated that Nixon and McGovern voters had sharp issue disagreements on five key issue areas (social programs, welfare, size of government, school integration, and the Cold War), and these disagreements among voters corresponded to differences between the candidates. In other words, voters voted for the candidate with whom they agreed on these issues.[18] Similarly, studies of the 1988 Bush–Dukakis campaign revealed strong relationships between voters' economic and foreign policy views and their votes.[19]

American voters often fall short of the well-informed ideal, but these shortcomings can be overcome *if* voters see the issues and the election as important to them. That "if" can be a big one.

Anticipated Reactions

How does the general public influence policy makers' decisions if citizens are frequently not paying attention? How do voters influence a legislator's vote on a bill when most voters will not know how the legislator votes on this bill and perhaps half of the people back home do not even know who their representative is? Carl Friedrich coined the term **anticipated reactions** to describe how even uninformed voters exercise some control over elected officials.[20]

To illustrate this concept, imagine that Mr. Smith earns a college degree, gets a job, and moves to a new city. He finds an apartment he can afford and begins settling in. Unfortunately, he has moved into a high-crime area. Every night he hears glass breaking, shouts, police sirens, and worse. He can't sleep. One morning he goes to the pet shop on the corner. He tells the proprietor he wants the most ferocious watchdog in the store. He leaves with ninety pounds of snarling muscle and teeth. "Perfect," Smith thinks. That night, for the first night in weeks, Smith sleeps soundly. So does the dog. While they sleep, two burglars pick the lock to Smith's front door. They open the door and notice the snoring dog on the floor in front of them. They enter anyway, quietly step over the dog, and proceed to burglarize the apartment. They take Smith's credit cards, cash, baseball cards, and comic book collection. On their way out they quietly step over the still-sleeping watchdog and close the door behind them. The next morning Smith is outraged when he discovers what happened. He takes the dog back to the pet shop and demands a refund. The owner tells Smith to calm down and explains that if the dog had not been "on duty," things would have been worse. The thieves would have taken Smith's television, stereo, and other bulky items too, but they didn't want to wake up the dog. Even though the dog was asleep, he still influenced the burglars' behavior. Smith may or may not have found this argument convincing, but it does illustrate the concept of anticipated reactions rather well. The burglars anticipated how the dog would have reacted if he had awakened and tried to prevent a "negative" reaction.

Following analogous reasoning, we can say that the public is often sleeping while important public policy issues are being debated, reported, and decided. But if the public awakens, some public officials will lose their positions. If a public official becomes involved in a scandal or takes positions unpopular back in the home district, voters might find out and react. Office holders try to head off trouble before it arises. They anticipate how the public would react to their deeds if the public found out about them. How do voters find out? Several ways:

1. Most people may not follow politics closely, some people do. They read newspapers and magazines, watch the news and C-SPAN. They follow politics like some people follow sports. These **opinion leaders** will notice and will spread the word when a public figure gets out of line.

2. To lose a seat, an elected official does not have to alienate everyone who voted for him or her last time. A shift of a few thousand votes from candidate A to candidate B can change the outcome. For this reason, elected officials try to anticipate the reactions of **interested minorities.**

3. An **opposing candidate** will scrutinize an incumbent's record in search of an unpopular vote or action and will publicize any potentially damaging information.

4. The **media** will report on elected officials' actions, especially scandalous ones.

In these ways even a slumbering, inattentive electorate can be awakened and exercise some control over public officials. Still, politicians may be anticipating what they can get away with rather than calculating what is best for the people at home. In the watchdog analogy legislators are cast in the role of burglars. The more informed and attentive the voters are, the more control they have over these officials.

Democracy Unplugged: How Active Are American Voters?

Low Turnout

As noted the ideal democratic voter is well-informed and active. Frequently, people are poorly informed, especially in elections below the presidential level. Is the ideal met in the second sense? How active are American voters? Not very. Low **turnout levels** are the norm rather than the exception. Table 4.2 demonstrates that voting-age people who do not vote in presidential elections regularly outnumber those who vote for the winning candidate. To put it another way, nonvoters have in effect "won" every presidential election since 1932!

The raw numbers displayed in table 4.3 make this point even more vividly. In 1980 Ronald Reagan was widely reported to have won in a popular-vote "landslide." But while he outpolled President Carter by more than eight million popular votes, approximately seventy-two million voting-age citizens did not vote at all! Reagan's 42.9 million popular votes pale by comparison. The same pattern has followed in subsequent elections. President Clinton failed to win more than 50 percent of the popular vote in 1992 and again in 1996. Both times, he was elected with a plurality rather than a majority of the popular vote. More telling, however, is the fact that there were about *twice* as many nonvoters as Clinton voters in 1996.

A quiet day at the polls.

© Bob Daemmrich/Stock Boston.

Table 4.2

		Voters	Nonvoters
		(% of voting-age population)	
1932	Roosevelt-Hoover	52.4%	47.6%
1936	Roosevelt-Landon	56.0	44.0
1940	Roosevelt-Wilkie	58.9	41.1
1944	Roosevelt-Dewey	56.0	44.0
1948	Truman-Dewey	51.1	48.9
1952	Eisenhower-Stevenson	61.6	38.4
1956	Eisenhower-Stevenson	59.3	40.7
1960	Kennedy-Nixon	62.8	37.2
1964	Johnson-Goldwater	61.9	38.1
1968	Nixon-Humphrey-Wallace	60.9	39.1
1972	Nixon-McGovern	55.2	44.8
1976	Carter-Ford	53.5	46.5
1980	Reagan-Carter-Anderson	54.0	46.0
1984	Reagan-Mondale	53.1	46.9
1988	Bush-Dukakis	50.2	49.8
1992	Clinton-Bush-Perot	55.9	44.1
1996	Clinton-Dole-Perot	49.0	51.0

Voter Turnout in Presidential Elections: Percentages

Source: Federal Election Commission; Commission for the Study of the American Electorate.

Off-Year Congressional Elections

Fewer people vote in congressional elections than in presidential elections. In off-year congressional elections, turnout drops by about 15 percent. In primaries and local elections, turnout is usually even lower. Voter interest in an election is related to the level of media coverage, the perceived importance of the office and the issues, the attractiveness of the candidates, and the competitiveness of the race. Accordingly, voters tend to view presidential contests as **high-stimulus elections** and other races as **low-stimulus elections.**[21] This distinction contributes to the so-called **coattail effect.** The president's party usually loses seats in the House of Representatives in off-year elections. In fact, from 1906 through 1996, the president's party lost an average of almost thirty-four House seats in off-year elections. Why? One theory is that weak partisans and independents are drawn to the polls in presidential elections. Once in the voting booth, they also cast ballots in congressional races. When the

QuotableQuote

Bad officials are the ones elected by good citizens who do not vote.
—George Nathan

Table 4.3

Voter Turnout in Presidential Elections: Raw Numbers

		Popular Votes (in millions)
1976	Carter	40.8
	Ford	39.15
	Nonvoters	69.5
1980	Reagan	43.9
	Carter	35.4
	Anderson	5.7
	Nonvoters	72.4
1984	Reagan	54.5
	Mondale	37.6
	Nonvoters	81.3
1988	Bush	48.9
	Dukakis	41.8
	Nonvoters	90
1992	Clinton	44.9
	Bush	39.1
	Perot	19.2
	Nonvoters	82
1996	Clinton	47.4
	Dole	39.2
	Perot	8.1
	Nonvoters	98.6

Source: *World Almanac and Book of Facts,* 1999 (Mahwah, NJ: World Almanac Books, 1999) p. 494; *Statistical Abstract of the United States 1998: The National Data Book,* 118th ed. (United States Department of Commerce, 1998) Tables 458 and 459, p. 279.

winning presidential candidate's supporters decide to assist the candidate by voting for fellow party members, these congressional candidates may ride the winner's coattails into office. In a subsequent off-year election, however, many of these less committed voters, or **drop-off voters,** will fail to turn out. Without the artificial boost from a winning presidential candidate, some congressional incumbents will be unable to retain their seats.[22]

The 1998 election results were unusual in that President Clinton's fellow Democrats actually *gained* five seats in the House. Disappointed Republicans blamed Speaker of the House, Newt Gingrich, for overemphasizing Clinton's legal problems and impeachment prospects. Was there a "backlash" from voters? Gingrich decided to resign as Speaker and announced that he would leave Congress, in spite of the fact that he had been reelected by a large margin.[23]

The Right to Vote

So who votes? The Constitution left the question of who would have **the right to vote** to states. Most adults today are eligible to vote, but many do not. In colonial days and in the nation's early years, only **white, male, property owners** were eligible to vote. States varied with respect to the amount of property one had to own and with the enforcement of these restrictions. In the most permissive states, more than 80 percent of white male adults could vote, while in the most restrictive states, fewer than 10 percent were legally eligible. Gradually, suffrage was granted to all white males. **Black males** were enfranchised with the ratification of the Fifteenth Amendment in 1870. Blacks in the South were effectively disenfranchised in the late nineteenth and early twentieth centuries, however, through the use of white primaries, poll taxes, literacy tests, discriminatory administrative procedures, and intimidation. The Supreme Court ruled that white primaries are unconstitutional. Poll taxes became unpopular because white voters did not want to pay to vote. Literacy tests were abused as high standards of "civic literacy" were applied to blacks while whites were usually required merely to sign their names. The Voting Rights Act of 1965 addressed literacy test inequities. Registration rates for whites and blacks in the South today are approximately equal, and southern turnout rates are about the same as northern turnout rates in presidential elections. Another major expansion occurred in 1920 when the Nineteenth Amendment gave **women** the right to vote. The size of the electorate roughly doubled. In 1971 the Twenty-Sixth Amendment allowed **eighteen year olds** to vote. Remaining state restrictions on voting vary. In some states convicted felons cannot vote until after they have completed their sentences. In other states, felons permanently lose the right to vote. Residency and registration requirements vary. At present most adults have the legal right to vote. But who exercises this right?[24]

Who Votes?

Data from recent presidential and congressional races make some generalizations possible. This data are displayed in table 4.4 on pages 84 and 85.

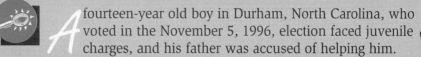

A fourteen-year old boy in Durham, North Carolina, who voted in the November 5, 1996, election faced juvenile charges, and his father was accused of helping him. The boy registered to vote at a rock concert. He used his own name but listed his birth year as 1956, which would have made him forty. He went with his father to vote. The boy was charged with felony counts of illegal voting and providing false information on a voter registration card. The father was charged with being an accessory after the fact of voter fraud and with a misdemeanor charge of contributing to the delinquency of a minor.

Both father and son voted straight Republican ballots.

- Whites are more likely to register and vote than blacks are.
- Blacks are more likely to register and vote than Hispanics are.
- Registration and turnout differences between men and women are insignificant.
- Eighteen to twenty year olds are least likely to register and vote.

Although young people are slightly less politically interested than older people of similar education levels, much nonvoting among younger people can be attributed to the unsettled circumstances of the age group. Military service, being away at college, failure to meet residency and registration requirements are voting barriers that affect the young more than older citizens.[25] The likelihood of voting increases with age until age sixty-five. At this point turnout declines somewhat, but the decline is more attributable to physical difficulties in getting to the polls than to a decline in interest in political affairs. Employed and educated people are more likely to vote than are unemployed people with less education.

By age thirty-five most people become at least occasional voters. Habitual nonvoters who repeatedly fail to vote account for about 5 percent of the total electorate.[26] Who votes? white, working, well-educated people. High-income, white-collar professionals. Who doesn't vote? Minorities, younger citizens

Table 4.4

Voting-Age Population Registered and Voting, Cross Sections, 1976–1994[a] (percent)

| | Percentage Reporting They Registered | | | | | | | | | |
| | Presidential Election Years | | | | | Congressional Election Years | | | | |
	1976	1980	1984	1988	1992	1978	1982	1986	1990	1994
Race/ethnicity										
White	68	68	70	68	70	64	66	65	64	64
Black	59	60	66	65	64	57	59	64	59	58
Hispanic origin[b]	38	36	40	36	35	33	35	36	32	30
Hispanic citizen[b]	51	54	59	57	59	48	52	54	52	53
Sex										
Male	67	67	67	65	67	63	64	63	61	61
Female	66	67	69	68	69	63	64	65	63	63
Region[c]										
Northeast	66	65	67	65	67	62	63	62	61	61
Midwest	72	74	75	73	75	68	71	71	68	69
South	68	64	64	66	67	60	62	63	61	61
West	63	63	65	63	64	59	61	61	58	58
Age										
18–20	47	45	47	45	48	35	35	35	35	37
21–24	55	53	54	51	55	45	48	47	43	46
25–34	62	62	63	58	61	56	57	56	52	52
35–44	70	71	71	69	69	67	68	68	66	63
45–64	76	76	77	76	75	74	76	75	71	71
65 and older	71	75	77	78	78	73	75	77	80	76
Employment										
Employed	69	69	69	67	70	63	66	64	63	63
Unemployed	52	50	54	50	54	44	50	49	45	46
Not in labor force	65	66	68	67	67	63	64	66	63	62
Education (years)										
8 or less	54	53	53	48	44	53	52	51	44	40
1–3 of high school	56	55	55	53	50	53	53	52	48	45
4 of high school	67	66	67	65	65	62	63	63	60	59
1–3 of college	75	74	76	74	75	69	70	70	69	68
4 or more college	84	84	84	83	85	77	78	78	77	76
Total	67	67	68	67	68	62	64	64	62	62

[a]Data for earlier years can be found in previous editions of *Vital Statistics on American Politics.*
[b]Persons of Hispanic origin may be of any race.
Sources: U.S. Bureau of the Census, Current Population Reports, *Voting and Registration in the Election of November 1976* (Washington, D.C.: U.S. Government Printing Office, 1993), Series P-20, no. 322, 11-12, 14-21, 57, 61; *November 1978,* no. 344, 8, 11-19, 60, 65; *November 1980,* no. 370, 10-20, 50, 56; *November 1982,* no. 383, 1-12, 46, 49; *November 1984,* no. 405, 13-24, 59; *November 1986,* no. 414, 11-22, 29, 31; *November 1988,* no. 440, 13-24, 48, 50; *November 1990*

Percentage Reporting They Voted

Presidential Election Years					Congressional Election Years				
1976	1980	1984	1988	1992	1978	1982	1986	1990	1994
61	61	61	59	64	47	50	47	47	47
49	51	56	52	54	37	43	43	39	37
32	30	33	29	29	24	25	24	21	19
43	44	48	46	48	34	37	36	34	34
60	59	59	56	60	47	49	46	45	44
59	59	61	58	62	45	48	46	45	45
60	59	60	57	61	48	50	44	45	45
65	66	66	63	67	51	55	50	49	49
55	56	57	55	59	40	42	43	42	41
58	57	59	56	59	48	51	48	45	46
38	36	37	33	38	20	20	19	18	17
46	43	44	38	46	26	28	24	22	22
55	55	55	48	53	38	40	35	34	32
63	64	64	61	64	50	52	49	48	46
69	69	70	68	70	59	62	59	56	56
62	65	68	69	70	56	60	61	66	61
62	62	62	58	64	47	50	46	45	45
44	41	44	39	46	27	34	30	28	28
57	57	59	57	59	46	49	48	47	45
44	43	43	37	35	35	36	33	28	23
47	46	44	41	41	35	38	34	31	27
59	59	59	55	58	45	47	44	42	40
68	67	68	65	69	52	53	50	50	49
80	80	79	78	81	64	67	63	63	63
59	59	60	57	61	46	49	46	45	45

no. 453, 1-2, 4, 13-14, 17; *November, 1992*, no. 466, v-vii, 1, 5; "Voter Turnout in November 1994 Election," press release, 8 June 1995, from the November 1994 Current Population Survey on Internet (http://www.densus, gov/org/pop)as cited in Harold W. Stanley and Richard G. Niemi, *Vital Statistics on American Politics, (5th ed.)*, *(Congressional Quarterly, 1995)*, p. 79.

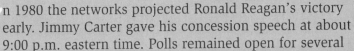
(including many college students), the unemployed, and the uneducated. Because education, employment status, and income tend to go together, people who vote are relatively "better off" in socioeconomic terms than are nonvoters.

Why Not Vote?

Next question: Why don't people vote? Answers, explanations, and excuses abound.

- Some people don't vote because of peer pressure. If your friends and colleagues think that voting is a waste of time, this attitude may rub off on you.
- Some people don't vote if the weather is bad.
- Some don't vote if they believe their favorite candidate can't win (or lose, for that matter).

QuotableQuote

Meet the new boss.
Same as the old boss.
—Peter Townshend

- Some, in effect, defer to the "experts." They reason along these lines: "The budget deficit is a complex problem. I don't know how to fix it. It would be irresponsible for me to vote for one of the offered alternatives."
- Some nonvoters reject both candidates: "They are both bums. Why vote?"
- Some are alienated or cynical: "My one vote won't decide the outcome." "All the candidates are alike." "It doesn't matter who wins."[27]

- Some don't vote because they failed to register. Or they moved and missed the residency requirement. Or they are away from home and failed to get an absentee ballot. Or they won't register in the hope that this will help them avoid jury duty.
- Many don't vote because they are "too busy."[28]

No doubt, the preceding list could be expanded. It suffices, however, to make the point that people have many reasons for not voting, and they will vote if they perceive an election as important to them. This behavior brings up another questions: Is not voting rational?

Rationality is often defined in **cost-benefit terms.** If the benefits associated with an action outweigh the costs, the action is rational. If the costs outweigh the benefits, it is irrational. What **costs** are associated with voting?

- You have to make sure you are registered.
- You have to travel to the polls.
- You might have to wait in line.
- You might be late for work, or maybe you will have to leave work a little early.
- You might have to take your kids with you.
- Maybe it's raining and you will get wet.

Now consider the **benefits.** Do you think your one vote will decide the outcome? Probably not. It seems that the costs of voting outweigh the benefits. Voting appears irrational!

Why Vote?

So why vote? David Letterman proposed that turnout would increase if we gave people toasters and other small appliances when they voted. In the absence of such inducements, does it make sense to vote? Numerous arguments can be advanced. Keep in mind that democratic citizens have rights and obligations. Voting is *both* a right and an obligation. Voting is a matter of civic duty. It is one of our most important duties, one of the easiest ones to fulfill, yet one of the most neglected. Do you find politics boring and disgusting? Guess what? Many things in life are unpleasant. Do you enjoy going to the dentist or getting a medical examination? There are things that we do because we *should*. Vote because participation is valuable in its own right. Write in

QuotableQuote

There is . . . a price to freedom. Freedom doesn't just happen automatically—and in much of the world, it doesn't happen at all. . . .

Our children's future depends on our citizenship today, just as our own freedom is a result of American lives sacrificed in the past on battlefields far from home.

Maybe you can't get away to walk through those fields of crosses at Normandy. But perhaps there is a military cemetery not too far from where you live. Sometime you might take a walk down those long rows of crosses.

Look at the dates of birth and death. Notice how old they were—or rather, how young they were—when their lives were snuffed out. Then go home and look into the mirror and say that you don't have the time to keep up with issues that affect the future of this country. Say that you find this stuff boring or that you have other things to do.
—**Thomas Sowell**[29]

U.S. Military Cemetery, Normandy, France.

© Bachman/Photo Researchers.

a protest candidate if you are dissatisfied with the choices but vote to demonstrate your support for elections as a means of selecting leaders. In this way leaders must continue to anticipate how you would react to their misdeeds if you found out about them. Voting preserves accountability.

Anything else? By voting you can promote policies that will benefit *you*. If you and your peers do not vote, then elected officials can safely ignore you and cut *your* programs when pressed to reduce spending. Knowing that eighteen to twenty year olds vote less frequently than retirees vote makes it a lot easier to cut student loans than to cut Medicare. Further, low turnout adds to the clout of an intense minority group in your community. Perhaps some radicals in your town are pushing their extreme political agenda. They will vote. You have a chance to offset them. Will

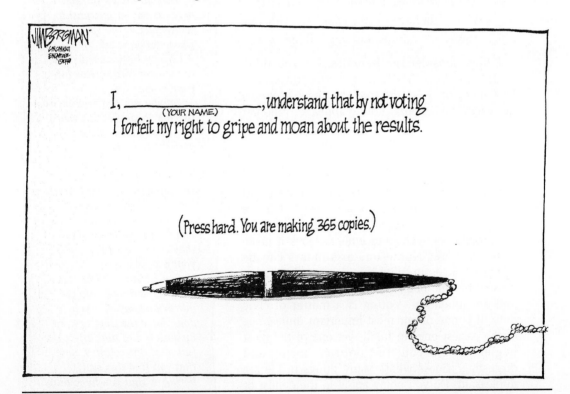

I, _____ , understand that by not voting
        (YOUR NAME)
I forfeit my right to gripe and moan about the results.

(Press hard. You are making 365 copies.)

"Sign Your Name."

As Published in Altoona Mirror, November 3, 1998, A6. Reprinted with special permission of King Features Syndicate.

n 1996 Congressman Robert K. "Bob" Dornan, a Republican representing California's forty-sixth district, narrowly lost his seat in the general election to Democrat Loretta Sanchez. Dornan held a 233-vote lead after the initial count, but Sanchez pulled ahead by a few hundred votes after mailed-in ballots were counted.

Republican Jon D. Fox, a Republican representative from Pennsylvania, initially won reelection over Democrat Joseph M. Hoeffel by a mere ten votes. Hoeffel conceded on November 14, 1996, after a final count put Fox up by eighty-four votes.

Some local races have been even closer. Here are some examples from 1997 primaries in western Pennsylvania:

David Schade and Fred Swanson sought to become the Democratic candidate in the race for mayor of Brentwood, a Pittsburgh suburb. They tied at 877 votes each. In accordance with state law, they drew lots to break the tie. Each shook a marble-sized ball from a leather flask, and Schade won by drawing the higher number.

Pauline Abdullah tied with Thomas Napolitano in their race for the Democratic mayoral nomination in Braddock, Pennsylvania. Abdullah won by drawing a higher-numbered ball.

In Warren County candidates rolled a single die to decide a tie for the Republican nomination to elect a new county school board president.

In Loretto, Pennsylvania, William Toth received forty-three votes to David J. Eckenrode's forty-two votes in their race for the Democratic mayoral nomination.

Does a single vote decide an election? It happens.

you take it? Voting is also the easiest way for average citizens to express their views, including their frustrations, to the government. Some argue that if you don't vote, you have no right to complain afterwards. Vote or shut up. Furthermore, some elections (especially local ones) are decided by slim margins. Here your single vote can be critical.

Calvin and Hobbes
by Bill Watterson

"Calvin & Hobbes."

Key Terms

Notes

Collective Links to Public Officials: Parties and Interest Groups

Political Parties and Party Identification

More people identify themselves as Democrats than as Republicans. We have already seen that college-educated, upper-income, white-collar professionals tend to identify with the Republican Party, and such people are most likely to vote. One reason that Republican candidates often do well in national elections, despite the Democrats' superior numbers, is that Republicans have higher turnout rates. In 1976 Jimmy Carter and Walter Mondale advocated voter registration reform to make it easier for people to vote. They argued that turnout was too low in the United States and that their proposal was nonpartisan. Do you find it coincidental that Democrats led this attempt to increase turnout?

Congress, with President Clinton's support, adopted the **motor-voter law** in 1993. The law, which took effect in 1995, requires states to

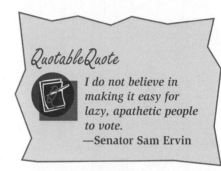

QuotableQuote

I do not believe in making it easy for lazy, apathetic people to vote.
—**Senator Sam Ervin**

- Allow citizens to register to vote when they apply for a driver's license
- Provide voter registration forms at military recruitment offices
- Permit registration by mail
- Allow citizens to register to vote at welfare and disability benefits offices

In opposition, Republicans predicted that the bill would pad the voting rolls with poorer people who tended to support Democrats.

Liberals and Conservatives

Liberals are more likely to be Democrats, and conservatives are more likely to be Republicans. Generally, **liberals** favor social change, advocate equality, and support government involvement in providing social services. **Conservatives** promote traditional values, advocate law and order, call for freedom from economic regulation, and envision a more limited social role for government.[1] As demonstrated in table 5.1, self-described liberals have declined in number since 1973, whereas the number of conservatives has increased.

Independents

Another important generalization is that the percentage of people identifying themselves as Democrats or Republicans has decreased since 1952, while the percentage of people identifying themselves as independents has increased.

Table 5.1

Liberal or Conservative Self-Identification, 1973–1996 (Percent)

Date	Extremely Liberal	Liberal	Slightly Liberal	Moderate	Slightly Conservative	Conservative	Extremely Conservative	Don't Know	Number of Interviews
March 1973	4	14	13	36	13	13	3	6	1,484
March 1974	1	14	14	38	15	11	2	5	1,480
March 1975	3	12	13	38	16	10	2	5	1,478
March 1976	2	13	12	37	15	13	2	6	1,494
March 1977	2	11	14	37	16	12	3	5	1,524
March 1978	1	9	16	36	17	12	2	5	1,505
March 1980	2	8	14	40	18	12	3	2	1,451
March 1982	2	9	15	39	14	13	4	4	1,495
March 1983	2	8	12	40	18	13	2	4	801
March 1984	2	9	12	39	19	13	3	4	1,462
March 1985	2	11	11	37	18	14	3	4	1,525
March 1986	2	9	12	39	16	14	3	5	1,468
March 1987	2	12	13	37	16	12	2	4	1,437
March 1988	2	12	13	35	17	15	2	4	1,472
March 1989	3	12	12	37	16	13	2	6	1,530
March 1990	3	10	13	35	18	14	4	4	1,368
March 1991	2	10	14	39	14	14	3	4	1,513
March 1993	2	11	13	36	17	16	3	3	1,597
March 1994	2	11	13	35	16	16	3	3	2,980
March 1996	2	10	12	36	16	16	3	5	2,898

Note: Question: "We hear a lot of talk these days about liberals and conservatives. I'm going to show you a seven-point scale on which the political views that people might hold are arranged from extremely liberal—point 1—to extremely conservative—point 7. Where would you place yourself on this scale?"

Source: General Social Survey, National Opinion Research Center, University of Chicago, as cited in Harold W. Stanley and Richard G. Niemi, *Vital Statistics on American Politics*, 6th ed. (Congressional Quarterly, 1998), p. 112.

Table 5.2 shows that in 1952 forty-seven percent of the people identified themselves as strong or weak Democrats, 28 percent identified themselves as strong or weak Republicans, and 23 percent identified themselves as independents (some of whom "leaned" in a Democratic or Republican direction). In 1994 only 39 percent identified themselves as strong or weak Democrats (a drop of 8 percent). Twenty-eight percent identified themselves as strong or weak Republicans (no change), and 34 percent identified themselves as independents (an increase of 11 percent). This increase in the percentage of independent identifiers supports the claim that a **dealignment** is taking place and that parties are dying. Are parties becoming obsolete? What is the **independent message?**

First, take a closer look at the data. If one concentrates on voter **behavior** and not merely on how people identify themselves, the decline of parties is not so dramatic. Including independents who leaned in their direction in 1996, 53 percent of those surveyed favored the Democrats, 39 percent favored the Republicans, and 9 percent were truly independent. In 1952 six percent of the respondents could be classified as hard-core independents. Their numbers have increased, but not as markedly as it appears at first glance.

- More than one-third of people who identify themselves as independents regularly vote for Democrats.
- Another third or more of these independents regularly vote for Republicans.
- The remaining genuine independents who do not predictably vote for either party often have little interest in politics.
- To put it another way, nine out of ten voters continue to behave as though party labels matter to them. Many so-called independents are **closet partisans.**

Split-ticket voting has increased since the early 1970s.[2] Such voters do not vote for all the candidates on a single party's ticket. Does this behavior signify party decline? Not necessarily. Given the high visibility of presidential elections, it is not surprising that voters need not base their decisions on the party label. In less visible, lower-level elections, however, party-line voting remains common. Further, the data in table 5.3 show that even at the presidential level voters usually support their own party's candidate.

QuotableQuote

Some problems are so complex that it takes high intelligence just to be undecided about them.
—**Anonymous**

In the 1960s and early 1970s, **cross-cutting political issues** like United States involvement in the Vietnam War were dominant. These issues cut across traditional party lines and pitted Democrat against Democrat and Republican against Republican. At such times it is understandable that many voters found party labels to be relatively unimportant. In more recent years **traditional political issues** have regained their centrality as much public debate focuses on jobs, welfare, and the budget deficit. Such issues traditionally find Democrats on one side and Republicans on the other. These issues reinforce party differences.

Finally, independents are somewhat younger than their more partisan counterparts. Party ties usually strengthen with age. As the electorate ages, party identification should also strengthen. In sum, the obituary notices for parties seem premature.[3]

Table 5.2

Partisan Identification, National Election Studies, 1952–1996 (Percent)

Year	Democrat			Independent	Republican			Apolitical	Total	Number of interviews
	Strong	Weak	Independent	Independent	Independent	Weak	Strong			
1952	22	25	10	6	7	14	14	3	101	1,784
1954	22	25	9	7	6	14	13	4	100	1,130
1956	21	23	6	9	8	14	15	4	100	1,757
1958	27	22	7	7	5	17	11	4	100	1,808
1960	20	25	6	10	7	14	16	2	100	1,911
1962	23	23	7	8	6	16	12	4	99	1,287
1964	27	25	9	8	6	14	11	1	101	1,550
1966	18	28	9	12	7	15	10	1	100	1,278
1968	20	25	10	11	9	15	10	1	101	1,553
1970	20	24	10	13	8	15	9	1	100	1,501
1972	15	26	11	13	10	13	10	1	99	2,694
1974	17	21	13	15	9	14	8	3	100	2,505
1976	15	25	12	15	10	14	9	1	101	2,850
1978	15	24	14	14	10	13	8	3	101	2,283
1980	18	23	11	13	10	14	9	2	100	1,613
1982	20	24	11	11	8	14	10	2	100	1,418
1984	17	20	11	11	12	15	12	2	100	2,236
1986	18	22	10	12	11	15	10	2	100	2,166
1988	17	18	12	11	13	14	14	2	101	2,032
1990	20	19	12	11	12	15	10	2	101	1,991
1992	17	18	14	12	13	15	11	1	101	2,487
1994	15	19	13	10	12	15	16	1	101	1,795
1996	19	20	14	9	11	15	13	0	101	1,695

Note: Question: "Generally speaking, do you consider yourself a Republican, a Democrat, and Independent, or what?" If Republican or Democrat: "Would you call yourself a strong (R/D) or a not very strong (R/D)?" If Independent or other: "Do you think of yourself as closer to the Republican or Democratic party?"

Source: Calculated by the editors from National Election Studies data, Center for Political Studies, University of Michigan, as cited in Harold W. Stanley and Richard G. Niemi, *Vital Statistic on American Politics*, 6th ed. (Congressional Quarterly, 1998), p. 108.

Table 5.3

Vote for Presidential Candidates by Party Identification, 1968–1992

Election	Candidates	Democrats	Republicans	Independents
1968	Hubert H. Humphrey (D)	74%	9%	31%
	Richard Nixon (R)	12	86	44
	George C. Wallace (AI)	14	5	25
1972	George McGovern (D)	67	5	31
	Richard Nixon (R)	33	95	69
1976	Jimmy Carter (D)	82	9	38
	Gerald R. Ford (R)	18	91	57
	Eugene J. McCarthy (I)	—	—	4
1980	Jimmy Carter (D)	69	8	29
	Ronald Reagan (R)	26	86	55
	John B. Anderson (I)	4	5	14
1984	Walter F. Mondale (D)	79	4	33
	Ronald Reagan (R)	21	96	67
1988	Michael S. Dukakis (D)	85	7	43
	George Bush (R)	15	93	57
1992	Bill Clinton (D)	82	7	39
	George Bush (R)	8	77	30
	Ross Perot (I)	10	16	31

Note: D = Democratic; R = Republican; AI = American Independent; I = Independent; — = less than 1 percent. Percentages have been rounded to the nearest whole number.
Source: Gallup Organization as cited in Michael Goldstein, *Guide to the 1996 Presidential Election* (Congressional Quarterly, 1995), p. 56.

Party Organizations

The Constitution does not mention political parties. The seeds for political parties, however, were planted when **Federalists** and **Anti-Federalists** debated over the ratification of the Constitution. American distrust of parties runs deep. In his famous farewell address, **President Washington** warned of "the baneful effects of the spirit of party."[4] Yet parties have flourished in this country and have proven to be essential to the functioning of a large-scale democracy. The country's first organized parties grew out of a division in Washington's cabinet. To get his proposals through Congress, Washington had to build coalitions among different factions. **Alexander Hamilton,** Washington's treasury secretary, built an informal party to this end. Hamilton's group came to be known as the **Federalist Party. Thomas Jefferson,** Washington's secretary of state, often disagreed with Hamilton on policy matters but remained in the cabinet out of loyalty to Washington.

When Jefferson left the cabinet in 1793, he and others who opposed Federalist economic and foreign policies consolidated their forces and were known as the **Republicans** (and later as the **Democratic-Republicans** and still later as the **Democrats**).[5]

Party Functions

Campaign volunteers working at a "phone bank."

© *Michael Hayman/Stock Boston.*

What do political parties do? What functions do they perform in the American political system?

- Parties **recruit candidates** for local, state, and national offices.
- Parties help to **train** these candidates and **assist** them in various ways during the campaign. Parties **raise and spend campaign funds.**
- Parties help **attract voters** for candidates through grassroots volunteer organizations, phone banks, and so on.
- Parties **streamline or simplify elections** in that voters are not asked to choose their favorite presidential candidate from a field of two hundred names; instead, each party nominates a single candidate.

In short, party organizations try to **win elections.** This function is one of the chief ways in which parties can be distinguished from interest groups. While parties and interest groups seek to advance the policy views of their supporters, interest groups do not formally nominate and sponsor their own candidates.

QuotableQuote

I have only one firm belief about the American political system, and that is this: God is a Republican and Santa Claus is a Democrat.

God is an elderly or, at any rate, middle-aged male, a

Parties perform additional functions.
- Parties **link** the masses to their government. President Clinton is a Democrat. Maybe your congressperson, governor, and you are Democrats, too. You share the same party label. You have something in common.
- Parties **take positions on issues** and publicize these issues. When voters learn of these positions, some will feel more comfortable with one party than another. They share views and have more in common.
- The **party label** can serve as a shorthand **cue** that helps voters make decisions.
- Parties engage in **interest aggregation** or **conflict resolution** when they try to bring diverse voters

together under a big party umbrella. A party tells voters with diverse interests that voting for the party's candidates will help the voters satisfy their own interests. Narrow and, perhaps, conflicting interests are combined in this way as the party tries to forge a winning coalition. Generally, Democrats are more diverse than Republicans. This factor can make it difficult for Democrats to run unified and cohesive campaigns.

- Parties engage in **interest representation** in that parties and their candidates emphasize different values, principles, and positions. Sometimes the differences seem slight, but there are at least differences in emphasis.[6]

To summarize, parties function to win elections. The party label provides guidance for some voters. The parties' candidates champion certain interests. And the parties try to fashion winning coalitions.

Party Structures

What do party organizations look like?

- Delegates to **national party conventions** meet every four years to nominate presidential and vice-presidential candidates (or to ratify candidates already selected through primaries and caucuses), approve party platforms, and make rules.
- The **national committee** takes care of day-to-day operations. Its main focus is on winning the presidency.
- The national committee selects a **national party chair,** but in reality, the party's presidential nominee usually chooses the chair. The chair plays a large role in the national campaign and in fund-raising. If the presidential campaign ends in defeat, the national committee generally elects a new chair.

stern fellow, patriarchal rather than paternal and a great believer in rules and regulations. He holds men strictly accountable for their actions. He has little apparent concern for the material well-being of the disadvantaged. He is politically connected, socially powerful and holds the mortgage on literally everything in the world. God is difficult. God is unsentimental. It is very hard to get into God's heavenly country club.

Santa Claus is another matter. He's cute. He's nonthreatening. He's always cheerful. And he loves animals. He may know who's been naughty and who's been nice, but he never does anything about it. He gives everyone everything they want without thought of a quid pro quo. He works hard for charities, and he's famously generous to the poor. Santa Claus is preferable to God in every way but one: There is no such thing as Santa Claus. . . .

Democrats are also the party of government activism, the party that says government can make you richer, smarter, taller and get the chickweed out of your lawn. Republicans are the party that says government doesn't work, and then they get elected and prove it.
—P.J. O'Rourke

- Senators select members for their party's **senatorial campaign committee,** and House members do likewise for their party's **congressional campaign committee.** These committees recruit congressional candidates, provide training, and help with fund-raising.
- States have **state committees** headed by a **state chair.** State laws regulate the operations of these committees, and the differences between and among states can be great.
- **County committees** recruit candidates for some local and countywide offices. In areas where the party has difficulty winning elections, finding people willing to run for office can be very hard. This situation is one reason that so many elections feature candidates running unopposed.
- **Precinct and ward committee persons** operate at the neighborhood level. These individuals organize volunteers to make phone calls, place lawn signs, distribute literature, register people to vote, and help voters get to the polls on election day.

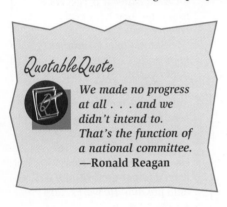

QuotableQuote

We made no progress at all . . . and we didn't intend to. That's the function of a national committee.
—Ronald Reagan

Despite appearances, with the national committee at the apex of the pyramid and precinct committee persons at the base, the party structures are not truly hierarchical. Nevertheless, the national party has considerable **influence.** For example, it can make **soft money** available for general party activities as long as this money is not spent directly on a particular candidate. But the national party organization does not run the whole show. The national party does not directly control party operations in the states, counties, and communities. A good deal of variation and independence exists across state party organizations.

Different Kinds of Party Systems

In a **single-party system,** one party dominates elections. Examples include the Communist Parties in the People's Republic of China, Cuba, and North Korea. Little suspense surrounds the outcome of elections. For years states in the American south were so solidly Democratic that the region virtually functioned as a single-party one. This era was the age of **yellow-dog Democrats,** of whom it was said that "they would vote for a yellow dog that was a Democrat before they would vote for a Republican." Elections were competitive; the real competition, however, occurred in the **primaries** when the Democrats selected their candidates. During the 1960s many white southern males became frustrated with some of President Johnson's social programs, and the Democrats lost their hold on the region. In a **two-party system,** two major parties compete in elections. In a **multiparty system,** several parties are competitive. Most democracies have multiparty systems. Examples include Italy, Israel, Switzerland, and the Netherlands. Such arrangements are common in countries with **parliamentary systems.**

- The majority party in the legislature or parliament elects one of its members to serve as prime minister.

- If no party has a majority of the seats in parliament, a coalition of parties with enough votes to give them a majority is assembled. This **coalition government** then selects a prime minister.
- Such coalitions can be fragile, making multiparty parliamentary systems relatively unstable.

Party systems can also be classified as strong or weak. In a **strong party system,** a party has a clearly defined platform that can be made binding on members of the party. There is **party discipline** in that party leaders can force party members to work and vote together. Strong party systems are also called **responsible** party systems. The parties' positions are clearly delineated on election day. Voters know where the respective parties stand. The party winning a majority of the seats has the discipline to work toward achieving the party's objectives. Next election, if the voters are unhappy with how things worked out, it is reasonable for them to hold the majority party "responsible" for its failures. In contrast, in a **weak party system** the parties lack a single, clearly defined party program. There is little or no party discipline.

Third Parties

The United States has a weak, two-party system, but **minor parties** or **third parties** have played a role. **Protest parties** have been built around popular individuals to advance positions not addressed by the major parties. Examples include the Populists in the 1890s and the Progressives in the 1920s. Minor-party presidential candidates have included Theodore Roosevelt in 1912 (the Bull Moose Party), George Wallace in 1968 (the American Independent Party), John Anderson in 1980 (the National Unity Party), and H. Ross Perot in 1992 (the United We Stand, America group) and in 1996 (the Patriot or Reform Party).

As shown in table 5.4, some minor-party presidential candidates have won impressive numbers of popular votes.

These parties usually drop off the radar screen when the candidate fades from public view. Furthermore, major parties are adept at responding to some of the positions advanced by such candidates if those positions strike a responsive chord with the voters.

Another kind of third party is organized around a goal or ideology that persists for some time. These are called **ideological parties.** Examples include the Communist Party, the

Presidential candidate H. Ross Perot on the campaign trail.

© *AP/Wide World Photos.*

Table 5.4

Third Parties in Presidential Elections

Year	Party	Candidate	Percent of Vote	Electoral Vote
1832	Anti-Masonic	William Wirt	7.8	7
1856	Know Nothing	Millard Filmore	21.5	8
1860	Secessionist	J.C. Breckinridge	18.1	72
1860	Constitutional Union	John Bell	12.6	39
1892	Populist	James B. Weaver	8.6	22
1912	Bull Moose (Progressive)	Theodore Roosevelt	27.4	88
1912	Socialist	Eugene Debs	6.0	0
1924	Progressive	Robert M. La Follette	16.6	13
1948	States' Rights	Strom Thurmond	2.4	39
1968	American Independent	George C. Wallace	13.5	46
1980	National Unity	John B. Anderson	6.6	0
1992	United We Stand, America	H. Ross Perot	18.9	0
1996	Patriot/Reform	H. Ross Perot	8.6	0

Socialist Workers Party of the United States, and the Libertarian Party. They entertain no realistic chance of winning national elections, but they see elections as vehicles for attracting publicity for their ideas. They will not sacrifice ideological purity by watering down their message to win a few more votes. Why bother? Instead, they run candidates in elections to **publicize** their ideas. If some of their ideas catch on with voters, the major parties can be expected to address them later. For this reason, these parties are sometimes called **issue finders** for the major parties. Women's suffrage and bargaining rights for labor are two issues that third parties originally promoted. Eventually, major parties "found" them.

Why Does the United States Have a Two-Party System?

The United States has a two-party system for several reasons:

- Major parties have been sufficiently **flexible** to adapt to new ideas advanced by third parties.
- Institutional or structural factors also play a role. In multiparty systems legislators are often elected according to **proportional representation** where parties receive legislative seats in proportion to the parties' share of the vote. In

*C*onsider some of the implications of a two-party system. Such a system encourages broad parties. In a multiparty system, each party tries to win votes from its natural constituents—labor, farmers, business, and so on. In a two-party system, one party cannot win a majority by appealing only to labor, only to farmers, or only to business. Both Democrats and Republicans must appeal to a wide variety of groups and interests. This factor encourages the major parties to take moderate stands on issues.

The *disadvantage* is that when issue differences are blurred, voters see elections as presenting "choices" between Tweedle Dum and Tweedle Dee. The outcome does not seem to make much difference. The *advantage* is that moderate policies produce stable and centrist government. What do you think of this trade-off?

such systems, even minor parties get some seats. The United States uses a **winner-take-all** system to fill congressional seats. Only the candidate with the most votes in a district gets a seat. Minor parties are usually shut out.

- **Campaign finance laws** also make it difficult for minor party presidential candidates to qualify for public funds.
- Major party candidates have automatic **access to the ballot,** whereas minor party candidates must circulate petitions and overcome formidable administrative hurdles just to get their names listed.

Interest Groups

Some people criticize the inordinate power that special-interest groups have over policy makers. Others say that interest groups give people with intense feelings a democratic way to emphasize their views to public officials. Groups are "good" when they give the public a way to participate in policy making; groups are "bad" when certain groups become so powerful that they dominate policy makers' attention. Good or bad, interest groups are not new. In *The Federalist*, Number 10, James Madison explained that self-interested individuals form **factions** in the pursuit of their shared interests. In an "extended republic" many such factions—or groups—form and compete. A competitive balance results, preventing any single group from becoming tyrannical. This reasoning is very similar to contemporary **interest group pluralists** who maintain that multiple

The NRA is large, but it falls far short of speaking for a majority of the national population. The interest group system enables a minority of the population to prevail against the stated preferences of the majority. Is this situation fair? Maybe it is. After all, compared to the general public, members of the group know more and care more about their issue. This feature of the political system helps account for the wishes of an intense minority.

(or plural) interest groups compete to influence policy makers. Consequently, no single group becomes too powerful, and good public policy results.

The National Rifle Association: A Case Study in Group Power

In fact, interest groups can be quite powerful. The National Rifle Association (NRA) provides a case in point. After the assassinations of John F. Kennedy, Robert Kennedy, and Martin Luther King Jr. and after the attempted assassinations of George Wallace, Gerald Ford, and Ronald Reagan, polls showed wide public support for strong federal gun-control laws. Congress passed a gun-control measure in 1968, but prior to the enactment of the "Brady Bill" in 1993, efforts to strengthen federal gun-control laws were relatively unsuccessful. Reacting to the shooting of a prominent figure, people tell pollsters that there ought to be stronger gun-control laws. For most, it ends there. We go on with our lives.

The NRA, however, focuses narrowly on the gun-control issue:

- It devotes all of its attention and resources to influencing policy in this area.
- It is stable, well organized, well financed, and technologically sophisticated.
- It rapidly sends out information alerts to members notifying them of pending changes in gun-control laws and provides members with postcards to send to their congresspeople urging them to oppose such changes.
- Congresspeople understand that many NRA members are willing to vote against representatives who come down on the "wrong" side on this single issue.
- It usually takes a long time for a bill to move through the committee system and become a law. Although the attention of the general public is diverted, the NRA remains focused and sustains its intensity over time.

All these factors contribute to the NRA's effectiveness.

More recently, competing groups like Handgun Control, Incorporated, have emerged to represent those who intensely favor stronger gun-control laws. Some stronger state-level gun laws have been enacted, as have new limits on importing

On the side of the NRA headquarters building in Washington are these words from the Second Amendment: ". . . the right of the people to keep and bear arms, shall not be infringed." These words are presented as evidence that the framers of the Constitution recognized an individual's right to keep and bear arms.

Omitted are the Second Amendment's opening words: "A well regulated militia, being necessary to the security of a free state . . ." When these missing words are added, does the meaning of the Second Amendment change? Some observers believe that the framers recognized only a collective right of *the people* (not individuals) to keep and bear arms as part of the militia.

assault weapons. In 1993 Congress passed the Brady Bill, named for President Reagan's former press secretary, James Brady, who was seriously wounded in a 1981 assassination attempt on Reagan. The bill requires a five-day waiting period before purchasing handguns and required states to conduct background checks on purchasers.[7]

Types of Interest Groups

Many types of interest groups are at work. **Economic interest groups** act to protect their members' economic self-interests. Economic groups represent large corporations like Chrysler, IBM, and Sunoco. The AFL-CIO's Committee on Political Education (COPE) is an example of an economic interest group representing a labor union. Professional associations like the American Bar Association and the American Medical Association also promote the economic interests of their members. **Ideological interest groups** work to promote their members' positions on public policy issues. Examples include the American Civil Liberties Union, the National Association for the Advancement of Colored People, the Christian Coalition, Operation Rescue, and the National Rifle Association. **Public interest groups** like Common Cause pursue reforms designed to improve government. Such good-government groups are sometimes called "goo-goos." There are even **government interest groups,** like the National Governors' Association and the National League of Cities, which seek to advance the interests of their members.

Ingredients of Interest Group Power

A group is **influential** if it is able to get policy makers to do something that they would not otherwise have done.[8] Several factors help policy makers resist group pressure:

- If public figures hold relatively **insulated positions,** groups have little influence over them. Federal judges are a case in point. They are appointed, not elected, and many enjoy lifetime tenure.
- If **competing interest groups** are active, policy makers can play one group off against another, reducing the influence of any single group.
- If the public is **attentive,** policy makers can resist group pressure, secure in the knowledge that voters will reward them.

On the other hand, interest groups have various **power resources** as they attempt to influence policy makers:

- **Large size** contributes to a group's effectiveness. If large groups can persuade their members to vote in bloc fashion, elected officials will pay attention. Large groups can also raise substantial amounts of money.
- **Geographic concentration** helps groups become very influential within their communities. Tobacco farmers, oil companies, and automobile manufacturers are especially powerful in some states.
- The **high prestige** of professional associations like the National Education Association, the American Federation of Teachers, or the American Medical Association also helps them get publicity, influence public opinion, and gain access to decision makers.
- **Financial strength** is another important ingredient of group power. Financial resources can be used to hire professional lobbyists, make campaign contributions, and generate public relations campaigns.
- Leaders of **unified groups** with **highly motivated members** can more easily mobilize the group in pursuit of its objectives.
- In the most effective groups, **supportive members** give leaders leeway in making day-to-day tactical decisions. Such groups can act quickly and decisively while competing groups are busy surveying members for directions and approval.
- Concentrating on a **narrow range of interests** allows a group to devote all of its resources to influencing policy in that area. Competing groups may have to spread their resources over a wider variety of issue areas. Recall the National Rifle Association example on this point.
- **Duration and stability** also contribute to group effectiveness. Experienced groups know the ropes. Newly organized groups require time to get up to speed.
- Groups are most effective if they pursue relatively **conventional objectives.** A well-organized, well-financed, narrowly focused group pursuing objectives far out of step with mainstream popular opinion will have limited effectiveness.

When individuals organize, they have more power collectively than they did individually. Group opinions look more formidable than individual opinions. Information costs are broadly distributed. You do not have to do your own policy research; just wait for your organization's newsletters and action calls. In sum, **organization** is the key to political effectiveness.

Interest Group Tactics

Possessing resources like money, a narrow focus, motivated members, and so on is one thing; such resources, however, must be converted into actual power. How? Groups use various **tactics** in their efforts to influence policy makers. **Direct bribery** would be the most obvious way for a group to win a public official's cooperation. Disadvantages include the fact that bribery is expensive and illegal, and if the group is caught, it will have a major public relations problem. **Indirect forms of bribery** may be another matter. The group can make **campaign contributions** to candidates to win their support or at least to ensure future access. Sometimes groups **create conflicts of interest** by giving business to the hometown law firms of key policy makers. For years groups invited congresspeople to deliver speeches at conferences and paid handsome honoraria. Such honoraria have since been banned as a form of bribery. In the late 1980s the House Ethics Committee investigated then-Speaker of the House Jim Wright (D-TX) after learning that Wright's supporters bought copies of his book in unusually high numbers. The committee concluded that the purchases were an indirect way of providing financial rewards to the Speaker. Wright left Congress in the wake of this scandal.[9]

Campaign Finance and Political Action Committees

Groups sometimes try to influence the selection of policy makers. In an election the group can try to persuade members to vote as a bloc or to volunteer for campaign work. The group may publicize its endorsement of a favored candidate. Or the group can make campaign **contributions** that go toward expenses such as media advertising, paid staffers, and direct-mail promotions. Campaign costs are high and getting higher. Wealthy candidates have a competitive advantage over opponents with more limited personal resources unless the latter are able to raise funds from contributors. The concern in the first instance is that a wealthy candidate might be able to "buy" an

Quotable Quote

[W]e have a responsibility to make our democracy work better for America, by limiting the influence of special interests and expanding the influence of the American people. Special interests have too much power in the halls of government. They often operate in secret and have special privileges ordinary Americans do not even know exist. Elections have become so expensive that big money can sometimes drown out the voices of ordinary voters—who should always speak the loudest.
— **1996 Democratic National Platform**

election; the concern in the second instance is that wealthy contributors might be able to buy themselves a candidate—even a president.

Such concerns prompted the drafting of the 1971 **Federal Election Campaign Act (FECA).** The Act was amended in 1974 and 1976.

- The Act established a six-member bipartisan Federal Election Commission (FEC).
- The Commission regulates and keeps track of funds spent in federal elections.
- Presidential and congressional candidates are required to make **public disclosures** of their contributions and spending.
- **Campaign contribution limits** also apply in congressional and presidential races. Individuals are limited to contributing $1,000 per candidate for each primary, general, or runoff election.

Political Action Committees (PACs) have become increasingly important. PACs raise money and make contributions to political candidates. FECA encourages the development of PACs because it allows for a $5,000 contribution per candidate per election as opposed to the $1,000 limit on individual contributions. To qualify as a PAC, the organization must adhere to the following:

- Receive contributions from fifty or more people
- Be registered with the FEC for six months
- Make contributions to five or more federal candidates

In the early 1970s about 150 PACs existed; today the number exceeds 4,000. There are two kinds of PACs:

- The first type is affiliated with corporations, labor unions, or trade associations. Corporate PACs outspend the others. Such PACs were created to get around the legal prohibition on direct corporate, bank, or union contributions to federal candidates.
- The second kind is the independent or unaffiliated PAC. These independent committees raise funds for political parties and restrictions on them are less stringent than the restrictions on affiliated PACs.

Public financing is available for presidential candidates who qualify for matching funds. This provision is designed to prevent presidential candidates from becoming too indebted to private contributors. Candidates who accept public funds must also agree to abide by overall **spending limits.** FECA originally imposed spending limits on congressional campaigns too, but congressional candidates were not eligible for federal funds. In 1976 the Supreme Court treated candidate spending as a First Amendment issue and overturned congressional spending limits. The Court reasoned that individuals have the right to advance their political views by spending their money to get elected. Spending limits for presidential candidates were upheld, however, if the candidate accepts federal funds. Why? It is reasonable to attach strings to federal money.[10] Presidential candidates who do not want to be encumbered by spending limits should not apply for federal funds.[11]

Independent expenditures are not legally restricted. Individuals or PACs can spend money on billboards, television and radio ads, and the like to help a candidate as long as this spending is not coordinated with the candidate's campaign. If you want to advance your political views by conducting your own ad campaign in support of a favored candidate, you have the legal right to do so. Another loophole in federal campaign finance laws involves **soft money.** There is a legal limit of $5,000 per year on individual contributions to PACs and $20,000 per year on individual contributions to the national committee of a political party. However, individuals can give money to state or local party organizations, where disclosure requirements are generally lax, and such funds can be used for "party-building activities." The line between activities that strengthen the party and those that help a party's candidate can be indistinct.

The more PACs proliferate, the less influence any individual PAC has. . . . Their influence is diminished by their proliferation.
—**Representative Henry Hyde (R-IL)**

How much influence do PACs have over policy makers? Do PACs "buy" elected officials? It is difficult to prove conclusively that a specific contribution caused a policy maker to vote a certain way. PACs do not always win. Often PACs contribute to the reelection campaigns of lawmakers who already agree with them on the issues, regardless of the contribution. Furthermore, legislators receive contributions from various—and sometimes competing—PACs. While a politician may receive a great deal of PAC money, a relatively small portion will come from a single PAC.

On the other hand, context is important. Some studies have demonstrated a relationship between PAC contributions and congressional committee treatment.[12] In congressional, state, and local races, an amount of money that would be insignificant in a nationwide presidential race may be very important. Further, the same contribution to a United States Senate candidate in Montana will go a lot further than it would in California, even though a senator from Montana casts just as many policy votes as a senator from California. While a PAC contribution does not guarantee an official's vote, it at least provides **access.** Senator Charles Mathias (R-MD) observed that

An official may not change his or her vote solely to accommodate the views of . . . contributors, but often officials, including myself, will agree to meet with an individual who made a large contribution so the official can hear the contributor's concerns and make the contributor aware these concerns have been considered. . . . Since an elected official has only so much time available, the inevitable result of such

QuotableQuotes

You can't take thousands of dollars from a group and not have it affect you.
—**Representative Barney Frank (D-MA)**

Dialogue with politicians is a fine thing, but with a little money they hear you better.
—**Justin Dart**

Politics is the gentle art of getting votes from the poor and campaign funds from the rich, by promising to protect each from the other.
—**Oscar Ameringer**

special treatment for the large contributor is that other citizens are denied the opportunity they otherwise would have to confer with the elected official.[13]

PACs are practical in their contribution patterns; they want access to policy makers, not access to losing candidates.

- PACs with vast financial resources can contribute to *both* candidates to ensure the eventual victor's indebtedness.
- Some PACs wait until after the election and contribute to help the winner retire outstanding campaign debts.
- PACs usually support incumbents.

By some estimates PACs give more than 80 percent of their contributions to incumbents and only 10 percent or less to challengers.[14] This pattern reinforces the advantage that incumbents have over their opponents.

PACs also **target** their efforts, contributing primarily to congresspeople serving on relevant committees. For example, Congressman John Murtha (D-PA) is the ranking minority member on the House Defense Appropriations Subcommittee. He receives more money from defense PACs than any other representative in the state. Congressman Bud Shuster

(R-PA) chairs the House Public Works and Transportation Committee. He receives substantial contributions from trucking, air transport, and railroad PACs.

Campaign finance reform issues figured prominently in the 1996 presidential campaign. Some of Clinton's opponents raised questions about efforts of Chinese contributors to influence United States policy through contributions to the Democrats. Questions were also raised about President Clinton's invitations of donors to the White House. Such matters were subsequently discussed at congressional hearings and various reform proposals have been explored. Concern has been pronounced, commentary extensive, and cynicism widespread. Although many Americans say they care about campaign finance reform, however, is this really the kind of issue that, in the final analysis, determines how you vote?

Additional Tactics

Interest groups also try to influence the selection of **appointed officials.** Groups seek to influence the president who makes nominations but getting access can be difficult. Therefore, groups try to influence presidential advisors who assist in the search for nominees. Interest groups also try to influence senators who participate in the confirmation process. Groups are most effective in influencing the appointment of people to fill bureaucratic posts. Agency executives need specialized expertise. For this reason, they often have worked in the area they will be regulating and return to such private-sector positions after leaving their appointed posts. Because these executive positions usually undergo little press and public scrutiny when they are being filled, presidents do not have to worry very much about public backlash if they listen to a group's appointment suggestions.

Groups also try to influence **public opinion.** When the **North American Free Trade Act (NAFTA)** was being considered, supporters and opponents launched massive public relations campaigns to generate support for their respective positions. Political candidates, in turn, took up the issue. During the 1992 presidential campaign, both Bill Clinton and George Bush favored NAFTA on grounds that it would stimulate trade and create jobs. Ross Perot opposed the pact with the colorful prediction that the "giant sucking sound" that will be heard is the sound of American jobs being sucked away to Mexico.[15]

Public relations are important to a group's effectiveness. A group's tactics should not offend the public. To this end groups try to neutralize public opinion on an issue, create a generally favorable image over time, and/or repair a damaged public image. Exxon's advertising campaigns following the wreck of its oil tanker, the *Valdez*, off the coast of Alaska attempted to repair the company's damaged public image. One reason to avoid offering bribes is that there will be a severe public backlash if the bribery is revealed.

Civil rights leader, Martin Luther King Jr., advocated nonviolent resistance to publicize the injustices of racial discrimination. Such means educate and alert the general public without alienating potential supporters. Even in the service of a just cause, violence is counterproductive.

Ralph Reed, former executive director of the Christian Coalition, explained that the "religious right" had to learn this lesson:

> [R]eligious conservatives must shun harsh language on critical issues—chiefly abortion, Clinton-bashing, and homosexuality—and learn to speak of our opponents with charity. . . . To change public attitudes, we must also repudiate the demonization of women who are pregnant out of wedlock, condemn violence at abortion clinics in unequivocal terms, and pour our greatest efforts into education, persuasion, and prayer—not politics alone.[16]

Interest groups employ professional **lobbyists** to influence public policy on behalf of the group. Washington's K Street is home to numerous so-called legislative consultants, trade representatives, government relations specialists, corporate counsels, and others who sell their experience in the ways of government to those who value their knowledge and contacts. Lobbyists are often former public servants.

- Some served as congressional staffers or White House aides.
- Some were agency executives or bureaucrats.
- Some were even elected officials.
- But as lobbyists they work for interest groups. Often they work for one of the groups they dealt with when they were government employees. They almost certainly command higher salaries as lobbyists than they did as public officials.

Policy networks, or **iron triangles,** develop among agency bureaucrats, congressional committees, and lobbyists working in the same issue area. An oil company might value the experiences of an Energy Department officer, a House Energy and Commerce Committee staffer, or a Senate Energy and Natural Resources Committee aide and might recruit that person. Some individuals pass through a **revolving door** when they leave their government jobs to become lobbyists.

Publicly, lobbyists testify at congressional and administrative hearings. They orchestrate letter-writing campaigns to give elected officials the impression that there is a groundswell of support for the group's position. They run public relations campaigns promoting the group's interests. Privately, lobbyists try to build a close relationship with legislators on the committees most relevant to their interests. To this end lobbyists must be honest, courteous, and well-informed. Providing false information is the easiest way for a lobbyist to ruin a relationship with a legislator. If a lawmaker, over time, comes to trust the lobbyist's information, that lawmaker will be willing to listen when the lobbyist wants to talk about the group's position on a bill. This kind of relationship does not develop overnight.

After Congress drafts legislation and the president approves it, **bureaucratic agencies** administer the programs. A group can seek the most favorable application possible. Here, too, lobbyists cultivate close working relationships with agency professionals. Agencies publish proposed regulations and rule changes in the *Federal Register* and invite interested parties to react. Lobbyists submit written recommendations and testify at hearings. The specialized and technical nature of many regulations, together with a general lack of public scrutiny, contributes to the effectiveness of lobbyists in this area.

Groups also try to influence **federal court decisions.** As appointed and long-tenured officials, federal judges enjoy insulation from group pressure. Nevertheless

- Groups like the American Civil Liberties Union, the National Rifle Association, and the National Organization of Women sponsor **test cases** that raise issues the group wants a court to address.
- The group's lawyers file **friend-of-the-court** or *amicus curiae* **briefs** in which they try to persuade judges to decide the case in a desired way.
- The group can ask **legal scholars** to write journal articles favoring their position.
- The group can try to influence **public opinion** in the hope that judges will notice and be affected.
- The group can try to influence the **appointment process** to try to get sympathetic judges selected in the first place.[17]

Evaluating Interest Groups: Good News and Bad News

Interest groups make some positive contributions to the American political system.

- Interest groups represent the interests of members to policy makers between elections. They provide vehicles for public participation.
- Interest groups give members the feeling that they can make a difference and enhance feelings of political efficacy. When people feel that they can make a difference, they are more likely to try to do so. That is, they are more likely to participate in political activities.
- Interest groups provide information for policy makers that would otherwise be unavailable or difficult to obtain.
- Interest groups focus public attention on political issues and educate members about policy developments.
- Interest groups provide campaign contributions, enabling people of modest means to run for office.
- When plural groups compete in their efforts to influence policy makers, no single group becomes too powerful. The system is "safe" in that members of group X have overlapping memberships; they belong to groups Y and Z as well. If the leaders of group X go too far and propose actions contrary to the interests of groups Y and Z, some group X members will stand up and restrain their leaders. Potential groups are also important. If group X takes steps injurious to the interests of an unorganized segment of the public, these people will be motivated to organize and defend themselves.
- Interest groups give additional weight to the feelings of intense minorities.

In short, because of the group system, those who know and care the most about an issue have the most influence.

On the negative side, critics point to assorted undesirable consequences of group activities.

- The group system enables a minority to negate the will of the majority, as the NRA often does on gun-control issues. No matter how much you dress it up with talk about differences in knowledge and intensity, there is something fundamentally wrong when the minority defeats the majority.
- Groups also engage in unethical behavior. If I help you, I expect you to help me. Such a system encourages direct and indirect bribery.
- When government policy results from bargains struck with interest groups, the formal policy-making processes are replaced by informal negotiating. The group system defines the "common good" as a competitive balance. No single group speaks for the interest of the public at large. Policy that does promote the common good—and not just the interest of the strongest group—is an accident. This condition is sometimes called the no government leadership problem.
- The alleged merits of the group system are based on the premise that groups compete. But sometimes, groups do not compete on equal footing. Some groups

James Madison expected that self-interested persons would form factions in the pursuit of their objectives. In The Federalist, Number 10, he outlined his ideas for curbing the mischiefs of faction. How well have his ideas worked?

are more powerful than others. In such uncompetitive circumstances one group can rout another.

- Groups do not always compete; sometimes they cooperate or collude. Oil company lobbyists will join forces to battle a perceived common foe such as an environmental interest group.

- The internal organization of the most effective groups is relatively oligarchical or authoritarian. In such groups members have little day-to-day influence over group leaders. Critics complain that you cannot build a democratic structure out of such undemocratic building materials.

- Some critics charge that the group system is biased in favor of business and upper-class interests. As E. E. Schattschneider put it, "The flaw in the pluralist heaven is that the heavenly choir sings with a strong upper-class accent. Probably about 90% of the people can't get into the pressure system."[18]

Key Terms

Notes

chapter 6

Elections: Presidential and Congressional

Help Wanted

Four-year position available. May be renewed. Applicant must at least be thirty-five years of age, a natural born United States citizen, and a resident within the United States for fourteen years. Salary: $200,000 per year. Housing and weekend camp included. Transportation provided, including use of own airplane. Position for spouse possible. Good communication skills and ability to work with other people necessary.

Staff assistance available. Full health care, life insurance, ample pension, and other fringe benefits. Relevant experience preferred. Good opportunity for the right person.

Of course, we do not select the president of the United States by conducting an executive job search like those undertaken by corporations when they seek chief executive officers. It is, nevertheless, instructive to reflect on what we are looking for when we choose our presidents.

Reviewing the resumes of our last nine presidents, we see that

- One was a former general (Dwight D. Eisenhower).
- Five served in Congress (John F. Kennedy, Lyndon Johnson, Richard Nixon, Gerald Ford, and George Bush).
- Three had been governors (Jimmy Carter, Ronald Reagan, and Bill Clinton).
- Three had extensive prior experience in the federal government (Johnson, Nixon, and Bush).

There are similarities and differences in their backgrounds; there is no single path to the White House.

Presidential Character

Given the demands of the presidency, what kind of person do we want to be president? As we contemplate competing promises, issue positions, advertising campaigns, speeches, charisma, and the confusion that characterize presidential elections, how can we predict who would be the best president? How important is a candidate's **character**?

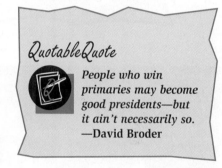

QuotableQuote

People who win primaries may become good presidents—but it ain't necessarily so.
—**David Broder**

Character means different things to different people. In 1996, Bob Dole's supporters equated it with personal morality in the belief that voters would view Dole as superior to President Clinton in this regard. Because many questions surrounded Clinton's personal conduct, his supporters preferred to define character differently. Pointing to his first-term budget battles with Republicans in Congress, Clinton supporters defined character as the willingness to stand up and fight for important positions.

Is character best defined as a matter of personal integrity and ethical behavior? Or is character best defined as steadfastness and fortitude? For that matter, is it necessarily an either-or proposition? The 1996 presidential campaign is an instructive case in point.

1996 Presidential Campaign

A joke made the rounds during the campaign that went something like this. Newt Gingrich, Dan Quayle, and Bill Clinton went to see the Wizard of Oz. Gingrich asked for a heart,

During his 1998 grand jury testimony in the Paula Jones sexual harassment suit, President Clinton testified under oath that he never had sexual relations with former White House intern, Monica Lewinsky. He testified under oath that he could not recall having met privately with her around the Oval Office. He testified under oath that he did not encourage anyone to lie. Seven months later, after having assured his advisors and congressional supporters repeatedly that he was telling the truth, he changed his story. He revealed that he had, in fact, had a physical relationship with Ms. Lewinsky that was "not appropriate." He admitted that he had "misled" people. In 1998, after Clinton resisted calls for his resignation, the House impeached him for high crimes and misdemeanors. Disturbing conduct and disturbing questions. Was this controversy really about the President's private sex life, or was it about perjury and obstruction of justice? What do you think?

Bill and Hillary Clinton with Al and Tipper Gore celebrating their renomination at the 1996 Democratic National Convention.

© *Reuters/Eric Miller/Archive Photos.*

Quayle asked for a brain, and Clinton asked for Dorothy. In light of Clinton's 1998 impeachment, a telling anecdote. "There's no one in politics to make you proud anymore," said Tom DiEugenio, a shoemaker in Erie, Pennsylvania.[1] Many voters were frustrated and angry as they contemplated their choices. When Colin Powell declined to seek the Republican nomination, many voters expressed disappointment that a man of his stature would not run in 1996.

In 1969 Ted Kennedy drove off a bridge, and his female passenger drowned. Senator Kennedy did not report the accident until the following day, and his presidential chances were effectively finished. In the 1970s the Watergate scandal brought down a presidency. In the 1980s a presidential commission concluded that congressional policies had

"So, who cares about the other stuff?

Steve Benson, reprinted by permission of United Feature Syndicate.

been circumvented during the Iran-Contra affair. In 1987 Gary Hart's presidential campaign self-destructed when reporters revealed that he was engaged in an extramarital affair with Donna Rice. Joe Biden's 1988 presidential bid crashed when he was caught plagiarizing portions of a speech by a British politician, Neil Kinnock, and when we learned that he had made exaggerated statements about his academic record. In 1988 candidates Al Gore and Bruce Babbitt had to explain their previous use of marijuana. When Congresswoman Susan Molinari (R-NY) agreed to keynote the 1996 Republican Convention, she answered similar questions. And back in 1992 Bill Clinton first explained that he never violated the drug laws of *this* country. He later conceded that he had smoked pot while he was in England as a student. He then hastened to add that he did not enjoy it, and besides, he did not inhale. Not surprisingly, political opponents nicknamed him "Slick Willie." Gennifer Flowers told reporters that she and Clinton had an affair. Clinton went on *60 Minutes* with his wife, Hillary, at his side and denied the claims. He won in 1992. Paula Jones sued Clinton for sexual harassment. Her suit was eventually dismissed. Political advisors watched for additional "bimbo eruptions," as they came to be called. We heard about the Whitewater investigation, Travelgate, Filegate, and other "gates." And Clinton became the first Democrat to be reelected to the presidency since Franklin D. Roosevelt.[2]

Presidential campaigns are grueling. We place the candidate and the candidate's family and finances under intense public scrutiny. The same tabloids that regularly report

"Unless we all sleep together . . ."

As published in Newsweek, *June 9, 1997, p. 27.*

sightings of Elvis on Mars are taken seriously when they report allegations of candidate misconduct. Some capable people refuse to run this presidential gauntlet. Perhaps Mario Cuomo, Colin Powell, and others wanted to *be* president but concluded that the price of *becoming* president was just too high. Negative campaigning is common. When polled, people regularly say that they disapprove of mudslinging, character assassination, and negativity. They say that they want a candidate to tell them what he or she will do, not what's wrong with the other candidate(s). This attitude sounds good, even noble. But who do you think is reading all those tabloids? Negative campaigning often works. We say that we don't like it, but we remember the charges and allegations. They stick. For this reason, as Michael Dukakis learned the hard way in 1988, negative charges must be answered. Now candidates prepare response ads even *before* an opponent can launch an attack. Candidates say that they reject character attacks, that the campaign is about issues and ideas, not personalities and insults.[3] Then surrogates for the candidates make the attacks for them. It has become fashionable to use women's voices to soften the tone of the attacks.[4] The damage is done. The message gets out. And as long as the attack did not come from the candidate's own lips, he or she can avoid blame.[5]

What about character? Is it relevant to presidential campaigns? Should we examine the private lives of presidential candidates? Do we have a responsibility to assess candidates on the basis of what we know about their characters? Most of us would agree that we have a right to be informed about a candidate's health because a person's physical capacity for the job is relevant.

By the same token, should we also know whether the candidate has a tendency to embellish—or even abandon—the truth? Should we care whether the candidate is indiscreet, has a passion for secrecy, or is dishonest? We concede that a president will not be perfect, but do we have a right to insist on certain standards of good character?

"Higher Standards Limbo Competition."

As published in Altoona Mirror, *January 12, 1997, B6.*

These expectations seem eminently sensible. But take a closer look. First, a character trait that is laudable in private life may prove counterproductive in public life. Some maintained that President Bush was too loyal to Vice President Quayle in 1992. If Bush had dropped Quayle from the ticket and replaced him with a more popular running mate, Bush might have had a better chance of being reelected to a second term. Another example of an admirable trait being countproductive in public life: although honesty and candor are generally admired, might not a president occasionally have to maintain secrecy and even mislead the press and the public in the interests of national security?[6]

Second, is there not a distinction between public and private lives? between personal character and public character? Is everything about a presidential candidate our business? Is nothing private? Do we really have to know whether President Clinton prefers briefs or boxers? Compare the Watergate scandal (involving a sitting president, obstruction of justice and other felony charges, congressional committee approval of three articles of impeachment, federal criminal convictions, and a presidential resignation) with Gary Hart's tryst with Donna Rice (involving behavior that was wrong but which was of questionable relevance to the public at large). Is there not a qualitative distinction between the two "scandals"? How do we decide whether the misconduct in question is *relevant* to one's ability to function as president? William Bennett, who argues that the issue of public character is relevant to presidential campaigns, says that he does not believe that a person's private life should be subjected to political scrutiny: "Unless private foibles have clear public implications, they should not be the focus of inquiry."[7] Against this standard, was Clinton's apparent lack of candor under oath about his "inappropriate" relationship with Monica Lewinsky an instance of private or public misconduct?

Third, does it matter whether the candidate puts otherwise private matters into public play by personally bringing them up for political gain? On one hand a candidate's marital infidelity might be considered a private matter for the candidate and spouse to resolve. But what if this candidate hypocritically runs on a family values platform while engaging in extramarital affairs? At this point formerly private conduct becomes a matter of public concern. Recall Vice President Gore's heartrending speech at the 1996 Democratic Convention when he spoke of his sister's death from smoking. There were few dry eyes in Chicago's United Center when he finished. His purpose? To dramatize the Democrats' pledge to take on the tobacco companies. He used a personal tragedy for political ends, thus converting the private into the public. As a result, he should not have objected when reporters questioned him about why he continued to accept support from the tobacco industry for some years following his sister's death.[8]

Fourth, as we search for character flaws, we should remember that we are electing a president, not a pope. Honesty alone does not qualify a person to be president. Conversely, should ethical imperfection disqualify an otherwise accomplished person from the presidency? Logically, character can be relevant without making it the exclusive criterion for selecting presidents.[9] A flawed individual might become a reasonably effective president. It is up to us to decide how flawed is too flawed.

So what about the 1996 campaign? Bob Dole's advisors urged him to emphasize character and to stress his campaign theme, "A better man for a better America." But Elizabeth Dole worried that, after a lifetime of public service, her husband might destroy his reputation in a desperate bid for victory at all costs.[10] If voters decided solely on the basis of character, Dole's chances improved markedly. An NBC-*Wall Street Journal* poll found that

- Dole had a two-to-one advantage over Clinton when people were asked which candidate was more honest.
- Dole had a thirty-point edge when people were asked which candidate had higher ethical and moral values.
- Dole also had a big lead when people were asked which candidate stuck by his beliefs.

But many voters who said they had serious questions about Clinton's character, morals, and honesty also said that they would vote to reelect Clinton anyway because he had better ideas than Dole had and was more in tune with their everyday concerns. As Democratic pollster Peter Hart said before the election, "Dole has elements people respect, but he is having trouble turning that into votes."[11]

Why? In 1992 Democratic strategist Jim Carville posted a sign in the campaign "war room" to keep the staff focused. The sign had three statements: "Change versus more of the same," "Don't forget health care," and "It's the economy, stupid!"[12] In 1996 it was still the economy, and there was nothing stupid about it.

- Personal economic anxiety had diminished for many voters.
- The "misery index," which adds the inflation rate to the unemployment rate, was down.

"It's the economy, stupid."

Steve Benson, reprinted by permission of United Feature Syndicate.

- President Clinton was able to repeat Ronald Reagan's question from 1980: "Ask yourself, am I better off now than I was four years ago?" Most voters answered in the affirmative.[13]

In 1998 a healthy economy helped President Clinton resist calls for his removal.

Character issues can swing a close election. It is very difficult, however, to unseat an incumbent president during times of relative peace and prosperity. Although we care about character and would prefer heroic leaders to scoundrels, most of us vote on the basis of bread-and-butter issues.

QuotableQuote

Clinton is so far ahead in the polls, he started dating again.
—Dennis Miller

James David Barber's Presidential Character Types

James David Barber equates presidential character with a president's orientation toward life—that is, the stance with which the president confronts experience.[14] Barber employs two "baselines" to describe four presidential character types.

- One baseline for defining presidential types is **activity-passivity.** How much energy does the president expend in doing the job?

- Another baseline is **positive-negative affect.** Does the individual enjoy serving as president?

Barber's basic character patterns are as follows:

- **Active-positive** presidents are active, and they enjoy the job. They seek results.
- **Active-negative** presidents expend great effort but reap little emotional reward. Their work has a compulsive quality. They seek to get and keep power.
- **Passive-positive** presidents are relatively less energetic, but they seek affection and exude hope. They want to be well regarded.
- **Passive-negative** presidents do little and enjoy it less. They are in politics out of a sense of duty.[15]

Table 6.1 classifies some former presidents according to Barber's character types.

Presidential Recruitment and Selection

Primaries and Caucuses

Securing a major party's **nomination** is the first step to becoming president. Candidates must start early to organize campaigns, recruit volunteers, collect signatures on ballot-access petitions, build name recognition, and, most important, raise money. Most declare their candidacies by June 30 of the year preceding the general election. Traditionally, the first contests are the Iowa **caucuses** and the New Hampshire **primaries.**[16] These states, with less than 2 percent of the nation's population, receive intense media attention. This scrutiny far exceeds the proportion of delegates selected in these small states as reporters compete for scoops and designate candidates "front-runners," "surprisingly strong contenders," or "disappointments." In an effort to get in on the action, other states have moved their own contests to earlier dates, and the nomination calendar has become increasingly front-loaded as a result.

Primaries became especially important following the 1968 presidential election. At the 1968 Democratic Convention in Chicago, the Democrats nominated Vice President Hubert

Table 6.1

Presidential Character: Barber's Categories

Active-Positives

Thomas Jefferson, Franklin D. Roosevelt, Harry S. Truman, John F. Kennedy, Gerald Ford, Jimmy Carter, George Bush

Passive-Positives

James Madison, William Howard Taft, Warren Harding, Ronald Reagan

Active-Negatives

John Adams, Woodrow Wilson, Herbert Hoover, Lyndon Johnson, Richard Nixon

Passive-Negatives

George Washington, Calvin Coolidge, Dwight Eisenhower

Humphrey as their candidate despite the fact that he had not formally entered a single primary. Supporters of Robert Kennedy, Eugene McCarthy, and other disgruntled Democrats pushed for **reforms.** Procedural details have fluctuated as new reforms were enacted following each subsequent convention. In general terms, however, the rules changes have

- Increased the representation of minorities and women at party conventions. Democrats require delegations to be evenly divided between men and women.
- Increased the role of rank-and-file voters in the selection process through an emphasis on primaries. Presidential primaries have proliferated.
- Decreased the power of party leaders to control the nomination.

As a result, candidates must start earlier in the campaign cycle to win mass support in each state, campaigns have become more expensive, media coverage has intensified, and party conventions have diminished in importance as candidate-selection devices.[17]

Party Conventions

Following the early primary season, the parties hold **national conventions** in the summer. In past years convention deals were sometimes made by delegates and party bosses to give the nomination to a particular candidate. Multiple ballots were sometimes necessary to reach a decision. Suspense and anticipation were high, and media coverage was extensive and intense. In more recent times the primary-determined nominee has been known in advance. Instead of candidate **selection** conventions, parties have held "coronations" or **ratifying conventions** where the delegates made things official. Nevertheless, conventions are still important.

Democratic National Convention, Chicago, 1996.

© CORBIS/Wally McNamee.

- Conventions enable delegates to get acquainted and plan for the fall campaign.
- Conventions provide a forum for debating and modifying rules and procedures.
- Convention delegates approve a **platform** that is presented to voters to signal party positions and beliefs.
- Conventions give party luminaries a chance to speak to the assembled delegates and to address the viewing public.
- The party views the convention as a pep rally for "the troops" and as a four-day infomercial for the public, a chance to impress voters with the party's candidates, messages, and unity.

Conventions are heavily scripted and staged with television in mind. Who will be speaking when prime-time cameras are on? What will the viewers at home see? What will they think of this party and its candidates? The parties try to minimize dissension and rancor and to demonstrate unity and resolve.

On the other hand, journalists look for news. Conflict makes for more interesting stories than harmony. The interests of party leaders and reporters are at odds. The irony is that if party leaders succeed in staging a "good show," networks are less interested in covering it. In 1996 newsman Ted Koppel left the Republican Convention in San Diego, complaining that nothing newsworthy was going to happen there. He did not even bother to attend the Democratic Convention in Chicago later in August. Koppel is not the only journalist to feel this way. Network coverage has declined and will probably continue to do so under existing circumstances. Of course, for political junkies, C-SPAN provides gavel-to-gavel coverage of the proceedings.

The General Election

The **general election campaign** follows the conventions. The nominees travel around the country like rock stars on tour. They make speeches and television commercials. They provide local newspersons with sound bites and photo opportunities and spend millions of dollars. Their every utterance is reported and scrutinized. For that matter, so are their haircuts. Candidates hold televised debates, and audiences approach Super Bowl-like numbers. Finally, election day arrives on the Tuesday following the first Monday in November. At that point our next president is elected. Right? Well, not exactly. The American people do not elect the president; we elect **electors** who elect the president on our behalf.

The Electoral College

The framers of the Constitution had difficulty agreeing on how to elect the president. Some wanted Congress to elect the president, but this plan was rejected to preserve executive independence and separation of powers. Some favored a direct popular vote, but opponents feared that the masses might be too uninformed to meet this responsibility. Communications systems were so primitive that even the most astute citizens would have trouble getting information about candidates from distant states. This situation would give an unfair competitive advantage to candidates from the most populous states. As a compromise the framers agreed that state legislators would choose special presidential "electors." These electors would be drawn from the ranks of the wisest members of the community, but the electors could not be members of Congress or federal officials. We continue to elect presidents indirectly. The operations of the **electoral college** are relatively straightforward.

- Each state has the same number of electoral votes as it has representatives and senators. Delaware has two senators and one representative, so it has three electoral votes. Pennsylvania has two senators and twenty-one representatives, so it has twenty-three electoral votes. Nationwide, there are one hundred senators, 435 representatives, and the District of Columbia gets three electoral votes for a grand total of 538 available electoral votes.
- Most states award electoral votes according to a **unit rule**.[18] The candidate who wins a *plurality* of the popular votes in a state (that is, more popular votes than anyone else even if this total falls short of a 50 percent plus one majority)receives *all* of that state's electoral votes. As such, if Bill Clinton defeated Bob Dole by a single popular vote in Pennsylvania, the unit rule would give Clinton all twenty-one of Pennsylvania electoral votes and Dole would receive none.
- To win the presidency, a candidate needs a *majority* of the 538 electoral votes available nationwide—270 electoral votes.
- If there are multiple candidates and no candidate receives 270 electoral votes, the House of Representatives selects the president from the top three presidential electoral-vote recipients. In this case each state's congressional delegation casts a single vote. The votes of twenty-six states are needed to declare a winner. Meanwhile, the Senate selects the vice president from the top two vice-presidential electoral-vote recipients. If the House is unable to agree on a president by inauguration day, the vice president serves as acting president.

Does this system sound complicated? Here is the electoral college in a nutshell: Each state has electoral votes equaling its number of senators and representatives. In most cases the *popular* vote winner in a state gets all of that state's *electoral* votes. It takes 270 electoral votes to win the presidency. Otherwise, the election goes to Congress. Table 6.2 display each state's number of electoral votes.

Table 6.2

Electoral Votes

State	Electoral Votes	State	Electoral Votes
Alabama	9	Montana	3
Alaska	3	Nebraska	5
Arizona	8	Nevada	4
Arkansas	6	New Hampshire	4
California	54	New Jersey	15
Colorado	8	New Mexico	5
Connecticut	8	New York	33
Delaware	3	North Carolina	14
District of Columbia	3	North Dakota	3
Florida	25	Ohio	21
Georgia	13	Oklahoma	8
Hawaii	4	Oregon	7
Idaho	4	Pennsylvania	23
Illinois	22	Rhode Island	4
Indiana	12	South Carolina	8
Iowa	7	South Dakota	3
Kansas	6	Tennessee	11
Kentucky	8	Texas	32
Louisiana	9	Utah	5
Maine	4	Vermont	3
Maryland	10	Virginia	13
Massachusetts	12	Washington	11
Michigan	18	West Virginia	5
Minnesota	10	Wisconsin	11
Mississippi	7	Wyoming	3
Missouri	11	**TOTAL:**	**538**

What can go wrong with the electoral college? Several things. First, parties identify people to serve as electors. These electors meet in their respective state capitals in mid-December to cast their electoral votes. Most states pledge their electoral votes to their popular-vote winner, but the electors themselves are not bound by the Constitution nor by federal law to cast their votes as they are pledged. In some states electors are "bound" only by custom, tradition, and political pressure. This arrangement gives rise to the occasional **faithless elector,** who decides to vote for someone other than the popular-vote winner in his or her state.[19] In this case, the electoral votes are counted as they are cast.

Another problem is the possibility that a presidential election could go to the House of Representatives. In 1824 no candidate received a majority of the nationwide electoral vote. In the House, Henry Clay's and William Crawford's backers agreed to support John Quincy Adams, giving Adams the presidency over Andrew Jackson. It is offensive to the democratic sensibilities of many to think that a president could again be selected through so indirect a method. Further, there is neither constitutional nor statutory guidance for representatives as to how they should vote if they are called to do so. Should a representative from Pennsylvania's twenty-one-member congressional delegation vote for his or her party's candidate? for his or her district's choice? for his or her personal choice?[20]

This situation brings us to the most dramatic problem. Including President Clinton, we have had sixteen plurality presidents. They received more popular votes nationwide than anyone else, but they fell short of 50 percent of the total popular vote. But at least they won the popular vote. Three times in our history, the electoral college has awarded the presidency to the nationwide popular-vote *loser*. This happens when a candidate wins large, electoral-vote-rich states by slim popular-vote margins while losing smaller, electoral-vote-poor states by large popular-vote margins.

- In 1824 Andrew Jackson won the popular vote nationwide, but electoral-vote totals sent the election to the House where John Quincy Adams was selected president.[21]
- In 1876 Rutherford B. Hayes, a Republican, received fewer popular votes nationwide than his Democrat opponent, Samuel J. Tilden. However, Hayes won the presidency by one electoral vote.[22]
- In 1888 the Republican, Benjamin Harrison, won the presidency in the electoral college despite receiving fewer popular votes nationwide than his Democrat opponent, Grover Cleveland.[23]

Electoral college malfunctions have been rare, but they are possible every four years. **Reform proposals** are many.

- Some of the most common reform proposals include calls to abolish the electoral college outright. Its critics contend that it may have served a purpose in the nation's early days when communications were limited and the wisdom of informed elites was at a premium, but it has long outlived its usefulness. Abolish this archaic institution and select the president through a direct popular vote.[24]
- Less dramatic proposals include abolishing the unit rule so a state's electoral votes would be awarded in **proportion** to a candidate's share of that state's popular vote. In this way the electoral vote would more closely reflect the popular vote.
- Another proposal is to eliminate the faithless elector problem in one of two ways: legally bind all electors to vote as they are pledged or eliminate the electors and award electoral votes automatically.

While many agree that reform is needed, agreement over the details is lacking. Unless malfunctions once again rock the electoral college, reform will remain troublesome. Why? The reform proposals are not neutral. They would advantage certain interests and disadvantage other interests. Further, the electoral college itself is not neutral.

The electoral college has not produced a president who lost the nationwide popular vote since 1888. In 1976, however, we had a close call. Jimmy Carter received 40,828,587 popular votes and 297 electoral votes. Gerald Ford received 39,147,613 popular votes and won states with a total of 241 electoral votes. Carter won the popular vote and the electoral vote. What's the problem? Several states, including Ohio and Hawaii, were close. They both eventually went to Carter and with them went their then-combined 29 electoral votes.[25] However, had just 9,246 Carter voters in these states switched to Ford, Ford would have won both states. Nationwide, the popular-vote results would not have changed; Carter would have remained the popular-vote winner. But a loss of 29 electoral votes would have left Carter with only 268 electoral votes and, apparently, would have given Ford 270. There is more. In mid-December a Ford elector in Washington state voted for Ronald Reagan instead. The vote was counted as it was cast, meaning that Ford's official electoral vote total was 240, not 241. Following this scenario, the official electoral vote would have stood: Ford = 269; Carter = 268; and Reagan = 1. At this point the House of Representatives would have been called on to select the president from among the top three electoral-vote recipients—including Ronald Reagan.[26]

Consider some of the effects of the electoral college. A candidate needs 270 electoral votes to win the presidency. A candidate has limited campaign time and money and must expend these resources judiciously. Former New York Knick, Charles Oakley, once observed, "[y]ou can't throw a hook on the side of the road and expect to catch a fish in the grass."[27] Translation: "Fish where the fish are." Similarly, candidates campaign most heavily where the electoral votes are. The nine largest states (see table 6.3) have 243 electoral votes among them.

Candidates are also well-advised to campaign most heavily in competitive states. Imagine that candidate A's polls show that he is far behind in state X. He calculates that intensive campaigning could narrow the margin. In the final analysis, however, the candidate would still lose the state. Under these circumstances he should forget about state X and go on to the next one. Whether he loses by a single popular vote or by one million popular votes, he still receives zero electoral votes. Conversely, if

Table 6.3

Electoral-Vote-Rich States

State	Electoral Votes
California	54
New York	33
Texas	32
Florida	25
Pennsylvania	23
Illinois	22
Ohio	21
Michigan	18
New Jersey	15
TOTAL:	**243**

presidents were elected through a direct popular vote, it would be sensible for the candidate to try to win as many popular votes as possible wherever he could get them. Next imagine that candidate B's polls show that she is far ahead in state Y. If she were to ignore state Y for the rest of the campaign, her lead would shrink, but she would still win the state. Under such circumstances she should ignore the state and concentrate more heavily on competitive states where her campaigning would make the biggest difference.

The nine states listed in table 6.3 are both large and generally competitive. These are key battleground states in presidential elections. If candidate A had the extreme misfortune of losing California by a single popular vote, losing New York by a single popular vote, losing Texas by a single popular vote, and so on through all nine states, he would be behind by a mere nine popular votes overall—a virtual tie. In the electoral college, however, he would be behind by a count of 243 to 0. Good luck in trying to rally from such a deficit! As a result, candidates campaign most extensively in certain states and are very sensitive to the interests of people who live there.[28]

The electoral college contributes to the power of large, industrialized states.[29] If the electoral college were abolished (or if the unit rule were abolished so that electoral votes more closely reflected the popular vote), large states would become relatively less powerful. The unfortunate candidate A from the preceding example would be only nine popular votes behind after his series of close defeats in the big states. He would be very interested in winning popular votes from Alaska, Delaware, Montana, Nevada, North Dakota, South Dakota, Vermont, and Wyoming. Candidates would try to secure as many popular votes as possible from any and all sources regardless of state lines. In this way, then, the electoral college makes states important as states.[30] Critics sometimes charge that the electoral college is *undemocratic* in that the nationwide popular vote winner can be denied the presidency. Martin Diamond responds that the popular vote winner always wins the electoral vote—in that *state*. As such the debate about reforming the electoral college is not about democracy; it is about *federalism*. It is about whether or not we want states to remain important as states in presidential elections.[31]

The electoral college also magnifies the power of minorities who are relatively small in number nationwide, but who are clustered in large numbers in some large states. The nationwide percentage of Jewish voters is fairly small, but many Jewish voters live in New York and Florida. Candidates seeking the combined fifty-eight electoral votes from these two states must be attentive to Jewish interests. Nationwide, the percentage of Hispanic voters is growing but remains relatively small. However, many Hispanics live in California, Texas, Florida, and New York—states with 144 electoral votes among them. It is no accident that the parties prominently feature Hispanic speakers at their conventions and that candidates who can speak Spanish or who have Hispanic in-laws make sure that the voters know. It is no accident that candidates must be attuned to Hispanic interests.

The electoral college also reinforces the two-party system in that a respectable showing by a third-party candidate is not good enough. That candidate must *win* a state outright to receive any electoral votes. In 1992 H. Ross Perot won an impressive 18.9 percent of the nationwide popular vote (to Clinton's 43 percent and Dole's 37.4 percent), but he failed to win a single state and wound up with zero electoral votes.[32] Some voters report that they are dissatisfied with major-party candidates, and they consider casting "protest votes" for third-party candidates. But when such voters acknowledge the distinct possibility that their protest candidate will fail to win any electoral votes, they decide against throwing away their votes, figuratively hold their noses, and vote for the lesser of major-party evils. Under a direct popular vote-system, such voters would have a greater incentive to vote for a protest candidate in an effort, at minimum, to force an eventual runoff between the two major-party candidates.

Types of Presidential Elections

Walter Dean Burnham described different types of presidential elections in his book, *Critical Elections and Mainsprings of American Politics*.[33] Presidents are not elected through a **normal vote,** which would occur if everybody voted, all partisans supported their party's candidate, and the Independents evenly split their votes. Because Democrats continue to outnumber Republicans, normal votes would always produce Democratic presidents. Obviously, Democrats do not always win. Salient issues and attractive candidates swing votes across party lines. Turnout fluctuates and varies from party to party and election to election. Instead, we can distinguish among four types of presidential elections:

- In a **maintaining election** the larger party (the Democrats) maintains control of the presidency. The larger party holds the White House. Not enough votes shift to the Republicans to give the smaller party the presidency. Examples include 1964, when Lyndon Johnson (Democrat), succeeded John F. Kennedy (Democrat), and 1996, when Bill Clinton (Democrat) was reelected.

- In a **deviating election** enough votes shift to the smaller party to give it the presidency, but it remains the smaller party. Many may vote for the Republican candidate, but do not subsequently become Republicans. Examples include 1952, when Dwight D. Eisenhower (Republican) succeeded Harry S. Truman (Democrat), and 1968, when Richard Nixon (Republican) succeeded Johnson (Democrat).

- In a **reinstating election** the larger party, which was turned out of power in a deviating election, returns to power. The larger party recaptures the presidency. Examples include 1960, when Kennedy (Democrat) succeeded Eisenhower (Republican); 1976, when Jimmy Carter (Democrat) succeeded Gerald Ford (Republican); and 1992, when Clinton (Democrat) succeeded George Bush (Republican).

- In a **realigning** or **critical election,** the smaller party wins the presidency and enough voters change their party registrations so that this party becomes the new majority party. The party that entered an election cycle as the smaller party emerges as the larger one as opposing party members, and especially Independents, switch. There is a "realignment" in party strength. A realignment occurred in the 1930s. Franklin Roosevelt (Democrat) succeeded Herbert Hoover (Republican) in 1932. Roosevelt won reelection in 1936. The Democrats had been the smaller party during the Hoover years but became the larger party during Franklin D. Roosevelt's presidency.

In 1980 Ronald Reagan (Republican) defeated Jimmy Carter (Democrat) in a landslide. Technically, the 1980 election was a deviating election. But Republican numbers began to grow and continued to grow throughout the 1980s. At the same time, the number of people identifying themselves as Democrats declined. Had a realignment occurred? As of this writing Democrats continue to outnumber Republicans, but the margin is smaller than it was prior to Reagan's election. Whatever one chooses to call the 1980 election, it was certainly an important one.

In the year 2000 the Democrats will be hoping for another maintaining election. Republicans will be hoping for a deviating election. The most optimistic Republicans will be hoping for a realigning election.

Congressional Elections

Constitutional Provisions

Article 1, Section 2 provides that members of the House of Representatives are elected through a direct popular vote. Seats are apportioned among the states on the basis of population, but every state is entitled to at least one seat in the House. Representatives serve two-year terms. Representatives must meet the following criteria:

- Be at least twenty-five years of age
- Have been United States citizens for at least seven years
- Be inhabitants of the states that elect them

Article 1, Section 3 specifies that each state has two senators. Senators serve six-year terms. One-third of the seats in the Senate are contested every two years. Senators must meet the following criteria:

- Be at least thirty years of age
- Have been United States citizens for at least nine years
- Be inhabitants of the states that elect them

The Seventeenth Amendment provides for a direct popular vote in Senate elections.

Presidential Influence

As discussed elsewhere, turnout in off-year congressional races is lower than congressional-election turnout in presidential years. During a presidential year some successful congressional candidates ride into office on the president's coattails. In off-year races many weak partisans stay home and some congresspeople who won narrow victories with the president's assistance are unable to hold their seats. This pattern explains, in part, why the president's party usually loses seats in the House in off-year congressional elections.[34]

Presidents campaign for their party's congressional candidates. They raise campaign funds for candidates. They visit districts and appear with the candidates. They send other administration officials out onto the campaign trail to help candidates. However, these tactics work only if the president is popular. In light of various political and legal problems facing President Clinton in 1998, some Democratic candidates, who normally would have welcomed the President's support, tried to keep their distance from him.[35]

Profile of Members of Congress: Who Wins Elections?

New members of Congress being sworn in.

© AP/Wide World Photos.

Occupation, Race, and Gender

The **average congressperson** is a well-educated, middle-aged, middle- or upper-income, white, male Protestant. He is probably a lawyer, businessman, or banker. He is a former member of the armed services and is still a resident and political activist in the town where he spent his formative years. Table 6.4 provides information on members' backgrounds.

The number of women in Congress approximately doubled in the 1990s, but there are still far fewer women in Congress than in the general population. The same

Table 6.4

Members of Congress: Seniority and Occupation, 1987–1997

Representatives

Seniority and Occupation	100th (1987)	101st (1989)	102d (1991)	103d (1993)	104th (1995)	105th (1997) Dem.	105th (1997) Rep.	105th (1997) Total
Seniority[a]								
Under 2 years	51	38	55	115	92	46	33	79
2–9 years	221	230	176	139	189	84	129	214[b]
10–19 years	114	117	149	134	109	48	52	100
20–29 years	37	35	42	34	36	22	12	34
30 years or more	12	13	13	13	9	5	1	6
Total	435	435[c]	435	435	435	205	227	435[c]
Occupation								
Agriculture	20	19	20	19	19	8	14	22
Business or banking	142	138	157	131	163	55	126	181
Education	38	42	57	66	76	40	33	74[b]
Journalism	20	17	25	24	15	4	7	12[b]
Law	184	184	183	181	170	87	85	172
Public service/politics	94	94	61	86	102	54	46	100

Senators

Seniority and Occupation	100th (1987)	101st (1989)	102d (1991)	103d (1993)	104th (1995)	105th (1997) Dem.	105th (1997) Rep.	105th (1997) Total
Seniority[a]								
Under 2 years	14	11	6	15	12	7	9	16
2–9 years	41	34	33	31	37	13	26	39
10–19 years	36	43	47	38	31	14	12	26
20–29 years	7	10	10	11	15	7	7	14
30 years or more	2	2	4	5	5	4	1	5
Total	100	100	100	100	100	45	55	100
Occupation								
Agriculture	5	4	8	9	9	2	6	8
Business or banking	28	28	31	27	24	8	25	33
Education	12	11	10	12	10	5	8	13
Journalism	8	8	10	8	8	2	7	9
Law	62	63	61	58	54	26	27	53
Public service/politics	20	20	4	12	12	9	17	26

Note: Members of Congress may state more than one occupation; therefore, sum may be greater than total. Not all occupations reported are listed. Data for earlier years can be found in previous editions of *Vital Statistics on American Politics*.

[a] Represents consecutive years of service.

[b] Includes Rep. Bernard Sanders (I-VT).

[c] Includes two vacancies.

Sources: U.S. Bureau of the Census, *Statistical Abstract of the United States, 1988* (U.S. Government Printing Office, 1987), 244; *Congressional Quarterly Weekly Report*, (1988), 3295; (1989), 41–44; (1990), 3837; (1991), 127–130; (January 16, 1993. Supplement), 13, 170–173; (Novemeber 12, 1994, Supplement), 11; (1995), 550–553; (1997), 29, 506–509. As cited in Harold W. Stanley and Richard G. Niemi, *Vital Statistics on American Politics*, 6th ed. (Congressional Quarterly, 1998), p.198.

holds true for blacks, Hispanics, and other minorities. Table 6.5 summarizes some of the data through the 105-year Congress. In the 106th Congress there are fifty-eight female representatives and nine female senators.

Name Recognition

Some **celebrities** capitalize on their name recognition to win election to Congress. Some came to Congress from the sports world.

- Representative **Steve Largent** (R-OK) was a wide receiver for the Seattle Seahawks. He ended his fourteen-year NFL career with 819 catches; 13,089 yards, 100 touchdowns, 177 consecutive games with a reception; and ten 50-catch seasons.
- Representative **J. C. Watts** (R-OK), former University of Oklahoma quarterback, led the Sooners to consecutive Orange Bowl victories in 1980 and 1981 and was named most valuable player in both games.
- Representative **Jim Ryun** (R-KA) was a world-class runner, Olympian, and world-record holder in the mile.
- Senator **Jim Bunning** (R-KY) pitched for three teams but is best known for the perfect game he pitched for the Philadelphia Phillies over the New York Mets on June 21, 1964. Bunning also threw a no-hitter for the Detroit Tigers against the Boston Red Sox in 1958.
- **Bill Bradley** (D-NJ) served in the United States Senate from 1979 until 1997, following his NBA career with the New York Knicks and his Hall of Fame collegiate career at Princeton University.
- Former representative and vice-presidential candidate **Jack Kemp** (R-NY) was a quarterback for the Buffalo Bills.
- Former representative **Tom McMillan** (D-MD) was an NBA player for the Washington Bullets (as they were then known), in addition to several other teams, and held the Pennsylvania high school career scoring record until 1998.

Some came to Congress from the entertainment world.

- Senator **Fred Thompson** (R-TN) was an actor who appeared in numerous movies.
- The late representative **Sonny Bono** (R-CA) was a singer and television performer.[36]
- Former representative **Fred Grandy** (R-IA) played Gopher on *The Love Boat*.
- Former representative **Ben Jones** (D-GA) played Cooder on *The Dukes of Hazzard*.
- Although she did not win, **Nancy Kulp** ran for Congress in Pennsylvania. She played Miss Hathaway on *The Beverly Hillbillies*.

Advantages of Incumbency and the Debate over Term Limits

Another generalization that can be made about the members of Congress is that once they are elected, they are usually successful in getting reelected. An incumbent is most

Table 6.5

Members of Congress: Female, Black, Hispanic, Marital Status, and Age, 1971–1997

Congress	Female	Black	Hispanic	Not Married[a]	Under 40	40–49	50–59	60–69	70–79	80 and over
Representatives										
92d (1971)	12	12	5	26	40	133	152	86	19	3
93d (1973)	14	15	5	34	45	132	154	80	20	2
94th (1975)	18	16	5	54	69	138	137	75	14	2
95th (1977)	18	16	5	56	81	121	147	71	15	0
96th (1979)	16	16	6	69	86	125	145	53	14	0
97th (1981)	19	16	6	86	94	142	132	54	12	1
98th (1983)	21	20	10	68	86	145	132	57	13	1
99th (1985)	22	19	11	69	71	154	131	59	17	2
100th (1987)	23	22	11	64	63	153	137	56	24	2
101st (1989)	25	23	11	—	41	163	133	74	20	2
102d (1991)	29	25	10	—	39	153	133	86	20	4
103d (1993)	48	38	17	—	47	152	129	91	13	3
104th (1995)	49	39	18	—	53	153	136	80	12	1
105th (1997)	51	37	18	—	47	145	147	82	10	2
Senators										
92d (1971)	1	1	1	3	4	24	32	23	16	1
93d (1973)	0	1	1	4	3	25	37	23	11	1
94th (1975)[b]	0	1	1	6	5	21	35	24	15	0
95th (1977)	0	1	0	9	6	26	35	21	10	2
96th (1979)	1	0	0	5	10	31	33	17	8	1
97th (1981)	2	0	0	7	9	35	36	14	6	0
98th (1983)	2	0	0	10	7	28	39	20	3	3
99th (1985)	2	0	0	8	4	27	38	25	4	2
100th (1987)	2	0	0	11	5	30	36	22	5	2
101st (1989)	2	0	0	—	0	30	40	22	6	2
102d (1991)	2	0	0	—	0	22	47	24	5	2
103d (1993)	6	1	0	—	1	16	49	22	11	1
104th (1995)	8	1	0	—	1	14	41	27	16	1
105th (1997)	9	1	0	—	1	21	39	26	12	1

Note: "—" indicates not available. As of beginning of first session of each Congress. Figures for representatives exclude vacancies. The counts above exclude nonvoting delegates and commissioners from American Samoa, Guam, Puerto Rico, the Virgin Islands, and Washington, D.C.

[a]Single, widowed, or divorced.

[b]Includes Sen. John Durkin (D-NH), seated September 1975.

Sources: Hispanic (1971–1985): Congressional Quarterly, *American Leaders, 1789–1987* (Congressional Quarterly, 1987), 55; female and black (1971–1997) and Hispanic (1987–1997), *Congressional Quarterly Weekly Report* (1970), 2756; (1972), 2991; (1974), 3104; (1976), 3155; (1978), 3252; (1980), 3318; (1982), 2805; (1984), 2921; (1986), 2863; (1988), 3294; (1990), 3835–3836; (January 16, 1993, Supplement), 12; (November 12,, 1994, Supplement), 10; (1997), 28; not married and age (1971–1989); U.S. Bureau of the Census, *Statistical Abstract of the United States, 1988* (U.S. Government Printing Office, 1987), 244: *1990, 257;* age (1991–1997); calculated by the editors from *Congressional Quarterly Weekly Report* (1991), 118–127; (January 16, 1993, Supplement), 12, 160–168; (1995), 541–549; (1997), 497–505. As cited in Harold W. Stanley and Richard G. Niemi, *Vital Statistics on American Politics,* 6th ed. (Congressional Quarterly, 1998), p. 197.

Table 6.6

House and Senate Incumbents Reelected, Defeated, or Retired, 1946–1996

Chamber/Years	Retired[a]	Number Seeking Reelection	Defeated Primaries	Defeated General Election	Reelected Total	Reelected Percentage of Those Seeking Reelection
House						
1946	32	398	18	52	328	82.4
1948	29	400	15	68	317	79.3
1950	29	400	6	32	362	90.5
1952	42	389	9	26	354	91.0
1954	24	407	6	22	379	93.1
1956	21	411	6	16	389	94.6
1958	33	396	3	37	356	89.9
1960	26	405	5	25	375	92.6
1962	24	402	12	22	368	91.5
1964	33	397	8	45	344	86.6
1966	22	411	8	41	362	88.1
1968	23	409	4	9	396	96.8
1970	29	401	10	12	379	94.5
1972	40	390	12	13	365	93.6
1974	43	391	8	40	343	87.7
1976	47	384	3	13	368	95.8
1978	49	382	5	19	358	93.7
1980	34	398	6	31	361	90.7
1982	40	393	10	29	354	90.1
1984	22	411	3	16	392	95.4
1986	40	394	3	6	385	97.7
1988	23	409	1	6	403	98.3
1990	27	406	1	15	390	96.0
1992	65	368	19	24	325	88.3
1994	48	382	4	35	347	90.8
1996	45	379	2	21	358	94.5

likely to lose in his or her *first* reelection campaign. After that, reelection rates are very high, especially for representatives. About one-third to one-half of senators seeking reelection attract strong, well-funded, well-known challengers. Sitting governors and current House members frequently vie for Senate seats. In contrast, House elections often lack credible challengers—or any challengers. Many House elections go uncontested. Others feature little-known and poorly financed challengers. Most challengers spend little money, run weak campaigns, and lose badly. Since 1970 more than 90 percent of House incumbents seeking reelection have won. In 1996 approximately 95 percent of House incumbents and 92 percent of Senate incumbents seeking reelection won. Table 6.6 tracks the electoral fate of congressional incumbents over a fifty-year period.

| Chamber/Years | Retired[a] | Number Seeking Reelection | Defeated | | Reelected | |
			Primaries	General Election	Total	Percentage of Those Seeking Reelection
Senate						
1946	9	30	6	7	17	56.7
1948	8	25	2	8	15	60.0
1950	4	32	5	5	22	68.8
1952	4	31	2	9	20	64.5
1954	6	32	2	6	24	75.0
1956	6	29	0	4	25	86.2
1958	6	28	0	10	18	64.3
1960	5	29	0	1	28	96.6
1962	4	35	1	5	29	82.9
1964	2	33	1	4	28	84.8
1966	3	32	3	1	28	87.5
1968	6	28	4	4	20	71.4
1970	4	31	1	6	24	77.4
1972	6	27	2	5	20	74.1
1974	7	27	2	2	23	85.2
1976	8	25	0	9	16	64.0
1978	10	25	3	7	15	60.0
1980	5	29	4	9	16	55.2
1982	3	30	0	2	28	93.3
1984	4	29	0	3	26	89.6
1986	6	28	0	7	21	75.0
1988	6	27	0	4	23	85.2
1990	3	32	0	1	31	96.9
1992	7	28	1	4	23	82.1
1994	8	26	0	2	24	92.2
1996	13	20	1	1	19	92.3

[a]Does not include persons who died or resigned from office before the election.

Sources: 1946–1992; Norman J. Ornstein et al., ed., *Vital Statistics on Congress, 1993–1994* (Congressional Quarterly, 1994), 58, 59; *Congressional Quarterly Weekly Report* (1994), 2995, 3232, 3240; (1996), 3225, 3232, 3233. As cited in Harold W. Stanley and Richard G. Niemi, *Vital Statistics on American Politics*, 6th ed. (Congressional Quarterly, 1998), pp. 47–48.

Incumbents have several advantages over their challengers. Incumbents have **name recognition.** They enjoy **credibility** that comes from holding the office; no on-the-job-training period is necessary if the incumbent is reelected. Incumbents have greater **access to the media** than their challengers have and enjoy advantages over their challengers when it comes to **fund-raising.**[37]

Campaign costs have risen in recent years. Television advertising, polling, focus-group research, and direct-mail fund-raising appeals have become increasingly important and expensive. A successful Senate campaign generally costs several million dollars. It is not unusual for successful House campaigns to cost $500,000. Table 6.7 summarizes campaign spending by winning congressional candidates over a two-decade period.

The irony here is that it costs money for an unknown challenger to build name recognition. Generally, challengers need to spend more money to win than incumbents do, yet incumbents find it easier to raise funds.[38] Campaign reform advocates sometimes complain that election campaigns cost too much and propose that congressional spending limits should be imposed. In light of a challenger's relatively greater need to spend to become known and wage a serious campaign, what do you think the effect of such spending limits would be? Would the reform benefit incumbents? challengers? Or would it be neutral?

Table 6.7

Campaign Spending for Winning Congressional Candidates, 1975–1996

Chamber/Years	Receipts[a]	Expenditures[a]	Total[a]	Political Action Committee Contributions Percentage of Receipts
House				
1975–1976	$42.5	$38.0	$10.9	25.6
1977–1978	60.0	55.6	17.0	28.3
1979–1980	86.0	78.0	27.0	31.4
1981–1982	123.1	114.7	42.7	34.7
1983–1984	144.8	127.0	59.5	41.1
1985–1986	172.7	154.9	72.8	42.2
1987–1988	191.0	171.0	86.4	45.2
1989–1990	198.3	179.1	91.5	46.1
1991–1992	235.9	243.6	97.7	41.4
1993–1994	245.8	230.6	97.6	39.7
1995–1996	321.9	297.2	122.8	38.1
Senate				
1975–1976	21.0	20.1	3.1	14.8
1977–1978	43.0	42.3	6.0	14.0
1979–1980	41.7	40.0	10.2	24.5
1981–1982	70.7	68.2	15.6	22.1
1983–1984	100.9	97.5	20.0	19.8
1985–1986	106.8	104.3	28.4	26.6
1987–1988	121.7	123.6	31.8	26.1
1989–1990	121.5	115.4	31.1	25.6
1991–1992	118.5	123.7	32.2	27.2
1993–1994	151.0	150.7	32.7	21.7
1995–1996	124.9	128.0	29.6	23.7

[a]In millions of current dollars.

Sources: 1975–1980: Federal Election Commission, "1994 Congressional Fundraising Climbs to New High," press release, April 28, 1995, 2; 1981–1996: "Congressional Fundraising and Spending up Again in 1996," press release, April 14, 1997, 2; percentages calculated by the editors. As cited in Harold W. Stanley and Richard G. Niemi, *Vital Statistics on American Politics*, 6th ed. (Congressional Quarterly, 1998), p. 90.

*I*n a 1994 Senate race in California, Michael Huffington spent more than $20 million of his own money in an attempt to unseat the incumbent senator, Diane Feinstein. He lost.

Approximately 40 percent of all campaign funds come from individual contributors.

- Direct-mail solicitations produce most of these contributions.
- PACs provide about 30 percent of campaign funds.
- PACs contribute more than five times as much money to incumbents as they do to challengers.[39]

Congressional leaders often raise funds for the campaigns of their parties' incumbents and challengers, who will remember this help if they are elected. Thus PACs have another way to contribute, and leaders have another way to solidify their support from other members of Congress.[40]

In addition, congresspeople have given themselves allowances to cover telephone, travel, staff, office, and mailing expenses.[41] They also have generous health care and retirement plans, free parking and subsidized meals in the House and Senate dining rooms; television and radio recording studios in the Capitol and professionals to assist members in producing their media spots; and other **fringe benefits.**[42] Furthermore, an incumbent continues to draw a salary while campaigning for reelection, whereas challengers often take leaves of absence from their jobs to campaign. Such considerations contribute to the popularity of **term limits.**[43]

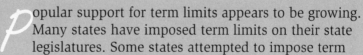

Something to Think About

*P*opular support for term limits appears to be growing. Many states have imposed term limits on their state legislatures. Some states attempted to impose term limits on their congressional representative, but the Supreme Court ruled that this action was unconstitutional.[44]

Proponents of term limits say that the system is rigged against challengers. Incumbents are almost immortal. Challengers don't even bother to run. Voter participation declines. Most turnover results from voluntary retirements, not from election defeats. Term limits, advocates claim, will make elections more competitive and meaningful; enable fresh ideas to enter Congress; allow citizen-legislators to replace professional, lifetime representatives; and make Congress more accountable to the public.

Critics of term limits argue that we already have term limits. It is called "voting." If we disapprove of our incumbent's performance, vote him or her out. But if we approve of the incumbent's work, we should have the right to reelect. To deny us this right is an undemocratic restriction on voter choice. Perhaps incumbents are so successful because they are already accountable to the people and respond to the wishes of their constituents. Further, term limits will cause Congress to lose some experienced, knowledgeable, responsible members. They will be replaced by inexperienced newcomers who will depend heavily on unelected staff assistants to teach them the ropes. In the meantime lobbyists and bureaucrats will find it easier to have their way with inexperienced congresspeople. Besides, the Republicans didn't need term limits to unseat enough Democrats in 1994 to become the majority party.

Does inexperience matter? About twenty first-term House members were asked, "Do you approve of what we're doing to stop what's going on in Freedonia?" or "Do you approve of what we're doing to stop ethnic cleansing in Freedonia?" Replies included "take action" and "it's a different situation than the Middle East." None of the twenty House freshmen recognized the fictitious nation of "Freedonia" from the 1933 Marx Brothers movie *Duck Soup*. The joker was *Spy* magazine, whose national editor, Jamie Malanowskie, characterized the responses as "completely understandable." "In campaigning," he said, "they are asked a lot of dumb questions, and they are all used to supplying answers."[45]

What do you think about term limits?

Incumbent reelection statistics inflate an incumbent's reelection chances to some degree. Some turnover takes place when incumbents die or seek other offices. Additional turnover results when incumbents retire instead of running in elections they might lose. Redistricting, which occurs once every ten years, also produces higher than average turnover.[46] Redistricting threatens incumbents when new district lines are less friendly to them than the old ones were. Some incumbents inevitably decide to retire or move on,

Table 6.8

Turnover in the House of Representatives, by Decade and Party System, 1789–1996

	Total Turnover	Deaths	Retired/ Resigned[a]	Denied Renomination	General Election Defeat	Unknown/ Other[b]
Decade						
1790s	.387	.015	.169	.002	.028	.173
1800s	.358	.016	.145	.001	.034	.161
1810s	.491	.020	.178	.009	.067	.218
1820s	.390	.014	.134	.002	.080	.161
1830s	.485	.023	.176	.005	.122	.159
1840s	.584	.023	.250	.010	.099	.203
1850s	.577	.014	.248	.014	.143	.157
1860s	.488	.020	.229	.027	.121	.090
1870s	.476	.018	.214	.035	.148	.061
1880s	.436	.016	.189	.047	.128	.055
1890s	.386	.017	.169	.044	.128	.028
1900s	.269	.025	.110	.033	.087	.014
1910s	.287	.028	.111	.028	.115	.006
1920s	.216	.029	.073	.026	.087	.000
1930s	.280	.037	.078	.047	.117	.000
1940s	.247	.026	.083	.032	.106	.000
1950s	.170	.025	.074	.014	.056	.000
1960s	.167	.016	.072	.022	.058	.000
1970s	.188	.010	.112	.014	.052	.000
1980s	.122	.010	.072	.006	.032	.000
1990s	.219	.005	.134	.019	.060	.000
Overall						
1789–1996	.347	.020	.144	.021	.089	.073
Party system						
First, 1789–1824	.408	.017	.161	.003	.045	.182
Second, 1825–1854	.518	.020	.201	.007	.113	.176
Third, 1855–1896	.475	.017	.214	.035	.136	.073
Fourth, 1897–1932	.270	.027	.101	.034	.099	.009
Fifth, 1933–1964	.219	.028	.078	.027	.085	.000
Sixth, 1965–1996	.165	.009	.095	.013	.046	.000

Note: Figures are proportions of the original House membership for each Congress failing to return to the following Congress, averaged across all Congresses within a decade (or a party system). Decades are defined by the first year of a Congress (e.g., the 1980s includes 1981–1982 through 1989–1990); each decade mean is based on five Congresses, except for the 1790s (six) and the 1990s (three). Results reflect the final disposition of challenged elections. Data are current through January 27, 1997.

[a]Includes retirements from public office, retirements to seek or accept other elective office (including the Senate), retirements to accept federal executive branch appointments, and resignations.

[b]"Unknown" are cases in which the member was not a candidate in the next general election but it could not be determined whether he or she was denied renomination or deliberately chose not to seek reelection. "Other" refers mainly to expulsions (almost all of which were connected with disloyalty in the Civil War).

Source: Revised from John W. Swain, Stephen A. Borrelli, Brian C. Reed, and Sean F. Evans, "U.S. House Turnover, 1789–1995: Toward a "Systemic' Perspective," paper presented at the annual meeting of the American Political Science Association, 1996. As cited in Harold W. Stanley and Richard G. Niemi, *Vital Statistics on American Politics,* 6th ed. (Congressional Quarterly, 1998), p. 43.

rather than risk electoral defeat. Over a period of several elections, many congressional seats change hands.[47] Table 6.8 tracks turnover in the House over time.

Put the pieces all together, and it is evident that the average member of Congress (who is white, male, highly educated, and a white-collar professional) does not look like most Americans. Because he may feel closest to those constituents who share this profile, some constituents are likely to be more influential than others. The poor, the young, the elderly, the uneducated, the unemployed, women, minorities, and others are frequently "represented" by congressmen who may not be able to understand their needs.[48]

QuotableQuote

Maybe 125 new members can make a difference. But somehow that sounds to me like if you scramble eggs the cholesterol will disappear.
— **Representative Dennis Eckart (D-OH)**

Key Terms

Notes

Governmental Institutions

About This Section

This section looks at the institutions that convert inputs into policy outputs (conversion functions). Article 1 of the Constitution established Congress, Article 2 the presidency, and Article 3 the courts. This section considers the three branches in the same order as the framers did.

chapter 7 Congress

Addresses the history, structures, and operations of the United States Congress. Individual members of Congress represent the people back in the home districts (interest representation). Congress as a whole makes public policy (rule initiation) for the entire nation. Conflicts between these two roles are highlighted.

chapter 8 The American Presidency

Reviews the historical origins of the presidency. Could a president become an American king? Popular expectations, contrasting presidential views of the office, bargaining, presidential powers and limits, and the foreign affairs presidency are among the topics discussed.

chapter 9 The Federal Bureaucracy

Describes how the government applies general rules to specific cases (rule application). The chapter supplies some theoretical background and explores bureaucratic structures, functions, and malfunctions.

chapter 10 The Federal Court System

Explains how federal judges interpret the law to resolve legal disputes (rule interpretation). The chapter includes these questions: What do federal courts look like? What cases can they hear? How does the Supreme Court work? How are federal judges appointed? What is "judicial review"?

part 3

chapter 7

Introduction: Congressmen and Congresswomen versus Congress

Start with an important observation: Congress is made up of congressmen and congresswomen. I know. You are probably thinking, "I had to buy a textbook to learn this?" Actually, the above statement is not as trite as it appears. Let me explain.

uppose that new research conclusively demonstrates the dangers of smoking. Even you, a long-time skeptic (and smoker), are convinced. Congress considers legislation outlawing tobacco. This legislation would advance the national interest.

Now suppose that you are a member of Congress, you are from North Carolina, and most of your constituents depend on tobacco production for their livelihoods. When the legislation comes to a floor vote, what will you do?

The United States Congress is the national legislature. We expect Congress to pass laws for the good of the entire country. But the individual members of Congress are elected by voters in states and local districts. These voters expect the individual members to represent the interests of their home districts. This **local** orientation of individual members undercuts the ability of Congress to promote the **national** interest. Local interests and national interests sometimes conflict. For example, stronger regulations on offshore drilling operations might serve national environmental interests, but a representative from an oil state may feel obliged to resist such legislation.

There is more to it. Members of Congress are expected to be residents of their home districts. They maintain and staff district offices to care for the needs of constituents. But they perform most of their legislative work in the nation's capital and are discouraged by their colleagues from running home on a weekly basis. Washington runs on political debate, news, gossip, and speculation. Over time, members of Congress may become preoccupied with **beltway issues** that seem important to people who work inside the City but are less important to middle America. In short, congressmen and congresswomen can lose touch with their home districts and their constituents. We face two paradoxical points:

- Congress is expected to **legislate** to advance national interests, but individual members of Congress can be so district oriented in **representing** their constituencies that Congress as a whole cannot function in this fashion.
- Conversely, living and working in Washington can make members of Congress lose touch with the folks back home.

Congressional Functions

Rule initiation is one of Congress's most important functions. While policy proposals may originate with interest groups, the president, and others outside Congress, it is

U.S. Capitol Building.

© *Bohdan Hrynewych/Stock Boston.*

Congress that ultimately shapes, rejects, or enacts new policies. We expect Congress to be our national legislature, to pass laws advancing national interests. **Interest representation** is another important role. Districts are diverse. Agricultural concerns dominate some districts; labor interests and service professions dominate others. Ethnic, racial, and economic compositions vary widely. Members of Congress are expected to represent these diverse interests. But as we have seen, when members represent their home districts, it is difficult for Congress as a whole to transcend local perspectives to further national interests. In addition, Congress engages in **rule application** when it tries to influence bureaucratic operations through appropriations processes and oversight committees. Further, Congress is involved in **rule interpretation** when the Senate conducts hearings and confirms federal court appointments.[1]

    Constituency service is another important congressional function. Incumbent congresspeople who seek reelection usually win. Morris Fiorina thinks that one reason incumbents are hard to beat is that they perform many services for the voters back home.[2] When a legislator takes a position on a policy issue, someone will disagree. No matter what position the legislator takes, somebody will not like it. On s a "legislator" Congressman Ron Dellums (D-CA) generally opposed defense spending. He voted to cut the number of B-2 bombers down to 20 at a time when the Pentagon wanted 130. He helped reduce spending on the Strategic Defense Initiative and voted to reduce the United States military presence in Europe. His position was that money spent on defense programs could be better spent on programs to aid the poor and disadvantaged. In 1993 President Clinton proposed closing some military bases to save money. Alameda County, which Dellums represents, ranked first on the list of recommended base closings. Dellums insisted that the proposed closings were a form of political retribution. As a "representative" he opposed these closings and mounted an effort to save his local bases.

the other hand, providing valued services for constituents brings pure profit. One can make friends without simultaneously making enemies. Many Democrats in the home district will support their Republican incumbent if they conclude that the experienced legislator can win more tangible rewards for the district than a rookie Democrat could. An experienced lawmaker will be more successful in obtaining federal money for new highways, bus terminals, airports, research facilities, post offices, and military contracts for the home district. Such projects boost the local economy. Members of Congress have caseworkers and other staffers to attend to such matters.

- Some members of Congress receive more than ten thousand letters per week. Few of these correspondents are writing merely to send their regards; most are writing to ask for something.
- Some want help in untangling some bureaucratic red tape.
- Some want information.
- Some are feeling patriotic and are asking for an American flag that flew above the Capitol.
- Some are writing to request recipes!

The bottom line is that most of these people want something. Members of Congress sometimes complain that they feel like glorified errand boys or errand girls. A practical response: "It's better to be reelected as an errand boy or girl than not to be reelected at all."

The Senate and the House: Similarities and Differences

Congress is a **bicameral legislature,** consisting of an upper chamber (the Senate) and a lower chamber (the House of Representatives). Both houses must approve a bill for it to become a law. The houses differ in critical ways. James Madison described some of these differences in *The Federalist Papers.*[3]

The **Senate** was designed to be less directly responsive to the people.

QuotableQuote

The necessity of a senate is . . . indicated by the propensity of all single and numerous assemblies, to yield to the impulse of sudden and violent passions, and to be seduced by factious leaders into intemperate and pernicious resolutions. . . . [A] body which is to correct this infirmity ought . . . be less numerous. It ought, moreover, to possess great firmness, and . . . hold its authority by a tenure of considerable duration.
—James Madison, *The Federalist,* Number 62

- Senators were elected by state legislators, not through a direct popular vote. This arrangement did not change until the Seventeenth Amendment took effect in 1913.
- Senators serve six-year terms.
- Senators "represent" statewide constituencies. Naturally, a state has more voters than a congressional district has. As such a wider variety of views will vie for expression. In such a setting, the senator is not a slave to any single interest and might be able to play one interest off against another. If the senator offends some segment of the population, she or he might not have to worry about reelection for another six years. These factors contribute to a senator's policy independence.
- The Senate, with only one hundred members, is smaller than the House.
- The Senate is also less formal in its procedures. For example, the Senate allows "unlimited debate."

- Senators have opportunities to study and act on a wide variety of pressing national issues. There is less specialization in the Senate than in the House because the Senate has fewer people to cover the workload.
- Media coverage of the Senate is relatively more extensive.
- Senators are often well-known beyond their home states. This national visibility encourages some senators to run for the presidency.

In short, senators are expected to exercise their informed judgments on behalf of their states and the Nation.

On the other hand, the aptly named **House of Representatives** was designed to be more directly representative of the people.

- Members are elected through a direct popular vote.
- They serve relatively short, two-year terms.
- The House, with 435 seats, is larger than the Senate.
- Seats are apportioned among the states on the basis of population, with large states having more seats than small states.
- The House of Representatives is more formal than the Senate. For example, debate is limited and takes place according to a rule.
- There is more specialization in the House because more members do its work.
- Generally, representatives are not as well-known nationally as their Senate counterparts.
- Representatives from states with two or more seats represent congressional districts rather than entire states. Thus their constituencies are smaller and less diverse. They have less ability to play interests off against one another and enjoy less freedom in taking issue positions than senators do.

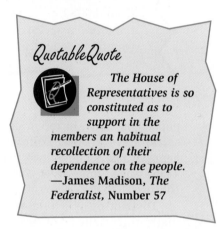

QuotableQuote

The House of Representatives is so constituted as to support in the members an habitual recollection of their dependence on the people.
—James Madison, *The Federalist,* Number 57

Apportionment and Districting

Apportionment involves the question, How many seats in Congress will each state have? Recall that the delegates at the Constitutional Convention faced this question in 1787. They decided that each state would have two seats in the Senate and representation in the House would depend on population, with every state guaranteed at least one seat. As a result, California, with more than 31.5 million people, has two United States senators. Delaware, with fewer than eight hundred thousand people, also has two senators. If some issue motivated the fifty-two senators from the twenty-six smallest states to pool their votes, they could outvote the forty-eight senators from the twenty-four most populous states. On the other hand, California has fifty-two seats in the House of Representatives, while Delaware has just one. Every ten years, a **national census** is taken. Subsequently, the 435 House seats are reapportioned to reflect n the early 1980s the Republicans controlled the Pennsylvania state legislature. While redistricting to account for population and seat losses, they decided to combine parts of the old twenty-first district with the old twelfth district. Don Bailey, a Democrat, represented the twenty-first and John Murtha, also a Democrat, represented the twelfth. The two Democrats had to face each other in a primary. Murtha won and remained a secure fixture in the House. Either way, one less Democrat would return to Congress.

population shifts. In recent decades snowbelt states have lost population, and sunbelt states have grown. Following the 1990 census Illinois, Michigan, Ohio, and Pennsylvania each lost two seats in the House. New York lost three seats. Conversely, Texas gained three seats, Florida gained four, and California gained seven. This trend is expected to continue.[4]

Districting is a related matter. Senators serve statewide constituencies, so districting issues are not important. Drawing district lines for the House of Representatives, however, generates much controversy. After determining how many House seats a state will have, state legislators may have to redraw district lines to reflect changes. These lines affect the prospects of different candidates. If all of a state's black voters are clustered within a single district, the district's representative must be attuned to their interests. But representatives from other parts of the state need not be so attuned. Or a Republican-controlled state legislature might redraw a Democrat incumbent's House district in ways that make it difficult for him or her to be reelected.[5]

Gerrymandering

When state legislators redraw congressional district lines, astute politicians have maneuvered to inflate or deflate the voting strength of certain interests. This practice is called **gerrymandering.** The term dates back to a political map redrawn in 1812 to favor Massachusetts governor, Elbridge Gerry. A newspaper editor thought that the map looked like a salamander and coined the term "gerrymander." In 1957 the Alabama state legislature redrew the political boundaries of the city of Tuskegee. The City, which had been square in shape, was transformed into an irregular, many-sided figure. The result was to render most of the City's black population ineligible for voting in municipal elections. Courts have barred such blatant racial gerrymandering.

More subtle is **silent gerrymandering,** or the underrepresentation of cities and the overrepresentation of rural areas that occurs when people move from rural to urban areas but the state legislature fails to redistrict to account for these changes. Such patterns occurred in several states from the early to mid-twentieth century. For example, the Illinois state legislature had not redrawn congressional district lines since 1901. In ensuing decades rural populations decreased, and urban populations increased, but the state legislature did not redraw district lines. Chicago voters complained that their votes did not have equal weight with those of rural voters. One congressional district in Chicago had more than nine hundred thousand people, while a district in southern Illinois had just slightly more than one hundred thousand people! Urban voters maintained that this arrangement deprived them of **equal protection of the laws** as guaranteed by the Fourteenth Amendment and the **republican form of government** guaranteed by Article 4 of the United States Constitution.

In *Colegrove* v. *Green* (1946),[6] Justice Frankfurter wrote that "it is hostile to a democratic system to involve the judiciary in the politics of the people." Article 1, Section 4 of the Constitution provides that "[t]he times, places and manner of holding elections for Senators and Representatives, shall be prescribed in each State by the legislature thereof, but the *Congress* may . . . make or alter such regulations" [emphasis added]. In Frankfurter's view the text of the Constitution gave this political question to Congress, not the courts; Chicago voters should take their concerns to Congress, not the Supreme Court. He concluded that "Courts ought not to enter this political thicket."

Frankfurter's opinion was compelling in theory. In practice, however, he was telling dissatisfied voters to take their complaints about the electoral processes to elected officials who were themselves products of this tainted electoral machinery. If a state legislator or United States representative from an urban district tried to increase the power of urban voters, legislators from rural areas could block them to protect the clout of their own home bases. Not surprisingly, problems of this type continued.

One Person, One Vote

In 1962 the Supreme Court agreed to enter Frankfurter's political thicket in *Baker* v. *Carr.*[7] Similar population shifts had occurred in Tennessee. Writing for the Court, Justice Brennan concluded that the Fourteenth Amendment's equal protection clause guarantees that votes be weighted equally. The failure of the Tennessee legislature to redistrict violated the one person, one vote principle. Now districts must be approximately equal in population.[8]

Informal Norms

In all human institutions unwritten understandings define appropriate and inappropriate behavior. **Informal norms** can influence behavior as much as formal rules can. Individuals who fail to conform to informal mores will find **sanctions** taken against them. Think of college residence halls with formal rules about overnight visits by members of the opposite sex. Here a common informal expectation is that neighbors should not report infractions of this rule. Violate this norm, and you will be ostracized (perhaps severely and creatively).

Informal rules in Congress include an expectation that members **work hard** at their legislative tasks. Regular long weekends in the home district, coupled with grandstanding and posturing for headlines, is frowned upon if the member neglects important legislative responsibilities. Congresspeople are also encouraged to **specialize,** especially in the House. Policy areas are many, and no individual can keep up with all policy fronts. Specialization ensures that some lawmakers will always have needed expertise. New legislators learn that they should not seek to become Jacks and Jills of all trades. Rather, they gain respect and power by becoming authorities in specialized policy areas. **Honesty** is another important informal norm. Members are expected to be true to their word. Because lawmakers cannot keep up with everything, they must trust one another when they seek guidance from colleagues. Misleading a fellow member is a serious breach. Legislators are also expected to treat one another with **courtesy.** Personal attacks are unacceptable. Policy disagreements will be frequent, but policy coalitions will shift from day to day. Today's opponent may be tomorrow's ally. As such it is important to be able to disagree without being disagreeable. The **reciprocity** norm is also important. Help colleagues whenever possible. Vote for another member's pet bill, if you can. Supply some information when requested. Provide such favors, and you can expect the same in return.

In the past newcomers were expected to serve **apprenticeship periods** when they quietly observed their elders and learned the ropes. This norm is no longer important. Freshmen are now active participants from the start.

Members of Congress who violate these informal norms will encounter social pressure. A veteran member of the party or state delegation will take the offending member aside and explain the facts of legislative life. If the message does not get through, the offending legislator will find it difficult to get cooperation, win support for bills, and obtain desired committee assignments as more formal sanctions are

There have been some dramatic violations of the "courtesy norm." In 1832 Representative Sam Houston caned Representative William Stanbery on a Washington street. Stanbery pulled a gun and tried to shoot Houston, but the gun misfired.

In 1856 Representative Preston Brooks attacked and beat Senator Charles Sumner on the Senate floor.

More recent breeches of courtesy have also occurred. In 1985 there was a confrontation between Representatives Bob Dornan (R-CA) and Thomas Downey (D-NY). Dornan, a former conservative talk-show host, called Downey, who had been elected to Congress at age twenty-five and who did not serve in the military, a "draft-dodging wimp." Downey demanded an apology. Dornan aide, Brian Bennett, replied that it would be "a cold day in hell before he gets an apology from Bob Dornan." Subsequently, Downey approached Dornan while the two men were on the House floor. Dornan grabbed Downey's tie and threatened him. Learning of the incident, then-House Speaker Thomas ("Tip") O'Neill (D-MA) told the two congressmen that they could "settle it outside in the street, but don't settle it on the House floor."

There have been other recent confrontations. Just off the House floor, Representative Sam Gibbons (D-FL) pulled the tie of Representative Bill Thomas (R-CA). Representative Jim Moran (D-VA) scuffled with Representative Randy (Duke) Cunningham (R-CA) after Cunningham questioned Moran's support for U.S. troops. Democrats angered Republicans when they placed a cartoon poster of Speaker Newt Gingrich dressed in a diaper and crying on the Speaker's chair.

applied. Informal norms enable 435 representatives and one hundred senators of diverse backgrounds, interests, political beliefs, and personalities to work together.

The norms, however, discourage rocking the boat and, as a result, may contribute to a leisurely pace that some younger and less patient members may find disconcerting.[9]

Norms change. Some Washington observers believe that congressional manners have been worsening. Why? Possible explanations include the following:

"Cry Baby."

© *New York Daily News. L.P. reprinted with permission.*

- Volatile issues like abortion, school prayer, and welfare reform
- Increasing numbers of junior members who are not steeped in parliamentary traditions
- Televised debate
- Inconsistent enforcement of rules
- Increased partisan animosity following Republican victories in 1994, which made the Democrats the minority party in the House for the first time in forty years
- Inadequate education of new members by the parties on proper decorum
- Scandals
- Decreasing respect for tradition in society at large
- Some combination of the above

Whatever the reasons members of Congress have acknowledged a problem. In 1997 a privately financed retreat was held in an attempt to restore congressional civility. The Pew Charitable Trusts sponsored the three-day conference in Hershey, Pennsylvania, and the Aspen Institute, a nonprofit educational organization, was in charge of the program. Members rode together by train to Hershey. Historian David McCollough spoke on the history of congressional norms. Participants included House Speaker Newt Gingrich (R-GA), House Majority Leader Dick Armey (R-TX), House Minority Floor Leader Richard Gephardt (D-MO), and House Minority Whip David Bonior (D-MI).

Party Leaders

In a **responsible party system,** parties have clear programs, and leaders can compel members to work together. As noted, the United States does not have a responsible party system. Instead, it has a **weak party system,** where programs contain ambiguities, generalities, and contradictions and party members need not vote with their partisan colleagues. Within this context congressional **party leaders** use their powers to try to get their members to cooperate.

In the **House of Representatives,** the most powerful leader is the **Speaker of the House.** The Speaker is a member of the **majority party** in the House. The Republicans have held a majority of House seats since 1994. Currently, Dennis Hastert (R-IL) is the Speaker. He is the presiding officer of the House and serves as a public spokesperson for his party and, to some extent, for the House as a whole. He has the power to recognize members during floor debate; refers bills to committees; and appoints members to special investigating committees, ad hoc committees, and conference committees. He helps assign members to permanent standing committees, though the Speaker lost the power to make these assignments independently in 1911. Now the Republican Committee on Committees and the Democratic Steering and Policy Committee make such assignments. The Speaker's actual power depends on the skillful use of formal powers to bargain with House colleagues.

The **majority floor leader** is Richard Armey (R-TX). He is the leader and spokesman of his party during floor debates. He serves as a general assistant to the Speaker. He helps to schedule floor debates, confers with congressional leaders, committee chairs, and other Republicans about his party's "program." He also helps to round up votes on bills. His actual power depends on his personal bargaining skills and on his relationship with the Speaker.

The **majority whip** is Thomas DeLay (R-TX). The term **whip** comes from the British fox-hunting term *whipperin,* which refers to the person who makes sure that the hounds do not stray during a hunt. He serves as a liaison between party leaders on one hand and rank-and-file members of his party on the other. His main responsibility is to round up votes on bills. He is assisted in his efforts to persuade party members to vote together by deputy and regional whips.

On the **minority** side no Democrat holds a position comparable to Speaker. The top leadership post for the minority party is **minority floor leader.** Currently, Richard Gephardt (D-MO) holds this position. His powers and duties are similar to those of the majority floor leader. Because the minority floor leader does not stand as a general assistant to a Speaker of his own party, however, his is the top leadership position in his party.

The **minority whip** is David Bonior (D-MI). Like the majority whip, he attempts to convince his party colleagues to vote together on key bills.

Party Leaders in the Senate

In the **Senate** there is no position comparable to Speaker of the House. The **vice president** of the United States is constitutionally designated to serve as president of the Senate. The vice president (currently Al Gore) presides over Senate sessions when he attends and votes in the event of a tie. He is not actually a member of the Senate, does not participate in debates, has little real Senate power, and seldom bothers to attend.

The **president pro tempore** is Strom Thurmond (R-SC). He is the presiding officer of the Senate in the vice president's absence. The position itself carries little real power. President pro tempore is primarily an honorary position that is usually given to

S trom Thurmond is the Senate's elder statesman. He was born on December 5, 1902. A former governor of South Carolina, he was first elected to the Senate in 1954 as a Democrat. He switched to the Republican Party in 1964. Promising that this would be his last term, he was reelected to the Senate in 1996. He is the oldest person to have been elected to the Senate. If he completes his term, he will be one hundred years old when he leaves the Senate.

the most senior member of the majority party. As in the House, the Republicans hold a majority of Senate seats.

The real party leaders in the Senate are the **majority floor leader** (Trent Lott, R-MS); the **majority whip** (Don Nickles, R-OK); the **minority floor leader** (Thomas Daschle, D-SD); and the **minority whip** (Harry Reid, D-NV). Their powers and responsibilities are similar to those of their House counterparts. Because there is no "Speaker of the Senate," however, the majority floor leader is this body's most powerful party leader.

Selecting Party Leaders

Methods of selection vary. The **entire membership** of their respective chambers formally elect the Speaker of the House and the president pro tempore of the Senate. In this way it is technically accurate to say that Dennis Hastert is Speaker of the House and not just the "Majority Speaker."

In reality, however, the majority party chooses a nominee for each position at the start of each session. The minority party nominates its own candidate. When the full membership votes, the members traditionally vote along straight party lines and the majority party's candidate wins. As of 1995 the Speaker is limited to four consecutive two-year terms.

To be chosen Speaker, a lawmaker should have a good deal of House experience, be generally respected, and be a person whom different factions in the party can "live with." Sometimes the Speaker is not a first choice of most party colleagues but emerges as a consensus candidate after others fail to garner enough support. Well-honed political skills are a must for the Speaker. Often a floor leader becomes Speaker when the previous Speaker leaves, but such a line of succession is not automatic.[10] Their respective parties formally select floor leaders and whips at the start of each session. These contests are often heated, and there is no guarantee of reelection.[11]

The Committee System

To perform their legislative tasks, the House and Senate divide labor into specialized committees where bargains are struck and deals are made. Without such deliberation and compromise, disagreements cannot be resolved, support coalitions cannot be built, and legislation cannot be enacted. These "little legislatures" are essential to congressional operations.

The House has nineteen **standing committees,** and the Senate has seventeen standing committees. In addition, there are several special, select, and joint committees. Table 7.1 lists the House and Senate standing committees.

Standing committees are usually responsible for specialized policy areas such as agriculture, banking, commerce, foreign relations, small business, veterans' affairs, and so on. After a bill is introduced, it is sent to a committee for consideration.

QuotableQuote

Congress in session is Congress on public exhibition, while Congress in committee rooms is Congress at work.
—Woodrow Wilson

- The committee can report the bill out to the full House or Senate for debate and a vote.
- The committee can first amend the bill and then report it to the full House or Senate for debate and vote.
- The committee can decide not to report the bill to the full House or Senate.
- Most legislation that fails to win passage dies at the committee stage.

How a Bill Becomes a Law

The process by which a bill becomes a law illustrates Committee powers and procedures. Article 1, Section 7 of the Constitution provides that "all bills for raising revenue shall originate in the House of Representatives." Otherwise, bills can originate in either chamber. Any member in the House and Senate can **introduce** a bill. The Speaker in the House and the majority and minority floor leaders in the Senate then assign the bill to a committee.[12]

The committee chair can assign the bill to a **subcommittee.** Here the bill receives its most intensive scrutiny.

- The subcommittee holds **public hearings** at which lobbyists, bureaucrats, and other interested parties speak about the bill.
- The subcommittee holds a **mark-up session** at which members discuss the bill and revise it.
- The subcommittee then **votes** on whether to report the bill to the full committee.
- At this point a handful of congresspeople can effectively kill the bill by voting to hold it in subcommittee.

Table 7.1

Congressional Committees

Senate Standing Committees
(as of Oct. 1997)

Agriculture, Nutrition, and Forestry
Chairman: Richard G. Lugar, IN
Ranking Dem.: Tom Harkin, IA

Appropriations
Chairman: Ted Stevens, AK
Ranking Dem.: Robert C. Byrd. WV

Armed Services
Chairman: Strom Thurmond, SC
Ranking Dem.: Carl Levin, MI

Banking, Housing, and Urban Affairs
Chairman: Alfonse M. D'Amato, NY
Ranking Dem.: Paul S. Sarbanes, MD

Budget
Chairman: Pete V. Domenici, NM
Ranking Dem.: Frank R. Lautenberg, NJ

Commerce, Science, and Transportation
Chairman: John McCain, AZ
Ranking Dem.: Ernest F. "Fritz" Hollings, SC

Energy and Natural Resources
Chairman: Frank H. Murkowski, AK
Ranking Dem.: Dale Bumpers, AR

Environment and Public Works
Chairman: John H. Chafee, RI
Ranking Dem.: Max Baucus, MT

Finance
Chairman: William V. Roth, Jr., DE
Ranking Dem.: Daniel Patrick Moynihan, NY

Foreign Relations
Chairman: Jesse Helms, NC
Ranking Dem.: Joseph R. Biden, DE

Governmental Affairs
Chairman: Fred Thompson, TN
Ranking Dem.: John Glenn, OH

Indian Affairs
Chairman: Ben Nighthorse Campbell, CO
Ranking Dem.: Daniel K. Inouye, HI

Judiciary
Chairman: Orrin G. Hatch, UT
Ranking Dem.: Patrick J. Leahy, VT

Labor and Human Resources
Chairman: Jim Jeffords, VT
Ranking Dem.: Edward M. Kennedy, MA

Rules and Administration
Chairman: John W. Warner, VA
Ranking Dem.: Wendell H. Ford, KY

Small Business
Chairman: Christopher "Kit" Bond, MO
Ranking Dem.: John F. Kerry, MA

Veteran's Affairs
Chairman: Arlen Specter, PA
Ranking Dem.: John D. Rockefeller IV, WV

Senate Special Committee
(as of Oct. 1997)

Aging
Chairman: Charles E. Grassley, IA
Ranking Dem.: John B Breaux, LA

Senate Select Committees
(as of Oct. 1997)

Ethics
Chairman: Robert Smith, NH
Ranking Dem.: Harry M. Reid, NV

Intelligence
Chairman: Richard C. Shelby, AL
V. Chairman: Bob Kerrey, NE

House Select Committee
(as of Oct. 1997)

Intelligence
Chairman: Porter J. Goss, FL
Ranking Dem.: Norman Dicks, WA

Joint Committees of Congress
(as of Oct. 1997)

Economic
Chairman: Rep. Jim Saxton, NJ
V. Chairman: Sen. Connie Mack, FL

Library
Chairman: Rep. Bill Thomas, CA
V. Chairman: Sen. Ted Stevens, AK

Printing
Chairman: Sen. John W. Warner, VA
V. Chairman: Rep. Bill Thomas, CA

Taxation
Chairman: Rep. Bill Archer, TX
V. Chairman: Sen. William V. Roth, Jr., DE

House Standing Committees
(as of Oct. 1997)

Agriculture
Chairman: Robert F. (Bob)
  Smith, OR
Ranking Dem.: Charles W.
  Stenholm, TX

Appropriations
Chairman: Robert L. "Bob"
  Livingston, LA
Ranking Dem.: David R. Obey, WI

Banking and Financial Services
Chairman: Jim Leach, IA
Ranking Dem.: Henry B.
  Gonzalez, TX

Budget
Chairman: John R. Kasich, OH
Ranking Dem.: John M. Spratt, SC

Commerce
Chairman: Thomas J. "Tom" Bil-
  ley, Jr., VA
Ranking Dem.: John D.
  Dingell, MI

Education and the Workforce
Chairman: Bill Goodling, PA
Ranking Dem.: William L.
  Clay, Sr., MO

**Government Reform
  and Oversight**
Chairman: Dan Burton, IN
Ranking Dem.: Henry A.
  Waxman, CA

House Oversight
Chairman: Bill Thomas, CA
Ranking Dem.: Sam
  Gejdenson, CT

International Relations
Chairman: Benjamin A.
  Gilman, NY
Ranking Dem.: Lee H.
  Hamilton, IN

Judiciary
Chairman: Henry J. Hyde, IL
Ranking Dem.: John
  Conyers, Jr., MI

National Security
Chairman: Floyd D. Spence, SC
Ranking Dem.: Ronald V.
  Dellums, CA

Resources
Chairman: Don Young, AK
Ranking Dem.: George Miller, CA

Rules
Chairman: Gerald B. H.
  Solomon, NY
Ranking Dem.: John Joseph
  Moakley, MA

Science
Chairman: F. James
  Sensenbrenner, Jr., WI
Ranking Dem.: George E.
  Brown, Jr., CA

Small Business
Chairman: James M. Talent, MO
Ranking Bem.: John J.
  LaFalce, NY

Standards of Official Conduct
Chairman: James V. Hansen, UT
Ranking Dem.: Howard L.
  Berman, CA

**Transportation and Infrastruc-
ture**
Chairman: Bud Shuster, PA
Ranking Dem.: James L.
  Oberstar, MN

Veterans' Affairs
Chairman: Bob Stump, AZ
Ranking Dem.: Lane A. Evans, IL

Ways and Means
Chairman: Bill Archer, TX
Ranking Dem.: Charles B.
  Range, NY

Source: *The World Almanac and Book of Facts*, 1998, p. 87.

If the subcommittee reports the bill back to the full committee, the full committee may schedule additional hearings.

- The committee holds another mark-up session.
- The committee votes on whether or not to report the bill out of committee to the full House or Senate, respectively. Once again, a relatively small number of congresspeople on a full committee can block legislation.

In the Senate bills are put on the schedule and go to the floor for **unlimited debate** and a vote. In the House most bills must first pass through the **Rules Committee.** The House Rules Committee

- Has no legislative field of specialization
- Schedules full House consideration of bills

While they were in the minority, House Republicans had complained that Democrats used the rules to inhibit Republican input on the floor. When the Republicans became the majority in 1995, they promised open rules that would enable bills to be amended on the floor with few restrictions. The outgoing Rules Committee chairman, Joe Moakley (D-MA), was asked how long the Republicans would believe in open rules. He replied, "Until they report one out." He said legislation had become so complex and members so skilled at parliamentary maneuvers that debate could be endless.

In January 1995 the Republicans brought up a package of reforms from their Contract with America. They brought these reforms up under a *closed* rule that prevented floor amendments.

The rules affect one's chances of getting policies passed. When there is a choice between "purifying" the rules and winning policy victories, reformers find themselves in a difficult position.

- Limits the amount of time that members can speak about bills
- Limits the kinds of floor amendments that can be offered

Given the size of the House, some such organizational body is needed to direct traffic. When the Rules Committee **grants a rule,** the bill goes to the floor for debate and a vote according to the rule. But the Rules Committee is not neutral. Rules Committee members evaluate the content of a bill. If committee members oppose the bill, they can

- Kill it by refusing to grant a rule
- Delay it
- Frustrate the bill's supporters by granting a rule that opens the bill up to floor amendments

On the other hand, if Rules Committee members support the bill, they can grant a rule favorable to quick passage. Once again, a relatively small group of representatives serving on the Rules Committee can block legislation.[13] The atmosphere is ripe for bargaining and compromise. Rules Committee members may be able to persuade the bill's sponsors to make certain changes in return for a favorable rule.

House and Senate majorities must approve a bill. If, after having gone through numerous debates and amendments, the two versions of the bill **differ,** a joint **House-Senate Conference Committee** is appointed to work out the differences. Members are usually drawn from the committees that originally considered the bill.

- The conference committee's compromise bill is reported to the House and Senate for debate and vote.
- No amendments can be offered at this time.
- If either chamber rejects the bill, it goes back to the conference committee one more time.
- The conference committee's second compromise bill is then reported to the House and Senate.
- If either body rejects this version of the bill, the bill is killed.

Once again, a small number of lawmakers are so positioned that they can block legislation.

If House and Senate majorities approve the conference committee's compromise bill, it is sent to the **president** for **signature or veto.** If the president signs it, the bill becomes a law. But if the president vetoes the bill, it is returned to Congress. In this instance, one person—the president—can block legislation. It takes a two-thirds vote of the House and Senate to **override** a presidential veto.

Finally, the law could be challenged in a case brought to the Supreme Court, and the justices could declare the law unconstitutional.

The rules and procedures are such that a bill must run an obstacle course or traverse a mine field to win passage. The bill can blow up at many points along the way. A handful of strategically situated individuals can block legislation. Supporters of a bill must accommodate potential opponents by making concessions to them. An important fact of congressional life is that it is easier to block legislation than to pass it. The result is that many bills that are passed go through so many modifications that they bear faint resemblance to the bills that were originally introduced.

Committee Chairpersons

Though the **powers** of **committee chairpersons** wax and wane over time, chairs remain powerful and are central actors to the legislative process. Throughout most of the twentieth century, committee chairs

- Set committee **agendas.** Chairs sometimes used this power to block consideration of bills they opposed.
- **Appointed subcommittees** and assigned members to them.
- Appointed **subcommittee chairpersons.**
- Assigned committee **staff** and indebted overworked congresspeople by providing such assistance.
- Controlled **proxy votes** for absent members and cast those votes as they (the chairs) saw fit.

The Changing Powers of Committee Chairpersons

In 1973 the House Democrats adopted a **Subcommittee Bill of Rights** to prevent chairpersons from abusing their powers. Chairs were required to hold **regularly**

scheduled meetings and were required to hold **hearings** on a bill if so requested by a majority of the committee members. These changes remain in place. Several other changes, however, were reversed by the Republicans after they assumed majority-party status in 1995.[14]

- They reinstated committee chairpersons' authority to make staff decisions.
- They again authorized committee chairs to select subcommittee chairpersons.
- They reduced the number of subcommittees and committees, decreasing the total number of available chairmanships.
- They eliminated proxy voting.
- They limited Chairpersons to six-year terms.

Freshman Republicans supported these changes, and some assumed subcommittee chairmanships immediately. Relatively speaking, some of these reforms appeared to weaken chairpersons and strengthen the Speaker. This point should not be overstated, however. The legislative process will not function without the committee system, and committee chairs remain at center stage.

The Seniority System

The **seniority system** has been important to the selection of committee chairpersons throughout most of the twentieth century. During the nineteenth century, congressional turnover was relatively high. Legislators did not accumulate as much seniority as they do now. Through 1910 the Speaker of the House personally selected committee chairpersons. A "revolt" against then-**Speaker Joseph Cannon** removed this power from his hands. A search for suitable alternatives commenced. Around this time members of Congress were beginning to acquire more seniority, and it emerged as a critical selection criterion for choosing chairpersons. Under the seniority system the most senior majority party member on a committee automatically chaired that committee.[15]

The seniority system proved controversial. Supporters of the seniority system made several arguments:

- Long experience was equated with probable expertise on the part of chairpersons.
- Automatic selection would avoid potentially divisive political battles over the selection of chairpersons.
- Special interest groups would not be able to lobby for their favorite committee member.
- Automatic selection would keep chairpersons independent from party leaders. If party leaders picked committee chairs, the president could pressure party leaders to influence legislative deliberations inside the committee rooms. Such presidential influence would threaten constitutional separation of powers.

Critics of the seniority system answered with their own arguments:

- Long tenure is just as likely to produce senile committee chairpersons as it is to produce expert ones. The fact that someone has been around for a long time does not necessarily mean that the person is good at the job. It only means that the individual has been around a long time. Period.

- Sometimes the best person for the chairmanship is not the most senior member of the committee. Why should Congress deny itself his or her leadership?
- The most senior members of Congress come from the safest districts. Their reelection is virtually assured. They become less responsive to changing circumstances and public sentiments than they should be.
- Under the seniority system special interest groups could continue to support their favorite committee members in the knowledge that they would become committee chairs eventually.

In 1973 House Democrats modified the seniority system. Members of the majority party still chair committees, but seniority status no longer guarantees a chair. The Democrats, who were then in the majority, determined that the entire Democratic caucus would approve chairpersons. All members of the party would have a vote. They usually selected the most senior committee member of their party, but there were several notable exceptions.[16]

The Senate Filibuster

Unlike the House of Representatives, the Senate has **unlimited debate.** For this reason, the United States Senate has been called "the greatest debating society on earth." When some senators oppose a bill that will soon be coming to a vote but are too few in number to defeat it, they can prevent a vote from being taken by engaging in a **filibuster.**[17] A senator is recognized, takes the floor, and talks. And talks. And talks. When fatigue sets in, she or he can yield to an ally who will continue the filibuster.[18] Because the Senate allows unlimited debate, filibustering senators are not restricted to talking about the bill in question. They can talk about anything. Some have read from telephone books and cookbooks. The greatest debating society on earth?

The bill's supporters have several options:

- They can give up and say, "You win. Please. Just stop talking!"[19]

Jimmy Stewart engaged in a filibuster, from the film, "Mr. Smith Goes to Washington."

© *Kobal Collection.*

- They can work out a compromise with the bill's opponents in exchange for an end to the filibuster. Sometimes the threat of a filibuster is enough to win some concessions from the bill's sponsors.

- They can try to outlast the filibustering senators by keeping a quorum on hand and staying in session around the clock. In the past, Senators did not actually have to listen to the filibuster. They read. They slept. When the talking senators wore down, an immediate vote was taken. Some reformers seek to bring back these round-the-clock filibusters.

- They can impose **cloture,** which is a formal way to break a filibuster. Cloture is a special vote that interrupts a filibuster. If three-fifths of the Senate agree (sixty members), debate is closed and a vote on the bill is taken.[20]

Sarah Binder and Steven Smith point out that filibusters have increased in number since the 1960s. In the early nineteenth century, only twenty-three filibusters took place. Between 1970 and 1994 there were 191 filibusters. From 1991 through 1994, fifty-six filibusters occurred.[21] Through the filibuster mechanism, a relative handful of legislators can block a bill. This fact stands as further evidence that it is easier to block legislation than to pass it.

Congressional Decision Making

Why does a lawmaker vote yes or no on a particular bill? There is no single answer to this question. John Kingdon's interviews with representatives revealed that various factors influence legislative decisions.[22] Although the relative importance of different factors varies with the circumstances, some generalizations are possible.

- **Constituents** are influential when members of Congress make their voting decisions. Of course, different people want different things, and legislators cannot satisfy everybody. Further, not all constituents are equally vocal and/or interested on all issues. Consequently, members often try to guess at the decision that will be most acceptable to the folks back home. Given long experience and close ties to the home district, reasonably educated guesses are possible.
- **Legislators** influence each other. Members of Congress specialize. One member cannot be an expert in all policy areas. Sometimes members must vote on unfamiliar issues. In such situations members turn to trusted colleagues with relevant expertise and with whom they generally agree on policy matters. They seek advice or cues from these peers. The expectation is that when their roles are reversed, the "cue getter" will return the favor and will act as "cue giver."
- **Interest groups** influence members of Congress. Groups hire lobbyists, make campaign contributions, provide information, and testify at hearings in an effort to sway congressional votes.
- **Political parties** influence congressional voting decisions. Although strict party discipline is absent and both parties have mavericks, legislators are usually more likely to vote with their party than with the opposition.[23]
- **Party leaders** use their resources to try to persuade members to vote together.
- The **president** also has some influence over congressional voting. On some issues the president will personally lobby members of Congress in an attempt to win their votes.[24]
- Congressional **staffers** are influential. Legislators depend heavily on their aides for research assistance and advice.
- **Bureaucrats** wield some influence when they provide needed information or cooperate as a member of Congress attempts to untangle some red tape to help a constituent.
- And legislators also account for their **personal beliefs** when they make policy decisions. When interviewed, most say that they follow their own beliefs at least in part.[25]

The degree to which any single factor motivates a congressional voting decision varies from legislator to legislator and from issue to issue. On matters of national security and international relations, members of Congress often put most weight on their own policy beliefs. On domestic matters involving jobs in the home district, constituents may be more influential. Lawmakers do not respond to any single set of inputs. They have some flexibility in making legislative decisions, and this flexibility is an important ingredient in **bargaining.**

Bargaining: Compromise, Logrolling, and the Congressional Pork Barrel

Congressional power is unevenly distributed. Committees vary in prestige and status. Power shifts with the issues. Legislation can be stalled at numerous points. To pass legislation, sponsors must mobilize support over and over again. Support coalitions must be built in subcommittee, in committee, and on the floor. Forging coalitions takes time, patience, and skill. It requires bargaining and negotiation. Sometimes, bargains are the products of **compromise.** A compromise represents an attempt to find some middle ground. For example:

- Congressman Smith wants to appropriate $400 million for a project.
- Congresswoman Jones wants to appropriate $800 million for that project.
- They compromise and agree to appropriate $600 million.

Other times, bargains are the result of **logrolling.** Logrolling is the legislative equivalent of the phrase "You scratch my back and I'll scratch yours." The word derives from America's frontier past. When pioneers needed to clear the land to build their homes, neighbors set aside their differences and disputes and helped one another handle the heavy timber. When legislators engage in logrolling, they cooperate and support legislation that has something in it for all of them.

An example of logrolling is **pork barrel legislation.** The *pork barrel* is a legislator's term for the national treasury. Trying to get federal money for projects that benefit one's home district—highways, dams, museums, and so on—is called "dipping for pork." Powerful legislators become adept at "bringing home the bacon." The term comes from a common practice in the pre-Civil War South of distributing pieces of salted pork to slaves from huge barrels. Slaves, often desperate for food, would rush to the barrel and fight over portions of the pork.

QuotableQuote

Laws are like sausages. It is better not to see them being made.
—Otto von Bismark

Effective legislators are good at building coalitions, winning support from undecided legislators, and countering the objections of opponents. The most effective legislators know how to compromise and work well with other people. Realistically speaking, it is unlikely that legislators representing constituents with diverse viewpoints and interests will be able to accomplish much without compromising. Compromise is a fact of legislative life. Of course, compromising over legislative details is different from compromising over matters of principle. Critics maintain that legislators lose sight of this distinction.

*O*n March 26, 1998, House Transportation Committee Chairman Bud Shuster (R-PA) angrily responded to charges from younger Republican colleagues that he was trading highway projects for votes. The Committee had approved a $217 billion surface transportation bill. Shuster had set aside about $9 billion for "special projects" personally requested by members. It included about one thousand projects in 350 districts.

Three Republican members of the Class of 1994—Representatives Steve Largent (R-OK), Tom Coburn (R-OK), and Sue Myrick (R-NC)—claimed that they were offered about $15 million each in road projects for their districts in exchange for their votes. All three had come to Congress criticizing pork-barrel politics, promising to cut federal spending, and pledging to change old-style practices where veteran politicians made sure that they and their friends got plenty of federal money for their home districts. Coburn said, "I think the system stinks. It's being used for political patronage and to keep you entrenched in office."

Shuster took the House floor and accused the three young Republicans of a "blatant falsehood" in suggesting that his Committee promised highway money in exchange for votes and threatened to withhold that money if they opposed the bill. He challenged "these members to name one person, one person whom I went to and said you will get a project in exchange for your vote." Shuster explained that projects were chosen on the basis of a fourteen-point checklist to determine their need. Shuster made the following observation:

> Sometimes it seems as though the smaller the minority they represent, the more incensed they become because they view themselves as more pure, more righteous, more sanctimonious than the larger majority of us who are mere mortals. Now I don't ascribe any of these motives to our colleagues. I prefer to believe that they are simply misinformed.[26]

Representative James Oberstar (D-MN), ranking Democrat on the Transportation Committee, supported Shuster's version of the story. Oberstar said he was "offended by the use of language, by the accusations made."

This dispute over what may or may not have been logrolling, depending on whom you listen to, divided the participants by generation rather than by party. It also illustrates that junior congresspeople have less patience with the reciprocity norm—with the notion that to get along, one should go along—than their predecessors had.

Representation

What does it mean to say that a member of Congress "represents" his or her district? There are different styles of representation.

- Some representatives see themselves as **instructed delegates.** They feel bound by the wishes of their constituents and follow instructions from home. They vote their constituencies, not their consciences.
- Some view themselves as **trustees.** They think that they should base decisions on their own views, experiences, judgments, and wisdom. They do what they think is best. Unlike instructed delegates, they vote their consciences, not their constituencies.
- Some see themselves as **brokers** or **politicos.** They try to account for *all* competing interests from the home district, not just the most vocal ones. They try to ignore their own preferences and, instead, take positions that accommodate as many interests from the home district as possible.
- Some see themselves as **errand boys** or **errand girls.** They emphasize casework, cutting red tape for constituents, and performing varied services for the people back home.

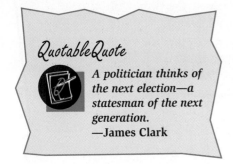

Quotable Quote

A politician thinks of the next election—a statesman of the next generation.
—**James Clark**

In fact, mixed types of representation are common. Most members of Congress provide services but place different degrees of emphasis on this role. On foreign policy and national security matters, many lawmakers act primarily on the basis of their own views. On domestic matters they may be more inclined to defer to constituent preferences. However, these preferences are not always clear, so representatives try to make reasonably educated guesses.

Congress in Change

1994 Congressional Elections

The Republicans won control of both houses of Congress in the **1994 elections,** winning fifty-three seats in the House and eight in the Senate. The victories brought their Senate total to fifty-three seats. Democratic defections brought Republican n 1997 a balanced budget amendment was before the Senate. Freshman Senator Robert Toricelli (D-NJ) announced that he would cast the deciding vote to kill the amendment. Earlier versions of the amendment had been popular among New Jersey voters. When he was in the House, Toricelli voted for the amendment. In his campaign for the Senate, he promised to support the amendment. In the final analysis, he changed his mind and voted no. Why? He explained his vote as follows:

> I want people to remember this vote as a time when I simply decided I'd do the right thing. Politics involves sometimes making compromises of which you are not always proud. But I also realize in dealing with the Constitution of the United States, the standards are different.

Toricelli had won by more than a 10 percent margin in 1996. Recognizing that he would not face reelection again until 2002, he reasoned that he could survive the political fallout from his decision to oppose the amendment. Toricelli pointed to another freshman, Senator Tim Johnson (D-SD), as a real "voice of courage" in the debate.

While in the House, Johnson also attempted to protect himself against conservative criticisms by voting for the amendment. In the Senate, however, Johnson voted against the amendment. The Republican National Committee immediately began running ads saying that "Tim Johnson broke his promise to you." Johnson conceded that the "easy thing politically would be to support the amendment," but Johnson was convinced that the amendment would mar the Constitution: "There are some issues worth losing an election over. In future years, when I'm no longer here and talking to my grandchildren, I want to be proud of what I did here."[27]

Recall the observation that it is easier for a senator to act like a trustee than it is for a representative to do so.

strength to 233 House seats by mid-1995. Not a single Republican incumbent lost. Democrats found themselves in the minority in the House for the first time in forty years. More than half of all House members in the 104th Congress arrived in the 1990s. The Republican freshmen were young and inexperienced, with more than half under forty-five years of age, and almost half first-time officeholders.

The face of Congress was changing.

Newt Gingrich and the Contract with America

Newt Gingrich, *Time* magazine's Man of the Year in 1994, provided leadership and coherence by articulating a series of policy proposals in the **Contract with America**.[28] More than three hundred Republican House candidates signed this contract that promised voters that a Republican majority would bring the Contract's proposals to floor votes.

- The Contract's proposals included a balanced budget constitutional amendment, a line-item veto for the president, welfare reform, capital-gains tax reductions, and term limits for congresspeople.
- The Contract also promised floor votes on procedural reforms including a reduction in the number of House committees and committee staffs, term limits for committee chairs, the elimination of proxy votes in committees, a requirement that committee meetings be open to the public, and a requirement for a three-fifths majority vote to pass tax increases.

Only Republican House members signed the Contract; Senators did not. Nevertheless, items approved by the House made their way to the Senate for consideration. As such the Contract was an extremely specific exercise in agenda setting. Instead of a confusing transition with new Republican committee chairs pursuing different objectives, the Contract provided focus for the Republican Party.

The 104th Congress opened with a remarkably active first one-hundred days. The House convened at noon on January 4, 1995, and elected Gingrich to be Speaker. The House quickly passed a series of rules changes[29] and the Congressional Accountability Act, requiring Congress to comply with laws it enacts for the general citizenry. Instead of the usual perfunctory first day, the House kept working until 2:30 in the morning! The pace did not slow substantially over the next ninety-nine days.

- The House approved a balanced budget amendment (defeated by a single vote in the Senate), a ban on unfunded mandates, the presidential line-item veto, tax cuts, crime legislation, product liability and tort reform, a national security bill, and welfare reform.
- The Republicans met their contract pledge to vote on the items mentioned. They did not promise to pass all of them.

Congressional term limits failed in the House. Welfare reform and the line-item veto[30] became law, and unfunded mandate reforms were enacted. Other Contract items did not become law.

A Bumpy Ride: Some Are Deciding to Get Off

Without the Contract to sustain their focus and unity, the remainder of the 104th Congress returned to business as usual.[31] Public support declined. Gingrich, whose Contract pledged to "end [Congress's] cycle of scandal and disgrace," encountered ethics problems of his own. By 1997 he was struggling to hold onto his leadership post. He was charged with having used tax-exempt projects, including a college course that he taught, for political purposes. Gingrich admitted to having failed to seek proper legal

Something to Think About

ollowing a disappointing showing in the 1998 congressional elections—the Republicans *lost* five House seats amid expectations that they were poised to register substantial gains—Gingrich took the blame, resigned as Speaker, and gave up his House seat. *Time's* 1994 Man of the Year was depicted on the cover of the November 16, 1998, issue of *Newsweek* under the banner, "The Loser."

Bob Livingston (R-LA) was selected as Speaker-designate. In December, faced with published accusations of marital infidelity, he announced that he would not serve as Speaker, gave up his House seat, and called upon President Clinton to follow his example by submitting his own resignation.

advice on such projects and that inaccurate statements had been submitted to the ethics investigators over his signature. He agreed to submit to a reprimand by the House and to pay a $300,000 penalty as punishment for violating House rules. By agreeing to these sanctions, Gingrich was permitted to remain as Speaker.

Many senators and representatives who voluntarily left Congress expressed disappointment with congressional developments and directions. Senator Sam Nunn (D-GA) left Congress in 1996 following twenty-four years in the Senate. He was a widely respected chair of the Senate Armed Services Committee. Even Republican colleagues asked him to reconsider when he announced his retirement plans. Nunn found it strange that term-limit advocates had come to view politicians as tainted by experience:

> The younger members expect to come in on at least the same level [as veteran members] and sometimes they think they've just been elected and therefore they have a mandate from the people and therefore they know everything. It's a little different psychology than it used to be. It's very naive. . . . Just because somebody gets elected doesn't give them the ability to come in here and know what's going on in Vietnam and NATO or the way the Pentagon works. They eventually learn that. Most of the time it's the hard way, and most of the time it's too painful and embarrassing to admit it.[32]

He objected to politicians' increasing reliance on polling because it substitutes "following" for "leadership." Citing the need for campaign reform, he said that most of his colleagues are honest, but "can you retain your intellectual honesty if next week you're hoping to raise $50,000 from the people who run restaurants?"[33]

Senator James Exon (D-NB) cited the "ever-increasing vicious polarization of the electorate" when he announced his plans to retire after the 1996 elections.

Senator Nancy Kassebaum (R-KS) cited the volume of mail, faxes, and e-mail messages; the proliferation of committee work; and the lack of time for reflection in her retirement comments. She hoped that new senators would "keep a bridge between the two parties and not just throw brickbats." The new House Republicans brought a lot of energy, she offered, but "they also brought a lot of in-your-face."[34]

On the House side Representative Patricia Schroeder (D-CO), first elected in 1972, also stepped down following the 1996 elections. Changes in Congress took a toll on her:

> There's this angry populism targeted at government. It's mindless. I get up every day and that's the forum I'm operating in. Get mad about this. Blow up that. We're in kill-or-be-killed politics now. People take every issue and think, what kind of 30-second ad would that make? It's gotten so surly and so mean.[35]

Of course, some leave for new opportunities with think tanks, corporate boards, universities, or the media. Representative Susan Molinari (R-NY) was a rising star in the Republican Party. The Party highlighted Molinari by choosing her to deliver the keynote address at the Republican National Convention in San Diego in 1996. She left Congress for a position on *CBS News Saturday Morning.* From politician to television personality—the line between politics and the media continues to blur.

Some Things Never Seem to Change

Republican party control, procedural reforms, and other changes have occurred, but three important things have not changed.

1. Blocking legislation remains easier than passing it, which makes compromise essential.
2. The fact that individual members represent home districts makes it difficult for Congress to legislate for the nation as a whole.
3. Incumbents defeat challengers more often than not.

In conclusion, many of us judge Congress harshly—see Mark Twain's comment—when we think of Congress as a whole. But when we consider our own congressperson's service for our district, we usually decide to send the incumbent back to Washington to accumulate additional seniority and power for use on our behalf.

QuotableQuote

Suppose you were an idiot. . . . And suppose you were a member of Congress. . . . But I repeat myself.
—Mark Twain

Key Terms

chapter 8

The American Presidency

Some Presidential Functions

The president performs various functions in the American political system and is involved in all four steps through which inputs are converted into public policy outputs.

- The president represents interests **(interest representation)** by calling attention to certain policy demands from the public. President Ronald Reagan represented

White House.

© *Owen Franken/Stock Boston.*

interests when he declared war on drugs, President George Bush did so when he said he wanted to be known as the "environmental president," and President Bill Clinton did so when he made health care reform a high priority. Presidents represent interests by placing certain issues on the national policy agenda.

- The president initiates rules **(rule initiation)** by recommending legislation to Congress and prodding the legislature to enact these initiatives. President Clinton initiated rules when he asked Congress to approve the North American Free Trade Agreement (NAFTA). All presidents initiate rules when they send their annual budget request to Congress.

- The president applies rules **(rule application)** by acting as administrator or chief executive officer of the federal bureaucracy. Bureaucratic agencies report to the president, and the president influences and directs bureaucratic operations through appointees.

- The president indirectly interprets rules **(rule interpretation)** by nominating federal judges and top regulatory agency officials. These appointees, in turn, interpret rules when disputes arise.

Presidents also perform **systems maintenance functions** that help the system survive.

When President Clinton signs a bill in a ceremonial fashion, he uses a different pen to sign each letter of his name. Because "William Jefferson Clinton" contains twenty-three letters, he is able to produce twenty-three commemorative pens with a single signature. President Johnson used fifty pens to sign the Voting Rights Act of 1965.

President Clinton signing a bill.

© AP/Wide World Photos.

- The president **resolves conflict** by taking sides in a dispute. In 1993 President Clinton became involved in a flight attendants' strike when he asked the airline to accept binding arbitration. In 1994 the Black Coaches Association threatened to boycott the NCAA basketball playoffs in opposition to a proposal that would have reduced the number of athletic scholarships. Clinton offered to help mediate the dispute, and the boycott was averted. In 1996 American Airlines pilots went on strike but President Clinton imposed a sixty-day cooling-off period to halt a walkout and help the two sides resolve their differences. In each instance the president participated in conflict resolution.

- The president **generates support** for the political system by lending the tradition and prestige of the office to a program. President Clinton "humanizes" the government when he jokes, jogs, frequents McDonald's, or teaches his daughter to drive. These actions, encourage citizens to identify with and relate to the government.

- The president **creates legitimacy** by signing a bill in a ceremonial way, inviting interested parties to the bill-signing ceremony, and distributing souvenir pens to commemorate the event.[1]

Historical Origins of the Presidency

The Articles of Confederation did not provide for a separate presidency. The central government was weak, and the fact that no single person was charged with leading it compounded that weakness. We have already seen that some critics of the Articles of Confederation wanted a stronger central government that could regulate commerce and provide for common defense. But with the memory of King George III and English rule still fresh, distrust of central power was widespread. During the 1780s, there was a desire for a stronger—but limited—central government. There was also a desire for a formidable—but accountable—presidency. Central power was limited through an intricate system of checks and balances. Still, concerns remained regarding centralized power and a president who conjured up memories of the king.

Constitutional Powers

Article 2 provided that the executive power of the United States would be vested in a president who would faithfully execute the laws. It has been argued that the framers gave the president certain **implied powers.** That is, it can be inferred that presidents can do whatever they think necessary to preserve national security because only then can laws be executed faithfully. Article 2 also provided **express** or **enumerated powers.** Some powers relate to **foreign affairs:**

- The president is **commander in chief** of the armed forces.
- The president has the power to make **treaties** with the advice and consent of the Senate.
- The president can nominate, and with the advice and consent of the Senate, **appoint ambassadors,** public ministers, and consuls.
- The president is authorized to **receive ambassadors** and public ministers.

Additional powers have a more **general** scope:

- The president has the power to grant **reprieves and pardons** for offenses against the United States except in cases of impeachment.
- The president can **nominate,** and with the advice and consent of the Senate, **appoint** federal judges and other officers of the United States.
- The president is charged with giving Congress information on **the state of the Union** and can **recommend legislation** at other times.
- In addition, Article 1 describes the president's power to **veto** legislation submitted by Congress, subject to congressional override.

George Clinton

George Clinton, the first governor of New York after Independence, opposed ratification of the Constitution. In his 1787 letter "To the Citizens of the State of New York,"[2] he raised a series of objections.

- There were no limits on presidential eligibility for reelection. Citing Montesquieu's observation that "the greatness of the power must be compensated by the brevity of the duration,"[3] he found danger in extended presidential tenure.

- Influence over appointments, control of troops, power to grant pardons, and duration in office of four years or more give a president "possessed of ambition . . . power and time sufficient to ruin his country."[4]
- The vice presidency is "as unnecessary as it is dangerous."[5] The vice president's service as presiding officer of the Senate represented a dangerous "blending of the executive and legislative powers."[6]
- The electoral college's manner of selecting presidents is too indirect.
- Powers over war and peace, treaties, embassies, and the armed forces should be left to the legislature.

All in all Clinton maintained that the president would "differ but very immaterially from the . . . monarchy in Great Britain."[7]

Alexander Hamilton

A few months later, **Alexander Hamilton** responded to Clinton's arguments in *The Federalist*, Number 69.[8] Most state governors of the time were weak and subordinate to state legislatures in a number of ways. In many states the legislature selected the governor, he served a very brief term, and his salary could be reduced by legislative vote. New York was an exceptional state in that its governor was relatively powerful. Hamilton told his New York readers that the presidency had been modeled largely after their own governorship. He addressed Clinton's points and argued that the president would not become an American king; rather, the president would more closely resemble a national version of New York's own governor.

Some felt that a **plural executive** would be preferable to a single executive. With such an executive committee, the threat of an individual assuming monarchical powers would be removed. Hamilton responded to such concerns in *The Federalist*, Number 70.[9] A plural executive, he argued, would provide "a feeble execution of the government. A feeble execution is but another phrase for a bad execution; and a

George Washington had informed Hamilton that he was
willing to accept the presidency if the electors selected
him. The fact that this heroic, patriarchal figure
seemed certain to become the first president eased apprehensions
to a large degree. It would be ludicrous to claim that Washington
would become a tyrannical King George IV.
But what about his successors?

government ill executed, whatever it may be in theory, must be, in practice, a bad government."[10]

If several people wielded executive power, they might disagree. If they disagreed at a critical time, they might split the community into "irreconcilable factions."[11] But Hamilton's weightiest objection to a plural executive was that it could "conceal faults and destroy responsibility."[12] Executives might blame one another when things went wrong, and how could the public judge? In extreme cases how could the public decide which culprit to impeach? A single executive is easier to watch. As such Hamilton believed that a single president would be safer and more efficient than a plural executive would be.

Paradoxical Popular Expectations of the Presidency

The framers, in short, recognized that the country needed a strong central government and a strong presidency, but they were afraid of creating an American king. The presidency was founded on a basic paradox: People simultaneously desired and feared strong leadership. Thomas Cronin has argued that the American people continue to have exaggerated, paradoxical, or even contradictory expectations of presidents.[13]

- We want our presidents to be decent and honorable, and at the same time we expect them to be tough, decisive, and guileful. Polls show that we want our president to be both "sinister" and "sincere" "a kindhearted son of a bitch."[14] It is difficult for a single person to satisfy such desires.
- We want our presidents to be "programmatic" (committed to policies in a detailed way) and "pragmatic" (flexible, willing and able to compromise).[15]
- We want our presidents to lead us, but we also want them to represent, listen to, and follow us.
- We want our presidents to inspire us, to raise our hopes and our aspirations. Many admired President Reagan's optimism and affability (recall his campaign slogan: "It's morning in America!"). However, too much inspiration can lead to disillusionment and cynicism.

One night in September 1996, President Clinton told reporters on Air Force One that he was trying to lead the American people away from their "funk," which he described as anger about government, unease with technological change, and fear for their jobs. Parallels were drawn between Clinton's comment and President Jimmy Carter's earlier efforts to lead America out of its "malaise," a downbeat theme that plagued his unsuccessful reelection campaign in 1980.

Worried about these comparisons, Clinton held a press luncheon in the White House and explained that he had made a poor choice of words, he was "very optimistic" and "feeling good," and the country was not in a funk.

During his October 6, 1996, debate with Senator Bob Dole, Clinton observed, "It's not midnight in America"—a take-off on Reagan's earlier message.

Cronin tells a story of President Lincoln having taken a vote at a cabinet meeting that went entirely against him. He announced the result this way: "Seven nays and one aye, the ayes have it."[16] Would your reaction to this story be the same if the featured character were a less-admired president?

- We worry about concentrated power and generally oppose secrecy, yet we admire dynamic, aggressive, heroic presidents.
- We want presidents to be above partisan politics. They are presidents of all the people of the United States, not just of their fellow Democrats or Republicans. But we expect our presidents to be gifted and savvy politicians who can broker deals with Congress and get things done.
- We want our president to be a "common person," but we demand uncommon performance.

In May 1996 President Clinton accepted an invitation to speak at Pennsylvania State University's graduate school commencement ceremonies. Despite the fact that he was in the middle of a reelection campaign, some of the graduates complained to reporters that some people in the audience seemed to be more interested in the President than in the graduates. One graduate noted that she thought the President's speech was "too political."

Maureen Delaney, a third-grade teacher in Pennsylvania, regularly asks her students to write essays on what they would do if they were president. Some sample excerpts follow.

If I Were President

- There would be no more nuclear war bombs and no hunting.
- Kids nine and over would be able to drive.
- As for criminals, I would put them in jail and make them stay there for seven years and give them bread and water to eat and drink.
- People who killed other people I would put in a torture chamber.
- There would be less guns, twice as many police, no Ku Klux Klan, and a stronger penalty for committing suicide should be passed.
- We kids could vote at the age of eight.
- There would be the death penalty for these things: drug abuse and murders of fifteen to twenty people.
- If somebody shot me, I would put them in jail for the rest of their life. I would take guns away from people who shoot people a lot. Then I would put them in jail.
- Kids would have rights like having their own credit cards.
- I would move away from the White House and build a new one in Florida. I would try to get more football games on TV.

- Everything would cost a penny. There would be less guns to kill animals because they need their fur and we don't.
- I would give one million dollars to everyone in the United States. Then I would be a poor president.
- There wouldn't be any taxes, poor people, or robbers. Everything would be free. The White House would be painted green so it would be called the Green House.

Out of the mouths of babes. What's the point? Kids expect a lot of the President. So do adults. Our consideration of the presidency should help us to form realistic expectations.[17]

- We want our president to be one of us, yet also to be something more. We like the idea that anyone can become president, but we don't want a president who is too common or ordinary: "We are inconsistent; we want our presidents to be one of the folks but also something special. If a president gets too special, however, he gets clobbered. If he tries to be too folksy, people get bored."[18]

In sum, the ideal president is kind but tough, common but competent. This balance is difficult to strike.

Presidential Job Description

Here's how Clinton Rossiter described the president's jobs in *The American Presidency:*[19]

- The president serves as **chief of state;** that is, the president greets visitors, hosts state dinners, bestows medals, lights the national Christmas tree, tosses the first pitch of the baseball season, and performs other such symbolic and ceremonial tasks.
- The president serves as **chief executive;** that is, the president oversees and attempts to direct the federal bureaucracy.
- The president serves as **chief diplomat,** negotiates treaties and executive agreements, mediates disputes, appoints and recognizes ambassadors, and conducts other business with foreign nations.
- The president serves as **commander in chief** of the armed forces, oversees the nation's defenses, and deploys troops during hostilities.
- The president serves as **chief legislator,** delivers a State of the Union address, presents budget proposals to Congress, and otherwise recommends legislation.

On August 23, 1996, donors were invited to the White House for coffee. The Democratic National Committee (DNC) campaign chairman requested the event because the DNC was not meeting its fund-raising targets in Texas. The Committee estimated that such "coffees" would bring in $500,000 in donations. According to the files of Harold Ickes, a key figure in President Clinton's 1996 reelection campaign, such events were an important part of campaign fund-raising.

Documents released by the Clintons on February 25, 1997, reveal that some 938 guests were invited to spend the night at the White House between 1992 and 1996. The fact that big financial donors and fund-raisers were frequent overnight guests in the Lincoln Bedroom generated much controversy.

Chelsea Clinton celebrated her seventeenth birthday on March 2, 1997. When asked what he and Mrs. Clinton would be getting their daughter for her birthday, the President replied, "We're going to let her sleep in the Lincoln Bedroom for free." (just kidding)

- The president serves as **manager of prosperity,** prepares a budget, appoints the secretary of the treasury (and, occasionally, the chairman of the Federal Reserve Board), confers with the Council of Economic Advisors, and takes other steps to protect the economic health of the nation.
- The president serves as **chief of party.** A popular president can effectively endorse and campaign for party members and can be a formidable fund-raiser.

Rossiter's treatment of the presidency is idealized,[20] but he does acknowledge that the president's roles **overlap.** Being a successful party leader contributes to the president's effectiveness as chief legislator. Sometimes roles **conflict.** For example, while we want our president to be a forceful chief diplomat, we hope that presidential decisions are designed to advance the interests of the nation, not just the interests of the party. The president's "job" is, in fact, many jobs. But a common thread runs

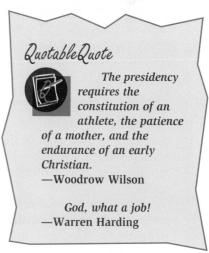

The presidency requires the constitution of an athlete, the patience of a mother, and the endurance of an early Christian.
—Woodrow Wilson

God, what a job!
—Warren Harding

through these diverse activities: A president is expected to provide **leadership.** The president articulates goals and uses resources to enlist the cooperation of others in achieving them. By saying, "These are the goals of my administration. These are the goals our political system should pursue," the president is providing leadership. Not everyone will agree, but we are more likely to tolerate disagreements and even forgive errors than we are to accept presidential indecisiveness.

Contrasting Views of the Presidency

Like other American citizens, presidents have a variety a views of the office. President **William Howard Taft** had a **restricted view** of presidential power. He rejected the notion that presidents possessed powers beyond those specifically granted in constitutional or statutory provisions. He maintained that there was no "undefined residuum of power" that presidents could tap to further the public interest. Without an "affirmative constitutional or statutory provision," a presidential power simply did not exist.[21]

Taft's predecessor, **Theodore Roosevelt,** expressed a very different view of the office. Roosevelt's **stewardship doctrine** held that presidents possess undefined or implicit powers that they can wield in the national interest. As a steward of the people, a president should actively do everything possible for the good of the people and should not be content with "keeping his talents undamaged in a napkin." Unlike Taft, who would act only if he were explicitly *authorized* to do so by the Constitution or statute, Roosevelt believed that it was the president's "duty to do anything that the needs of the nation demanded unless such action was forbidden by the Constitution or the laws." For Roosevelt, then, presidents possess **unwritten powers,** and they should "serve the people affirmatively in cases where the Constitution does not explicitly forbid him to render the service."[22]

President **Abraham Lincoln's executive prerogative view** of presidential power exceeded even Roosevelt's and that of any subsequent president to date. While presiding over the Civil War, Lincoln authorized suspension of the right of *habeas corpus,* blockaded ports, and seized blockade-running ships. He also called for the emancipation and arming of slaves who agreed to fight for the Union. When questioned about the source of his authority to take such steps, he explained that he took an oath to "preserve, protect, and defend the Constitution of the United States." The oath did not enable him to act on the basis of his own abstract moral judgments concerning slavery. It did, however, impose upon him duties to the government and the nation, for which the Constitution serves as "organic law." Lincoln posed the question, "Was it possible to lose the nation and yet preserve the Constitution?" He reasoned that sometimes a limb must be amputated to save a life. Similarly, sometimes an otherwise unconstitutional act becomes lawful if it is necessary to preserve the nation.[23]

Presidential power meant very different things for these presidents. Presidential power continues to vary from president to president, making generalizations difficult. Nevertheless, it is important to examine some common sources of presidential power.

Many fear concentrated power and worry about presidential abuses, but surveys reveal that the presidents regarded as "great"—Lincoln, Franklin Roosevelt, Washington, Jefferson, Theodore Roosevelt, Wilson— were presidents who used their powers vigorously. (See Table 8.1.) They did not keep them undamaged in a napkin. This ambivalent attitude is yet another paradox.

Table 8.1

Ranking United States Presidents

The Greats

President in Order of Overall Ranking	Leadership Qualities	Accomplishments and Crisis Management	Political Skill	Appointments	Character and Integrity
Lincoln	2	1	2	3	1
F. Roosevelt	1	2	1	2	15
Washington	3	3	7	1	2
Jefferson	6	5	5	4	7
T. Roosevelt	4	4	4	5	12
Wilson	7	7	13	6	8
Truman	9	6	8	9	9
Jackson	5	9	6	19	18
Eisenhower	10	10	14	16	10
Madison	14	14	15	11	6

The Failures (listed chronologically)

Pierce, Buchanan, A. Johnson, Grant, Harding, Hoover, Nixon

Source: "Rating the Presidents," AP/T.Durand (as published in *Altoona Mirror,* February 8, 1997, A8.)

O n June 30, 1921, eight years after his term as president ended, William Howard Taft was appointed chief justice of the Supreme Court by President Warren Harding. He served as chief justice until 1930 and once commented happily, "In my present life, I don't remember that I ever was President."

In 1926 the Supreme Court decided the case *Myers* v. *United States*. President Woodrow Wilson removed a federal postmaster from his job without obtaining the Senate approval required by the Tenure of Office Act. Wilson claimed the *implied* constitutional power to remove such subordinates so the president can faithfully execute the laws.

Chief Justice Taft wrote the Court's majority opinion. To the surprise of those familiar with Taft's earlier limited views of presidential power, he *accepted* President Wilson's assertion of implied power. Maybe he "did not remember" his reservations.

Presidential Power

Informal Sources of Presidential Power

Presidents have both formal and informal sources of power. **Informal sources of presidential power** are varied.

- A president with **public support** has more leverage in dealing with other political actors. Although presidential popularity fluctuates throughout a president's term, presidents are generally most popular early in their terms during their "honeymoon period." For this reason, presidents are well-advised to have clear early policy agendas and to be prepared to "hit the ground running" immediately after assuming office so as not to squander this asset.
- A good relationship with the **press** can also contribute to a president's power. President Eisenhower enjoyed a cordial relationship with the press. According to some accounts, reporters sometimes polished Eisenhower's press conference remarks to help him deliver his message to the public. By contrast, President Nixon had a hostile relationship with the press. After losing a California gubernatorial election, he told reporters he was through with politics and they

"Spiro Agnew."

Steve Benson reprinted by permission of United Feature Syndicate.

would not have "Nixon to kick around anymore." Later his vice president, Spiro Agnew, criticized the press in his alliterative style as "nattering nabobs of negativism" and "hopeless, hysterical hypochondriacs of history." When scandals forced both men to resign their offices, press coverage was mostly unsympathetic.

- **Events** also affect presidential power. Presidents who serve during times of tension and crisis have more opportunities to exhibit heroic leadership than do presidents who serve during tranquil years.

- Some presidents are able to capitalize on the inherent **prestige** of their office to get things done. Regardless of policy differences, the office of president commands a degree of respect.

- Presidents can also address the public from the presidential **bully pulpit,** as Theodore Roosevelt called it, or the "electronic throne." A president with effective communication skills can build support for programs by communicating with the nation on television.

Formal Sources of Presidential Power

There are also **formal sources of presidential power.** Formal powers come from the Constitution, special legislation, or court decisions supporting presidents claiming "inherent powers." As described earlier, Article 2 of the Constitution names the president commander in chief of the armed forces. It gives the president the power to negotiate treaties and to appoint and receive ambassadors and public ministers. It authorizes the president to grant n 1993 President Clinton presented Congress with a national health care plan. On September 29, 1993, he delivered a televised speech in which he said that the existing health care system "is badly broken, and it is time to fix it." President Reagan frequently used anecdotes about individuals to make his proposals more comprehensible and attractive. Taking a page from Reagan's book, Clinton personalized this complex subject by telling stories about people who had lost their health insurance or had to choose between medicine and food. Support for Clinton's health care plan *tripled* over night. His overall approval rating also exceeded his disapproval rating for the first time in several months.

Ultimately, President Clinton was unable to secure congressional passage of his health care reform plan. But his televised speech built temporary support and momentum.[24]

reprieves and pardons for offenses against the United States (except in cases of impeachment), to recommend legislation, and to deliver a State of the Union message. It also gives the president the power to appoint various federal officials with the advice and consent of the Senate.[25] Article 1, Section 7, clause 2 outlines the president's **veto power.**

- A president has ten working days to sign or veto a bill after receiving it from Congress.
- If the president vetoes the bill, the entire bill goes back to the originating house. The president's veto message will carry specific objections to the bill.
- Congress can **override** a presidential veto by a two-thirds vote in the House and the Senate, often times a difficult proposition. More than 80 percent of presidential vetoes succeed.[26]
- Sometimes Congress attaches controversial **riders** to a bill the president wants in the expectation that the president will accept the riders to approve the rest of the bill.
- Another option is the **pocket veto.** If a president neither signs nor vetoes a bill within ten working days and Congress remains in session, the bill becomes a law without the president's signature.[27] But if the president neither signs nor vetoes the bill within ten days—in effect, places the bill in a pocket and keeps it there— and Congress *adjourns,* the bill is killed.
- If a president threatens Congress with a veto, Congress must either modify the bill or amass enough votes to override the veto.

The veto is be an important bargaining tool for presidents. They can also use the veto to protect a minority against hastily crafted legislation drafted to appease an agitated majority.[28]

Converting Potential Power into Actual Power

Presidents have formidable **potential powers,** but these resources must be converted into **actual power.** Richard Neustadt explains that presidents do not obtain results by giving orders. They do not get "action without argument." Instead, "presidential power is the power to persuade."[29] Contemplating an Eisenhower presidency, President Truman said, "[h]e'll sit here and he'll say 'Do this! Do that!' *And nothing will happen.* Poor Ike—it won't be like the Army. He'll find it very frustrating."[30]

Presidents find that they must convince others in the executive branch that it is in their own interests to do what the president wants. A former aide to President Franklin Roosevelt put it this way:

> Half of a president's suggestions . . . can be safely forgotten by a Cabinet member. And if the President asks about a suggestion a second time, he can be told that it is being investigated. If he asks a third time, a wise Cabinet officer will give him at least part of what he suggests. But only occasionally, except about the most important matters, do Presidents ever get around to asking three times.[31]

QuotableQuote

I sit here all day long trying to persuade people to do the things they ought to have the sense to do without my persuading them. . . . That's all the powers of the president amount to.
—**President Dwight David Eisenhower**

Dealing with Congress can be even more challenging for presidents because members of this separate branch are under no obligation to comply with presidential directives. Persuasion requires **bargaining,** and presidents have "currency" to use in such negotiations. As a coach driver can employ a carrot or a stick, presidents can offer rewards or threaten sanctions to win congressional cooperation. Presidential aides, and even the president, work the phones feverishly as critical votes draw near in Congress. A president offers campaign assistance, desired appointments, or similar inducements in return for a congressperson's support. On the other hand, a president can threaten to withhold such favors.[32] More dramatically, a president might draw up an **enemies list** and target those listed for denial of federal grants, investigations, press leaks, litigation, prosecution, tax audits, and so on. To be sure, such actions cross ethical lines and contributed to the demise of Richard Nixon's presidency. These steps illustrate powerfully, however, the importance that presidents attach to persuasion and bargaining.

The point is not that presidents are weak; it is that their powers are not self-executing. They must be willing to coax, cajole, persuade, and bargain to secure the cooperation of other key actors, and they must be able to do so skillfully to lead. As such, presidential power is largely a function of the personal bargaining skills and inclinations of particular presidents.

In June 1973 President Nixon's former counsel, John W. Dean III, gave the Senate Watergate Committee a memo proposing the use of "available federal machinery to screw our political enemies." An accompanying document named twenty "enemies" and two hundred other people who were regarded as unsympathetic to the Administration. Next to each name was a remark written by the President's special counsel, Chuck Colson, suggesting actions to be taken. For example, next to the name of Morton Halperin, an executive with Common Cause, appeared the comment "A scandal would be most helpful here."

The preceding year Colson had boasted that he would "walk over his grandmother if necessary to get Nixon reelected." Colson's tough talk made him a forceful presence in the White House. He was eventually sentenced to Allenwood Prison to serve time for crimes he committed. There he became a born-again Christian. More than two decades of commitment eased the skepticism of those who questioned the sincerity of his conversion. In 1993 he received the Templeton Prize for Progress in Religion, which carries a one million dollar award. Previous recipients included Mother Teresa and the Reverend Billy Graham.

Limits on Presidential Power

Modern presidents regularly complain that their responsibilities exceed their powers.

- President Kennedy sought the removal of a large sign pointing out the location of the Central Intelligence Agency's Langley, Virginia, headquarters. He thought it curious to advertise the address of this secret spy agency. An aide directed the Interior Department to remove it. Nothing happened. The instruction was repeated. Nothing happened. Finally, Kennedy personally called the official in charge of signs and demanded action. Only then was the sign removed.[33]

- President Johnson commented in frustration, "Power? The only power I've got is nuclear . . . and I can't use that."[34]

- President Carter encountered an extreme example of presidential limits. A mouse died inside an Oval Office wall, and the odor became offensive. The General Services Administration (GSA) was called to remedy the problem, but the GSA refused. The GSA explained that it had already exterminated in the White House, the mouse must have entered from outside the building, and then the mouse was under the jurisdiction of the Department of the Interior. The Interior Department responded that it did not deal with mice *inside* buildings. Carter angrily told his press secretary, Jody Powell, "I can't even get a damn mouse out of my office" and established an interagency task force to remove the mouse.[35]

Of course, presidential complaints can be self-serving. If we are persuaded that presidents lack power, perhaps we will lower our expectations. And sometimes, presidents get *too much* cooperation. President Carter's daughter, Amy, asked her mother for help with her homework on the industrial revolution. Mrs. Carter asked an aide if she knew anything about the subject. The aide called the Labor Department. Two days later help arrived in a truck carrying a massive printout prepared by a team of analysts. Amy received a C on her assignment.[36]

Formal Limits

Formal limits include the fact that presidential appointments require Senate approval, as do treaties. Presidents can recommend legislation, but Congress must be persuaded to pass it. Presidents can veto bills, but Congress can override vetoes. The Supreme Court might rule against a president, ordering the president to turn over tape recordings of conversations with aides for use as evidence in a pending criminal trial.

The **Twenty-Second Amendment,** limits Presidents to two terms. Various arguments are advanced in support of the two-term limit. For example:

- We need this additional check and balance to control the presidency. Voters might reelect the same president repeatedly out of habit.
- Parties are forced to develop qualified candidates to succeed the current president instead of becoming overly dependent on one leader.
- The demands of the presidency are great, and the risk of presidential burnout is severe. It is unlikely that presidents can be very effective beyond two terms.

On the other hand, critics say the Twenty-Second Amendment reflects an undemocratic distrust in the ability of voters to make reasoned decisions.

- In a crisis keeping the same president in office might be more desirable than changing command.
- Further, presidents who are no longer eligible for reelection are less accountable to us than they should be.
- Conversely, such lame-duck presidents are weakened in the sense that other political actors know the presidents will be gone soon.

In extreme circumstances, Article 2, Section 4 of the Constitution provides that the president can be **impeached** (by a majority vote in the House) and convicted and removed from office (by a two-thirds vote in the Senate) for "treason, bribery, and other high crimes and misdemeanors." Article 1, Section 3 states that removal by the Senate disqualifies the person from holding any other office of "honor, trust, or profit under the United States." If convicted and removed from office, a former president is subject to "indictment, trial, judgment and punishment, according to law."

n 1980 Ronald Reagan supported the two-term limit. In 1985, as he began his second term, he suggested that the Twenty-Second Amendment should be repealed.

Paula Jones.

© *AP/Wide World Photos.*

QuotableQuote

I have never had sexual relations with Monica Lewinsky.
—**President William Clinton**
January 17, 1998, sworn deposition

I did not have sexual relations with that woman, Miss Lewinsky.
—**President Clinton**
January 26, 1998, speech

The Impeachment of President Clinton

In 1994 Paula Jones brought a sexual harassment suit against President Clinton for an incident that allegedly occurred in an Arkansas hotel room in 1991. There, she claimed, Clinton propositioned her and exposed himself to her. At that time Clinton was governor of Arkansas, and Jones was a state employee. Clinton denied the charges and asked the Supreme Court to delay the suit until the end of his presidency. In 1982 the Court had ruled that presidents are immune from suits for their official acts. But what about *unofficial* acts that occurred *before* the president assumed office? Should presidents be immune from civil suits during their tenure in office?

In 1997 the United States Supreme Court ruled that Jones could press forward with her sexual harassment case against President Clinton without waiting for him to leave office. Writing for the unanimous Court, Justice Stevens observed that "[t]he high respect that is owed to the office of the chief executive, though not justifying a rule of categorical immunity, is a matter that should inform the conduct of the entire proceeding, including the timing and scope of discovery."[37]

Had there been a pattern of sexual misconduct in Clinton's past? Conservatives asked liberal feminists why they embraced the sexual harassment charges that Anita Hill brought against Clarence Thomas during his 1991 confirmation hearings, but did not support Jones. The Paula Jones suit was eventually dismissed, but not before President Clinton and former intern Monica Lewinsky denied, under oath, that they had engaged in sexual relations.

After receiving immunity, Lewinsky changed her story and testified to independent counsel Kenneth

Starr's Whitewater grand jury that she and President Clinton had had a number of sexual encounters.[38] Federal courts ruled that Starr had authority to subpoena the President to testify before the grand jury, but Clinton agreed to appear voluntarily.

From 1797 through 1998 the House impeached sixteen federal officials, including one president—Andrew Johnson in 1868—one cabinet officer, one senator, and thirteen federal judges. Johnson, whose impeachment involved a power struggle over his authority to remove cabinet officers without congressional approval, survived when the Senate fell one vote short of the two-thirds majority needed to remove him. The Senate has convicted and removed only seven officials—all of them federal judges. The most recent was U.S. District Judge Walter L. Nixon Jr., who was impeached, convicted, and removed for perjury.

President Clinton hugging Monica Lewinsky.

© AP/Wide World Photos.

On December 19, 1998, the House of Representatives impeached President Clinton for lying under oath before a grand jury ("perjury") and attempting to cover up his activities by tampering with witnesses and hiding evidence ("obstruction of justice"). President Clinton refused to resign, fought against his removal, and welcomed a lesser sanction such as censure.[39]

On February 12, 1999, the Senate acquitted President Clinton of perjury and obstruction of justice. Senators voted 50-50 on the obstruction of justice article. Five Republicans—John Chafee (RI), Susan Collins (ME), James Jeffords (VT), Olympia Snowe (ME), and Arlen Specter (PA)—joined with the 45 Democrats. Senators rejected the perjury charge by a 55-45 vote. Ten Republicans—Slade Gorton (WA), Richard Shelby (AL), Ted Stevens (AK), Fred Thompson (TN), John Warner (VA), Chafee, Collins, Jeffords,

QuotableQuote

Indeed, I did have a relationship with Miss Lewinsky that was not appropriate. In fact it was wrong. . . . I know that my public comments and my silence about this matter gave a false impression. I misled people, including even my wife.
—**President Clinton**
August 17, 1998, speech

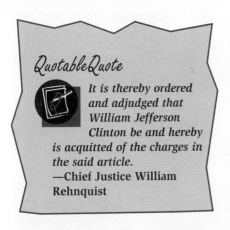
Snowe, and Specter—joined the 45 Democrats. As such, both charges fell short of the 67 votes required for conviction.

Throughout the proceedings, opinion polls showed that most of the public gave the President low scores for morality and personal trust. But with the booming economy and peace abroad, President Clinton enjoyed high job approval ratings. Presidents can be dismissed from office for *high* crimes and misdemeanors. The court of public opinion concluded that the sex and cover-up scandal was not serious enough to justify presidential removal. In the final analysis, the Senate agreed.

Informal Limits

There are also **informal limits** on presidential power. **Public opinion** can limit (as well as aid) presidents. A president might think that a balanced budget is necessary but, fearing public backlash, be unwilling to recommend a tax increase. **Events** beyond the president's immediate control can also limit Presidential power. For example:

- A new foreign leader rejects previously existing agreements with the United States.
- An existing social program is expensive and of questionable effectiveness, but it is too popular to cut.
- A bureaucratic agency is too entrenched to eliminate.
- A careless foreign alliance is difficult to undo.

Another factor that limits presidents is their **isolation.** They can become detached from reality. Presidents cannot do everything themselves and so must depend on advisors for information and expertise. But advisors who are selected by the president, who lack independent support bases, and who serve solely at the president's will derive their own power from the president's continued support. Such advisors may be reluctant to bring the president bad news.

- Irving Janis observes that devil's advocates are rare at staff meetings. When a group of people gather to make important decisions, **groupthink** sets in as members suppress their misgivings about the group's consensus. Such artificial unanimity reduces stress in the face of risk.[40] When groupthink occurs in the White House, presidents act on the basis of incomplete, biased, and inaccurate information.
- Consider also the trappings and prestige of the office: Air Force One, Camp David, Secret Service agents, pageantry, and all the rest. (Does a band strike up "Hail to the Chief" when you enter a room?) It is easy to see how presidents can lose touch with reality and public feelings.
- George Reedy, press secretary for Lyndon Johnson, argues that presidents attract sycophants. Presidents surround themselves with "yes men" and "yes women" and do not handle bad news well.[41]

Forces inside the executive branch can also limit presidents. The executive bureaucracy is so large and complex that presidents cannot follow up on everything to be sure that their directions are followed and their plans implemented. Key officials—even presidential appointees—sometimes develop independent support bases and are able to resist the president.

- It might be politically difficult for a president to fire a popular department secretary.
- Key career civil servants have long tenure, established ties, job security, and know-how. They may not enthusiastically embrace the current president's goals, resulting in half-hearted cooperation.

The federal bureaucracy limits the president's efforts to direct and mold it.

W hen the Lyndon Johnson Presidential Library was dedicated, former Johnson aides and assistants were invited to the ceremony. One notable omission from the guest list: George Reedy.

Structure of the Presidency

The number of employees working under the president has increased since the New Deal era when the Brownlow Commission reported that "the President needs help."[43] The president is surrounded by advisors and aides—**a presidential establishment.** Cronin finds this "swelling of the presidency"[44] disturbing; an "inner sanctum" of government has developed. That inner sanctum is

> isolated from traditional, constitutional checks and balances. Under some presidents it was common practice for anonymous, unelected, unratified aides to negotiate sensitive international commitments by means of executive agreements that are free from congressional oversight. Other aides in the presidential orbit were able to wield fiscal authority over billions of dollars that Congress had appropriated . . . all with no semblance of public scrutiny.[45]

Although a president needs help, it is important to strike a balance to ensure that the presidential machinery assists but does not dominate the president.

The structure of the presidency is a general concept. It varies from president to president as each president develops a unique decision-making style. Nevertheless, Louis Koenig spoke in general terms about a number of concentric circles surrounding the president.[46] Moving outward from the president, one encounters the following:

- The **inner circle** of advisors is, in fact, closest to the president. These confidants may come from cabinet, staff, or other positions. First Lady Hillary Clinton could be considered a member of President Clinton's inner circle.[47]

- The **White House staff** includes the president's **personal** aides. They serve at the presidents pleasure and are chosen for their loyalty, support, and long-standing relationship with the president. Chances are, many of the staffers served the president previously when the president was a governor or member of Congress. The president's chief of staff and his press secretary are such staffers.

- The **Office of Management and Budget (OMB)** was known as the Bureau of the Budget until 1970. The president appoints top administrators in the OMB, but its rank-and-file employees are civil servants who work under various presidents.

The OMB helps the president prepare the annual budget by coordinating agency budget requests and reviewing them to determine whether agencies are operating within the president's overall policy and fiscal objectives. The OMB also coordinates agency testimony at congressional hearings and funnels agency advice on pending legislation to the president. This Office is an important tool for presidents as they try to oversee bureaucratic operations.

- **Economic advisors** assist presidents. President Clinton established a National Economic Council. When economic matters become pressing, the importance of economic advisors grows. Of course, presidents can reject sound economic advice for political reasons. Economists might urge immediate steps to reduce the deficit, but the president may refrain from supporting a tax increase for fear of voter backlash. Recall how President Bush's 1988 campaign pledge—"Read my lips: No new Taxes."—came back to haunt him when he later supported tax increases.[48]

- The president, vice president, secretary of state, secretary of defense, and others drawn from offices and agencies that touch on national security affairs serve on the **National Security Council (NSC).** The creation of the NSC in 1947 recognized that national security issues are not just military issues. Economic, diplomatic, and other factors are also relevant. Some presidents (like Richard Nixon) relied heavily on the NSC; other presidents (like John F. Kennedy) used it infrequently.

- President Nixon established the **Domestic Council** to advise him on domestic affairs. It is to domestic affairs what the NSC is to international affairs.

- The **vice president's** role in an administration depends on the president. John Nance Garner, a vice president under President Franklin Roosevelt, said, "the vice-presidency is worth a pitcher of warm spit." After he left his position as Republican floor leader in the House of Representatives to become President Nixon's vice president, Gerald Ford remarked, "I've got all the perks. But power? Power is what I left up there on Capitol Hill."[49] Formally, vice presidents can preside over Senate sessions, but they rarely attend. They can vote to break a tie, but rarely get this opportunity. When it does happen, it makes for high drama.[50] Vice presidents stand the proverbial "heartbeat away" from the presidency, ready to assume the office in the event of the president's death, resignation, or incapacity. John Adams, the nation's first vice president, described his status this way: "I am nothing, but I may be everything."[51] Presidents can assign ceremonial tasks to their vice presidents, but presidents do not generally like to give their power away. For years vice presidents were rarely, if ever, "second in command." President Franklin Roosevelt largely ignored Vice President Truman. Only after he became president

QuotableQuote

The man with the best job in the country is the vice president. All he has to do is get up every morning and say, "How is the president?"
—**Will Rogers**

he NSC is supposed to function in a purely advisory capacity. During President Reagan's second term, controversy surrounded an NSC that crossed this advisory line and began implementing policy clandestinely. Televised congressional hearings into the Iran-Contra Affair drew big audiences.

The presidentially appointed Tower Commission released a report that concluded that the administration attempted to trade arms for hostages while publicly asking allies to refrain from supplying arms to Iran. In violation of congressional policy, proceeds from the arms sales were then channeled to support the "Contras" fighting to overthrow the Communist Sandinista government in Nicaragua. The NSC ran the program outside of established channels. The commission said that it was "plausible to conclude that [President Reagan] did approve [arms sales to Iran] in advance" and that there was "considerable evidence . . . of a diversion [of money] to support the Contras." However, the NSC pointed out, Oliver North had destroyed much of the supporting evidence before leaving his NSC job. The commission was also critical of the CIA director, William Casey, for failing to investigate more thoroughly, and Chief of Staff Donald Regan, for failing to ensure that proper disclosures were made in orderly fashion.

At best, President Reagan was depicted as a person who took too little interest in details and overdelegated responsibility to aides who served him poorly.

following Roosevelt's death did Truman learn of the existence of the atomic bomb.[52] When President Eisenhower was asked to give one example of a contribution Vice President Nixon had made to Eisenhower's decision making, he replied, "Give me a week and I might think of one."[53] Since Walter Mondale's vice presidency, however, the office has been growing in importance.[54] Often vice presidents are selected as running mates to broaden the appeal of the ticket. Massachusetts governor Michael Dukakis added balance to his ticket by selecting the more conservative senator from Texas, Lloyd Bentsen, to be his running mate in 1988. George Bush countered with the younger, more conservative senator from Indiana, Dan Quayle.[55]

- The Constitution does not provide for **the cabinet,** but all presidents have had one. It consists of the president, vice president, the heads of the fourteen administrative departments, and a few others. Recent presidents have attempted to use the cabinet as an advisory sounding board or even a decision-making group. Presidents Carter and Reagan held frequent cabinet meetings during their first few years. The meetings grew less frequent when they discovered that the specialization of *individual* members makes it difficult for the cabinet to function effectively as a *group.* The secretaries often function as advocates for their own departments, seeking resources first and worrying about the big picture later. Does it really make sense to have the secretaries of defense, agriculture, and education participate in meetings on nuclear disarmament? Presidents Kennedy, Johnson, and Nixon did not think so. In George Reedy's words, "The cabinet is one of those institutions in which the whole is less than the sum of the parts."[56] *Individual* cabinet members, however, may become trusted presidential advisors and members of the inner circle.

- **Miscellaneous agencies** and special **presidential commissions** constitute the outer circles. The Brownlow and Tower Commissions are examples.[57] Sometimes commissions are established to influence public opinion by showing presidential "concern" about some problem. After Los Angeles Lakers point guard Earvin "Magic" Johnson was diagnosed as HIV positive, President Bush appointed him to a commission on AIDS. Johnson served for a time but resigned when he concluded that the commission's main importance was in the public relations arena.

It bears repeating that presidential structure varies from president to president. One president relies heavily on the vice president, but another does not. One president tries to revive cabinet government, but another does not. One president relies heavily on the National Security Council, but another does not.

Presidential Power in Foreign Affairs

The Two Presidencies

In an article entitled "The Two Presidencies," Aaron Wildavsky argued that

[t]he United States has one President, but it has two presidencies; one presidency is for domestic affairs, and the other is concerned with defense and foreign policy. Since World War II, Presidents have had much greater success in controlling the nation's defense and foreign policies than in dominating its domestic policies.[58]

The **foreign affairs presidency** is strong because of the complexities of international relations, public support, and the need for quick action and coherent policies. Congress is a deliberative body. It is difficult for Congress to respond rapidly to international crises. In light of the need for the Nation to speak with a single and decisive voice, Congress often provides at least temporary support for presidents at such times. Furthermore, the president's constitutional powers in foreign affairs are

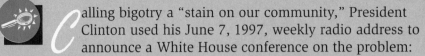

alling bigotry a "stain on our community," President Clinton used his June 7, 1997, weekly radio address to announce a White House conference on the problem: "It is time for us to mount an all-out assault on hate crimes, to punish them swiftly and severely, and to do more to prevent them from happening in the first place." Prejudice-motivated crimes are directed against blacks, Jews, homosexuals, and other minorities. The conference would bring together victims of hate crimes, lawmakers, religious leaders, and law enforcement officials to search for solutions.

Presidential leadership in such areas is important. However, a president could point to such a conference or commission as evidence of his deep concern, reap some public relations benefits, and do little else. Symbolism can go a long way in politics.

substantial. The president serves as commander in chief of the armed forces, appoints and receives ambassadors, and negotiates treaties.[59] In **domestic affairs** the president's constitutional powers are less imposing, popular support is not as readily available, and conflicting demands from contending constituencies pull the president in different directions.

In *United States* v. *Curtiss Wright Export Corporation*,[60] Justice Sutherland spoke of the "plenary and exclusive power of the President as the sole organ of the Federal government in the field of international relations." Sutherland added that "the President alone has the power to speak or listen as a representative of the nation." The sole organ of the federal government in the field of international relations? Sutherland overstated the case. Congress also has international relations powers.

- The Senate ratifies treaties and diplomatic appointments.
- Congress declares war.
- Congress raises and supports armies, provides and maintains a navy, and appropriates money to these ends.
- Congress regulates the armed forces and provides for calling forth the militia.

Curtiss Wright is significant, however, because it illustrates the judicial impulse to support and cooperate with the president in foreign affairs.

The general **public** also gives the president more leeway in foreign affairs.[61]

- In 1979 President Carter's approval ratings temporarily climbed after Americans were taken hostage in Iran.

*I*tem One: On August 17, 1998, President Clinton admitted that he misled people about his inappropriate relationship with Monica Lewinsky.

Item Two: On August 20, 1998, President Clinton ordered U.S. missile strikes against a terrorist camp in Afghanistan and a chemical weapons plant in the Sudan. The strikes were in retaliation for terrorist bombings of American embassies in Kenya and Tanzania less than two weeks previously.

Question: Were the two items related? Senators Arlen Specter (R-PA) and Dan Coats (R-IN) seemed to think so. Less than two hours after the missile strikes, almost before the smoke had cleared, both Senators publicly questioned the President's motives. They suggested that the President might have been trying to divert public attention from his other problems, much as the fictional president in the film *Wag the Dog* had done.

Item Three: On December 16, 1998—on the eve of a House vote on impeachment—President Clinton ordered missile attacks against Iraq. Secretary of Defense William S. Cohen and Secretary of State Madeline Albright were among those who claimed that there was no ulterior motive in the timing of the military action. Others disagreed. Senate Majority Leader Trent Lott said that "both the timing and the policy are open to question." Some members of Congress thought that the President was taking the country to war to fend off impeachment. Some sample comments:

- "For this sort of thing to come to a head on the eve of an impeachment vote is highly suspicious." (Bob Barr, R-GA)

- "The suspicion some people have about the President's motives in this attack is itself a powerful argument for impeachment. After months of lies, the President has given millions of people around the world reason to doubt that he has sent Americans into battle for the right reasons." (House Majority Leader Richard Armey, R-TX)

- "If the President is audacious enough to start a war to stop this [impeachment], we will probably have to deal with it." (Dennis Hastert, R-IL)

- "The fact is that we have either had hostilities or threatened hostilities at interesting times throughout the year." (Robert Livingston, R-LA)

- "Suddenly, on the eve of a vote to impeach him, after six years of a weak approach to Saddam Hussein, we are now told bombing is an urgent necessity." (Matt Salmon, R-AZ)
- "You'd have to be basically retarded to think there wasn't some manipulation [by Clinton] going on." (Mike Oxley, R-OH)
- "Not that Saddam Hussein doesn't deserve it. But why now?" (Gerald Solomon, R-NY)

Plausible? The fact that such reservations were voiced so publicly and quickly demonstrates how serious it is when a president's credibility is damaged.

Item Four: The House postponed impeachment proceedings for one day. On December 19, 1998, President Clinton was impeached. A few hours later he announced that U.S. and British forces had inflicted serious damage on Iraq's military establishment, immediate objectives had been accomplished, and Operation Desert Fox was being suspended.[62]

- In 1983 United States troops were deployed to Grenada. Support for the action rose by about 30 percent after President Reagan went on television to explain his rationale.
- In September 1994 public support for President Clinton's handling of tensions in Haiti improved by almost 20 percent following his televised speech.
- In 1991, before President Bush ordered military action to force Iraq to withdraw from Kuwait, almost 50 percent of the public wanted to give economic sanctions more time to work. After Bush ordered the troops into combat, more than 80 percent of the public supported his decision.[63]

Americans sense that it is their patriotic duty to "rally 'round the flag" and support presidents in foreign affairs. Criticizing the president's handling of foreign affairs in the face of some immediate international threat is considered disloyal, un-American, and irresponsible. However, presidents learn that this support is temporary.[64]

The War Powers Act

Although presidents are relatively more powerful in foreign affairs than in domestic affairs, they are far from omnipotent. If Congress declares war, the president serves as commander in chief and is entitled to whatever tactical discretion the position entails. But what if the president wants to deploy troops and Congress has *not* declared war? In today's world of intercontinental ballistic missiles and thermonuclear devices, it might

U.S. missiles strike Baghdad, December 1998.

© *Scott Peterson/Liaison Agency.*

not be possible for Congress to convene and provide the president with a declaration of war in time to counter enemy aggression. Does the Constitution have enough slack to cover such contingencies? Questions about presidential war powers in the absence of formal declarations of war have generated much debate.

In the summer and early fall of 1972, President Nixon thought that his national security advisor, Henry Kissinger, would be able to get a peace treaty with North Vietnam before the November elections. When that effort failed and the North Vietnamese proved unreceptive to new efforts in December, Nixon ordered a massive air strike that became known as the "Christmas bombing." The size of the attack shocked many in Congress and an attempt soon began to limit presidential war powers in the absence of formal declarations of war. When the story of the Watergate scandal began to unfold in the spring and summer of 1973, the president lost additional political support. Sentiment to limit executive authority mounted. Against this backdrop Congress approved the **War Powers Resolution.** Nixon vetoed it as an unconstitutional interference with the president's necessary discretion as commander in chief. Congress overrode his veto on November 7, 1973.

The law attempts to spell out the conditions under which a president can deploy troops and commit them to hostilities. The law tries to strike a balance between presidential and congressional war powers stating that "the collective judgment of both ritics said the War Powers Resolution inhibits the president's ability to act with the force and speed necessary to protect national security. Furthermore, it may be unwise to impose time limits on troop commitments. One should not tell an enemy who is shooting at you that, no matter what happens, your troops may be withdrawn in X days.

Supporters note that the law does permit the president to respond quickly through its sixty-day provision. It merely specifies that unilateral presidential action will not be tolerated indefinitely. In a checked-and-balanced system, questions of war and peace cannot be left to a single individual—even the president. The resolution permits Congress to play a meaningful role, while enabling presidents to deal with emergencies.

What do you think?

the Congress and the president will apply to the introduction of United States armed forces into hostilities."[65]

- The law requires that the president, in every possible instance, consult with Congress *before* introducing the armed forces into hostilities. Congress concedes that prior consultation is not always feasible. In any event, however, the president must, within forty-eight hours, report to Congress the reasons for these actions, cite the constitutional authority for doing so, and estimate the scope and duration of the hostilities.
- The president is required to provide periodic status reports to Congress.
- The law provides for the withdrawal of troops in two ways. First, Congress can pass a concurrent resolution ordering the president to withdraw the troops.[66] Second, the law provides that within sixty days after a report is submitted (or is required to be submitted), the president must terminate use of United States armed forces unless Congress has specifically authorized their continued use.[67]

The president and Congress have war powers of their own. The War Powers Resolution attempts to clarify the roles and their relationship. It succeeds, in part, but it continues to generate a good deal of controversy.[68] President Kennedy said that the difference between domestic and foreign policy was the difference between a bill being defeated and the country being wiped out.[69] This reality ensures that, regardless of the presidential-congressional balance that is achieved, presidents will continue to be very powerful in foreign affairs.

Key Terms

chapter 9

The Federal Bureaucracy

Bureaucratic Functions

What do bureaucratic agencies do? They perform various functions in the political system, but **rule application** is their most important role. Bureaucrats take general rules enacted by Congress and apply them to particular cases. Congress might get too bogged down in details if it always tried to establish programs with precise wording. Instead, Congress sometimes sets broad program goals—reducing environmental

Department of Commerce.

© CORBIS/Bettmann.

pollution, producing safer cars, and so on—leaving important application questions to the discretion of the bureaucratic experts administering those programs.

This situation implies that bureaucrats engage in **rule interpretation.** They must interpret congressional intentions and rules before applying them, making judgment calls. In this sense it can be argued that bureaucrats do not merely carry out policy; rather, they *make* it.

Bureaucrats play a role in **rule initiation** when they testify at congressional hearings and when they make policy recommendations to the president. Congresspeople and presidents can benefit from the expertise of those who will be charged with administering the programs under consideration. It makes sense to ask for and listen to such advice.

Bureaucrats even engage in **interest representation** when they act as advocates for the interests of their clients. For example, officials in the Department of Veterans Affairs may ask Congress to increase funding for programs that benefit disabled veterans. In turn, the Department would expect political support from its veteran clients should it someday be targeted for budget cuts.

Bureaucratic agencies also perform some **systems maintenance functions.** Although we hear much public criticism of "the bureaucracy" in general, people are generally supportive of the specific agencies with which they have dealings.[1] On an agency-by-agency basis, then, these agencies help **generate support** for the system.

Further, bureaucrats sometimes resolve conflicts between competing parties (**conflict resolution**). If twenty colleges and universities apply for the same grant and officials in the Department of Education award the funds to college X, a "conflict" is resolved.

Some Preliminary Observations

Do Bureaucrats Make Public Policy?

Since the Great Depression of the 1930s, the American public has generally agreed that government should regulate businesses to maintain competition, promote safety, and provide services that the private sector will lack incentives to provide. The United States has become a nation with numerous federal laws and enormous programs. Congress delegates considerable discretion to bureaucratic experts in taking care of technical program details.

As the executive bureaucracy has grown, the president's ability to control it has been challenged. Congress is supposed to make the laws. The president is supposed to execute them. Do these suppositions match reality? If not, are other assumptions about democratic accountability in doubt? In a democratic system policy makers are elected to make them accountable to the public. We do not elect bureaucrats. Instead, they take exams and are tested for merit to ensure that they will have the training and skills to perform their jobs. If these bureaucrats merely *administer* programs that are made by elected officials, there is nothing to worry about. On the other hand, if these unelected bureaucrats have so much discretion that they are, in effect, *making* public policy decisions, then we have a problem.[2]

> ### QuotableQuote
>
> *Congress does not any longer make laws, nor does the President execute them. Laws are now largely made by the bureaucrats who also execute them.*
> —**Phillip Kurland**

Are Government Agencies and Regulations Necessary?

Another observation: Bureaucracy is unpopular. Bureaucracy bashing is as common in political campaigns as it is on Rush Limbaugh's radio talk show. Candidates routinely promise to make the government more efficient and more responsive, to eliminate waste and fraud, to cut it down to size through streamlining and privatization, or, as Bill Clinton and Al Gore promised, to "reinvent government."[3] Yet bureaucracy seems a necessary evil. Governmental programs do not administer themselves. The government cannot function without dedicated public servants to run its programs.

Does the government regulate too much? Since the 1970s government regulation of commercial activities on behalf of the public interest has increased. Regulatory agencies affect the food we eat, the air we breathe, the water we drink, the cars we drive, and the toys our children play with.

n 1998 the Occupational Safety and Health Administration (OSHA) issued rules requiring bathroom breaks for workers. Federal law requires employers to have enough bathrooms, but it did not say anything about allowing workers to use them. Is this an example of government meddling and overregulation?

Consider the Iowa teacher who brings her entire class with her to the bathroom when she has to go and cannot find a substitute to watch her students. Or the North Carolina meatpacker who had to wait so long for permission that she soiled herself. Or California's Central Valley where labor contractors often do not provide enough toilets for farm workers. Of nearly eight hundred female public school teachers surveyed in Iowa in 1996, more than half said that they tried not to drink liquids during the school day. OSHA officials were convinced that the problem is more widespread than imagined and that the issue is one of human dignity.

Jane Bryant Quinn's comment provides a sensible summary:

Some regulations improve our quality of life; some regulations are stupid, rigid, and expensive. Before you cheer a politician who promises to get government off our backs, decide what you intend. Fewer health-and-safety laws? Or just regulatory common sense?[4]

Critics argue that regulation inhibits innovation, discourages risk taking, reduces productivity, and leads to the loss of jobs. Further, federal regulatory agencies overregulate by specifying detailed standards for every aspect of manufacturing instead of setting general targets for businesses to meet. Businesses failing to meet such standards can be assessed fines and penalties. Additionally, it costs money to comply with these regulations. Businesses pass on these increased costs to consumers or lay off workers to contain operating expenses. Sometimes, critics observe, the government regulates businesses right out of business.

Supporters of government regulation say that it has made the environment healthier, has made the workplace safer, and has enhanced our quality of life. If profits are low, prices are high, and American companies have trouble competing with foreign firms, these supporters say that blaming government regulation is easier than admitting to mismanagement and inefficiency. Deregulation, they fear, would make us vulnerable to businesses that will expose us to dangers by cutting corners to hold down costs and maximize profits.

Despite heading a national task force on government efficiency, Vice President Gore experienced postal inefficiency on a large scale. Gore's staff mailed some ninety-five thousand Christmas cards by December 10, 1993. Many were not delivered until mid-February of the following year. I don't know about you, but I have not received mine yet!

A teacher and his class: are bathroom breaks for workers a legitimate area for regulatory concern?

© *Spencer Christopher Grant/Stock Boston.*

Both sides can marshall numerous examples to support their claims. On balance, there is a philosophical dispute here about the proper role of government. Critics of government regulation generally think that the government which governs least, governs best. On the other side are those who think that regulation is essential to protect the weak, the poor, and even the masses against those who would endanger them.

Coming into Contact with Civil Servants

Most contacts between citizens and their government involve civil servants. Government employees teach our children in public schools, clean our streets, plow snow from our roads, and provide police protection for our homes and communities. In some localities municipal employees collect our garbage, put out fires, and pump out our basements after storms. When Congress adjusts income tax rates, postal service workers deliver the revised tax booklets to us and forward our checks and refund requests to the Internal Revenue Service. If you are an impoverished student who runs afoul of the law, a public defender may be appointed to assist you, while the county prosecutor prepares a case against you.[5]

The Amazing, Colossal Bureaucracy

Brace yourself for a news flash. Ready? The bureaucracy is large. The executive branch of the federal government employs approximately 2.8 million civilians. These people administer laws, collect taxes, work in embassies, inspect fast-food restaurants, clean up toxic-dump sites, conduct occupational safety inspections, and perform a myriad of additional duties assigned to them. Collectively, they are known as the "federal bureaucracy." Another 1.8 million people are in the military. About one-third of civilian employees work for a defense agency of some kind. The scale of the bureaucratic establishment in Washington, D.C., is enormous. The image of hundreds of white-collar workers toiling in cubicles along endless halls is representative of any major bureaucratic installation in our nation's capital. But only 12 percent of career civil servants (about 350,000 in all) work in or around Washington. Many work in United States territories or in foreign countries. Most are scattered throughout field offices in communities around the country. In short, not all federal civil servants are secretaries, clerks, and lawyers working in Washington. Furthermore, about fifteen million people work in government at the state and local level. The point: Government employees are virtually everywhere!

Bureaucratic Organizations

Max Weber and the Ideal Bureaucratic Organization

The purpose of bureaucracy is to administer and execute large-scale programs efficiently. It does not matter whether the organization is producing automobiles or processing social security checks. Administering any large-scale enterprise efficiently requires that the individuals working toward this end be organized in some coherent fashion. **Max Weber,** a German sociologist, saw the **bureaucratic organization** as the most effective way to accomplish this task. Weber's analysis of bureaucracy, published in 1922, remains influential and serves as a convenient point of departure for any study of organizational design and behavior.[6]

Weber described an **ideal** bureaucratic organization.[7] He explained that such an organization would have several distinguishing characteristics. First, an ideal bureaucratic organization has a clear-cut **division of labor.** A **specialized** expert performs each task. Second, specialists are organized into **hierarchical arrangements.** They are assigned to clearly defined ranks, with lower ones subordinate to higher ones. Hierarchical superiors direct the activities of subordinates. In this way specialists can be **coordinated.** Third, **formal, written rules and regulations** govern bureaucratic procedures. Decisions are made in a standardized and consistent fashion, according to "the book." Fourth, **written files** are carefully maintained. When a formal rule is applied in a particular way, this precedent is recorded so that future cases can be handled in a consistent fashion. When members of the organization leave, replacements can be recruited and easily trained by familiarizing them with the rules and files. **Continuity** results. Fifth, officials make decisions in a **detached and rational** manner, not in an emotional or sentimental fashion. Decisions are based on the formal rules and an examination of objective facts. Sixth, employees are hired and promoted on the basis of their skill and ability. Competence, credentials, training, experience, and expertise count. Appearance, family connections, and other factors not directly related to job performance do not count. This **merit principle** determines personnel decisions in an ideal bureaucratic organization and provides the most qualified available personnel.[8]

Inefficiency in the Real World

The key factor underlying the above characteristics is **rationality.** For Weber a bureaucratic organization was one that employed specialization, hierarchy, formal rules and regulation, written files, impersonal decision making, and the merit principle to achieve the greatest possible efficiency. In the real world we find that bureaucratic organizations fall short of Weber's ideal. We find inefficiency where we hoped to find efficiency. We have all experienced lost mail, fouled-up credit-card and bank statements, mistakes in our class registration schedules, and the like. Why?

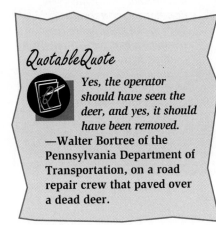

QuotableQuote

Yes, the operator should have seen the deer, and yes, it should have been removed.
—**Walter Bortree of the Pennsylvania Department of Transportation, on a road repair crew that paved over a dead deer.**

Sometimes bureaucratic inefficiency results when formal rules and regulations become overly cumbersome. There is such a thing as having too many rules or rules that are too detailed. Rather than expediting operations, rules can tangle actors in webs of **red tape.**

Sometimes, on the other hand, inefficiency results when informal norms and rules develop to rival the formal ones. In the name of efficiency, several bureaucrats might agree to handle a matter informally. The problem is that such informal arrangements produce gaps in the files and raise the possibility that favoritism, partiality, and other nonobjective factors might influence outcomes.

Another problem is that large organizations—government agencies, large companies, universities, and so on—can become too impersonal. Individuals may feel that they are nothing more than Social Security numbers to clerks who routinely process similar cases.[9] If a bureaucratic mistake is made, it can be difficult to obtain a "human" response. Standard routines simplify decision making and promote efficiency. The trade-off is that reliance on standardized operating procedures reduces flexibility and the ability to address individual circumstances.

A related problem is that bureaucrats grow accustomed to doing things a certain way. Bold innovation risks failure. Modest change, if any, is preferred. There are **sunk costs** in the established routine, making that which is known preferable to that which is unknown. This environment does not encourage adaptability and creativity.

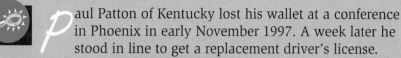
There may even be conflicts among some of Weber's ideal principles. One can argue that specialization undermines hierarchical authority. Subordinate experts possesses technical knowledge that their more generalized supervisors may lack. Not surprisingly, subordinates will occasionally resist their supervisors, believing that they (the subordinates) have more knowledge of how things should be done. In short, we should acknowledge that bureaucratic organizations have some important **dysfunctional consequences.**[10]

Incentives and Bureaucratic Decision Making

Weber's "ideal" bureaucratic organization celebrates rationality. The ideal bureaucrat was one who made the most rational decision possible. In the real world factors other than a desire to administer programs with maximum efficiency and rationality influence bureaucratic behavior. For instance, highly trained bureaucratic specialists might crave a sense of professional autonomy. They may bristle at hierarchical constraints and the limits that the chain of command places on their discretionary judgment.

The boss doesn't always call all the shots. A supervisor might depend on a subordinate's advice. Two peers might design informal ways to get jobs done more quickly. Such departures from formal expectations can be good or bad, depending on the circumstances.

Bureaucrats seek to protect their own agencies and their own jobs. Instead of cooperating to solve social problems, agencies may compete with one another for scarce budgetary resources. From a bureaucrat's point of view, it helps to have supportive clients who will come to the agency's defense if Congress threatens budget cuts. Bureaucrats have an incentive to show that they are *making progress*—and that they will make even *more* progress if they get *more* money next year. If an agency *solves* its assigned problem, we will no longer need the agency.

Such peculiar incentives produce irrational bureaucratic behavior. When viewed against the backdrop of the bureaucratic incentive structure, however, such behavior may be well-advised.

Some Administrative Theory

Woodrow Wilson and the Distinction between Politics and Administration

In 1887 **Woodrow Wilson** published an essay entitled "The Study of Administration."[11] It has become customary to trace the origins of public administration as an academic discipline to this article. Today it is common to urge American business executives to study and emulate the practices of some of their foreign counterparts. Wilson made similar arguments more than one hundred years ago in an attempt to improve administrative efficiency in the **public** sector. Wilson maintained that Americans devoted insufficient attention to how governments are administered. He drew an important distinction between politics and administration:

> Administrative questions are not political questions. Although politics sets the tasks for administration, it should not be suffered to manipulate its offices. . . . Politics is thus the special province of the statesman, administration of the technical official. . . . The broad plans of governmental action are not administrative; the detailed execution of such plans is administrative.[12]

If this **politics-administration dichotomy** proved sound, it would be possible for administrators in a democratic **political** system to "borrow" **administrative** ideas from other nations, even undemocratic ones. After all, "politics" relates to the setting of policy goals and ends; "administration" relates merely to means, to the implementation of policy goals established elsewhere. Can public administrators in the United States be instructed by their French or German counterparts? Wilson thought so:

> We borrowed rice, but we do not eat it with chopsticks. . . . If I see a murderous fellow sharpening a knife cleverly, I can borrow his way of sharpening the knife

without borrowing his probable intention to commit murder with it. . . . [B]y studying administration as a means of putting our own politics into convenient practice, as a means of making what is democratically politic towards all administratively possible towards each, we are on perfectly safe ground, and we can learn without error what foreign systems have to teach us.[13]

Wilson's suggestion that we study foreign administrative practices remains intriguing. In light of the extent to which bureaucrats exercise discretion in applying ambiguous program mandates from Congress, however, the line between politics and administration is less clear for us today than it was for Wilson.

Schools of Thought: Classical Approaches to Scientific Management

Frederick Taylor was another early voice. Taylor is sometimes called the "father of scientific management." **Scientific management** promised to increase productivity by discovering the most efficient, least fatiguing, **one best way** to proceed. His studies at the Bethlehem Steel Works were illustrative. Taylor advised managers to conduct careful **time and motion studies** to determine the best way to perform a task. Thus managers carefully observed shovelers under varying conditions as they employed different shoveling techniques. Managers also kept meticulous records and charted productivity. Through such studies scientific managers learned that regardless of the material being shoveled, workers should be supplied with shovels designed to carry precisely 21.5 pounds of matter. The steps of scientific management are as follows:

1. Perform time-motion studies to discover the one best way to do a job.
2. Select workers who are willing and able to work in the prescribed manner. These "elite" workers are paid more.
3. Train the elite workers.
4. Prepare a new division of labor. Managers make plans and recruit, train, monitor, and retrain workers and workers work in the prescribed fashion. They work hard, but not too hard because, a worker who is injured or exhausted today will not be productive tomorrow.

Increased productivity leads to increased profits which, in turn, leads to increased wages for management and labor. A new mental attitude develops. Managers and workers see one another as teammates, not adversaries. Workers accept the new system because they are rested, better paid, and happy. Taylor described scientific management as "kindness." However, he also observed that, "scientific management has nothing in it that is philanthropic. . . . The final test of any system is, does it pay?" Taylor concluded that scientific management does, in fact, pay.[14]

Taylor was one of the leading theorists in the **classical school** of administrative theory.[15] Supporters maintain that his ideas relate equally well to developing a science of processing Social Security checks. Critics call him a **machine model** theorist for treating people as extensions of mechanical equipment, as human cogs in organizational machines. Critics point out that this mechanistic approach overlooks the importance of the "human element."[16]

Later theorists criticized the classicists for placing too much emphasis on organizational structures and rules while neglecting the importance of **human relations.**[17] These theorists argued that economic incentives alone will not produce efficiency. Some human relations theorists stressed the importance of **social needs** and **group relations** to organizational members and performance.[18] Others emphasized the **psychological needs** of individuals in organizations. These **self-actualization theorists** highlighted the importance of finding fulfillment and satisfaction in one's work.[19] In short, these theorists held that to motivate members of an organization, they need opportunities to satisfy their social and psychological needs at work.

Modern Approaches: Contingency Theory

Warren Bennis predicted that bureaucracy, as we know it, would become outdated and would be replaced by new organizational structures.[20] He observed that modern organizations were becoming larger, more complex, and multinational in scope. Given the increased technical complexity of organizational tasks, highly skilled professionals would become more important than ever. However, they would be more committed to their professional careers than to the organization's goals. Temporary groups of specialists would work as teams, but these task groups would disband upon completion of the task, and new groups would form to deal with the next project. In such an **organic-adaptive structure,**[21] as Bennis called it, challenging tasks would provide specialists with intellectual stimulation, satisfaction, and motivation. Their commitment to work groups would be reduced, since the groups would be temporary. Members of such **modern organizations** would have to be flexible, able to tolerate change and uncertainty. Modern managers would be part diplomat and part philosopher. That is, they would have to be able to spot specialists with the needed skills and blend them together to form **"synergistic teams."**[22] For such teams the whole would be *greater* than the sum of the parts. Members would complement one another and collaborate so effectively that team members, in effect, "played over their heads." Modern managers, then, would have to recognize that the best way to proceed was **contingent** upon the circumstances. The best team depended on the task. As such, modern administrative theory is sometimes called **contingency theory.**

More Bureaucratic Problems

Parkinson's Law

Although Weber's bureaucratic ideal was intended to perform efficiently, actual bureaucratic agencies do not always do so.

Consider **Parkinson's Law.** In a satirical essay, C. Northcote Parkinson observed that "[w]ork expands so as to fill the time available for its completion."[23] Work is elastic. There is no relationship between the work to be done and the time it takes to do it. If you have a month to write a paper, you will take a month. If you have a week to write a paper, you will take a week. Similarly, there is little or no relationship between the work to be done and the size of the staff assigned to do it. The number of officials employed would be much the same whether the workload increased or decreased. Parkinson offered two related axioms: First, officials seek to multiply subordinates, not rivals. Second, officials make work for one another.

QuotableQuote

Nothing can go wrong . . . go wrong . . . go wrong. . . .
—**Line from the film** *Westworld*

Something to Think About

Imagine a civil servant, Andrews, who considers himself overworked. He could ask to share his responsibilities with a colleague, but this colleague would immediately become Andrews's rival. Instead, Andrews would prefer to have two assistants, Brown and Clark, assigned to help him. Andrews would remain the only person who comprehends the entire job. Brown and Clark would compete to impress Andrews. When Brown begins to complain of being overworked, he will seek two assistants of his own, Davis and Edwards. Seeing this, Clark will seek two assistants as well, Franklin and Griggs. Seven officials will now be doing what Andrews initially did alone. To justify their positions, Andrews's subordinates will generate mountains of paperwork, all of which he must review. They will become involved in interpersonal conflicts, and Andrews will have to keep the peace. Far more people will now take far longer to produce the same work. Meanwhile, Andrews will still feel overworked.[24]

Bureaucratic organizations expand not because of an increasing workload, but because officials seek to have additional subordinates hired. Such pointless growth is wasteful and inefficient. Is it inevitable?[25]

Peter cited Socrates as an example of an historical figure who rose to his level of incompetence, describing him as "a competent teacher who reached his level of incompetence when he became his own defense attorney."

The Peter Principle

Consider also the **Peter Principle.** Lawrence J. Peter and Raymond Hull maintained that "in a hierarchy, every employee tends to rise to his level of incompetence."[26] The authors were convinced that incompetence is everywhere. Private sector. Public sector. Nonprofit sector. It doesn't matter. Everywhere they looked, they saw persons who were in over their heads and who could not do their jobs. A competent person at one level is promoted when a higher position opens up. If the person proves competent at that level, additional promotions will occur until that person reaches a level of incompetence. She or he will stay there until retirement. The problem is that the skills that make a person competent at one level may not ensure success at the next level. Skills at one level can even become liabilities at another. A perfectionist mechanic's attention to detail may make that person a superb diagnostician. If promoted to repair shop supervisor, however, we might find the mechanic absorbed in a dismantled engine while work orders go unprocessed and angry customers discover that their cars are not ready.[27]

The Dilbert Principle

Scott Adams, the cartoonist of "Dilbert" fame, wrote an illuminating parody of workplace malfunctions.[28] In brief, Adams contends that Peter was too optimistic! Now, Adams claims, incompetent workers are promoted directly to management without ever passing through a temporary competence stage:

> [T]he Peter Principle has given way to the "Dilbert Principle." The basic concept of the **Dilbert Principle** is that the most ineffective workers are systematically moved to the place where they can do the least damage: management.

The Dilbert Principle.

© Dilbert reprinted by permission of United Feature Syndicate, Inc.

This has not proved to be the winning strategy that you might think.

Maybe we should learn something from nature. In the wild, the weakest moose is hunted down and killed by dingo dogs, thus ensuring survival of the fittest. This is a harsh system—especially for the dingo dogs who have to fly all the way from Australia. But nature's process is a good one; everybody agrees, except perhaps for the dingo dogs and the moose in question . . . and the flight attendants. But the point is that we'd all be better off if the least competent managers were being eaten by dingo dogs instead of writing Mission Statements.

It seems as if we've turned nature's rules upside down. We systematically identify and promote the people who have the least skills.[29]

Structural Organization

The *United States Government Manual* runs approximately nine hundred pages. It describes different bureaucratic agencies; provides agency names, addresses, and phone numbers; identifies some key personnel; and briefly explains the responsibilities of the agency. Nine hundred pages. We can condense the manual considerably by considering four types of bureaucratic structures.

Cabinet Departments

First, there are fourteen **executive** or **cabinet departments:** the Departments of State, Treasury, Defense, Justice, Interior, Agriculture, Commerce, Labor, Health and Human Services, Housing and Urban Development, Transportation, Energy, Education, and Veterans Affairs. Executive departments are headed by **secretaries**[30] who sit in the president's cabinet. These secretaries are appointed by the president, with the advice and consent of the Senate, and they are responsible to the president. An **undersecretary** or **deputy secretary** typically shoulders much of the administrative workload. **Assistant secretaries** in charge of specific programs report to the undersecretary or deputy secretary. These secretaries have staff assistants who work on planning, budgeting, legal, and public-relations matters. Departments are divided into **bureaus** based on functions, services, clients, or geography. Each bureau has a **director.** Below the bureaus are **branches, services,** and **sections. Supervisors** report to directors and oversee more specialized subordinates.

Departments are organized into large **pyramids,** with the technical specialists at the bottom, various layers of supervisors above them, and the cabinet secretary at the top. The pyramid reaches its apex as the fourteen secretaries report to their common superior, the president. In theory the president controls the departments through presidential appointees. In fact, each department develops entrenched bureaus and long-tenured civil servants who may prove to be resistant to presidential control.

Independent Agencies

Second, **independent agencies** report to the president in much the same manner as the cabinet departments do. Technically, however, these agencies do not enjoy cabinet status. Examples include the National Aeronautics and Space Administration, the Central Intelligence Agency, the General Services Administration, and the Environmental Protection Agency.

Government Corporations

Third, **government corporations** administer economic enterprises for the government. They appear to be part government agency and part business organization. Their operations are financed through a combination of congressional appropriations and customer payments. Examples include the Federal Deposit Insurance Corporation, the Corporation for Public Broadcasting, and Amtrak.

Independent Regulatory Commissions

Fourth, **independent regulatory commissions** exist because of the need for rule making and regulation in highly complex, technical areas. Examples include the Interstate Commerce Commission, the Federal Trade Commission, the Federal Communications Commission, the Securities and Exchange Commission, the Federal Elections Commission, the National Labor Relations Board, and the Federal Reserve Board. They perform **quasi-legislative** and **quasi-judicial** tasks. They hold hearings, make rules, and resolve disputes. Independent regulatory commissions are not purely executive or administrative. For this reason, they are administratively independent from any single branch. Their independence is protected in that they are often headed by several commissioners with overlapping terms, they often have bipartisan members by law, and members may be appointed for fixed terms. Further, the Supreme Court has ruled that whereas the president can remove purely executive appointees at will, the president cannot unilaterally remove commissioners from independent regulatory commissions.[31]

Recruitment and Selection: Hiring Bureaucrats

How are positions in bureaucratic agencies filled? A distinction can be made between **appointive positions** and **career civil service positions.**

Presidential Appointees

The president appoints about twenty-five hundred **political executives**. They enjoy substantial policy-making powers and are not covered by the civil service system. Such appointments are made at the cabinet level and at the federal administrative level (that is, just below the level of assistant secretary). Appointees often have backgrounds in law, business, and the social sciences. Such political executives get these positions by winning the favor of the president. Although they need not be members of the president's party, their **loyalty** to the president is very important. Presidents appoint these executives. When the president leaves office, they leave and the next president appoints a new "team." Through these appointees, in theory, the president controls the career bureaucrats. Two recent trends are apparent: First, the **number** of presidential appointees has **increased.** Franklin D. Roosevelt made about two hundred such appointments. Second, the **tenure** of these appointees has **decreased.** The average tenure of undersecretaries and assistant secretaries was estimated at twenty-two months.[32] The average tenure of political appointees in the Senior Executive Service (SES) was even less: about eighteen months in one position and even briefly in higher positions.[33] The higher political executive rise, the more likely they are to leave quickly.

Patronage

Historically, presidents have always cited **competency** as the basis for their appointment decisions. However, they seem to find it easier to recognize competency in their political supporters than in other potential appointees. **Patronage** or **political favoritism** characterized the filling of all federal service positions until 1883. Prior to 1829 white male elites held most of these positions. President Andrew Jackson wanted to bring more people from the middle and lower classes into government service. One of Jackson's supporters claimed, "to the victor belong the spoils." Thus the idea that the president's party loyalists should be rewarded with government positions is also called **the spoils system.** Although such a system encourages loyalty to the president, it does not ensure that appointees will have the requisite skills. After repeated efforts through the 1850s to make **merit** the basis of appointments, the **Civil Service Reform Act** (also known as the **Pendleton Act**) was passed in 1883. Just two years earlier President Garfield had been assassinated by Charles J. Guiteau, a disappointed seeker of a position in the diplomatic service.

Career Civil Service

The Civil Service Reform Act established a bipartisan **Civil Service Commission,** which administered tests to evaluate candidate qualifications. Federal employees were to be selected on the basis of their merit, not party loyalty. The Civil Service Commission functioned until 1978. Today the **Office of Personnel Management** administers civil service regulations and coordinates government personnel programs. A bipartisan **Merit Systems Protection Board** is responsible for protecting the merit system and the rights of federal employees. The board investigates employee complaints and prosecutes when officials violate civil service rules.

Today approximately 94 percent of federal bureaucratic positions are filled through the **merit selection** procedures. These are the **career civil servants.** Positions in the general civil service system are classified and covered by an eighteen-level **General Schedule (GS)** salary structure. Each level has several steps within it. In 1955 the **Federal Civil Service Entrance Exam** went into effect to screen applicants for management positions in the federal government. In 1974 that exam was replaced by another "universal" test, the **Professional and Administrative Career Examination (PACE).** Substandard performance by minorities led to charges that the PACE test was racially biased. In 1981 the **Office of Personnel Management (OPM)** agreed to eliminate this exam. From 1981 through 1990 applicants were hired by individual agencies on the basis of college grades, references, interviews, and, sometimes, specialized written tests developed for specific jobs. This decentralized system was extremely confusing. In 1987 a federal judge ordered that a new general exam be developed. In 1990 the OPM unveiled the **Administrative Careers with America**

Examination, a new universal test for applicants seeking entry-level management positions with the federal government. The OPM advertises positions, administers exams, and prepares a list of names of those who score well on the exams. Individual agencies have the responsibility for hiring their own new personnel. Agencies can promote people from within, or they can transfer civil servants from one position to another. If they want to screen "outside" applicants, they ask the OPM to certify several top applicants for the agency opening. The agency then makes its selection. **Service ratings** are generally used to determine promotions, pay increases, decreases, demotions, and dismissals.[34]

These civil servants are called "careerists" because they enjoy a good deal of job security. Few receive unsatisfactory service ratings from their supervisors. In fact, more than 80 percent get "above average" ratings. Think about that—how can 80 percent be above average? Only one in five hundred is rated "unacceptable."[35] Few civil servants quit voluntarily. They can be fired for cause (that is, for inefficiency, insubordination, and so on), but the procedures for firing incompetents are laborious. They can also lose their jobs through downsizing or "reductions in force."[36]

The Hatch Act

In 1939 the **Hatch Act** was passed to restrict the political activities of civil servants. On one hand it was designed to promote **neutral competence** by shielding civil servants from pressure to support certain political candidates and causes. On the other hand, it was designed to prevent the civil servants themselves from acting in ways designed to influence election outcomes. The act permitted federal workers to engage in "normal" political activities like voting and wearing campaign buttons but prohibited more active campaigning and running for partisan political offices. In 1993 Congress eased the Hatch Act's restrictions on the political activities of civil servants. President Clinton approved these revisions. Many forms of participation in partisan politics are now permissible. For example, civil servants may now seek and hold positions in political parties. However, some restrictions remain. Civil servants may not be candidates for public office in partisan elections. They can make campaign contributions, but they may not solicit campaign contributions from their subordinate employees nor from any person who has business before the employee's office. Additional restrictions apply for the CIA, FBI, Secret Service, and the IRS.[38]

Key Terms

Something to Think About

Frederick M. Malek was President Nixon's aide for recruiting political appointees. Frustrated with detailed procedures for firing people covered by the merit system, Malek proposed other ways to deal with unwanted civil servants. His recommendations were known as the "Malek Manual." Malek proposed that civil servants could be told to give up their present duties, move to makeshift jobs, and quietly resign. Their cooperation would be rewarded with "the finest recommendations, a farewell luncheon, and perhaps even a Department award." Another tactic would be to determine where the targeted civil servants would not want to live and transfer them there with promotions. Of course, they would not have to move if they resigned. Another approach was designed for employees with family responsibilities: promote them to jobs with extensive travel requirements to small towns with poor accommodations. Refusal to obey travel orders would be grounds for dismissal. Calling such moves "promotions" would help deflect charges of political witch hunting.[37]

Political hardball? Dirty tricks? Unethical? What do you think?

Something to Think About

$\mathcal{S}$ome argue that the government should make a special effort to hire members of socially disadvantaged groups that have endured racial, sexual, ethnic, or disability discrimination. Because of cultural biases in tests, inadequate educational opportunities, and social prejudice, the government should take affirmative steps to compensate the victims of such injustices. Bending the rules to assist such people is seen as a matter of social equity. Further, preferences should also be given to veterans, who risked their lives to defend this country. Such preferences can take the form of bonus points on entrance exams.

On the other hand, it is argued that hiring applicants whose test scores and educational backgrounds are relatively less impressive because the individuals are members of socially disadvantaged groups is wrong. To hire someone less qualified than another applicant is a disservice to the general public. Whether the top applicants became so because they were fortunate enough to have been born into circumstances that provided them with more breaks in life does not matter. Only the top applicants should be hired. Period.

Affirmative action versus the merit principle. What do you think?

chapter 10

The Federal Court System

Interpreting the Law

The Constitution is brief and has been amended infrequently over the years. As noted previously, it remains viable because many of its provisions were written in flexible language. Open-ended provisions require interpretation. As times change, courts are asked to reinterpret these constitutional rules to keep them current. In this sense **rule interpretation** is the primary **function** of courts in general and of the United States Supreme Court in particular.

We think of "the law" as clear, certain, and impartial. We speak almost reverently of being "a nation of laws, not men," meaning that everyone plays by the rules. No man or woman is considered to be above the law. Who we are does not matter. Who the judges are does not matter. The outcome of a case depends wholly on the law. Period. Some believe that when judges decide cases, they merely place the case facts on one side of a table and law books on the other side. They then search

U.S. Supreme Court Building.
© Robert E. Murowchick/Photo Researchers.

until they discover the written law that covers the facts at hand, apply these laws, and announce the result. But if this were all that the process entailed, computers could be programmed to decide cases for us. This view of judging is called **mechanical jurisprudence.**

Legal realists dispute the accuracy of this view. Laws as certain, objective entities do not really exist. Laws are often ambiguous. Constitutional provisions are often imprecise ("unreasonable" searches and seizures, "speedy" trials, "impartial" juries, "cruel and unusual" punishments). Facts are often in dispute. Law—like life—is not mechanical. And the judges who operate the legal mechanics of society are themselves not machines but human beings, men and women who make choices and exercise discretion as they render judgments. Not all judges will interpret a particular provision the same way. Through their actions judges can broaden or narrow the impact of a law, and in this sense judges "make policy."

Benjamin Cardozo was a member of the United States Supreme Court from 1932 through 1938. He said that, over time, he became reconciled to the uncertainty in the law that initially surprised and troubled him. At first, he was trying to reach "the solid land of fixed and settled rules." Eventually though, he accepted that the process of judging "in its highest reaches" is not just the "discovery" of law but its "creation."[1] By implication, the more unclear the law or the constitutional provision is, the more creatively powerful the judge becomes.

On the other hand, **Alexander Hamilton** described the judicial branch as "the weakest of the three departments of power" and as the "least dangerous" to the rights of the people. He explained that the judiciary would have influence over neither "the sword nor the purse." Courts possess "neither force nor will, but merely judgment" and depend on "the aid of the executive arm" to carry out their judgments.[2]

Courts are weak in the sense that they can react but cannot initiate. They offer opinions on

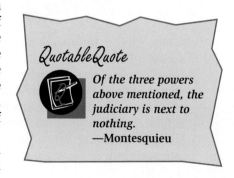

QuotableQuote

Of the three powers above mentioned, the judiciary is next to nothing.
—Montesquieu

matters of law when they are presented with cases raising such questions. Until a case is brought to a court, however, the judges wait in silence. They are not authorized to issue **advisory opinions** on legal issues in the absence of a case. Further, courts cannot enforce their own decisions. As Hamilton pointed out, they must depend on the cooperation of other branches. Such cooperation is not always forthcoming.

- In *Chisolm* v. *Georgia*[3] the Court ruled that Chisolm, a citizen of one state (South Carolina) could sue another state (Georgia) in federal court. This decision outraged states rights proponents. Opposition was immediate. The lower house of the Georgia state legislature approved a bill to punish by hanging "without benefit of clergy" any person aiding in the enforcement of the decision.[4] Just two days after the Court's decision, the Eleventh Amendment was introduced in both houses of Congress. The amendment modified the Supreme Court's original jurisdiction in such a way so as to reverse *Chisolm.*[5]

- *Worcester* v. *Georgia*[6] provides another example of the Court's dependence on other branches to enforce its decisions. Cherokee Indians were involved in a land dispute with Georgia. Chief Justice Marshall's opinion for the Court sided with the Cherokees and implied that the president was obliged to honor the Cherokee Nation's rights under federal law. President Andrew Jackson is reported to have exclaimed, "John Marshall has made his decision—*now let him enforce it!*"[7]

- In 1974 the Court prepared to rule on President Nixon's claim that tape recordings of his conversations with aides were protected by "executive privilege."[8] President Nixon suggested that he might refuse to comply with a "less than definitive" ruling from the Supreme Court. The Court "definitively" issued a unanimous ruling against the president.[9]

This situation brings us to a paradox: When the Constitution is most vague and the Court is at its most creatively powerful, its decisions are likely to be most controversial and hence, least legitimate, plausible, and persuasive. It is difficult for the Court simultaneously to be both creative and credible. For this reason, the judiciary has cultivated what some call **the cult of the robe,** the aim of which is to inspire public respect by elevating courts' prestige. The desire to inspire public respect is the reason that everyone rises when judges enter a court room, judges wear robes, wield gavels, and sit behind high benches. Courts want the broader public, including voters and public officials, to regard their decisions as legitimate and to assist in compliance.

Principles of Interpretation

When a judge **interprets** an unclear constitutional or statutory provision, the judge does not blithely decree, "I'm deciding this way because I feel like it! I had a bad day. My lunch is giving me indigestion. My new car won't start. My kids have the flu. I don't like liberal policies, and I don't like you!" It is considered improper for judges to substitute their own views of wise public policy for those of elected legislators. Instead, judges are supposed to base their decisions on the law. To do otherwise undermines judicial credibility. When judges interpret ambiguous provisions, they explain their interpretations by invoking some generally accepted **legal standards** or yardsticks.

Sometimes judges explain their decisions by referring to the **literal meaning** of the words of the text in question. A community might attempt to combat "hate speech" by imposing a speech code. Supporters of the code claim that it fosters sensitivity. Critics say it is an example of political correctness run amuck. But is it constitutional? A judge might read the First Amendment literally, conclude that the phrase *no law prohibiting freedom of speech* means "no law," and strike down the speech code. The literal text lends credibility to the decision. However, what is the literal meaning of "cruel and unusual punishment" or "due process of law"? Some texts have no literal meaning.

As judges interpret constitutional provisions or statutes, they sometimes refer to the **intent of the framers**.[10] Judges can then credibly argue that they are not simply writing their own policy preferences into the law; rather, they are relying on the authors of the text itself for guidance. Some problems with this approach include difficulty in ascertaining the framers' intent. Sometimes they disagreed. Sometimes they compromised. Sometimes they could not resolve certain issues clearly so they left things vaguely worded and passed the matter on to future generations. Sometimes the framers knew they could not foresee future details, so they laid down general concepts (prohibitions against unreasonable searches and seizures, for example) that could later be applied to specific cases. Furthermore, who do we mean when we speak of "the framers"?

- For constitutional purposes, are we talking about all the delegates who met in Philadelphia in 1787 or just those who signed the Constitution?
- Should we disregard the contributions that delegates who did not sign made to convention deliberations?
- Recall that the Constitution had to be ratified. What about the intentions of all the people who participated in state-level ratification conventions? If we had good records of all these meetings, would their intentions count?[11]

Sometimes judges explain their decisions by referring to previous cases or **precedents.** The term *stare decisis* means "let the decision stand." In other words, predictability and continuity should characterize the law. Today's decision should be consistent with yesterday's. However, sometimes judges find unclear or even conflicting precedents, and as times change, today's judges may decide that yesterday's decision no longer applies or that it was wrongly decided in the first place. At such times precedents can be overruled. Justice Holmes made the following statement in an 1897 address:

> It is revolting to have no better reason for a rule of law than that it was laid down in the time of Henry IV. It is still more revolting if the grounds upon which it was laid down have vanished long since, and the rule simply persists from blind imitation of the past.[12]

Sometimes judges base their decisions of prevailing **social or political needs.** They frame decisions in accordance with the times. During wartime, for example, judges are less likely to strike down governmental actions that they would disallow during peacetime. Following Japan's attack on Pearl Harbor in December of 1941, anti-Japanese sentiment ran high. President Roosevelt's 1942 executive order authorized military officials to designate certain military areas and to remove selected persons from those areas. In March 1942 the entire West Coast was so designated. All persons of Japanese ancestry were subjected to curfews and more than one hundred thousand persons were moved to relocation camps. Most were native-born Americans who had not been accused of any specific wrongdoing. Several cases challenged these regulations on grounds that they deprived American citizens of their civil rights without due process of law.[13] The Supreme Court generally accepted the military's contention that there was insufficient time to determine which Japanese Americans were loyal and which posed security risks. Individual rights were balanced against societal interests in conducting a successful war effort. Critics, including several dissenting justices, assailed the policy as racist and unconstitutional.

Such judicial standards are invoked by judges to enhance the credibility of their decisions and to protect the legitimacy of their courts. But the standards are flexible in their application. Judging is not a purely mechanical process. There is no getting away from the fact that "judging" requires the exercise of judgment, and different judges exercise their judgment in different ways.

Federal Court Structure and Jurisdiction

The United States has a **dual court system.** There are fifty state court systems and one federal court system. State court systems generally consist of

- Lower courts including **municipal courts, police courts, justices of the peace,** or **district magistrates.** The lowest courts in the state judicial hierarchy have limited jurisdiction in both **civil** and **criminal cases.**
- **Trial courts** with general jurisdiction. Most cases of a relatively serious nature begin in trial courts.
- **Intermediate appellate courts** to which trial court decisions can be appealed.
- A **state supreme court** or **court of appeals.** This court occupies the top position in the state judicial hierarchy.

The federal system forms a three-level pyramid.

- The **United States district courts** are at the bottom.
- The **United States courts of appeals** are in the middle.
- The **United States Supreme Court** is at the top.

A court cannot hear a case unless it has **jurisdiction** over the case. There are two kinds of jurisdiction: **original** and **appellate.**

- A case that is heard on original jurisdiction originates or starts in that court. It has not previously been heard in a lower court.
- A case heard on appellate jurisdiction has already been heard elsewhere, and it is now being heard on appeal.

Federal courts have jurisdiction over cases involving **federal parties** (ambassadors, public ministers, consuls, cases in which a state or the United States is a party, and some cases involving citizens of diverse states) or **federal questions** (questions involving the United States Constitution, federal laws or treaties, or admiralty and maritime law).

Article 3 is a natural starting point for an examination of the federal court system. Article 3, Section 1 of the U.S. Constitution provides that "[t]he judicial power of the United States shall be vested in one Supreme Court, and in such inferior courts as the Congress may from time to time ordain and establish." Article 3 also addresses judicial tenure, compensation, and federal court jurisdiction. Article 1, Section 8, clause 10 provides that, "[t]he Congress shall have the power [t]o constitute tribunals inferior to the Supreme Court." The federal court system was established under these provisions. Figure 10.1 provides a diagram of the federal court system.

The two main kinds of federal courts are: **constitutional** (or **judicial**) courts and **legislative** (or **administrative**) courts.

- **Constitutional courts** are created under Article 3 of the U.S. Constitution, and judges on these courts enjoy lifetime tenure (subject to impeachment) and irreducible salary to protect judicial independence.
- **Legislative courts** are created under Article 1 of the U.S. Constitution to perform quasi-legislative and administrative functions. Unlike constitutional courts, which can only decide cases and controversies, legislative courts can provide advisory opinions and perform other functions assigned to them by Congress. Although Congress can provide judges on these courts with protections like those enjoyed by judges on constitutional courts, judges on legislative courts usually serve fixed terms and their salaries are not protected. Further, judges on legislative courts can be removed for any reason by a simple majority vote of Congress.

Let's take a look at **federal constitutional courts,** starting with the **Supreme Court of the United States.** The United States Supreme Court is the only court explicitly mentioned in the Constitution.

- It was outlined in the Judiciary Act of September 24, 1789, and was organized on February 2, 1790.
- Its membership is fixed by Congress.
- It has had as few as five and as many as ten justices. Since 1869 the Court has had nine members, including a chief justice and eight associate justices.
- Six justices are needed for a quorum.
- The president nominates justices, and appointments are made with the advice and consent of the Senate.

Figure 10.1

Structure of the Federal Court System

State Courts	Federal Courts		
	Article 3 **Constitutional Courts**		**Article 1** **Legislative Courts**
State Court of Last Resort	Supreme Court of the United States Nine justices Original and appellate jurisdiction		U.S. Court of Appeals for the Armed Forces 1950 Five civilian judges Fifteen-year terms
	U.S. Courts of Appeals Thirteen courts 179 judges[1] Six to twenty-eight judges per court Appellate jurisdiction		U.S. Court of Federal Claims 1992 Sixteen judges Fifteen-year terms
			U.S. Court of Veterans Appeals 1988 Three to seven judges Fifteen-year terms
	U.S. District Courts Ninety courts 649 judges[1] Two to twenty-eight judges per court One to four courts per state Original jurisdiction	U.S. Court of International Trade 1980 Nine judges	
			U.S. Tax Court 1969 Nineteen judges Fifteen-year terms
			Territorial Courts Guam 1900 One judge, Ten-year term Virgin Islands 1917 Two judges, Ten-year terms Northern Mariana Islands 1978 One judge, Ten-year term Puerto Rico[2] 1900

[1] Does not include retired senior judges and bankruptcy judges.

[2] Unlike the other territories, Puerto Rico's court is a "constitutional" court so its judges serve life (or "good behavior") terms.

Source: *The United States Government Manual, 1998/99*, Office of the Federal Register, National Archives and Records Administration, Washington, D.C.

- Justices serve life (actually, "good behavior") terms, but they can retire at the age of seventy after serving ten years as a federal judge or at age sixty-five after serving for fifteen years.[14]

The Supreme Court has original and appellate jurisdiction.

- It has original jurisdiction in cases between the United States and a state; in cases between two (or more) states; in cases involving ambassadors, public ministers, or consuls; and in cases brought by a state against citizens of another state, aliens, or a foreign country. Congress has given federal district courts concurrent original jurisdiction in some such cases.
- It has appellate jurisdiction over cases heard in lower federal constitutional courts and some of the federal legislative courts. It can also hear appeals from the state court in which the parties have exhausted all of their state remedies if "substantial federal questions" are at issue.

The **United States courts of appeals** are intermediate appellate courts created by Congress on March 3, 1891. There are thirteen courts of appeals. The United States is divided geographically into twelve judicial circuits, including the District of Columbia. Each state is assigned to one of the circuits. Puerto Rico is assigned to the first circuit, the Virgin Islands to the third, and Guam and the Northern Mariana Islands to the ninth. The United States Court of Appeals for the Federal Circuit is the thirteenth circuit court. It was established in 1982 and has nationwide jurisdiction based on subject matter. Each circuit is traditionally headed by a Supreme Court justice who is said to be "riding circuit." Since the latter years of the nineteenth century, their actual participation in circuit court matters has been nominal. Except for the District of Columbia, judges must be residents of their assigned circuits. Each circuit court has a chief judge who is customarily the most senior judge under the age of sixty-five at the time of his or her assumption of the post. The chief judge may serve in this capacity for seven years. Each court has between six and twenty-eight judges. Usually, three judges sit to decide cases, but a quorum is two. Occasionally, the entire membership sits *en banc.* These are appellate courts, and proceedings are based on records established in lower courts.[15]

The Judiciary Act of 1789 established **United States district courts,** trial courts with general federal jurisdiction in civil and criminal cases. They are sometimes described as the workhorses of the federal court system. There are ninety district courts in the fifty states, the District of Columbia, Guam, Puerto Rico, the Virgin Islands, and the Northern Mariana Islands. Each state has at least one district court, and larger states have as many as four. Each district court has from two to twenty-eight judges. Customarily, one judge sitting with a jury presides over trials, unless a jury trial has been validly waived. The senior district judge who is under seventy years of age, who has been in office at least one year, and who has not previously held the position, serves as chief judge for a seven-year term. Congress has provided that, in some important instances, cases will be heard by special three-judge district courts. Such courts consist of two district judges and one circuit court judge. Decisions of three-judge district courts can be appealed directly to the U.S. Supreme Court.[16]

U.S. district courts have original jurisdiction only. Their jurisdiction extends to cases involving violations of federal laws; civil actions arising under the Constitution, federal laws or treaties; and cases involving citizens of different states. In civil suits the amount in controversy must exceed $75,000.[17] District courts also have jurisdiction over maritime, admiralty, and prize cases and can review and enforce actions of certain federal agencies. District courts have concurrent original jurisdiction with the U.S. Supreme Court over cases involving ambassadors and some cases in which a state is a party.

Other federal courts include the United States Court of International Trade, the United States Court of Federal Claims, the United States Court of Appeals for the Armed Forces, the United States Tax Court, the United States Court of Veterans Appeals, and territorial courts. All of these courts, with the exception of the United States Court of International Trade, are legislative courts.[18]

Justiciability

To summarize the preceding discussion, the Supreme Court has the power to interpret sometimes vague constitutional provisions. But the Court is weak, or dependent, in several ways.

- Congress established the federal court system itself and has the power to regulate the appellate jurisdiction of these federal courts.
- Courts do not initiate; they react. They must wait for cases to be brought to them before they can offer opinions on legal issues.
- They cannot enforce their own decisions.
- They cannot hear cases unless they have jurisdiction.
- Federal courts can only hear cases involving federal parties or federal questions.

There is more. Not only must a court have jurisdiction to hear a case; the issues themselves must be raised in ways that make them capable of judicial resolution. That is, the issues must be **justiciable.** There are several justiciability standards.

Constitutional courts cannot issue advisory opinions. They can only decide real cases. Before a court can act, it must be presented with a **real case or controversy.** The case must involve two adverse parties. Actual harm must be at issue. The dispute must be real, not contrived or hypothetical. Imagine that two students, Jane and John, read about a new law that Congress enacted. They do not like this law and think that a federal court would declare it unconstitutional if given a chance to review it. To that end they pretend to have a legal dispute involving the law and take their "case" to court. Their plan will not work because they have no real case or controversy. A court would find their dispute to be nonjusticiable.

Furthermore, a court will not deal with a question if the matter has become **moot.** A question is moot if it is too late for a court to provide the remedy being sought. For example, the Supreme Court was asked to render an opinion in an affirmative action case in *DeFunis* v. *Odegaard*.[19] DeFunis claimed that he had been unconstitutionally denied admission to the University of Washington Law School because of a program that gave preference to minority applicants. A lower state court agreed with DeFunis, and the State Supreme Court reversed. By the time the United States Supreme Court heard oral arguments, DeFunis was about to be graduated from law school. The Court observed it was now too late to provide DeFunis the legal remedy he was seeking—a legal education. He had already secured one on his own. The issue had become moot.

Consider another aspect of timing. If your case is moot, you do not have a case *anymore;* if your case lacks **ripeness** or **concreteness,** you do not have a case *yet.* Either way, a court cannot hear it. A court will not hear a case until the issues, facts, and controversy have become ripe, concrete, or fully developed. The controversy cannot be anticipatory or hypothetical. For example, if a student has tentative plans to go to law school some day, the student could not go to court today and ask that all affirmative action programs be declared unconstitutional so that she or he will not face the possibility of being disadvantaged by such a program in the future.

In addition, a court will not hear a case unless a party has **legal standing** to sue. It is not enough to say that you are abstractly interested in some law and would like to challenge its constitutionality. To bring a justiciable controversy to court, you must be able to show that you have suffered some direct injury or have some direct stake in the outcome of a case. If you step off a curb and a bus runs you over, you have suffered a direct injury and could have standing to sue (if not the physical ability to stand up). On the other hand, say you are a taxpayer who read that a new federal bus-testing center has been established in Altoona, Pennsylvania, and that all buses must be shipped to Altoona for a special inspection before they can be driven on the roads. You may object to this federal program, consider it a waste of federal tax dollars, and bring suit as a federal taxpayer. Have you suffered the kind of direct injury necessary to establish legal standing? This question is more difficult. Standing rules for taxpayer suits are more complicated than they are for cases involving physical injury.

Finally, courts will not deal with **political questions.** A political question is a question that the text of the Constitution gives to another branch of the government. Perhaps Congress is assigned constitutional responsibility for the matter in question. A political question is also a question that the court lacks "judicially manageable standards" to answer. The human mind can devise many fascinating questions, but not all of them belong in court. Does God exist? A profound question, to be sure, but a judge lacks judicial standards to supply an answer. Should prayer be allowed in public schools? Another important question, and in this case courts would be able to apply existing judicial standards. Will the Pirates win the World Series? (Don't laugh!) Courts lack judicial standards to answer such a question. However, Is baseball's new collective bargaining agreement legal? Is a question for courts.

Federal courts can only hear cases involving federal parties or federal questions. The issues also must be justiciable. In this sense, courts are **restrained.** However, courts themselves decide whether they have jurisdiction, and they decide whether the issues are justiciable. Justiciability standards can be manipulated to let courts get at cases they want to reach and to avoid cases they would prefer not to hear. For this reason, it is more accurate to speak of judicial **self-restraint.**

The Supreme Court at Work

The Court customarily begins its annual session on the first Monday of October and concludes in late June or early July. Each year the Court is asked to hear more than five thousand cases. In recent years it has been handing down full written and signed opinions in fewer than one hundred. The Supreme Court building was constructed in

Supreme Court courtroom.

© *Franz Jantzen/Collection of the Supreme Court of the United States.*

1935. Prior to that time the Court met in the Capitol. The justices sit behind a high bench of marble and mahogany in black leather, swivel chairs, which are arranged in order of seniority with the chief justice sitting in the center. The senior associate justice sits to the chief justice's immediate right, the second-ranking associate justice sits to the chief justice's left, and so on in declining order of seniority. The justices wear black robes but, unlike British judges, no wigs. Quill pens are placed at counsel tables every day. This fact was reported widely and with irony as the Court prepared to hear oral argument in *Reno* v. *American Civil Liberties Union*—a 1997 case challenging the constitutionality of congressional efforts to combat indecency on the Internet.

When a case is scheduled for consideration, records are sent up from lower courts. Most cases are appeals to lower court decisions. The Supreme Court does no independent fact-finding. It uses the evidence developed in lower courts and concentrates on legal issues. Both sides submit written **briefs** in which they present their arguments. Third parties who are interested in the outcome can also submit *amicus curiae,* or friend-of-the-Court, briefs. In this way interest groups can try to influence the Court's decision.

Oral arguments are heard over seven 2-week sessions from October through April.[20] There is a chance that a persuasive oral argument can sway the justices, but it is unlikely. The justices review written briefs before oral argument and come prepared to ask numerous pointed and probing questions. The pressure on attorneys arguing before the Court is enormous, and they must be prepared to think on their feet. In a speech to the American Bar Association, Chief Justice Rehnquist complained that big shot lawyers (for example, a state attorney general or a senior partner in a law firm) sometimes seize the opportunity to present oral arguments before the Supreme Court, even though they do little work on the cases. In Rehnquist's view "[t]his sort of insouciance offends the Court and can do nothing but harm to the client's case."[21] Rehnquist offered this advice:

> You don't have to be a Clarence Darrow or John W. Davis to successfully argue a case before us. But you do have to be prepared. . . . [Y]ou must expect hypothetical questions posing slightly different factual situations from yours, and be prepared to answer them. . . . You should also know from reading the recent decisions which of the members of the Court are apt to be sympathetic to your position, and which unsympathetic.
>
> You should recognize that questions coming from members of the Court whom you have reason to feel are unsympathetic to your position will not be designed to advance your cause, but will be more likely to be designed to expose perceived shortcomings or fallacies in your reasoning. . . . You are dealing with a Court consisting of nine justices and a concession or answer that pleases one may displease another. You must not shy away from giving answers which the questioner will not like, and you should never give an answer just to please the questioner.[22]

As Justice Felix Frankfurter put it, the Court does not see itself as "a dozing audience for the reading of soliloquies, but as a questioning body, utilizing oral argument as a means for exposing the difficulties of a case with a view to meeting them."[23]

Oral arguments are carefully timed.

- Each side is generally allotted thirty minutes.
- Attorneys stand at a lectern facing the justices. On the lectern are two lights.
- A white light flashes five minutes before time is up.
- When the red light flashes, the attorney is to stop instantly unless the chief justice gives permission to continue.

One of Chief Justice Hughes's law clerks said that Hughes was so strict about time limits that he once stopped a leader of the New York bar in the middle of the word *if.*[24]

On **conference days** the justices meet in an oak-paneled conference room on the second floor, adjacent to the chief justice's office. Following a tradition established by Chief Justice Fuller in 1888, the justices shake hands with one another when they enter the room.[25]

Conference meetings are private. The justices are not accompanied by their clerks. No records of discussions are kept. If a clerk brings a message to the conference room,

ustice Sandra Day O'Connor was questioning an attorney during an oral argument in April 1994.
Justice Ruth Bader Ginsburg, then a freshman on the Court, interrupted with her own question. "Excuse me!" snapped O'Connor, "Just let me finish." The next day Ginsburg interrupted Justice Anthony Kennedy. Several justices complained to Chief Justice Rehnquist about Ginsburg.

Like all human institutions, the Supreme Court has informal norms. One seems to be that while it is perfectly acceptable to interrupt attorneys delivering their oral arguments, one should never interrupt another justice in open court.

by custom the most junior justice serves as "doorkeeper" and retrieves the message. This way the justices can deliberate candidly and argue vigorously without fear of undermining public esteem. Legend has it that when Justice Black lay on his bed near death, he summoned his son and instructed him to burn his private papers to preserve the Court's secrets. Others have not been so circumspect. Some justices have published their papers upon retirement. In researching their book *The Brethren*, Bob Woodward and Scott Armstrong interviewed all the justices with the exception of then-Chief Justice Burger. They interviewed 170 former law clerks and somehow gained access to some of Justice Brennan's private notes and diaries.[26] These sources provide a glimpse into the conference meeting.

The chief justice customarily speaks first, identifying key issues and stating a personal position on them. The chief justice sets the agenda for the discussion. Next the associate justices give their views; they speak in *descending* order of seniority. The justices then cast a tentative **vote** in *ascending* order of seniority, with the least senior associate justice voting first, the most senior associate justice voting eighth, and the chief justice voting last.[27]

The next step is to assign **opinion writing.** If the chief justice is in the majority, the chief justice can personally write the Court's opinion or can assign it to another member of the majority. However, an exception is the tradition of letting every newcomer to the Court select the first opinion she or he will write. If the chief justice is on the minority side, the senior associate justice in the majority can write it him- or herself or can assign it to another member of the majority.

- Assignments are formally made by sending a note to the prospective author a few days after the conference meeting.
- Opinions are drafted and circulated to fellow justices for comments.

*U*nanimity was important when the Court ordered schools to desegregate in *Brown v. Board of Education* (1954). It was also important when President Nixon threatened to refuse to comply with a less than definitive decision ordering him to turn over subpoenaed tapes.

Unanimity was also important in 1993 when the Supreme Court considered a high-profile sexual harassment claim under Title 7 of the Civil Rights Act of 1964. In 1987 Teresa Harris quit her job in Nashville, Tennessee, claiming that her boss had sexually harassed her. Justice Clarence Thomas, whose own confirmation hearings nearly derailed following Anita Hill's charges of sexual harassment, did not speak during oral argument, nor did he write any portion of the opinion. He did join his fellow justices in a nine-to-zero vote in Harris's favor, however. Kathryn Abrams, a law professor at Cornell University remarked, "By acting quickly and unanimously, the Court clearly intended to send a message to the American public that the legal system will take women's claims of sexual harassment seriously."

- Numerous drafts may be produced in an attempt to pick up additional votes.
- If a draft is sufficiently persuasive, a justice might even switch his or her vote from the conference meeting.[28]

A **majority opinion** explains why the Court decided as it did. It serves as a guide for lower courts and lawyers and can be made on broad or narrow grounds. For this reason, the writer of the majority opinion is critical.

- A **concurring opinion** can be authored by a justice who agrees with the outcome of the case but for different reasons. Such justices may choose to go on record with their own reasons for reaching a decision. Concurring opinions can influence future opinions and can also lessen the impact of the majority opinion.
- **Dissenting opinions** are minority opinions. They are written by justices on the losing side and have no legal force. They may influence a future Court, however, if tomorrow's Court decides to overrule today's decision.[29] They can also serve to undermine the power of the majority opinion.
- **Unanimous opinions** have the most legitimacy and power. If the Court is divided and disappointed parties can point to dissenting and concurring justices

who are close to their position, their compliance may be reluctant. On the other hand, if the Court is united behind a clear and forceful opinion, noncompliance is out of the question.

On **opinion day,** tied in with oral argument days, the Court announces its decisions. Written opinions covering the Court's reasoning are filed with the court clerk. Starting with the junior justices and proceeding in ascending order of seniority, the justices deliver their opinions, in either summary or verbatim fashion. Sometimes only the decision is announced by the chief justice or the author. Most commonly, the author of the majority opinion simply summarizes the Court's decision.[30]

Selection and Appointment of Federal Judges

Unlike some state judges, federal judges are not elected. They are appointed by the president with the advice and consent of the Senate. Why? Two reasons:

1. The Constitution places limits on popular majorities. In protecting the rights of unpopular minorities, federal judges will sometimes interpret the Constitution in ways that frustrate the majority of the day. We appoint federal judges so they will have the **independence** needed to interpret such constitutional provisions objectively.
2. Federal judges need **technical skills, specialized training,** and **knowledge of legal precedents** to decide cases. Being able to win an election is not a sufficient credential.

So is the judicial selection system entirely based on merit? No. Partisan and other **political considerations** influence presidents and senators during the selection process. More than 90 percent of the time, presidents nominate members of their own party to federal judgeships. If merit were the sole selection criterion, this would not be the case.

Here is how the appointment process works at the **district court** level. When a vacancy occurs, local party officials (the president's party, that is) send a list of suggested nominees to the deputy attorney general of the United States. The Justice Department screens potential nominees for the president and then negotiates behind the scenes with senators from the state where the vacancy occurred, paying particular attention to senators who are members of the president's party.

- Because the district court in question is in a single state, senators from that state have a special stake in the appointment.
- Because of the custom of **senatorial courtesy,** other senators will defer to the home-state senators in the expectation that they will return this consideration when roles are reversed.
- In this way senators are able to reward some of their supporters with judicial appointments.

The **FBI** conducts background investigations, the nominee is formally named, and the **Senate Judiciary Committee** conducts public hearings at which the nominee and other interested parties testify. The **American Bar Association's Standing** udicial independence has been under attack. In January 1996 Federal Judge Harold Baer Jr., a Clinton appointee, ruled that police lacked probable cause to search two duffel bags. The bags contained eighty pounds of cocaine and heroin worth about $4 million. Republican presidential candidate, Bob Dole, immediately called for Judge Baer's impeachment. President Clinton's press secretary, Mike McCurry, suggested that Judge Baer should reverse his ruling or resign. Judge Baer reversed his ruling. Chief Justice Rehnquist observed that while criticism may be warranted at times, calls for resignation and impeachment should never come from responsible officials when they simply disagree with a judicial decision.[31]

In a related vein H. Lee Sarokin, who had been appointed to the U.S. Court of Appeals for the Third Circuit by President Clinton, retired after Senator Dole targeted him for criticism.

Representative Tom DeLay, the Republican majority whip from Texas, urged Congress to impeach federal judges whose decisions he disliked. Back in 1805 some congressmen critical of Justice Chase's opinions sought to remove him from the Supreme Court. Chief Justice John Marshall wrote to Chase that "[t]he present doctrine seems to be that a Judge giving a legal opinion contrary to the opinion of the legislature is liable to impeachment." Representative DeLay cited this letter in the apparent belief that Marshall's position supported his own. In fact, Marshall strongly opposed that effort as a threat to judicial independence.[32]

In 1997 the American Bar Association's Commission on Separation of Powers and Judicial Independence said that judges had been subjected to "misleading criticism, demagogic attacks and threats of impeachment from representatives of both political branches in both political parties." The commission, chaired by Edward W. Madiera Jr. of Philadelphia, said that "[a] public that does not trust its judges to exercise sound, even-handed judgment will look upon judicial independence . . . as a problem to be eradicated, rather than a virtue to be preserved."

What do you think?

Committee on the Federal Judiciary supplies evaluations. The committee, established in 1946, rates nominees as exceptionally well qualified, well qualified, qualified, not qualified, or not qualified because of age. These ratings can provide important leverage because it is politically difficult to support a nominee rated "not qualified" by the American Bar Association.[33] Following Judiciary Committee confirmation hearings, the full Senate votes on the nomination. Appointment requires a majority vote.

At the **United States Court of Appeals** level, individual Senators have relatively less power than at the district court level. The reason is that appellate courts generally span several states. The third circuit, for example, includes Pennsylvania, Delaware, New Jersey, and the Virgin Islands. When this court has a vacancy, senators from three states have a direct stake in the appointment. The influence of an individual senator is more diffuse or widely shared at this level. Otherwise, the process is similar. The president nominates a candidate, the Judiciary Committee holds hearings, and the full Senate votes on the appointment.

Individual senators have the least power in filling **Supreme Court** vacancies. Because the Supreme Court serves the entire nation, *all* senators have an equal stake in an appointment. Several factors influence presidents when they nominate someone for a seat on the Supreme Court. **Party,** once again, is a factor. Currently, only Justices Ginsburg and Breyer were appointed by a Democrat, and both were appointed by President Clinton. Justice Ginsburg succeeded Justice White, who had been appointed by President Kennedy in 1962. White noted that he wanted to delay his retirement until another Democratic president would have a chance to name his successor.

Personal friendship can also play a role. If other factors are equal or nearly so, a president might prefer to nominate a friend. Friendship is difficult to measure, but it probably influenced President Kennedy when he nominated White and President Johnson when he nominated his long-time friend Abe Fortas.

Sometimes presidents use the **EGG test**—they try to account for ethnic, gender, and geographical balance. In theory, such considerations should not matter. One need not be black to judge fairly in a race discrimination case, nor need one be female to judge fairly in a sex discrimination case. In practice, however, knowing that black, female, and other justices are on the Court may help some people accept the legitimacy of the Court's decisions. In light of the Court's institutional weakness and the pressures placed on candidates during presidential campaigns, such considerations are relevant.

President Johnson appointed the first black justice, Thurgood Marshall. Johnson did not deny that Marshall's race was a factor: "I believe it is the right thing to do, the right time to do it, the right man and the right place."[34]

When Marshall retired in 1991, President Bush nominated Clarence Thomas to replace him. When questioned by reporters, Bush insisted that he did not believe in racial quotas, Thomas was the most qualified person for the job, and Thomas's race had nothing to do with the nomination.[35] Bush's claims were greeted with skepticism, and it seems safe to say that there is now a "black seat" on the Supreme Court.

Something to Think About

Before joining the Court, Marshall was a prominent civil rights attorney. He also served as solicitor general of the United States. In both roles he argued frequently before the Court. Such experience was certainly a plus. But there was a downside, too. Justices are expected to avoid conflicts of interest. Justice Marshall found that he had to abstain, or "recuse" himself, frequently during his first term on the Court (1967–1968). In fact, he abstained in thirty-one of the first forty-four formally decided cases of his tenure!

When Justice William O. Douglas retired from the Supreme Court in 1975, President Ford named John Paul Stevens to replace him. Stevens's appointment was widely applauded, but feminists objected that Ford should have nominated a woman.[36] In 1981 President Reagan had his chance and appointed the first woman to the Supreme Court, Sandra Day O'Connor.

Geography sometimes plays a role. President Nixon wanted to appoint a southern conservative justice who would interpret the Constitution strictly. In 1969 he nominated Clement F. Haynsworth Jr. of South Carolina. The Senate rejected the nomination by a vote of fifty-five to forty-five. President Nixon countered by nominating G. Harrold Carswell of Florida. Carswell's nomination was defeated by a vote of fifty-one to forty-five.[37] Nixon later successfully appointed Lewis Powell, a Virginian, to the Court.

Religion can also be a factor. A "Catholic seat" has been held by Chief Justice Roger Taney, and by Justices Edward White, Joseph McKenna, Pierce Butler, Frank Murphy, William Brennan, and, presently, by Antonin Scalia. A "Jewish seat" has been held by Justices Louis Brandeis, Benjamin Cardozo, Felix Frankfurter, Arthur Goldberg, Abe Fortas, and presently, by Ruth Bader Ginsburg.

What about **objective merit**? When questioned, presidents routinely claim that they selected "the most qualified person for the job." When President Hoover was thinking about Oliver Wendell Holmes's successor on the Supreme Court, he was considering religion, geography, and other traditional factors. But professional and popular support for Benjamin Cardozo was overwhelming. Cardozo, New York State Court of Appeals judge, was widely regarded as the only capable successor to the great Justice Holmes. Hoover overcame his initial reluctance and appointed Cardozo to the Court. Observers hailed the appointment as Hoover's most significant act as president. Eventually, he came to agree with this assessment.

Something to Think About

O'Connor's nomination won overwhelming Senate confirmation. Some opposition came from those who questioned her positions on abortion and the Equal Rights Amendment. As a state legislator and state judge in Arizona, she had a public record on such topics. Additional concern was expressed over her lack of previous federal court experience.

The American Bar Association's Committee on the Federal Judiciary stated, in a letter to then-Senate Judiciary Committee Chairman Strom Thurmond, that Mrs. O'Connor meets the "highest standards of judicial temperament and integrity." But the message added, "Her professional experience to date has not been as extensive or challenging as that of some other persons who might be available for appointment to the Supreme Court."

Such a reservation must be kept in perspective. Four members of the Court at the time—Justices Brennan, White, Powell, and Rehnquist—brought no prior federal court experience with them either. As a matter of fact, White, Powell, and Rehnquist lacked even O'Connor's state court experience at the time of their appointments. Her lack of prior federal court experience was not unusual. Perhaps the recommendation said more about the committee than it did about O'Connor.[38]

QuotableQuote

[P]acking the Supreme Court simply can't be done. . . . I've tried it and it won't work. . . . Whenever you put a man on the Supreme Court, he ceases to be your friend.
—**Harry S. Truman**

But merit is not always first and foremost in a president's mind. Instead, the main concern for a president is his perception of the nominee's **real politics.**[39] Presidents can leave a lasting imprint on the nation through their Supreme Court appointments. Consider that William Rehnquist was appointed to the Court as an associate justice by President Nixon in 1971. Although presidents cannot force their appointees to decide cases in a certain way, they can try to guess how their appointees will act on the Supreme Court. They look for appointees who see the law and read the Constitution as they do. They look for judges who share their view of the role of government and the role of the individual. Presidents try to **pack** the Court with like-minded jurists. Presidents Bush and Reagan looked for justices who favored decentralization of the federal government and who took a "pro-life" position on the abortion issue. President Nixon sought "law and order" justices. To those who object that such litmus tests are inappropriate because they require judges to "prejudge" cases, it should be pointed out that none of this behavior is new. President Washington insisted that his appointees support the Jay Treaty and federalism, among other things. Further, despite presidents' best efforts to predict how their appointees will act, sometimes they guess incorrectly.

Teddy Roosevelt was surprised and disappointed when his recent appointee, Justice Holmes, voted against the government's position in a major antitrust case.[40] President Roosevelt complained, "I could carve out of a banana a judge with more backbone than that!"[41]

Evolution and Exercise of Judicial Power

Judicial Review

Article 3 provides that the judicial power of the United States extends to cases involving federal questions or federal parties. Question: *What* "judicial power"? What could federal courts do when a case was brought to them? The framers did not spell it out. Federal judicial power was open-ended.

In 1790 some of the men appointed to serve on the first United States Supreme Court met at the Royal Exchange Building in New York City. The occasion was greeted with pomp, ceremony, and press coverage as the third department of the American republic was preparing to get to work. But only four of the original six appointees showed up.[42] Early chief justices stayed for a short time, usually leaving for perceived greener judicial pastures at the state level. The future was uncertain. There was doubt that the Supreme Court would ever amount to much. But then **John Marshall** became chief justice in 1801, and he remained in that position until his death in 1835. He was succeeded by Roger Taney, who served as chief justice from 1836 through 1864. What happened? The Supreme Court began to realize and develop some rather formidable powers of its own. Chief among these powers was the power of **judicial review.** Judicial review is the power of a court to review the constitutionality of actions taken by other branches and officials when those actions are challenged in a real case that is brought to the Court.

Marbury v. Madison

The term *judicial review* is not found in the Constitution. Chief Justice Marshall asserted or created the power of judicial review in the landmark case *Marbury* v. *Madison.*[43] There were state court precedents for judicial review. Alexander Hamilton spoke favorably of it *The Federalist*, Number 78. Lower federal courts had previously reviewed congressional legislation. But *Marbury* v. *Madison* marked the first time that the Supreme Court clearly reviewed and invalidated an act of Congress on grounds that it violated the Constitution.

First some background. In the late 1790s two major political parties competed on the national level.

- The Federalists—including people like John Adams, Alexander Hamilton, and John Marshall—generally favored a strong national government.
- The Republicans—including people like Thomas Jefferson and James Madison—generally stressed states rights.

The Federalists controlled the presidency and Congress. Political relations between the two parties were strained, at best. In the November 1800 elections, Jefferson defeated Adams for the presidency, and the Republicans took control of Congress from the Federalists. Adams and his fellow Federalists did not have to leave office until March 1801. Jefferson would not be inaugurated until March 4, 1801.[44] The Federalists decided to make the most of their remaining time in power.

Congress passed the **Judiciary Act of 1801,** which established a number of new judgeships. Reasoning that they had lost control of the elected branches, the Federalists hoped to stock the judiciary with loyal partisans. In the closing days of his administration, President Adams tried to fill these newly created vacancies. He was still signing commissions on the eve of Jefferson's inauguration—hence the term **midnight judges.** One of Adams's late appointments was that of his secretary of state, John Marshall, to become chief justice of the United States Supreme Court. **William Marbury** was another of Adams's late appointees. He was named a justice of the peace for the District of Columbia. Adams signed Marbury's commission, but Secretary of State Marshall failed to deliver it. When Jefferson assumed office, he instructed his Secretary of State, James Madison, to withhold Marbury's undelivered commission.

The Republican Congress then repealed the Judiciary Act of 1801 and turned the impeachment power against some sitting Federalist judges. Marbury filed suit asking the Supreme Court to issue a **writ of mandamus** to force Madison to deliver the commission.[45] **Section 13** of the **Judiciary Act of 1789** authorized the Supreme Court to issue such writs on *original jurisdiction.* Marbury used Section 13 to bring his case to the Supreme Court. It was clear that President Jefferson would refuse to comply with a decision ordering his administration to give Marbury the commission. Further, it was widely assumed that if the Court issued such an order, the Republicans would try to impeach the new chief justice, John Marshall. On the other hand, if the young Court backed down in the face of such intimidating political forces, it might never recover its credibility.

Marshall wrote that the Court faced three questions. *First, did Marbury have a legal right to the commission?* The commission had been signed and sealed by President Adams, but it had never been delivered. Marshall answered that Marbury did, in fact, have a right to the commission. *Second, did Marbury have a legal remedy?* Marshall answered that he did, reasoning that where there is a legal right, there must be a corresponding legal remedy. *Third, was Marbury's appropriate legal remedy a writ of mandamus to be issued by the United States Supreme Court on original jurisdiction?* Marshall answered that whereas Marbury had a legal remedy, this was not it! Why not? Section 13 of the 1789 Judiciary Act supported Marbury's decision to seek this writ from the Supreme Court on **original** jurisdiction. Article 3 of the Constitution, however, only authorizes Congress to regulate the Court's **appellate** jurisdiction. As such Congress overstepped its constitutional authority by expanding the Court's original jurisdiction. Turning to Article 6, Marshall noted that the Constitution is the supreme law of the land. That which is inferior must fall before that which is superior. Therefore, when a congressional statute (Section 13) conflicts with a constitutional provision (Article 3), the Constitution prevails. Declaring that "it is emphatically the province and duty of the judicial department to say what the law is," Marshall concluded that "a law repugnant to the Constitution is void."

In this way Marshall asserted the Court's authority to interpret the Constitution and to determine whether or not challenged legislation was compatible with it. This power is potentially tremendous. Republicans were somewhat mollified by the fact that Marbury did not get his commission. But Marshall pulled off a major coup. He not only managed to avoid what would have been a disastrous showdown with President Jefferson; he established the Court's ability to review and, on occasion, invalidate legislation.[46]

United States v. Nixon

Another dramatic and more recent illustration of the Court's power to review the actions of other public officials occurred during the **Watergate scandals.** On June 17, 1972, seven men working for the Committee to Reelect the President (CREEP) were caught breaking into Democratic national party headquarters at the Watergate apartment and office complex in Washington, D.C. They were trying to install electronic listening devices to gather information about the Democrats' campaign plans. As the investigation proceeded, it seemed that high aides in the Nixon White House—and perhaps even President Nixon himself—had been involved and had attempted to conceal their involvement. The Administration denied such charges, but suspicions mounted that some of these officials were **obstructing justice**—a federal felony.

The Watergate Apartment and Office Complex.

© CORBIS/Adam Woolfitt.

Congressional investigating committees heard testimony from a variety of White House staffers and former aides. John Dean, former counsel to the President, provided some particularly damaging testimony. Dean testified that Nixon had congratulated him for having limited the case to the original seven defendants, discussed executive clemency and the possibility of providing "hush money" for these defendants, knew about the break-in early on, and actively participated in the cover-up. Again, the Administration denied the charges.

Alexander Butterfield then revealed to Congress that President Nixon tape-recorded conversations with his advisors in the Oval Office over the preceding two years. Were his conversations with Dean on tape? Such recordings could help determine who was

President Nixon's chief of staff, H. R. Haldeman, reported in his book, *The Haldeman Diaries*, that Nixon suggested they claim that the Democrats were "bugging" the Republican campaign too. Nixon offered that they might even plant some bugs themselves, find them, and then blame the Democrats!

telling the truth. The Senate investigating committee and Special Prosecutor Archibald Cox subpoenaed several tapes. Citing separation of powers, President Nixon refused to comply. In August 1973 a United States district court ordered Nixon to provide Cox with the tapes. Nixon ordered Cox, who technically worked out of the Justice Department, to drop the matter. When Cox refused, Nixon ordered that he and his staff be fired. Attorney General Elliot Richardson resigned, rather than carry out Nixon's order. Deputy Attorney General William Ruckleshaus was fired when he, too, refused to dismiss Cox. Finally, Solicitor General Robert Bork carried out the President's order on October 20. The press dubbed the episode the **Saturday Night Massacre.**

Widespread public criticism ensued, as did the start of formal **impeachment** proceedings in the House. A new special prosecutor, Leon Jaworski, was brought in, and Nixon agreed to turn over some of the tapes. Two were missing, and one contained a mysterious eighteen-minute gap. Additional **indictments** followed. Attorney General John Mitchell, White House Chief of Staff H. R. Haldeman, and Chief Domestic Advisor John Ehrlichman were among those charged with conspiracy to obstruct justice. Jaworski turned the tapes over to the **House Judiciary Committee** when he was finished with them. The House then subpoenaed forty-two more tapes, and Jaworski subpoenaed sixty-four more for use in preparing for prosecution. Nixon refused to supply them. Instead, in a move he called **Operation Candor,** he released **edited transcripts** of some of the conversations in question. These transcripts only increased public suspicion. At this point Nixon decided to carry questions about Jaworski's subpoena to the Supreme Court.

President Nixon made several arguments involving **separation of powers.** He maintained that a president cannot be forced to comply with a judicial order. One branch of the government lacks authority to give orders to another, coequal branch. Further, Nixon saw the dispute with the special prosecutor as an internal executive branch matter, as a dispute between the president and one of his subordinates. Did such arguments amount to an assertion that the president was above the law? Such a characterization may oversimplify Nixon's position, but such was the political climate at the time. President Nixon also invoked **executive privilege,** claiming that a president must be able to protect the confidentiality of his conversations with his advisors. Otherwise, they would not supply him with the full and candid advice he needs to meet his constitutional responsibility and to execute the laws faithfully.

Although the term *executive privilege* does not appear in the text of the Constitution, Nixon argued that it is an inherent, constitutionally based presidential power.[47]

The Court found Nixon's separation-of-powers arguments to be unpersuasive. However, the Court accepted Nixon's assertion that executive privilege exists and is constitutionally based. Further, although the Court was unwilling to say that this privilege "absolutely" protects the confidentiality of presidential conversations, the justices did agree that the privilege is **presumptive.** That is, in such controversies a court should presume that a president is justified in seeking to protect the confidentiality of conversations with advisors, and the heavier burden should be placed on the person seeking this information to show a specific and compelling need for it. In the present case the Court found that Jaworski had demonstrated such a need for the tapes and had successfully overcome the presumption that operated in Nixon's favor. Jaworski was able to show that the subpoenaed evidence was necessary to ensure that the defendants received their constitutionally guaranteed fair trials. Nixon was ordered to turn over the tapes, as the Court concluded that the president's "generalized assertion of privilege must yield to the demonstrated, specific need for evidence in a pending criminal trial."[48]

A few days after the Court's decision, the House Judiciary Committee approved three articles of impeachment against the President. As Nixon began to comply, it was evident that he knew about the break-in from the start and had misled his defenders. Impeachment by the full House seemed imminent. Before such a vote could be taken, Nixon **resigned** from office. He was **pardoned** by his successor, Gerald Ford.[49]

The Accountability of Federal Judges: Is Judicial Review Democratic?

Federal judges are not elected. They are not directly accountable to the public. Yet they possess great power, including the power to say what the law is. Critics make the following arguments:

- Federal judges have more power than they should in a democratic system;[50] the Supreme Court has set itself up as a "super legislature" that forces liberal decisions on the American people.
- The Court's decisions in the areas of school busing, prayer in public schools, and abortion could never have been approved through more "democratic" processes.
- Congress should remove the Court's jurisdiction over certain controversial social policy questions.
- Federal judges should be elected and should serve limited terms.
- Judges who act counter to the will of popular majorities be impeached.
- Congress should be able to overturn Supreme Court decisions.
- The public should be able to vote on whether or not Supreme Court decisions are correct.

In short, such critics argue that in a democracy, policy must reflect the will of the majority. When federal courts declare laws that had majority support unconstitutional,

In the wake of the Watergate scandal, twenty-one of Nixon's aides were convicted and sent to prison for their crimes. With the exception of G. Gordon Liddy, who was particularly uncooperative with investigators and who served fifty-two months, these men served prison terms ranging from four to twelve months. As noted, President Nixon himself received a pardon.

Nine years after Nixon's resignation, Frank Wills—the security guard who discovered the Watergate break-in—was arrested for shoplifting in Augusta, Georgia. Unemployed at the time, he had stolen a pair of shoes for his son. Unlike "the president's men," Mr. Wills received the maximum sentence: twelve months in prison for stealing a $12 pair of shoes.

they are acting in an undemocratic fashion. If democracy means majority rule, then judicial review by unelected judges is undemocratic.

One way to respond is to argue that federal judges *are* accountable to the public in indirect ways.

- Although we do not elect federal judges, elected officials—the president and senators—make judicial appointment decisions on our behalf.
- Further, federal judges undergo the same political socialization processes as the rest of us. In the process an "inner check" should develop that will prevent them from usurping powers reserved to other branches.
- Even more important, federal judges must be ever mindful of their institutional weakness, of their need to preserve their legitimacy and to protect the credibility of their decisions. In this vein we can expect federal judges to refrain from being too creative in their decisions for fear of injuring their credibility.

In sum, the common theme of these arguments is that judicial independence has been overstated and that unelected judges are, nevertheless, accountable to the public.

A very different kind of response is possible, however. A strong argument can be made that democracy means more than majority rule. It also means respect for the constitutional rights of all people. If federal judges are not directly accountable to the public, it is acceptable; they should *not* be directly accountable to public opinion. They are first and foremost accountable to the Constitution and to the democratic values it protects. The Constitution places limits on popular majorities. The Constitution signals that all individuals and minorities—no matter how unpopular they prove to be—have certain fundamental rights that must be recognized. Because federal judges interpret constitutional provisions protecting individuals and minorities against a majority, it would not make sense to make these judges answerable to the same majority. As

Justice Brennan pointed out, the Court must be able to review and interpret the Constitution. Otherwise, the Constitution will fall captive to "the anachronistic views of long-gone generations." Although it is generally desirable for public policy to be approved by popular majorities, unbridled majoritarianism will not do: "It is the very purpose of a Constitution—and particularly of the Bill of Rights—to declare certain values transcendent, beyond the reach of temporary political majorities."[51]

Key Terms

Conclusions

Informed Criticism

Many Americans are critical of their cars. They turn the key, but the car won't start. They try to turn the wheel, but the tires remain locked in place. They pull into a gas station and can't find the hood-release lever so they can check their oil. Is there something wrong with the car? *Maybe.* But maybe we have just become too impatient to read our owner's manuals. If we took the time to learn about our cars, they would serve us better. Does this mean that you have to learn how to overhaul your own engine? Of course not. But you should be sufficiently familiar with your car's mechanical systems to know what a flashing warning light on your dashboard means. Otherwise, prepare to call a tow truck.[1]

1992 Pontiac Bonneville S.E.—they run better if you read the owner's manual.

Courtesy, Joe Melusky.

Many American citizens are also critical of their political system and politicians. Is something wrong with the political system? *Probably.*[2] With some politicians? *Probably.* With all politicians? *No. Atlantic Monthly* Washington editor and former speech writer for President Carter, James Fallows, spoke at a *Providence Journal*/Brown University Public Affairs Conference entitled "Democracy in America: Does It Still Work?" Fallows blamed the media for many of democracy's problems, labeling the press as "sand in the gears" of the American political machinery.[3] While aiming some criticisms at the American educational system, foreign trade policies, and racial problems,

QuotableQuote

Politics is broken.
—Senator Bill Bradley

Fallows said that the press "has made the whole process harder than it needs to be."[4] Fallows spoke about the difference between skepticism and cynicism, citing a *Times/Mirror* poll that found that journalists "loved" politics and politicians. But their stories, in Fallows's opinion, did not reflect any of that love. "The stories were all about the disorder, the charlatanism, the braggadocio and the vanity. The message gotten across to the readers and viewers time and again is that this is ugly, this is corrupt."[5]

Fallows noted that political coverage in the news media tends toward "an unnatural and destructive emphasis on the process of politics rather than on its underlying substance."[6] He cited the reaction of "horse race" obsessed reporters to New Jersey Senator Bill Bradley's announcement that he would not seek reelection. Instead of paying attention to Bradley's criticisms of the political system, reporters asked, "Are you going to start a third party? Are you possibly slamming Bill Clinton? What about Colin Powell?"[7]

Speaking at the John F. Kennedy School of Government at Harvard University, Senator Bradley delivered a speech entitled "Freeing Democracy from the Power of Money."[8] Bradley was not content to point out that "politics is broken" and leave it at that; he offered a plan to effect repairs and outlined his proposal for reshaping the way in which political campaigns are financed. A summary of Senator Bradley's remarks is reprinted here.

Senator Bill Bradley
"Giving Elections Back to Citizens"
Summary Provided by Senator Bradley

This proposal would restore democracy to American elections by removing *all* the corrupting sources of money in campaigns and giving voters direct control over how much money is spent in a Senate election. It would not force taxpayers to fund politics through public financing, but it would equalize funding among candidates and provide free media time. Candidates would have to compete on their ideas, and once elected, to serve all their constituents without favoring contributors.

1. Constitutional amendment: Amend the Constitution to clarify that Congress has the power to set limits on contributions and expenditures in support of, or in opposition to, any candidate for Federal office. The spending limits implicit in the legislative proposal directly confront the Supreme Court's ruling in *Buckley* v. *Valeo* equating political money with free speech. If the Court will not reconsider this ruling, this amendment will correct it.

2. Tax check-off: Add a new Senate General Election Campaign Fund line to each tax return, and allow all filers to designate between $1 and $5,000 as an add-on to taxes. Funds added-on by taxpayers in each state will be designated for Senate elections in that state only.

3. Distribution of funds among candidates: Each Senate election year, one-half of the fund will be divided among all qualified candidates after the nomination process has been completed in each state. (The remaining half will be reserved for the next Senate election.) All qualifying party candidates and independents will receive an equal share. To qualify, a party or an independent candidate must obtain signatures of 5% of all registered voters in the state. Parties that have received 10% of the vote in two of the previous four Senate elections automatically qualify. No candidate may accept or spend funds from any source other than the common fund. All candidates must participate in at least two debates with all other candidates.

4. Broadcast time: Each broadcast licensee must make available to each eligible Senate candidate two hours of free broadcast time, of which at least one hour must be during prime time. Each broadcaster must make time available to candidates in all states in its broadcast area. Free time must be made available during the 90 days preceding the election. Appearances during news or public service programs will not count. Free broadcast time will be allocated in segments of 1–30 minutes, at the candidates' choice. The Federal Election Commission will also be required to develop a program of public service announcements providing basic information about voting requirements, voter registration, and election dates and locations, which broadcasters may carry in fulfillment of their basic public service requirements.

5. Nominating process: Candidates for any party's Senate nomination may accept only contributions of $100 or less. No candidate for a party's nomination may spend more than 50% of the total amount that will be available in the total fund for candidates in the general election, as estimated by the state on

January 1 of the election year. A candidate for nomination who did not comply with these rules would be ineligible for all funding and free broadcast time in the general election.

6. Party money/soft money: Contributions to state and national party organizations will be limited to $1,000 from individuals.

7. Independent expenditures: Broadcast licensees that accept independent expenditures for advertisements that make reference to any Senate candidate must provide equal, free time to allow any candidate mentioned negatively in the original ad to respond. If a candidate is mentioned positively, the licensee must allow all opponents the same amount of time to respond.[9]

Bradley focused directly on Senate campaign reform, but his remarks about the corrupting influence of political money could be extended to other campaigns as well. By banning outside contributions, his proposals would reduce the influence of wealthy contributors, political action committees, and "bundling" small contributions to evade existing PAC limits. Spending limits would reduce the advantage of wealthy candidates. Other reforms would target out-of-state money (money in the common fund would come from in-state taxpayers) and money funneled through party committees. Free airtime and mandatory participation in public debates would increase the visibility of all candidates.

Perhaps the American people are experiencing a crisis in confidence about our political institutions, a widespread feeling that the political system *has* broken down. Campaign reform *is* necessary. But campaign reform is difficult, messy, and complicated. Perhaps part of the appeal of term limits is that they are a simple kind of campaign reform. Support for term limits may reflect the sentiment that the political system has broken down. If so, the irony is that many Americans have concluded that to save democracy, we must curtail democracy. To ensure that elected representatives remain responsive to us, we must limit their terms, thereby limiting our own electoral options. Sensible? Robert W. Merry wrote that

> when democracies fade, it isn't usually because of external forces or cataclysmic events or tyrannies swooping down upon a people. Usually it is because the governed conclude that their government no longer works, that it needs to be replaced by something more efficient and workable even if it is less democratic. That's why it's important to consider what term limits reflect. They reflect just one tiny step down the road toward the idea that the salvation of democracy is less democracy. And if the problems of our governing system grow and voter frustrations expand, we can expect more and larger steps down that same road.[10]

If we are dissatisfied with how our political machinery is operating, we face some decisions. Will a tune-up suffice? Is a major overhaul in order? Or has the time come to declare the system irreparably broken and start shopping for a new one? Before answering, have we done our homework? Have we accurately diagnosed our current problems? Have we thoroughly researched the alternatives. As we comparison shop, are we aware of the costs—both apparent and hidden? In short, have we spent enough time learning how our political system operates? If we put in the time to become n 1998 the National Constitution Center released the results of its annual survey prior to Constitution Week, September 17–23, marking the 211th anniversary of the signing of the United States Constitution. The survey compared teenagers' knowledge of the Constitution to their knowledge of pop culture. The survey revealed that more teens can name the Three Stooges than can name the three branches of the government (59 percent to 41 percent). More know the Fresh Prince of Bel-Air than know the chief justice of the Supreme Court (94.7 percent to 2.2 percent). More know which city has the zip code 90210 than know the city in which the Constitution was written (75 percent to 25 percent). More know the father of the computer company Microsoft than know the father of the Constitution (58.3 percent to 1.8 percent). More know the name of the town in which Bart Simpson "lives" than know the town where Abraham Lincoln lived for most of his adult life (74.3 percent to 12.2 percent). More know what "The Club" protects than know what the Fifth Amendment protects (63.7 percent to 25 percent).[11]

"These results are alarming for everyone who cares about the future of our democracy," said Philadelphia Mayor Edward G. Rendell, Chairman of the National Constitution Center. "The Constitution doesn't work by itself. It depends on active, informed citizens. And that's who these kids are: our future citizens."[12]

functionally informed, our political system may serve us better. Informed political criticism is healthy; uninformed criticism is destructive.

This "owner's manual" for the American political system has emphasized the idea that the rules of the political game are not neutral. The electoral college. Congressional apportionment and districting practices. The seniority system. Term limits. Rules affect the distribution of political power—who has it and who doesn't. Rules operate to the advantage of certain parties and to the disadvantage of others. Similarly, reforms generally shift such advantages and disadvantages. It is prudent to evaluate the claims of reform proponents carefully. What will *they* get out of their reforms? What will *you* get out of their reforms? What will *the nation* get out of these reforms? Don't go along until you have asked these questions and received satisfactory answers.

Informed political criticism requires a basic understanding of rules and structures. We have seen that the design of the American political system separates, checks, and balances power. The virtue of such a system is **stability** and **safety.** It is difficult to disrupt the status quo in such a system, and it is difficult to abuse power without being contested by others who have power. On the other hand, such a system can be **sluggish, slow-moving,** and **prone to gridlock** when not faced with a crisis. Such apparent inefficiencies can be frustrating. But before you angrily vent these frustrations and call for streamlining, think things through. Think about why these problems exist. Think about the eventual consequences of your own suggestions. Think about whether these problems are really "problems" after all. A mechanical device that prevents an intoxicated driver from being able to drive his or her car immediately is a problem

The U.S. Constitution on display at the National Archives.

© Reuters/Anthony Hayward/Archive Photos.

from that would-be driver's point of view. When viewed from a broader societal perspective, however, maybe some built-in delays are good.

Question: Should You Care about Politics?

We have seen that many citizens don't care about politics. Since 1966 the Higher Education Research Institute at the University of California at Los Angeles has conducted an annual survey of college freshmen. The percentage of freshmen indicating that "keeping up to date with political affairs" is important has decreased over time. In 1998 only 25.9 percent of students saw such political awareness as important, as compared to 29.4 percent in 1996 and a record high of 57.8 percent in 1966.[13]

The story is much the same for the general public. In the 1996 presidential election, *98.6 million eligible voters did not vote.* Ninety-eight point six may be a normal temperature for a healthy adult, but it is difficult to believe that 98.6 million nonvoters is a signal of democratic health!

As citizens we have democratic rights. But we also have obligations and responsibilities.[14] Preservation of the democracy's electoral machine requires that citizens vote and that they vote in a reasonably informed way. If there are problems with the politicians and the processes, election day is an opportunity to express our displeasure. Vote against the incumbent. Write in a candidate of your own choosing. Write in your own name if you prefer! If you don't participate, some people will interpret your noninvolvement as satisfaction with the status quo. If that is untrue, *say so.* Why vote? Because the politician you hate hopes you will stay home.

Remember that whether you care about the political system or not, it can—and does—affect you. Political leaders can build new roads, change the speed limit, and affect the availability and price of gas. They can cut your student loans and send you to war. If you don't vote, they will be more likely to cut *your* program than someone else's when the time comes to save money. And if you don't vote, they won't even have to tailor their behavior with an eye toward anticipating how you *might* react. Without the voters, there are no reactions to anticipate.

What Difference Can an Individual Make?

If you think you can't make a difference, then you can't. It becomes a self-fulfilling prophecy. If you think you can't make a difference, you won't try. There is nothing that the folks in city hall like to hear more than people in the street saying, "You can't fight city hall." That statement is music to their ears because people who think they

QuotableQuote

Things don't just happen. They are made to happen.
—John F. Kennedy

can't fight city hall, won't try to stand up for themselves. They won't make phone calls to public officials. They won't write letters. They won't talk to their neighbors and attend public meetings. They won't call reporters at the local newspaper and television station to talk about concerns. They won't vote, and they won't inform their friends of city hall developments and encourage those friends to vote in bloc fashion. The smaller the town, the more influential the individual can be. But individuals who believe they can't fight city hall, won't try.[15]

Democracy works only if citizens are interested, informed, concerned, and attentive. It works best when citizens are skeptical rather than cynical, questioning rather than disillusioned. It is true that you don't have to pay close attention to political affairs. You don't have to understand what is going on in the political arena. You have a right to such choices, to choose ignorance over awareness and impotence over power. But it is also true that you don't have to enjoy the privilege of living in a political system where public officials must respond to your questions and challenges.

Recall that as Benjamin Franklin left the constitutional convention, he was asked to describe the system that the framers had devised. He explained that it was an indirect democracy, or a "republic." He then added, "It's a republic, if you can keep it."

It's time for you to respond to Mr. Franklin. Can you keep it?

As a citizen you have a right to speak and a right to complain, but you have a responsibility to do so reasonably and intelligently.

You don't have to know how to rebuild your car's engine, but you should know that you must use the clutch when you shift gears in a car with a five-speed transmission. You don't have to know how to change your own oil, but you should know that your car needs oil to run properly. Similarly, you don't have to follow the details of public policy debates on a full-time basis, but you should have a basic understanding of political developments in areas that are most relevant to you. Staying informed is the only way are to keep the political system out of the breakdown lane. Newspapers, television news, C-SPAN, and web sites make political information readily available. Becoming functionally informed does not take a great deal of effort.

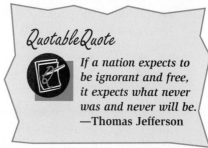

QuotableQuote

If a nation expects to be ignorant and free, it expects what never was and never will be.
—**Thomas Jefferson**

Key Terms

functionally informed	262	sluggish	263
stability	263	slow-moving	263
safety	263	prone to gridlock	263

Appendix:

In This Section

This section includes a "minichapter" on **public policy.** It also includes the **Declaration of Independence** (1776), the **United States Constitution** (1787), and selections from *The Federalist Papers.* Edited excerpts from *The Federalist* are included for your convenience. If you are interested in the full text of *The Federalist Papers,* you can access them at the following web sites:

http://lcweb2.loc.gov/const/mdbquery.html
http://www.mcs.net/ ~ knautzr/fed/fedpaper.html
http://www.law.ou.edu/ushist.html

The Federalist Papers were published in New York state newspapers in 1787 and 1788. These eighty-five letters were written by Alexander Hamilton, James Madison, and John Jay in an attempt to persuade New York citizens to support ratification of the Constitution. These letters remain one of the best sources for understanding what the framers of the Constitution had in mind.

In *The Federalist,* **Number 1,** Hamilton explained the reasons for writing *The Federalist Papers.*

James Madison is sometimes regarded as the architect of the American political system. In this sense *The Federalist,* **Number 10** can be seen as his blueprint. Here he discussed the problem of factions and ways to combat tyranny.

In *The Federalist,* **Number 51,** Madison elaborated and outlined a series of structural checks and balances to guard against the abuse of political power.

In *The Federalist,* **Number 69,** Hamilton argued against the fear that the president would become an American king. Instead, he suggested that the presidency was modeled after the governorship of New York. In *The Federalist,* **Number 70,** he maintained that a single president was preferable to an executive committee or council.

In *The Federalist,* **Number 78,** Hamilton predicted that the judiciary would be the "least dangerous" branch of the national government.

In *The Federalist,* **Number 84,** Hamilton argued unsuccessfully against the need for a written bill of rights. Hamilton contended that the Constitution already provided adequate protection for civil rights and liberties. Furthermore, he claimed that a written bill of rights might prove dangerous.

appendix

Minichapter,
Public Policy

Introduction

What is **public policy**? Hugh Heclo states that "policy is a course of action intended to accomplish some end. . . . [but] the term policy needs to be able to embrace both what is intended and what occurs as a result of the intention."[1] Charles Jones reserves the term *policy* for what is found in "studying government action on a public problem."[2] Theodore Lowi and Benjamin Ginsberg define public policy as "an officially expressed intention backed by a sanction, and that sanction can be a reward or a punishment."[3]

Public policy is one way the political system responds to forces brought to bear upon it from the environment.[4] Policy demands (inputs) come from various sources. Through a series of steps (conversion functions), these demands are transformed into public policies (outputs). These policies affect individuals and groups and they respond (feedback) by supporting the policy or demanding a change. This policy **cycle** continues.

This brief chapter focuses on policy-making **processes**.[5] No single policy-making process applies to all policy areas. Domestic policy making differs from foreign policy making. In the domestic arena we will consider regulatory, distributive (or promotional), and redistributive policies.[6] In the foreign policy arena, we will consider both crisis and noncrisis policy making.[7]

Domestic Policy Making

Regulatory Policies

Regulatory policies state what a person, group, or business may or may not do. Government can try to bring about certain behavior by providing rewards or punishments, carrots or sticks. Regulation is a **stick.** Conduct is mandated. Failure to comply will be met with **civil penalties** (such as fines) or **criminal penalties** (such as imprisonment). Regulatory policies require automobile manufacturers to meet emission-control standards and to install air bags. Regulatory policies prevent a drug company from marketing a diet pill, potency formula, or a new contraceptive until they receive Food and Drug Administration approval.

Regulatory policies distribute advantages and disadvantages to **competing groups** who demand **mutually exclusive policies.** There are clear winners and losers. Will the Federal Aeronautics Administration award a lucrative new air route between two cities to airline A or B? Will Congress eliminate restrictions on offshore oil drilling? Such policies directly distribute specific advantages and disadvantages to particular persons and groups.[8]

Distributive or Promotional Policies

Distributive or **promotional policies** provide benefits to persons or groups under conditions in which they are **not** in direct competition. Promotional policies are **carrots.** Promotional policies include subsidies, contracts, and licenses. **Subsidies** are government grants. They might encourage businesses to operate in inner cities or encourage farmers to reduce production of a certain crop. Government **contracts** are awarded to private firms that agree to conduct certain kinds of research and development or to produce new weapons systems. Government **licenses** permit individuals to practice medicine, to drive cabs, or to do something else that would otherwise be illegal.[9]

When Congress provides funds to build highways, truckers, drivers, and local businesses benefit. When Congress provides funds for a new museum, the modernization of an airport, or a beach-replenishment program following a hurricane, benefits are distributed unit by unit. Demands are **specific** and **nonconflicting.** A university in Texas gets a large research grant, Colorado gets a new dam, and New Hampshire gets a new post office. Everyone appears to be a winner, but appearances can be deceiving. There are always losers. Here the disadvantages include higher taxes for citizens. The advantages, however, are concrete and specific, whereas the disadvantages are diffuse and general.[10]

Redistributive Policies

Redistributive policies assign benefits to one large class at the expense of another class. A genuinely graduated income tax, with higher income persons paying substantially higher taxes than lower income persons, is an example. Here money is collected from one large group and redistributed to another in the form of public services. Winners and losers are **readily identifiable.** Such policy making is marked by **fierce struggle.** The battle lines often pit the rich against the poor, conservatives against liberals, business against labor, and Democrats against Republicans.[11]

Foreign Policy

Crisis Policy Making

A **crisis** presents a challenge to American policy that requires a quick response. The Japanese attack on Pearl Harbor, the placement of Soviet nuclear missiles in Cuba, the taking of American hostages by Iranian militants, and Iraq's invasion of Kuwait are examples. Some group takes hostile actions towards the United States. These actions are perceived as threats to American interests and national security. When such threats arise suddenly, they demand quick responses.

A crisis setting allows little time for debate, reflection, and deliberation. Existing national security policies, strategic alliances, and international relationships set the broad framework within which the governement makes immediate decisions. But the need for **speed,** and even for **secrecy,** increases the president's power. The president determines who will be consulted, for example, officials in the State Department, the Defense Department, and the Central Intelligence Agency. The president may rely on a national security advisor and the National Security Council. Typically, the president turns to an inner circle of close personal advisors and staffers and, if time permits, will broaden the conversations.[12] The president may confer with congressional leaders, foreign governments, the United Nations, or the North Atlantic Treaty Organization. In short, determining how to deal with an external demand on the American political system is largely up to the president.[13]

Noncrisis Policy Making

In a **noncrisis** situation the problem does not arise suddenly and does not demand a rapid response. The absence of a crisis enables a wide variety of persons and institutions to mobilize and express their positions. Foreign governments articulate their viewpoints over time. Diplomats and specialists in the State Department pass along information and recommendations. Members of Congress on foreign relations, armed services, intelligence, and other committees make their views known. Demands come from the military, intelligence agencies, and interest groups. Some groups want the government to raise tariffs to protect American workers. Others support multinational trade agreements to open up new markets and sources of cheap labor. Others promote Israeli security interests in the face of instability in the Middle East. Others seek to impose more restrictions on immigration.[14] In sum, more persons participate in noncrisis policy making than in crisis policy making.

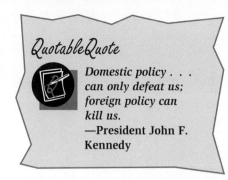

QuotableQuote

Domestic policy . . . can only defeat us; foreign policy can kill us.
—**President John F. Kennedy**

Key Terms

The Declaration of Independence

In Congress, July 4, 1776,

The Unanimous Declaration of the Thirteen United States of America

When, in the course of human events, it becomes necessary for one people to dissolve the political bands which have connected them with another, and to assume, among the powers of the earth, the separate and equal station to which the laws of nature and of nature's God entitle them, a decent respect to the opinions of mankind requires that they should declare the causes which impel them to the separation.

We hold these truths to be self-evident, that all men are created equal; that they are endowed by their Creator with certain unalienable rights; that among these, are life, liberty, and the pursuit of happiness. That, to secure these rights, governments are instituted among men, deriving their just powers from the consent of the governed; that, whenever any form of government becomes distructive of these ends, it is the right of the people to alter or to abolish it, and to institute a new government, laying its foundation on such principles, and organizing its powers in such form, as to them shall seem most likely to effect their safety and happiness. Prudence, indeed, will dictate that governments long established, should not be changed for light and transient causes; and, accordingly, all experience hath shown, that mankind are more disposed to suffer, while evils are sufferable, than to right themselves by abolishing the forms to which they are accustomed. But, when a long train of abuses and usurpations, pursuing invariably the same object, evinces a design to reduce them under absolute despotism, it is their right, it is their duty, to throw off such government and to provide new guards for their future security. Such has been the patient sufferance of these colonies, and such is now the necessity which constrains them to alter their former systems of government. The history of the present King of Great Britain is a history of repeated injuries and unsurpations, all having, in direct object, the establishment of an absolute tyranny over these States. To prove this, let facts be submitted to a candid world:

He has refused his assent to laws the most wholesome and necessary for the public good.

He has forbidden his governors to pass laws of immediate and pressing importance, unless suspended in their operation till his assent should be obtained; and, when so suspended, he has utterly neglected to attend to them.

He has refused to pass other laws for the accommodation of large districts of people, unless those people would relinquish the right of representation in the legislature; a right inestimable to them, and formidable to tyrants only.

He has called together legislative bodies at places unusual, uncomfortable, and distant from the depository of their public records, for the sole purpose of fatiguing them into compliance with his measures.

He has dissolved representative houses repeatedly for opposing, with manly firmness, his invasions on the rights of the people.

He has refused, for a long time after such dissolutions, to cause others to be elected; whereby the legislative powers, incapable of annihilation, have returned to the people at large for their exercise; the state remaining, in the meantime, exposed to all the danger of invasion from without, and convulsions within.

He has endeavored to prevent the population of these States; for that purpose, obstructing the laws for naturalization of foreigners, refusing to pass others to encourage their migration hither, and raising the conditions of new appropriations of lands.

He has obstructed the administration of justice, by refusing his assent to laws for establishing judiciary powers.

He has made judges dependent on his will alone, for the tenure of their offices, and the amount and payment of their salaries.

He has erected a multitude of new offices, and sent hither swarms of officers to harass our people, and eat out their substance.

He has kept among us, in time of peace, standing armies, without the consent of our legislatures.

He has affected to render the military independent of, and superior to, the civil power.

He has combined, with others, to subject us to a jurisdiction foreign to our Constitution, and unacknowledged by our laws; giving his assent to their acts of pretended legislation:

For quartering large bodies of armed troops among us:

For protecting them by a mock trial, from punishment, for any murders which they should commit on the inhabitants of these States:

For cutting off our trade with all parts of the world:

For imposing taxes on us without our consent:

For depriving us, in many cases, of the benefit of trial by jury:

For transporting us beyond seas to be tried for pretended offences:

For abolishing the free system of English laws in a neighboring province, establishing therein an arbitrary government, and enlarging its boundaries, so as to render it at once an example and fit instrument for introducing the same absolute rule into these colonies:

For taking away our charters, abolishing our most valuable laws, and altering, fundamentally, the powers of our governments:

For suspending our own legislatures, and declaring themselves invested with power to legislate for us in all cases whatsoever.

He has abdicated government here, by declaring us out of his protection, and waging war against us.

He has plundered our seas, ravaged our coasts, burnt our towns, and destroyed the lives of our people.

He is, at this time, transporting large armies of foreign mercenaries to complete the works of death, desolation, and tyranny, already begun, with circumstances of cruelty and perfidy scarcely paralleled in the most barbarous ages, and totally unworthy of the head of a civilized nation.

He has constrained our fellow citizens, taken captive on the high seas, to bear arms against their country, to become the executioners of their friends, and brethren, or to fall themselves by their hands.

He has excited domestic insurrections amongst us, and has endeavored to bring on the inhabitants of our frontiers, the merciless Indian savages, whose known rule of warfare is an undistinguished destruction of all ages, sexes, and conditions.

In every stage of these oppressions, we have petitioned for redress, in the most humble terms; our repeated petitions have been answered only be repeated injury. A prince, whose character is thus marked by every act which may define a tyrant, is unfit to be the ruler of a free people.

Nor have we been wanting in attention to our British brethren. We have warned them, from time to time, of attempts made by their legislature to extend an unwarrantable jurisdiction over us. We have reminded them of the circumstances of our emigration and settlement here. We have appealed to their native justice and magnanimity, and we have conjured them, by the ties of our common kindred, to disavow these usurpations, which would inevitably interrupt our connections and correspondence. They, too, have been deaf to the voice of justice and of consanguinity. We must, therefore, acquiesce in the necessity which denounces our separation, and hold them as we hold the rest of mankind, enemies in war, in peace, friends.

We, therefore, the representatives of the United States of America, in general Congress assembled, appealing to the Supreme Judge of the world for the rectitude of our intentions, do, in the name, and by the authority of the good people of these colonies, solemnly publish and declare, the these united colonies are, and of right ought to be, free and independent states: that they are absolved from all allegiance to the British Crown, and that all political connection between them and the state of Great Britain is, and ought to be, totally dissolved; and that, as free and independent states, they have full power to levy war, conclude peace, contract alliances, establish commerce, and to do all other acts and things which independent states may of right do. And, for the support of this declaration, with a firm reliance on the protection of Divine Providence, we mutually pledge to each other our lives, our fortunes, and our sacred honor.

The foregoing Declaration was, by order of Congress, engrossed, and signed by the following members:

John Hancock

New Hampshire
Josiah Bartlett
William Whipple
Matthew Thornton

Massachusetts Bay
Samuel Adams
John Adams
Robert Treat Paine
Elbridge Gerry

Rhode Island
Stephen Hopkins
William Ellery

New Jersey
Richard Stockton
John Witherspoon
Francis Hopkinson
John Hart
Abraham Clark

Pennsylvania
Robert Morris
Benjamin Rush
Benjamin Franklin
John Morton
George Clymer
James Smith
George Taylor
James Wilson
George Ross

Virginia
George Wythe
Richard Henry Lee
Thomas Jefferson
Benjamin Harrison
Thomas Nelson, Jr.
Francis Lightfoot Lee
Carter Braxton

North Carolina
William Hooper
Joseph Hewes
John Penn

Connecticut	Delware	South Carolina
Roger Sherman	Caesar Rodney	Edward Rutledge
Samuel Huntington	George Reed	Thomas Heyward, Jr.
William Williams	Thomas M'Kean	Thomas Lynch, Jr.
Oliver Wolcott		Arthur Middleton
	Maryland	
New York	Samuel Chase	Georgia
William Floyd	William Paca	Button Gwinnett
Philip Livingston	Thomas Stone	Lyman Hall
Francis Lewis	Charles Carroll, of Carrollton	George Walton
Lewis Morris		

Resolved, That copies of the Declaration be sent to the several assemblies, conventions, and committees, or councils of safety, and to the several commanding officers of the continental troops; that it be proclaimed in each of the United States, at the head of the army.

The Constitution of the United States of America[1]

We the People of the United States, in Order to form a more perfect Union, establish Justice, insure domestic Tranquility, provide for the common defence, promote the general Welfare, and secure the Blessings of Liberty to ourselves and our Posterity, do ordain and establish this CONSTITUTION for the United States of America.

Article 1

SECTION 1

All legislative Powers herein granted shall be vested in a Congress of the United States, which shall consist of a Senate and House of Representatives.

SECTION 2

The House of Representatives shall be composed of Members chosen every second Year by the People of the several States, and the Electors in each State shall have the Qualifications requisite for Electors of the most numerous Branch of the State Legislature.

No Person shall be a Representative who shall not have attained to the Age of twenty-five Years, and been seven Years a Citizen of the United States, and who shall not, when elected, be an Inhabitant of the State in which he shall be chosen.

[Representatives and direct Taxes[2] shall be apportioned among the several States which may be included within this Union, according to their respective Numbers,

---

[1]This version, which follows the original Constitution in capitalization and spelling, was published by the United States Department of the Interior, Office of Education, in 1935.
[2]Altered by the Sixteenth Amendment.

which shall be determined by adding to the whole Number of free Persons, including those bound to Service for a Term of Years, and excluding Indians not taxed, three fifths of all other Persons.][3] The actual Enumeration shall be made within three Years after the first Meeting of the Congress of the United States, and within every subsequent Term of ten Years, in such Manner as they shall by Law direct. The Number of Representatives shall not exceed one for every thirty Thousand, but each State shall have at Least one Representative; and until such enumeration shall be made, the State of New Hampshire shall be entitled to chuse three, Massachusetts eight, Rhode-Island and Providence Plantations one, Connecticut five, New York six, New Jersey four, Pennsylvania eight, Delaware one, Maryland six, Virginia ten, North Carolina five, South Carolina five, and Georgia three.

When vacancies happen in the Representation from any State, the Executive Authority thereof shall issue Writs of Election to fill such Vacancies.

The House of Representatives shall chuse their Speaker and other Officers; and shall have the sole Power of Impeachment.

SECTION 3

The Senate of the United States shall be composed of two Senators from each State, chosen by the Legislature thereof, for six Years; and each Senator shall have one Vote.

Immediately after they shall be assembled in Consequence of the first Election, they shall be divided as equally as may be into three Classes. The Seats of the Senators of the first Class shall be vacated at the Expiration of the second Year, of the second Class at the Expiration of the fourth Year, and of the third Class at the Expiration of the sixth year, so that one-third may be chosen every second Year; and if Vacancies happen by Resignation, or otherwise, during the Recess of the Legislature of any State, the Executive thereof may make temporary Appointments until the next Meeting of the Legislature, which shall then fill such Vacancies.

No Person shall be a Senator who shall not have attained to the Age of thirty Years, and been nine Years a Citizen of the United States, and who shall not, when elected, be an Inhabitant of that State for which he shall be chosen.

The Vice President of the United States shall be President of the Senate, but shall have no vote, unless they be equally divided.

The Senate shall chuse their other Officers, and also a President pro tempore, in the absence of the Vice President, or when he shall exercise the Office of President of the United States.

The Senate shall have the sole Power to try all Impeachments. When sitting for that purpose they shall be on Oath or Affirmation. When the President of the United States is tried, the Chief Justice shall preside: And no person shall be convicted without the Concurrence of two thirds of the Members present.

Judgment in Cases of Impeachment shall not extend further than to removal from Office, and disqualification to hold and enjoy any Office of Honor, Trust, or Profit

[3]Negated by the Fourteenth Amendment.

under the United States: but the Party convicted shall nevertheless be liable and subject to Indictment, Trial, Judgment and Punishment, according to Law.

SECTION 4

The Times, Place and Manner of holding Elections for Senators and Representatives, shall be prescribed in each State by the Legislature thereof; but the Congress may at any time by Law make or alter such Regulations, except as to the Places of Chusing Senators.

The Congress shall assemble at least once in every Year, and such Meeting shall be on the first Monday in December, unless they shall by Law appoint a different Day.

SECTION 5

Each House shall be the Judge of the Elections, Returns and Qualifications of its own Members, and a Majority of each shall constitute a Quorum to do Business; but a smaller number may adjourn from day to day, and may be authorized to compel the Attendance of absent Members, in such Manner, and under such Penalties, as each House may provide.

Each House may determine the Rules of its Proceedings, punish its Members for disorderly Behaviour, and, with the Concurrence of two thirds, expel a Member.

Each House shall keep a Journal of its Proceedings, and from time to time publish the same, excepting such Parts as may in their Judgment require Secrecy; and the Yeas and Nays of the Members of either House on any question shall, at the Desire of one fifth of those Present, be entered on the Journal.

Neither House, during the Session of Congress, shall, without the Consent of the other, adjourn for more than three days, nor to any other Place than that in which the two Houses shall be sitting.

SECTION 6

The Senators and Representatives shall receive a Compensation for their Services, to be ascertained by Law, and paid out of the Treasury of the United States. They shall in all Cases, except Treason, Felony and Breach of the Peace, be privileged from Arrest during their Attendance at the Session of their respective Houses, and in going to and returning from the same; and for any Speech or Debate in either House, they shall not be questioned in any other Place.

No Senator or Representative shall, during the Time for which he was elected, be appointed to any civil Office under the Authority of the United States, which shall have been created, or the Emoluments whereof shall have been increased, during such time; and no Person holding any Office under the United States shall be a Member of either House during his continuance in Office.

SECTION 7

All Bills for raising Revenue shall originate in the House of Representatives; but the Senate may propose or concur with Amendments as on other bills.

Every Bill which shall have passed the House of Representatives and the Senate, shall, before it becomes a Law, be presented to the President of the United States; if he approves he shall sign it, but if not he shall return it, with his Objections, to that House in which it shall have originated, who shall enter the Objections at large on their Journal, and proceed to reconsider it. If after such Reconsideration two thirds of that House shall agree to pass the bill, it shall be sent, together with the objections, to the other House, by which it shall likewise be reconsidered, and if approved by two thirds of that House, it shall become a Law. But in all such Cases the Votes of both Houses shall be determined by Yeas and Nays, and the Names of the Persons voting for and against the Bill shall be entered on the Journal of each House respectively. If any Bill shall not be returned by the President within ten Days (Sundays excepted) after it shall have been presented to him, the Same shall be a Law, in like Manner as if he had signed it, unless the Congress by their Adjournment prevent its Return, in which Case it shall not be a Law.

Every Order, Resolution, or Vote to which the Concurrence of the Senate and House of Representatives may be necessary (except on a question of Adjournment) shall be presented to the President of the United States; and before the Same shall take Effect, shall be approved by him, or being disapproved by him, shall be repassed by two thirds of the Senate and House of Representatives, according to the Rules and Limitations prescribed in the Case of a Bill.

SECTION 8

The Congress shall have Power To lay and collect Taxes, Duties, Imposts and Excises, to pay the Debts and provide for the common Defence and general Welfare of the United States; but all Duties, Imposts and Excises shall be uniform throughout the United States;

To borrow money on the credit of the United States;

To regulate Commerce with foreign Nations, and among the several States, and with the Indian Tribes;

To establish a uniform rule of Naturalization, and uniform Laws on the subject of Bankruptcies throughout the United States;

To coin Money, regulate the Value thereof, and of foreign Coin, and fix the Standard of Weights and Measures;

To provide for the Punishment of counterfeiting the Securities and current Coin of the United States;

To establish Post Offices and post Roads;

To promote the Progress of Science and useful Arts, by securing for limited Times to Authors and Inventors the exclusive Right to their respective Writings and Discoveries;

To constitute Tribunals inferior to the Supreme Court;

To define and punish Piracies and Felonies committed on the high Seas, and Offenses against the Law of Nations;

To declare War, grant Letters of Marque and Reprisal, and make Rules concerning Captures on Land and Water;

To raise and support Armies, but no Appropriation of Money to that Use shall be for a longer Term than two Years;

To provide and maintain a Navy;

To make Rules for the Government and Regulation of the land and naval forces;

To provide for calling forth the Militia to execute the Laws of the Union, suppress Insurrections and repel Invasions;

To provide for organizing, arming, and disciplining the Militia, and for governing such Part of them as may be employed in the Service of the United States, reserving to the States respectively, the Appointment of the Officers, and the Authority of training the Militia according to the discipline prescribed by Congress;

To exercise exclusive Legislation in all Cases whatsoever, over such District (not exceeding ten Miles square) as may, by Cession of particular States, and the acceptance of Congress, become the Seat of the Government of the United States, and to exercise like Authority over all Places purchased by the Consent of the Legislature of the State in which the Same shall be, for the Erection of Forts, Magazines, Arsenals, Dock-yards, and other needful Buildings;—And

To make all Laws which shall be necessary and proper for carrying into Execution the foregoing Powers, and all other Powers vested by this Constitution in the Government of the United States, or in any Department or Officer thereof.

SECTION 9

The Migration or Importation of such Persons as any of the States now existing shall think proper to admit, shall not be prohibited by the Congress prior to the Year one thousand eight hundred and eight, but a tax or duty may be imposed on such Importation, not exceeding ten dollars for each Person.

The privilege of the Writ of Habeas Corpus shall not be suspended, unless when the Cases of Rebellion or Invasion the public Safety may require it.

No bill of Attainder or ex post facto Law shall be passed.

No capitation, or other direct, Tax shall be laid unless in Proportion to the Census or Enumeration herein before directed to be taken.

No Tax or Duty shall be laid on Articles exported from any State.

No Preference shall be given by any Regulation of Commerce or Revenue to the Ports of one State over those of another: nor shall Vessels bound to, or from, one State, be obliged to enter, clear, or pay Duties in another.

No Money shall be drawn from the Treasury, but in Consequence of Appropriations made by Law; and a regular Statement and Account of the Receipts and Expenditures of all public Money shall be published from time to time.

No Title of Nobility shall be granted by the United States: And no Person holding any Office of Profit or Trust under them, shall, without the Consent of the Congress, accept of any present, Emolument, Office, or Title, of any kind whatever, from any King, Prince, or foreign State.

SECTION 10

No State shall enter into any Treaty, Alliance, or Confederation; grant Letters of Marque and Reprisal; coin Money; emit Bills of Credits; make any Thing but gold and silver Coin a Tender in Payment of Debts; pass any Bill of Attainder, ex post facto Law, or Law impairing the Obligation of Contracts, or grant any Title of Nobility.

No State shall, without the Consent of the Congress, lay any Imposts or Duties on Imports or Exports, except what may be absolutely necessary for executing its inspection Laws; and the net Produce of all Duties and Imposts, laid by any State on Imports or Exports, shall be for the use of the Treasury of the United States; and all such Laws shall be subject to the Revision and Control of the Congress.

No state shall, without the Consent of Congress, lay any duty of Tonnage, keep Troops, or Ships of War in time of Peace, enter into any Agreement or Compact with another State, or with a foreign Power, or engage in War, unless actually invaded, or in such imminent Danger as will not admit of delay.

Article II

SECTION 1

The executive Power shall be vested in a President of the United States of America. He shall hold his Office during the Term of four years, and, together with the Vice President, chosen for the same Term, be elected, as follows:

Each State shall appoint, in such Manner as the Legislature thereof may direct, a Number of Electors, equal to the whole Number of Senators and Representatives to which the State may be entitled in the Congress: but no Senator or Representative, or Person holding an Office of Trust or Profit under the United States, shall be appointed an Elector.

[The Electors shall meet in their respective States, and vote by Ballot for two persons, of whom one at least shall not be an Inhabitant of the same State with themselves. And they shall make a List of all the Persons voted for, and of the Number of Votes for each; which List they shall sign and certify, and transmit sealed to the Seat of the Government of the United States, directed to the President of the Senate. The President of the Senate shall, in the Presence of the Senate and House of Representatives, open all the Certificates, and the Votes shall then be counted. The Person having the greatest Number of Votes shall be the President, if such Number be a Majority of the whole Number of Electors appointed; and if there be more than one who have such Majority, and have an equal Number of Votes, then the House of Representatives shall immediately chuse by Ballot one of them for President; and if no Person have a Majority, then from the five highest on the List the said House shall in like Manner chuse the President. But in chusing the President, the Votes shall be taken by States, the Representation from each State having one Vote; a quorum for this

Purpose shall consist of a Member or Members from two-thirds of the States, and a Majority of all the States shall be necessary to a Choice. In every Case, after the Choice of the President, the Person having the greatest Number of Votes of the Electors shall be the Vice President. But if there should remain two or more who have equal votes, the Senate shall chuse from them by Ballot the Vice President.][4]

The Congress may determine the Time of chusing the Electors, and the Day on which they shall give their Votes; which Day shall be the same throughout the United States.

No person except a natural-born Citizen, or a Citizen of the United States, at the time of the Adoption of this Constitution, shall be eligible to the Office of President; neither shall any Person be eligible to that Office who shall not have attained to the Age of thirty-five years, and been fourteen years a Resident within the United States.

In Case of the Removal of the President from Office, or of his Death, Resignation, or Inability to discharge the Powers and Duties of the said Office, the same shall devolve on the Vice President, and the Congress may by Law provide for the Case of Removal, Death, Resignation, or Inability, both of the President and Vice President, declaring what Officer shall then act as President, and such Officer shall act accordingly, until the disability be removed, or a President shall be elected.

The President shall, at stated Times, receive for his Services a Compensation, which shall neither be increased nor diminished during the Period for which he shall have been elected, and he shall not receive within that Period any other emolument from the United States, or any of them.

Before he enter on the execution of his Office, he shall take the following Oath or Affirmation:—"I do solemnly swear (or affirm) that I will faithfully execute the Office of President of the United States, and will, to the best of my Ability, preserve, protect, and defend the Constitution of the United States."

SECTION 2

The President shall be Commander in Chief of the Army and Navy of the United States, and of the Militia of the several States, when called into the actual Service of the United States; he may require the Opinion, in writing, of the principal Officer in each of the executive Departments, upon any subject relating to the Duties of their respective Offices, and he shall have Power to Grant Reprieves and Pardons for Offenses against the United States, except in Cases of Impeachment.

He shall have Power, by and with the Advice and Consent of the Senate, to make Treaties, provided two-thirds of the Senators present concur; and he shall nominate, and by and with the Advice and Consent of the Senate, shall appoint Ambassadors, other public Ministers and Consuls, Judges of the supreme Court, and all other Officers of the United States, whose Appointments are not herein otherwise provided for, and which shall be established by Law: but the Congress may by Law vest the Appointment of such inferior Officers, as they think proper, in the President alone, in the Courts of Law, or in the Heads of Departments.

[4]Revised by the Twelfth Amendment.

The President shall have Power to fill up all Vacancies that may happen during the Recess of the Senate, by granting Commissions which shall expire at the End of their next Session.

SECTION 3

He shall from time to time give to the Congress Information of the State of the Union, and recommend to their Consideration such Measures as he shall judge necessary and expedient; he may, on extraordinary occasions, convene both Houses, or either of them, and in Case of Disagreement between them, with respect to the Time of Adjournment, he may adjourn them to such Time as he shall think proper; he shall receive Ambassadors and other public Ministers; he shall take care that the Laws be faithfully executed, and shall Commission all the Officers of the United States.

SECTION 4

The President, Vice President and all civil Officers of the United States, shall be removed from Office on Impeachment for, and Conviction of, Treason, Bribery, or other high Crimes and Misdemeanors.

Article III

SECTION 1

The judicial Power of the United States, shall be vested in one supreme Court, and in such inferior Courts as the Congress may from time to time ordain and establish. The Judges, both of the supreme and inferior Courts, shall hold their Offices during good Behaviour, and shall, at stated Times, receive for their Services, a Compensation, which shall not be diminished during their Continuance in Office.

SECTION 2

The judicial Power shall extend to all Cases, in Law and Equity, arising under this Constitution, the Laws of the United States, and Treaties made, or which shall be made, under their Authority;—to all Cases affecting ambassadors, other public ministers and consuls;—to all cases of admiralty and maritime Jurisdiction;—to Controversies to which the United States shall be a Party;—to Controversies between two or more states;—between a State and Citizens of another State;[5]—between Citizens of different States—between Citizens of the same State claiming Lands under Grants of different States, and between a State, or the Citizens thereof, and foreign States, Citizens, or Subjects.

[5]Qualified by the Eleventh Amendment.

In all Cases affecting Ambassadors, other public Ministers and Consuls, and those in which a State shall be Party, the supreme Court shall have original Jurisdiction. In all the other Cases before mentioned, the supreme Court shall have appellate Jurisdiction, both as to Law and Fact, with such Exceptions, and under such Regulations as the Congress shall make.

The trial of all Crimes, except in Cases of Impeachment, shall be by Jury; and such Trial shall be held in the State where the said Crimes shall have been committed; but when not committed within any State, the Trial shall be at such Place or Places as the Congress may by Law have directed.

SECTION 3

Treason against the United States, shall consist only in levying War against them, or in adhering to their Enemies, giving them Aid and Comfort. No Person shall be convicted of Treason unless on the Testimony of two Witnesses to the same overt Act, or on Confession in open Court.

The Congress shall have power to declare the Punishment of Treason, but no Attainder of Treason shall work Corruption of Blood, or Forfeiture except during the Life of the Person attainted.

Article IV

SECTION 1

Full Faith and Credit shall be given in each State to the public Acts, Records, and judicial Proceedings of every other State. And the Congress may by general Laws prescribe the Manner in which such Acts, Records and Proceedings shall be proved, and the Effect thereof.

SECTION 2

The Citizens of each State shall be entitled to all Privileges and Immunities of Citizens in the several States.

A Person charged in any State with Treason, Felony, or other Crime, who shall flee from Justice, and be found in another State, shall on demand of the executive Authority of the State from which he fled, be delivered up, to be removed to the State having Jurisdiction of the crime.

No Person held to Service or Labour in one State, under the Laws thereof, escaping into another, shall, in Consequence of any Law or Regulation therein, be discharged from such Service or Labour, but shall be delivered up on Claim of the Party to whom such Service or Labour may be due.

SECTION 3

New States may be admitted by the Congress into this Union; but no new State shall be formed or erected within the Jurisdiction of any other State; nor any State be formed by the Junction of two or more States, or parts of States, without the Consent of the Legislatures of the States concerned as well as of the Congress.

The Congress shall have Power to dispose of and make all needful Rules and Regulations respecting the Territory or other Property belonging to the United States; and nothing in this Constitution shall be so construed as to Prejudice any Claims of the United States, or of any particular State.

SECTION 4

The United States shall guarantee to every State in this Union a Republican Form of Government, and shall protect each of them against Invasion; and on Application of the Legislature, or of the Executive (when the Legislature cannot be convened) against domestic Violence.

Article V

The Congress, whenever two-thirds of both House shall deem it necessary, shall propose Amendments to this Constitution, or, on the Application of the Legislatures of two-thirds of the several States, shall call a Convention for proposing Amendments, which, in either Case, shall be valid to all Intents and Purposes, as part of this Constitution, when ratified by the Legislatures of three-fourths of the several States, or by Conventions in three-fourths thereof, as the one or the other Mode of Ratification may be proposed by the Congress; Provided that no Amendment which may be made prior to the Year One thousand eight hundred and eight shall in any Manner affect the first and fourth Clauses in the Ninth Section of the first Article; and that no State, without its Consent, shall be deprived of its equal Suffrage in the Senate.

Article VI

All Debts contracted and Engagements entered into, before the Adoption of this Constitution, shall be as valid against the United States under this Constitution, as under the Confederation.

This constitution, and the Laws of the United States which shall be made in Pursuance thereof; and all Treaties made, or which shall be made, under the Authority of the United States, shall be the supreme Law of the Land; and the Judges in every State shall be bound thereby, any Thing in the Constitution or Laws of any State to the Contrary notwithstanding.

The Senators and Representatives before mentioned, and the Members of the several State Legislatures, and all executive and judicial Officers, both of the United States and of the several States, shall be bound by Oath or Affirmation to support this Constitution; but no religious Tests shall ever be required as a qualification to any Office or public Trust under the United States.

Article VII

The Ratification of the Conventions of nine States shall be sufficient for the Establishment of this Constitution between the States so ratifying the same.

Done in Convention by the Unanimous Consent of the States present the Seventeenth Day of September in the Year of our Lord one thousand seven hundred and Eighty seven, and of the Independence of the United States of America the Twelfth. In Witness whereof We have hereunto subscribed our Names.[6]

George Washington
President and deputy from Virginia

New Hampshire
John Langdon
Nicholas Gilman

Massachusetts
Nathaniel Gorham
Rufus King

Connecticut
William Samuel Johnson
Roger Sherman

New York
Alexander Hamilton

New Jersey
William Livingston
David Brearley
William Paterson
Jonathan Dayton

Pennsylvania
Benjamin Franklin
Thomas Mifflin
Robert Morris
George Clymer
Thomas FitzSimmons
Jared Ingersoll
James Wilson
Gouverneur Morris

Delaware
George Read
Gunning Bedford, Jr.
John Dickinson
Richard Bassett
Jacob Broom

Maryland
James McHenry
Daniel of St. Thomas Jenifer
Daniel Carroll

Virginia
John Blair
James Madison, Jr.

North Carolina
William Blount
Richard Dobbs Spaight
Hugh Williamson

South Carolina
John Rutledge
Charles Coteworth Pinckney
Charles Pinckney
Pierce Butler

Georgia
William Few
Abraham Baldwin

Articles in Addition to, and Amendment of, the Constitution of the United States of America, Proposed by Congress, and Ratified by the Legislatures of the Several States, Pursuant to the Fifth Article of the Original Constitution[7]

Amendment I

Congress shall make no law respecting an establishment of religion, or prohibiting the free exercise thereof; or abridging the freedom of speech, or of the press; or the right of the people peaceably to assemble, and to petition the Government for a redress of grievances.

[6]These are the full names of the signers, which in some cases are not the signatures on the document.
[7]This heading appears only in the joint resolution submitting the first ten amendments, which are collectively known as the Bill of Rights. They were ratified on December 15, 1791.

Amendment II

A well regulated Militia, being necessary to the security of a free State, the right of the people to keep and bear Arms shall not be infringed.

Amendment III

No Soldier shall, in time of peace, be quartered in any house, without the consent of the Owner, nor in time of war, but in a manner to be prescribed by law.

Amendment IV

The right of the people to be secure in their persons, houses, papers, and effects, against unreasonable searches and seizures, shall not be violated, and no Warrants shall issue, but upon probable cause, supported by Oath or affirmation, and particularly describing the place to be searched, and the persons or things to be seized.

Amendment V

No person shall be held to answer for a capital or otherwise infamous crime, unless on a presentment or indictment of a Grand Jury, except in cases arising in the land or naval forces, or in the Militia, when in actual service in time of War or public danger; not shall any person be subject for the same offence to be twice put in jeopardy of life or limb; nor shall be compelled in any criminal case to be a witness against himself, nor be deprived of life, liberty, or property, without due process of law; nor shall private property be taken for public use, without just compensation.

Amendment VI

In all criminal prosecutions, the accused shall enjoy the right to a speedy and public trial, by an impartial jury of the State and district wherein the crime shall have been committed, which district shall have been previously ascertained by law, and to be informed of the nature and cause of the accusation; to be confronted with the witnesses against him; to have compulsory process for obtaining witnesses in his favour, and to have the Assistance of Counsel for his defence.

Amendment VII

In suits at common law, where the value in controversy shall exceed twenty dollars, the right of trial by jury shall be preserved, and no fact tried by a jury, shall be otherwise reexamined in any Court of the United States, than according to the rules of the common law.

Amendment VIII

Excessive bail shall not be required, nor excessive fines imposed, nor cruel and unusual punishments inflicted.

Amendment IX

The enumeration of the Constitution, of certain rights, shall not be construed to deny or disparage others retained by the people.

Amendment X

The powers not delegated to the United States by the Constitution, nor prohibited by it to the States, are reserved to the States respectively, or to the people.

Amendment XI [1798]

The Judicial power of the United States shall not be construed to extend to any suit in law or equity, commenced or prosecuted against one of the United States by Citizens of another State, or by Citizens or Subjects of any Foreign State.

Amendment XII [1804]

The Electors shall meet in their respective States and vote by ballot for President and Vice-President, one of whom, at least, shall not be an inhabitant of the same State with themselves; they shall name in their ballots the persons voted for as President, and in distinct ballots the person voted for as Vice-President, and they shall make distinct lists of all persons voted for as President, and of all persons voted for as Vice-President, and of the number of votes for each, which lists they shall sign and certify, and transmit sealed to the seat of the government of the United States, directed to the President of the Senate;—The President of the Senate shall, in the presence of the Senate and House of Representatives, open all the certificates and the votes shall then be counted;—The person having the greatest number of votes for President, shall be the President, if such number be a majority of the whole number of Electors appointed; and if no person have such majority, then from the persons having the highest numbers not exceeding three on the list of those voted for as President, the House of Representatives shall choose immediately, by ballot, the President. But in choosing the President, the votes shall be taken by states, the representation from each state having one vote; a quorum for this purpose shall consist of a member or members from two-thirds of the states, and a majority of all the states shall be necessary to a choice. And if the House of Representatives shall not choose a President whenever the right of choice shall devolve upon them, before the fourth day of March next following, then the Vice-President shall act as President, as in the case of the death or other constitutional disability of the President.—The person having the greatest number of votes as Vice-President, shall be the Vice-President, if such number be a majority of the whole number of Electors appointed, and if no person have a majority, then from the two highest numbers on the list, the Senate shall choose the Vice-President; a quorum for the purpose shall consist of two-thirds of the whole number of Senators, and majority of the whole number shall be necessary to a choice. But no person constitutionally ineligible to the office of President shall be eligible to that of Vice-President of the United States.

Amendment XIII [1865]

SECTION 1

Neither slavery nor involuntary servitude, except as a punishment for crime whereof the party shall have been duly convicted, shall exist within the United States, or any place subject to their jurisdiction.

SECTION 2

Congress shall have power to enforce this article by appropriate legislation.

Amendment XIV [1868]

SECTION 1

All persons born or naturalized in the United States, and subject to the jurisdiction thereof, are citizens of the United States and of the State wherein they reside. No State shall abridge the privileges or immunities of citizens of the United States; nor shall any State deprive any person of life, liberty, or property, without due process of law; nor deny to any person within its jurisdiction the equal protection of the laws.

SECTION 2

Representatives shall be apportioned among the several States according to their respective numbers, counting the whole number of persons in each State, excluding Indians not taxed. But when the right to vote at any election for the choice of electors for President and Vice-President of the United States, Representatives in Congress, the Executive and Judicial officers of a State, or the members of the Legislature thereof, is denied to any of the male inhabitants of such State, being twenty-one years of age, and citizens of the United States, or in any way abridged, except for participation in rebellion, or other crime, the basis of representation therein shall be reduced in the proportion which the number of such male citizens shall bear to the whole number of male citizens twenty-one years of age in such State.

SECTION 3

No person shall be a Senator or Representative in Congress, or elector of President and Vice-President, or hold any office, civil or military, under the United States, or under any state, who, having previously taken an oath, as a member of Congress, or as an officer of the United States, or as a member of any State legislature, or as an executive or judicial officer of any State, to support the Constitution of the United States, shall have engaged in insurrection or rebellion against the same, or given aid or comfort to the enemies thereof. But Congress may by a vote of two-thirds of each House, remove such disability.

SECTION 4

The validity of the public debt of the United States, authorized by law, including debts incurred for payment of pensions and bounties for services in suppressing insurrection or rebellion, shall not be questioned. But neither the United States nor any State shall assume or pay any debts or obligation incurred in aid of insurrection or rebellion against the United States, or any claim for the loss or emancipation of any slave; but all such debts, obligations, and claims shall be held illegal and void.

SECTION 5

The Congress shall have the power to enforce, by appropriate legislation, the provisions of this article.

Amendment XV [1870]

SECTION 1

The right of citizens of the United States to vote shall not be denied or abridged by the United States or by any State on account of race, color, or previous condition of servitude—

SECTION 2

The Congress shall have power to enforce this article by appropriate legislation.

Amendment XVI [1913]

The Congress shall have power to lay and collect taxes on incomes, from whatever source derived, without apportionment among the several States, and without regard to any census or enumeration.

Amendment XVII [1913]

The Senate of the United States shall be composed of two Senators from each State, elected by the people thereof, for six years; and each Senator shall have one vote. The electors in each State shall have the qualifications requisite for electors of the most numerous branch of the State legislatures.

When vacancies happen in the representation of any State in the Senate, the executive authority of such State shall issue writs of election to fill such vacancies: *Provided,* That the legislature of any State may empower the executive thereof to make temporary appointments until the people fill the vacancies by election as the legislature may direct.

This amendment shall not be so construed as to affect the election or term of any part of the Constitution.

Amendment XVIII [1919]

SECTION 1

After one year from the ratification of this article the manufacture, sale, or transportation of intoxicating liquors within, the importation thereof into, or the exportation thereof for the United States and all territory subject to the jurisdiction thereof for beverage purposes is hereby prohibited.

SECTION 2

The Congress and the several States shall have concurrent power to enforce this article by appropriate legislation.

SECTION 3

This article shall be inoperative unless it shall have been ratified as an amendment to the Constitution by the legislatures of the several States, as provided in the Constitution, within seven years from the date of the submission hereof to the States by the Congress.

Amendment XIX [1920]

The right of citizens of the Unite states to vote shall not be denied or abridged by the United States or by any State on account of sex.

Congress shall have power to enforce this article by appropriate legislation.

Amendment XX [1933]

SECTION 1

The terms of the President and Vice-President shall end at noon on the 20th day of January, and the terms of Senators and Representatives at noon on the 3d day of January, of the years in which such terms would have ended if this article had not been ratified; and the terms of their successors shall then begin.

SECTION 2

The Congress shall assemble at least once in every year, and such meeting shall begin at noon on the 3d day of January, unless they shall by law appoint a different day.

SECTION 3

If, at the time fixed for the beginning of the term of the President, the President elect shall have died, the Vice-President elect shall become President. If a President shall not have been chosen before the time fixed for the beginning of his term or if the President elect shall have failed to qualify, then the Vice-President elect shall act as President until a President shall have qualified; and the Congress may be law provide for the case wherein neither a President elect nor a Vice-President elect shall have qualified, declaring who shall then act as President, or the manner in which one who is to act shall be selected, and such person shall act accordingly until a President or Vice-President shall have qualified.

SECTION 4

The Congress may by law provide for the case of the death of any of the persons from whom the House of Representatives may choose a President whenever the right of choice shall have devolved upon them, and for the case of the death of any of their persons from whom the Senate may choose a Vice-President whenever the right of choice shall have devolved upon them.

SECTION 5

Sections 1 and 2 shall take effect on the 15th day of October following the ratification of this article.

SECTION 6

This article shall be inoperative unless it shall have been ratified as an amendment to the Constitution by the legislatures of three-fourths of the several States within seven years from the date of its submission.

Amendment XXI [1933]

SECTION 1

The eighteenth article of amendment to the Constitution of the United States is hereby repealed.

SECTION 2

The transportation or importation into any State, Territory, or possession of the United States for delivery or use therein of intoxicating liquors, in violation of the laws thereof, is hereby prohibited.

SECTION 3

This article shall be inoperative unless it shall have been ratified as an amendment to the Constitution by conventions in the several States, as provided in the Constitution, within seven years from the date of the submission hereof to the States by the Congress.

Amendment XXII [1951]

No person shall be elected to the office of the President more than twice, and no person who has held the office of President, or acted as President, for more than two years of a term to which some other person was elected President shall be elected to the office of the President more than once.

But this Article shall not apply to any person holding the office of President when this Article was proposed by the Congress, and shall not prevent any person who may be holding the office of President, or acting as President, during the term within which this Article becomes operative from holding the office of President or acting as President during the remainder of such term.

This article shall be inoperative unless it shall have been ratified as an amendment to the Constitution by the legislatures of three-fourths of the several states within seven years from the date of its submission to the states by the Congress.

Amendment XXIII [1961]

SECTION 1

The District constituting the seat of Government of the United States shall appoint in such manner as the Congress may direct:

A number of electors of President and Vice-President equal to the whole number of Senators and Representatives in Congress to which the District would be entitled if it were a State, but in no event more than the least populous State; they shall be in addition to those appointed by the States, but they shall be considered, for the purposes of the election of President and Vice-President, to be electors appointed by a State; and they shall meet in the District and perform such duties as provided by the twelfth article of amendment.

SECTION 2

The Congress shall have power to enforce this article by appropriate legislation.

Amendment XXIV [1964]

SECTION 1

The right of citizens of the United States to vote in any primary or other election for President or Vice President, for electors for President or Vice President, or for Senator or Representative in Congress, shall not be denied or abridged by the United States or any state by reason of failure to pay any poll tax or other tax.

SECTION 2

The Congress shall have the power to enforce this article by appropriate legislation.

Amendment XXV [1967]

SECTION 1

In case of the removal of the President from office or of his death or resignation, the Vice President shall become President.

SECTION 2

Whenever there is a vacancy in the office of the Vice President, the President shall nominate a Vice President who shall take office upon confirmation by a majority vote of both Houses of Congress.

SECTION 3

Whenever the President transmits to the President Pro Tempore of the Senate and the Speaker of the House of Representatives his written declaration that he is unable to discharge the powers and duties of his office, and until he transmits to them a written declaration to the contrary, such powers and duties shall be discharged by the Vice President as Acting President.

SECTION 4

Whenever the Vice President and a majority of either the principal officers of the executive departments or of such other body as Congress may by law provide, transmit to the President Pro Tempore of the Senate and the Speaker of the House of Representatives their written declaration that the President is unable to discharge the powers and duties of his office, the Vice President shall immediately assume the powers and duties of the office as Acting President.

Thereafter, when the President transmits to the President Pro Tempore of the Senate and the Speaker of the House of Representatives his written declaration that no inability exists, he shall resume the powers and duties of his office unless the Vice President and a majority of either the principal officers of the executive departments or of such other body as Congress may by law provide, transmit within four days to the President Pro Tempore of the Senate and the Speaker of the House of Representatives their written declaration that the President is unable to discharge the powers and duties of his office. Thereupon Congress shall decide the issue, assembling within forty-eight hours for that purpose if not in session. If the Congress, within twenty-one days after receipt of the latter written declaration, or, if Congress is not in session, within twenty-one days after Congress is required to assemble, determines by two-thirds vote of both Houses that the President is unable to discharge the powers and duties of his office, the Vice President shall continue to discharge the same as Acting President; otherwise, the President shall resume the powers and duties of his office.

Amendment XXVI [1971]

SECTION 1

The right of citizens of the United States, who are eighteen years of age or older, to vote shall not be denied or abridged by the United States or by any State on account of age.

SECTION 2

The Congress shall have the power to enforce this article by appropriate legislation.

Amendment XXVII [1992]

No law varying the compensation for the service of Senators and Representatives shall take effect until an election of Representatives shall have intervened.

The Federalist, Number 1 (Alexander Hamilton)

After an unequivocal experience of the inefficiency of the subsisting federal government, you are called upon to deliberate on a new Constitution for the United States of America. The subject speaks its own importance; comprehending in its consequences nothing less than the existence of the UNION, the safety and welfare of the parts of which it is composed, the fate of an empire in many respects the most interesting in the world. It has been frequently remarked that it seems to have been reserved to the people of this country, by their conduct and example, to decide the important question, whether societies of men are really capable or not of establishing good government from reflection and choice, or whether they are forever destined to depend for their political constitutions on accident and force. If there be any truth in the remark, the crisis at which we are arrived may with propriety be regarded as the era in which that decision is to be made; and a wrong election of the part we shall act may, in this view, deserve to be considered as the general misfortune of mankind.

This idea will add the inducements of philanthropy to those of patriotism, to heighten the solicitude which all considerate and good men must feel for the event. Happy will it be if our choice should be directed by a judicious estimate of our true interests, unperplexed and unbiased by considerations not connected with the public good. But this is a thing more ardently to be wished than seriously to be expected. The plan offered to our deliberations affects too many particular interests, innovates upon too many local institutions, not to involve in its discussion a variety of objects foreign to its merits, and of views, passions and prejudices little favorable to the discovery of truth.

Among the most formidable of the obstacles which the new Constitution will have to encounter may readily be distinguished the obvious interest of a certain class of men in every State to resist all changes which may hazard a diminution of the power emolument, and consequence of the offices they hold under the State establishments; and the perverted ambition of another class of men, who will either hope to aggrandize themselves by the confusion of their country, or will flatter themselves with fairer prospects of elevation from the subdivision of the empire into several partial confederacies than from its union under one government. . . .

And yet, however just these sentiments will be allowed to be, we have already sufficient indications that it will happen in this as in all former cases of great national discussion. A torrent of angry and malignant passions will be let loose. To judge from the conduct of the opposite parties, we shall be led to conclude that they will mutually hope to evince the justness of their opinions, and to increase the number of their converts by the loudness of their declamations and the bitterness of their invectives. An enlightened zeal for the energy and efficiency of government will be stigmatized as the offspring of a temper fond of despotic power and hostile to the principles of liberty. An overscrupulous jealously of danger to the rights of the people, which is more commonly the fault of the head than of the heart, will be represented as mere pretense and artifice, the stale bait for popularity at the expense of the public good. It will be forgotten, on the one hand, that jealously is the usual concomitant of love, and that the noble enthusiasm of liberty is apt to be infected with a spirit of narrow and illiberal distrust. On the other hand, it will be equally forgotten that the vigor of government is essential to the security of liberty; that, in the contemplation of a sound and well-informed judgment, their interest can never be separated; and that a dangerous ambition more often lurks behind the specious mask of zeal for the rights of the people than under the forbidden appearance of zeal for the firmness and efficiency of government. . . .

I propose, in a series of papers, to discuss the following interesting particulars:— THE UTILITY OF THE UNION TO YOUR POLITICAL PROSPERITY—THE INSUFFICIENCY OF THE PRESENT CONFEDERATION TO PRESERVE THAT UNION— THE NECESSITY OF A GOVERNMENT AT LEAST EQUALLY ENERGETIC WITH THE ONE PROPOSED, TO THE ATTAINMENT OF THIS OBJECT—THE CONFORMITY OF THE PROPOSED CONSTITUTION TO THE TRUE PRINCIPLES OF REPUBLICAN GOVERNMENT—ITS ANALOGY TO YOUR OWN STATE CONSTITUTION—and lastly, THE ADDITIONAL SECURITY WHICH ITS ADOPTION WILL AFFORD TO THE PRESERVATION OF THAT SPECIES OF GOVERNMENT, TO LIBERTY, AND TO PROPERTY.

The Federalist, Number 10 (James Madison)

Among the numerous advantages promised by a well constructed Union, none deserves to be more accurately developed than its tendency to break and control the violence of faction. The friend of popular governments, never finds himself so much alarmed for their character and fate, as when he contemplates their propensity to this dangerous vice. He will not fail, therefore, to set a due value on any plan which, without violating the principles to which he is attached, provides a proper cure for it. The instability, injustice and confusion introduced into the public councils, have, in truth, been the mortal diseases under which popular governments have everywhere perished; as they continue to be the favorite and fruitful topics from which the adversaries to liberty derive their most specious declamations. The valuable improvements made by the American constitutions on the popular models, both ancient and modern, cannot certainly be too much admired; but it would be an unwarrantable partiality, to contend that they have as effectually obviated the danger on this side, as was wished and expected. Complaints are everywhere heard from our most considerate and virtuous citizens . . . that our governments are too unstable, that the public good is disregarded in the conflicts of rival parties, and that measures are too often decided, not according to the rules of justice and the rights of the minor party, but by the superior force of an interested and overbearing majority. However anxiously we may wish that these complaints had no foundation, the evidence, of known facts will not permit us to deny that they are in some degree true . . . [P]revailing and increasing distrust of public engagements, and alarm for private rights, which are echoed from one end of the continent to the other . . . must be chiefly, if not wholly, effects of the unsteadiness and injustice with which a factious spirit has tainted our public administrations.

By a faction, I understand a number of citizens, whether amounting to a majority or minority of the whole, who are united and actuated by some common impulse of passion, or of interest, adverse to the rights of other citizens, or to the permanent and aggregate interests of the community.

There are two methods of curing the mischiefs of faction. The one, by removing its causes; the other, by controlling its effects.

There are again two methods of removing the causes of faction. The one, by destroying the liberty which is essential to its existence; the other, by giving every citizen the same options, the same passions, and the same interests.

It could never be more truly said, that of the first remedy, that it was worse than the disease. Liberty is to faction what air is to fire, an aliment, without which it instantly expires. But it would not be less a folly to abolish liberty, which is essential to political life because it nourishes faction, than it would be to wish the annihilation of air, which is essential to animal life, because it imparts to fire its destructive agency.

The second expedient is as impracticable, as the first would be unwise. As long as the reason of man continues to be fallible, and he is at liberty to exercise it, different opinions will be formed. . . .

The latent causes of faction are thus sown in the nature of man; and we see them everywhere brought into different degrees of activity, according to the different circumstances of civil society. A zeal for different opinions . . . divided mankind into parties, inflamed them with mutual animosity, and rendered them much more disposed to vex and oppress each other, than to co-operate for their common good. So strong is this propensity of mankind, to fall into mutual animosities, that where no substantial occasion presents itself, the most frivolous and fanciful distinctions have been sufficient to kindle their unfriendly passions, and excite their most violent conflicts. But the most common and durable source of factions has been the various and unequal distribution of property. Those who hold, and those who are without property, have ever formed distinct interests in society. . . . The regulation of these various and interfering interest forms the principle task of modern legislation. . . .

The inference to which we are brought is, that the *causes* of faction cannot be removed; and that relief is only to be sought in the means of controlling its *effects.*

If a faction consists of less than a majority, relief is supplied by the republican principle, which enables the majority to defeat its sinister views, by regular vote. . . . When a majority is included in a faction, the form of popular government, on the other hand, enables it to sacrifice to its ruling passions or interest, both the public good and the rights of other citizens. To secure the public good, and private rights, against the danger of such a faction, and at the same time to preserve the spirit and the form of popular government, is then the great object to which our inquiries are directed. . . .

By what means is this object attainable? Evidently by one of two only. Either the existence of the same passion or interest in a majority, at the same time must be prevented; or the majority, having such coexistent passion or interest, must be rendered, by their number and local situation, unable to concert and carry into effect schemes of oppression. If the impulse and the opportunity be suffered to coincide . . . neither moral nor religious motives can be relied on as an adequate control. . . .

From this view of the subject, it may be concluded, that a pure democracy, by which I mean a society consisting of a small number of citizens, who assemble and administer the government in person, can admit of no cure from the mischief of faction. A common passion or interest will, in almost every case, be felt by a majority . . . and there is nothing to check the inducements to sacrifice the weaker party, or an obnoxious individual. Hence it is, that such democracies have ever been spectacles of turbulence and contention; have ever been found incompatible with personal security, or the rights of property; and have, in general, been as short in their lives, as they have been violent in their deaths. . . .

A republic, by which I mean a government in which the scheme of representation takes place, opens a different prospect, and promises the cure for which we are seeking. . . .

The two great points of difference, between a democracy and a republic, are, first, the delegation of the government, in the latter, to a small number of citizens, and greater sphere of country, over which the latter may be extended.

The effect of the first difference is, on the one hand, to refine and enlarge the public views by passing them through the medium of a chosen body of citizens, whose wisdom may best discern the true interest of their community, and whose patriotism and love of justice, will be least likely to sacrifice it to temporary or partial considerations. Under such a regulation, it may well happen, that the public voice, pronounced by the representatives of the people, will be more consonant to the public good, than if pronounced by the people themselves, convened for the purpose. . . .

The other point of difference is, the greater number of citizens, and the extent of territory, which may be brought within the compass of republican, than of democratic government; and it is this circumstance principally which renders factious combinations less to be dreaded in the former, than in the latter. The smaller the society, the fewer probably will be the distinct parties and interests composing it; the fewer the distinct parties and interests, the more frequently will a majority be found of the same party; and the smaller the number of individuals composing a majority, and the smaller the compass within which they are placed, the more easily will they concert and execute their plans of oppression. Extend the sphere, and you take in a greater variety of parties and interests; you make it less probable that a majority of the whole will have a common motive to invade the rights of other citizens; or if such a common motive exists, it will be more difficult for all who feel it to discover their own strength, and act in unison with each other. . . .

Hence, it clearly appears, that the same advantage, which a republic has over a democracy, in controlling the effects of faction, is enjoyed by a large over a small republic—is enjoyed by the union over the states composing it. Does this advantage consist in the substitution of representatives, whose enlightened views and virtuous sentiments render them superior to local prejudices, and to schemes of injustice? It will not be denied, that the representation of the union will be most likely to possess these requisite endowments. Does it consist in the greater security afforded by a greater variety of parties, against the event of any one party being able to outnumber and oppress the rest? In an equal degree does the increased variety of parties, comprised within the union, increase this security? Does it, in fine, consist in the greater obstacles opposed to the concert and accomplishment of the secret wishes of an unjust and interested majority? Here, again, the extent of the union gives it the most palpable advantage.

The influence of factious leaders may kindle a flame within their particular states, but will be unable to spread a general conflagration through the other states. . . .

The Federalist, Number 51 (James Madison)

In order to lay a due foundation for that separate and distinct exercise of the different powers of government, which to a certain extent is admitted on all hands to be essential to the preservation of liberty, it is evident that each department should have a will of its own; and consequently should be so constituted that the members of each should have as little agency as possible in the appointment of the members of the others. Were this principle rigorously adhered to, it would required that all the appointments for the supreme executive, legislative, and judiciary magistracies should be drawn from the same fountain of authority, the people, through channels having no communication whatever with one another. Perhaps such a plan of constructing the several departments would be less difficult in practice than it may in contemplation appear. Some difficulties, however, and some additional expense would attend the execution of it. Some deviations, therefore, from the principle must be admitted. In the constitution of the judiciary department in particular, it might be inexpedient to insist rigorously on the principle: first, because peculiar qualifications being essential in the members, the primary consideration ought to be to select that mode of choice which best secures these qualifications; secondly, because the permanent tenure by which the appointments are held in that department, must soon destroy all sense of dependence on the authority conferring them.

It is equally evident that the members of each department should be as little dependent as possible on those of the others, for the emoluments annexed to their offices. Were the executive magistrate, or the judges, not independent of the legislature in this particular, there independence in every other would be merely nominal.

But the great security against a gradual concentration of the several powers in the same department, consists in giving to those who administer each department the necessary constitutional means and personal motives to resist encroachments of the others. The provision for defense must in this, as in all other cases, be made commensurate to the danger of the attack. Ambition must be made to counteract ambition. The interest of the man must be connected with the constitutional rights of the place. It may be a reflection on human nature, that such devices should be necessary to control the abuses of government. But what is government itself, but the greatest of all reflections on human nature? If men were angels, no government would be necessary. If angels were to govern men, neither external nor internal controls on government would be necessary. In framing a government which is to be administered by men over men, the great difficulty lies in this: you must first enable the government to control the governed; and in the next place oblige it to control itself. A dependence on the people is, no doubt, the primary control on the government; but experience has taught mankind the necessity of auxiliary precautions. . . .

The Federalist, Number 69 (Alexander Hamilton)

I proceed now to trace the real characters of the proposed executive, as they are marked out in the plan of the convention. This will serve to place in a strong light the unfairness of the representations which have been made in regard to it.

The first thing which strikes our attention is that the executive authority, with few exceptions, is to be vested in a single magistrate. This will scarcely, however, be considered as a point upon which any comparison can be grounded; for if, in this particular, there be a resemblance to the king of Great Britain, there is not less a resemblance to the Grand Seignior, to the khan of Tartary, to the Man of the Seven Mountains, or to the governor of New York.

That magistrate is to be elected for four years; and is to be re-eligible as often as the people of the United States shall think him worthy of their confidence. In these circumstances there is a total dissimilitude between him and the king . . . who is an hereditary monarch, possessing the crown as a patrimony descendible to his heirs forever; but there is a close analogy between him and a governor of New York, who is elected for three years, and is re-eligible without limitation or intermission. If we consider how much less time would be requisite for establishing a dangerous influence in a single state than for establishing a like influence throughout the United States, we must conclude that a duration of four years for the chief magistrate of the Union is a degree of permanency far less to be dreaded in that office, than a duration of three years for a corresponding office in a single state.

The president . . . would be liable to be impeached, tried, and, upon conviction of treason, bribery, or other high crimes or misdemeanors, removed from office; and would afterwards be liable to prosecution and punishment in the ordinary course of law. The . . . king . . . is sacred and inviolable; there is no constitutional tribunal to which he is amenable; no punishment to which can be subjected without involving the crisis of a national revolution. In this delicate and important circumstance of personal responsibility, the president . . . would stand upon no better ground than a governor of New York, and upon worse ground than the governors of Virginia and Delaware.

The president . . . is to have power to return a bill, which shall have passed the two branches of legislature, for reconsideration; but the bill so returned is not to become a law unless, upon that reconsideration, it be approved by two-thirds of both houses. The king . . . has an absolute negative upon the acts of the two houses of Parliament. . . . The qualified negative of the president differs widely from this absolute negative of the British sovereign and tallies exactly with the revisionary authority of the council of revision of this state, of which the governor is a constituent part. . . .

The president is to be the commander-in-chief of the army and navy of the United States, and of the militia of the several States, when called into the actual service of the United States. He is to have power to grant reprieves and pardons for offenses against the United States, except in cases of impeachment; to recommend to the consideration of Congress such measures as he shall judge necessary and expedient; to convene, on extraordinary occasions, both houses of the legislature, or either of them, and, in case of disagreement between them with respect to the time of adjournment, to adjourn them to such time as he shall think proper; to take care that the laws be faithfully executed; and to commission all officers of the United States.

In most of these particulars, the power of the president will resemble equally that of the king of Great Britain and of the governor of New York. The most material points of difference are these:

First. The president will have only the occasional command of such part of the militia of the nation as by legislative provision may be called into the actual service of the Union. The king . . . and the governor of New York have at all times the entire command of all the militia within their several jurisdictions. In this article, therefore, the power of the president would be inferior to that of either the monarch or the governor.

Second. The president is to be commander-in-chief of the army and navy of the United States. In this respect his authority would be nominally the same with that of the king of Great Britain, but in substance much inferior to it. It would amount to nothing more than the supreme command and direction of the military and naval forces, as first general and admiral of the Confederacy; while that of the British king extends to the declaring of war and to the raising and regulating of fleets and armies— all which, by the Constitution under consideration, would appertain to the legislature. The governor of New York, on the other hand, if by the constitution of the state vested only with the command of its militia and navy. But the constitutions of several of the states expressly declare their governors to be commanders-in-chief, as well of the army as navy; and it may well be a question whether those of New Hampshire and Massachusetts . . . do not, in this instance, confer larger powers upon their respective governors than could be claimed by a president. . . .

Third. The power of the president, in respect to pardons, would extend to all cases, except those of impeachment. The governor of New York may pardon in all cases, even in those of impeachment, except for treason and murder. Is not the power of the governor . . . on a calculation of political consequences, greater than that of the president? All conspiracies and plots against the government which have not been matured into actual treason may be screened from punishment of every kind by . . . pardoning. If a governor of New York, therefore, should be at the head of any such conspiracy . . . he could insure his accomplices and adherents an entire impunity. A president . . . on the other hand, though he may even pardon treason . . . could shelter no offender . . . from the effects of impeachment and conviction. . . .

Fourth. The president can only adjourn the national legislature in the single case of disagreement about the time of adjournment. The British monarch may prorogue or even dissolve the Parliament. The governor of New York may also prorogue the legislature of this state for a limited time; a power which, in certain situations, may be employed to very important purposes.

The president is to have power, with the advise and consent of the Senate, to make treaties, provided two-thirds of the senators present concur. The king . . . is the sole and absolute representative of the nation in all foreign transactions. He can of his own accord make treaties of peace, commerce, alliance, and of every other description. . . . In this respect, therefore, there is no comparison between the intended power of the president and the actual power of the British sovereign. The one can perform alone what the other can only do with the concurrence of a branch of the legislature. It must be admitted that in this instance the power of the federal executive would exceed that of any state executive. But this arises naturally from the exclusive possession by the Union of that part of the sovereign power which relates to treaties. If the Confederacy were to be dissolved, it would become a question whether the executives of the several states were not solely invested with that delicate and important prerogative.

The president is also to be authorized to receive ambassadors and other public ministers. This, though it has been a rich theme of declaration, is more a matter of dignity than of authority. It is a circumstance which will be without consequence in the administration of the government; and it was far more convenient that it should be arranged in this manner than that there should be a necessity of conveying the legislature, or one of its branches, upon every arrival of a foreign minister. . . .

The president is to nominate, and, with the advice and consent of the Senate, to appoint ambassadors and other public ministers, judges of the Supreme Court, and in general all officers of the United States established by law, and whose appointments are not otherwise provided for by the Constitution. The king . . . is emphatically and truly styled the fountain of honor. He not only appoints to all offices, but can create offices. He can confer titles of nobility at pleasure, and has the disposal of an immense number of church preferments. There is evidently a great inferiority in the power of the president . . . to that of the British king; nor is it equal to that of the governor of New York. . . . The power of appointment is with us lodged in a council, composed of the governor and four members of the senate, chosen by the assembly. The governor claims, and has frequently exercised, the right of nomination, and is entitled to a casting vote in the appointment. If he really has the right of nominating, his authority is in this respect equal to that of the president, and exceeds it in the article of the casting vote. In the national government, if the Senate should be divided, no appointment could be made; in . . . New York, if the council should be divided, the governor can turn the scale and confirm his own nomination. . . . [T]he power of the chief magistrate of this state, in the disposition of offices, must, in practice, be greatly superior to that of the chief magistrate of the Union.

Hence it appears that, except as to the concurrent authority of the president in the article of treaties, it would be difficult to determine whether that magistrate would, in the aggregate, possess more or less power than the governor of New York. And it appears yet more unequivocally that there is no pretense for the parallel which has been attempted between him and the king. . . . But to render the contrast . . . still more striking, it may be of use to throw the principal circumstances of dissimilitude into a closer group.

The president . . . would be an officer elected by the people for four years; the king . . . is a perpetual and hereditary prince. The one would be amenable to personal punishment and disgrace; the person of the other is sacred and inviolable. The one would have a qualified negative upon the acts of the legislative body; the other has an absolute negative. The one would have a right to command the military and naval forces of the nation; the other, in addition to this right, possesses that of declaring war, and of raising and regulating fleets and armies by his own authority. The one would have a concurrent power with a branch of the legislature in the formation of treaties; the other is the sole possessor of the power of making treaties. The one would have a like concurrent authority in appointing of offices; the other is the sole author of all appointments. The one can confer no privileges whatever; the other can make denizens of aliens, noblemen of commoners; can erect corporations with all the rights incident to corporate bodies. The one can prescribe no rules concerning the commerce or currency of the nation; the other is in several respects the arbiter of commerce, and in this capacity can establish markets and fairs, can regulate weights and measures, can lay embargoes for a limited time, can coin money, can authorize or prohibit the circulation of foreign coin. The one has no particle of spiritual jurisdiction; the other is the supreme head and governor of the national church! What answer shall we give to those who would persuade us that things so unlike resemble each other? The same that ought to be given to those who tell us that a government, the whole power of which would be in the hands of the elective and periodical servants of the people is an aristocracy, a monarchy, and a despotism.

The Federalist, Number 70 (Alexander Hamilton)

There is an idea, which is not without its advocates, that a vigorous Executive is inconsistent with the genius of republican government. The enlightened well-wishers to this species of government must at least hope that the supposition is destitute of foundation; since they can never admit its truth, without at the same time admitting the condemnation of their own principles. Energy in the Executive is a leading character in the definition of good government. It is essential to the protection of the community against foreign attacks; it is not less essential to the steady administration of the laws; to the protection of property against those irregular and high-handed combinations which sometime interrupt the ordinary course of justice; to the security of liberty against the enterprises and assaults of ambition, of faction, and of anarchy. Every man the least conversant in Roman story, knows how often that republic was obliged to take refuge in the absolute power of a single man, under the formidable title of Dictator, as well against the intrigues of ambitious individuals who aspired to the tyranny, and the seditions of whole classes of the community whose conduct threatened the existence of all government, as against the invasions of external enemies who menaced the conquest and destruction of Rome.

There can be no need, however, to multiply arguments or examples on this head. A feeble Executive implies a feeble execution of the government. A feeble execution is but another phrase for a bad execution; and a government ill executed, whatever it may be in theory, must be, in practice, a bad government.

Taking it for granted, therefore, that all men of sense will agree in the necessity of an energetic Executive, it will only remain to inquire, what are the ingredients which constitute this energy? How far can they be combined with those other ingredients which constitute safety in the republican sense? And how far does this combination characterize the plan which has been reported by the convention?

The ingredients which constitute energy in the Executive are, first, unity; secondly, duration; thirdly, an adequate provision for its support; fourthly, competent powers.

The ingredients which constitute safety in the republican sense are, first, a due dependence on the people, and secondly, a due responsibility.

Those politicians and statesmen who have been the most celebrated for the soundness of their principles and for the justice of their views, have declared in favor of a single Executive and a numerous legislature. They have with great propriety, considered energy as the most necessary qualification of the former, and have regarded this as most applicable to power in a single hand, while they have, with equal propriety, considered the latter as best adapted to deliberation and wisdom, and best calculated to conciliate the confidence of the people and to secure their privileges and interests. . . .

But one of the weightiest objections to a plurality in the Executive, and which lies as much against the last as the first plan, is, that it tends to conceal faults and destroy responsibility. Responsibility is of two kinds—to censure and to punishment. The first is the more important of the two, especially in an elective office. Man, in public trust, will much oftener act in such a manner as to render him unworthy of being any longer trusted, than in such a manner as to make him obnoxious to legal punishment. But the multiplication of the executive adds to the difficulty of detection in either case. It often becomes impossible amidst mutual accusations, to determine on whom the blame or the punishment of a pernicious measure, or series of pernicious measures, ought really to fall. It is shifted from one to another with so much dexterity, and under such plausible appearances, that the public opinion is left in suspense about the real author. The circumstances which may have led to any national miscarriage or misfortune are sometimes so complicated that, where there are a number of actors who may have had different degrees and kinds of agency, though we may clearly see upon the whole that there has been mismanagement, yet it may be impracticable to pronounce to whose account the evil which may have been incurred is truly chargeable. . . .

A little consideration will satisfy us, that the species of security sought for in the multiplication of the Executive, is unattainable. Numbers must be so great as to render combination difficult, or they are rather a source of danger than of security. The united credit and influence of several individuals must be more formidable to liberty, than the credit and influence of either of them separately. When power, therefore, is place in the hands of so small a number of men, as to admit of their interest and views being easily combined in a common enterprise, by an artful leader, it becomes more liable to abuse, and more dangerous when abused, than if it belonged in the hands of one man; who, from the very circumstance of his being alone, will be more narrowly watched and more readily suspected, and who cannot unite so great a mass of influence as when he is associated with others. The Decemvirs of Rome, whose name denotes their number, were more to be dreaded in their usurpation than any ONE of them would have been. No person would think of proposing an Executive much more numerous than that body; form six to a dozen have been suggested for the number of the council. The extreme of these numbers, is not too great for an easy combination; and from such a combination America would have more to fear, than from the ambition of any single individual. A council to a magistrate, who is himself responsible for what he does, are generally nothing better than a clog upon his good intentions, are often the instruments and accomplices of his bad and are almost always a cloak to his faults.

The Federalist, Number 78 (Alexander Hamilton)

We proceed now to an examination of the judiciary department of the proposed government.

In unfolding the defects of the existing Confederation, the utility and necessity of a federal judicature have been clearly pointed out. . . [T]he propriety of the institution in the abstract is not disputed; the only questions which have been raised being relative to the manner of constituting it, and to its extent. To these points, therefore, our observations shall be confined. . . .

Whoever attentively considers the different departments of power must perceive, that, in a government in which they are separated from each other, the judiciary, from the nature of its function, will always be the least dangerous to the political rights of the Constitution; because it will be least in a capacity to annoy or injure them. The Executive not only dispenses the honors, but holds the sword of the community. The legislature not only commands the purse, but prescribes the rules by which the duties and rights of every citizen are to be regulated. The judiciary, on the contrary, has no influence over either the sword or the purse; no direction either of strength or of the wealth of the society; and can take no active resolution whatever. It may truly be said to have neither FORCE nor WILL, but merely judgment; and must ultimately depend upon the aid of the executive arm even for the efficacy of its judgments.

This simple view of the matter suggests several important consequences. It proves incontestably, that the judiciary is beyond comparison the weakest of the three departments of power; that it can never attack with success either of the other two; and that all possible care is requisite to enable it to defend itself against their attacks. . . . It equally proves, that though individual oppression may now and then proceed from the courts of justice, the general liberty of the people can never be endangered from that quarter. . . . [F]rom the natural feebleness of the judiciary, it is in continual jeopardy of being overpowered, awed, or influenced, by its co-ordinate branches; and that as nothing can contribute so much to its firmness and independence as permanency in office, this quality may therefore be justly regarded as an indispensable ingredient in its constitution, and, in a great measure, as the citadel of the public justice and the public security.

The complete independence of the courts of justice is peculiarly essential in a limited Constitution. By a limited Constitution, I understand one which contains certain specified exceptions to the legislative authority; such, for instance, as that it shall pass not bills of attainder, no *ex-post-facto* laws, and the like. Limitations of this kind can be preserved in practice no other way than through the medium of courts of justice, whose duty it must be to declare all acts contrary to the manifest tenor of the Constitution void. Without this, all the reservations of particular rights or privileges would amount to nothing. . . .

There is no position which depends on clearer principles than that every act of a delegated authority, contrary to the tenor of the commission under which it is exercised, is void. No legislative act, therefore, contrary to the Constitution, can be valid. . . .

If it be said that the legislative body are themselves the constitutional judges of their own powers, and that the construction they put upon them is conclusive upon the other departments, it may be answered, that this cannot be the natural presumption, where it is not to be collected from any particular provisions in the Constitution. It is not otherwise to be supposed that the Constitution could intend to enable the representatives of the people to substitute their *will* to that of their constituents. It is far more rational to suppose that the courts were designed to be an intermediate body between the people and the legislature, in order, among other things, to keep the latter within the limits assigned to their authority. The interpretation of the laws is the proper and peculiar province of the courts. A constitution is, in fact, and must be, regarded by the judges as a fundamental law. It must therefore belong to them to ascertain its meaning, as well as the meaning of any particular act proceeding from the legislative body. If there should happen to be an irreconcilable variance between the two, that which has the superior obligation and validity ought, of course, to be preferred; in other words, the Constitution ought to be preferred to the statute, the intention of the people to the intention of their agents.

Nor does the conclusion by any means suppose a superiority of the judicial to the legislative power. It only supposes that the power of the people is superior to both; and that were the will of the legislature declared in its statutes, stands in opposition to that of the people declared in the Constitution, the judges ought to be governed by the latter, rather than the former. They ought to regulate their decisions by the fundamental laws, rather than by those which are not fundamental. . . .

If, then, the courts of justice are to be considered as the bulwarks of a limited constitution against legislative encroachments, this consideration will afford a strong argument for the permanent tenure of judicial offices, since nothing will contribute so much as this to that independent spirit in the judges which must be essential to the faithful performances of so arduous a duty. . . .

That inflexible and uniform adherence to the rights of the constitution, and of individuals, which we perceive to be indispensable in the courts of justice, can certainly not be expected from judges who hold their office by a temporary commission. Periodical appointments, however regulated, or by whomsoever made, would, in some way or other, be fatal to their necessary independence. If the power of making them was committed either to the Executive or legislature, there would be danger of improper complaisance to the branch which possessed it; if to both, there would be an unwillingness to hazard the displeasure of either; if to the people, or the persons chosen by them for the special purpose, there would be too great disposition to consult popularity, to justify a reliance that nothing would be consulted but the Constitution and the laws.

There is yet further and a weightier reason for the permanency of the judicial offices, which is deducible from the nature of the qualifications they require. It has been frequently remarked, with great propriety, that a voluminous code of laws is one of the inconveniences necessarily connected with the advantages of a free government. To avoid an arbitrary discretion in the courts, it is indispensable that they should be bound down by strict rules and precedents, which serve to define and point out their duty in every particular case that comes before them; and it will readily be conceived from the variety of controversies which grow out of the folly and wickedness of mankind, that the records of those precedents must unavoidable swell to a very considerable bulk, and must demand long and laborious study to acquire a competent knowledge of them. Hence it is, that there can be but few men in the society who will have sufficient skill in the laws to qualify them for the stations of judges. And making the proper deductions for the ordinary depravity of human nature, the number must be still smaller of those who unite the requisite integrity with the requisite knowledge. These considerations apprise us, that the government can have no great option between fit character; and that a temporary duration in office, which would naturally discourage such characters from quitting a lucrative line of practice to accept a seat on the bench, would have a tendency to throw the administration of justice into hands less able, and less well-qualified, to conduct it with utility and dignity. In the present circumstances of this country, and in those in which it is likely to be for a long time to come, the disadvantages on this score would be greater than they may at first sight appear; but it must be confessed, that they are far inferior to those which present themselves under the other aspects of the subject.

The Federalist, Number 84 (Alexander Hamilton)

The most considerable of the remaining objections is, that the plan of the convention contains no bill of rights. Among other answers given to this, it has been upon different occasions remarked, that the constitutions of several of the states are in a similar predicament. I add, that New York is of the number. And yet the persons who in the state oppose the new system . . . are among the most intemperate partisans of a bill of rights. To justify their zeal in this matter they allege two things: one is, that though the constitution of New York has no bill of rights prefixed to it, yet it contains in the body of it, various provisions in favor of particular privileges and rights, which, in substance, amount to the same thing; the other is, that the Constitution adopts, in their full extent, the common and statute law of Great Britain, by which many other rights, not expressed, are equally secured.

To the first I answer, that the Constitution offered by the convention contains, as well as the constitution of this state, a number of such provisions.

Independent of those which relate to the structure of the government, we find the following: Article I, section 3, clause 7. "Judgment in cases of impeachment shall not extend further than to removal from office, and disqualification to hold and enjoy any office of honor, trust, or profit under the United States; but the party convicted shall, nevertheless, be liable and subject to indictment, trial, judgment, and punishment, according to law." Section 9 of the same article, clause 2. "The privilege of the writ of *habeas corpus* shall not be suspended, unless when in cases of rebellion or invasion the public safety may require it." Clause 3. "No bill of attainder or *ex post facto* law shall be passed." Clause 7. "No title of nobility shall be granted by the United States; and no person holding any office of profit or trust under them, shall, without the consent of the congress, accept of any present, emolument, office, or title, of any kind whatever, from any king, prince, or foreign states." Article III, section 2, clause 3. "The trial of all crimes, except in cases of impeachment, shall be by jury; and such trial shall be held in the state where the said crimes shall have been committed; but when not committed within any state, the trial shall be at such place or places as the congress may by law have directed." Section 3 of the same article. "Treason against the United States shall consist only in levying war against them, or in adhering to their enemies, giving them aid and comfort. No person shall be convicted of treason, unless on the testimony of two witnesses to the same overt act, or on confession in open court." And clause 3 of the same section. "The congress shall have power to declare the punishment of treason; but no attainder of treason shall work corruption of blood, or forfeiture, except during the life of the person attained."

It may well be a question, whether these are not, upon the whole, of equal importance with any which are to be found in the constitution of this state. The establishment of the writ of *habeas corpus*, the prohibition of *ex post facto* laws, and of titles of nobility, *to which we have no corresponding provisions in our constitution,* are perhaps greater securities to liberty than any it contains. The creation of crimes after the commission of the fact, or, in other words, the subjecting of men to punishment for things which, when they are done, were breaches of no law; and the practice of arbitrary imprisonments have been, in all ages, the favorite and most formidable instruments of tyranny. . . .

To the second, that is, to the pretended establishment of the common and statute law by the Constitution, I answer, that they are expressly made subject "to such alterations and provisions as the legislature shall from time to time make concerning the same." They are therefore at any moment liable to repeal by the ordinary legislative power, and of course have no constitutional sanction. The only use of the declaration was to recognize the ancient law, and to remove doubts which might have been occasioned by the revolution. This consequently can be considered as no part of a declaration of rights; which under our constitutions must be intended to limit the power of the government itself.

It has been several times truly remarked, that bills of rights are . . . reservations of rights not surrendered to the prince. . . . Here, in strictness, the people surrender nothing; and as they retain everything, they have no need of particular reservations. "We the people of the United States, to secure the blessings of liberty to ourselves and our posterity do *ordain* and *establish* this constitution for the United States of America"; This is a better recognition of popular rights, than volumes of those aphorisms, which make the principal figure in several of our state bills of rights, and which would sound much better in a treatise of ethics, than in a constitution of government.

But a minute detail of particular rights is certainly far less applicable to a Constitution like that under consideration, which is merely intended to regulate the general political interests of the nation, than to one which has the regulation of every species of personal and private concerns. If therefore the loud clamors against the plan of the convention, on this score, are well founded, no epithets of reprobation will be too strong for the constitution of this state. But the truth is, that both of them contain all which, in relation to their objects, is reasonably to be desired.

I go further, and affirm, that bills of rights . . . are not only unnecessary in the proposed Constitution, but would even be dangerous. They would contain various exceptions to powers not granted, and on this very account would afford a colorable pretext to claim more than were granted. For why declare that things shall not be done which there is no power to do? Why, for instance, should it be said, that the liberty of the press shall not be restrained, when no power is given by which restrictions may be imposed? I will not contend that such a provision would confer a regulating power; but it is evident that it would furnish, to men disposed to usurp, a plausible pretense for claiming that power. They might urge with a semblance of reason that the Constitution ought not to be charged with the absurdity of providing against the abuse of an authority, which was not given, and that the provision against restraining the liberty of the press afforded a clear implication, that a right to prescribe proper regulations concerning it, was intended to be vested in the national government. This may serve as a specimen of the numerous handles which would be given to the doctrine of constructive powers, by the indulgence of an injudicious zeal for bills of rights. . . .

There remains but one other view of this matter to conclude the point. The truth is . . . that the Constitution is itself . . . a bill of rights. . . . Is it one object of a bill of rights to declare and specify the political privileges of the citizens in the structure and administration of the government? This is done in the most ample and precise manner in the plan of the convention; comprehending various precautions for the public security, which are not to be found in any of the state constitutions. Is another object of a bill of rights to define certain immunities and modes of proceeding, which are relative to personal and private concerns? This we have seen has been attended to, in a variety of cases, in the same plan. Advertising therefore to the substantial meaning of a bill of rights, it is absurd to allege that it is not to be found in the work of the convention. It may be said that it does not go far enough, though it will not be easy to make this appear; but it can with no propriety be contended that there is no such thing. It certainly must be immaterial what mode is observed as to the order of declaring the rights of the citizens, if they are provided for in any part of the instrument which establishes the government. Whence it must be apparent that much of what has been said on this subject rests merely on verbal and nominal distinctions, entirely foreign to the substance of the thing. . . .

Endnotes

Introduction

[1]The long-term effects of emerging technologies remain to be seen. Will the twenty-first century feature virtual citizenship in a cyberdemocracy?

[2]Harold Lasswell, Daniel Lerner, and C. Easton Rothwell, *The Comparative Study of Elites* (Stanford University Press, 1952), p. 7.

[3]Ibid.

[4]"Sovereignty," Microsoft (R) Encarta (Funk and Wagnalls, 1994).

[5]As of this writing, I am driving a 1992 Pontiac. The owner's manual is 320 pages long—considerably longer than the Articles of Confederation, Declaration of Independence, and the United States Constitution combined. It opens with the

statement "Many people read their owner's manual from beginning to end when they first receive their new vehicle." Not me. Maybe that is why I often find myself referring to "Part 5: Problems on the Road."

[6]Not "irrelevant"—**irreverent.**

[7]For the full text of the *Federalist Papers* and other important historical documents (the Declaration of Independence, the Articles of Confederation, the Constitution, and so forth), see THOMAS—U.S. Congress on the Internet at http://thomas.loc.gov/ and link to historical documents. If you prefer, go directly to http://lcweb2.loc.gov/const/mdbquery.html. Another web site for the *Federalist Papers* is http://www.mcs.net/~knautzr/fed/fedpaper.html. Another relevant site for historical documents is the University of Oklahoma Law Center's Chronology of U.S. Historical Documents at http://www.law.ou.edu/ushist.html.

[8]As far as I know, there is no such thing as "The Professional Political Scientist's Handbook." I made it up. If it turns out that such a book exists, please let me know. I should read it.

[9]The book is loosely organized around the system's framework. I use it at times to illustrate how the pieces of the political system "fit together." I try to keep the technicalities to a minimum. If you are a system's model purist, you may be disappointed by some of my simplifications.

Chapter One

[1]Alexander Astin, survey director, *The American Freshman: National Norms for Fall 1995* (Higher Education Research Institute, UCLA Graduate School of Education and Information Studies).

[2]As quoted in Jennings L. Wagoner Jr., *Thomas Jefferson and the End of a New Nation* (Phi Delta Kappa, 1976), p. 20.

[3]As quoted in Wagoner, p. 39.

[4]As quoted in Samuel Halperin, *A Guide for the Powerless and Those Who Don't Know Their Own Power* (Institute for Educational Leadership, 1981), p. 3.

[5]Frank Newman, *Higher Education and the American Resurgence* (Princeton University Press, 1985).

[6]David R. Hiley, "The Democratic Purposes of General Education," *Liberal Education* (Winter 1996), p. 25.

[7]Bruce Jennings, James Lindemann Nelson, and Erik Parens, "Values on Campus," *Liberal Education* (Winter 1996) p. 31.

[8]Julius Gould and William L. Kolb, *A Dictionary of the Social Sciences* (Free Press, 1965), p. 516.

[9]Vernon Van Dyke, "The Scope of Political Science," *The Conduct of Political Inquiry: Behavioral Political Analysis*, ed., Louis D. Hayes and Ronald D. Hedlund (Prentice-Hall, 1970), p. 27.

[10]Robert A. Dahl, *Modern Political Analysis*, 2nd ed. (Prentice-Hall, 1970), p. 6.

[11]Martin Meyerson and Edward C. Banfield, *Politics, Planning, and the Public Interest* (Free Press, 1955), pp. 303–12.

[12]Harold D. Lasswell, *Politics, Who Gets What, When, How* (McGraw-Hill, 1936).

[13]P. J. O'Rourke, *Parliament of Whores: A Lone Humorist Attempts to Explain the Entire U.S. Government* (Atlantic Monthly Press, 1991), p. 186.

[14]David Easton, *A Framework for Political Analysis* (Prentice-Hall, 1965), p. 50.

[15]Easton's work is probably the best introduction to the systems approach to political analysis. See also, Gabriel A. Almond and G. Bingham Powell, *Comparative Politics: A Developmental Approach* (Little, Brown, 1966) and William C. Mitchell, *The American Polity* (Free Press, 1962).

[16]Systems analysis is frequently criticized for having a built-in, politically conservative bias. Critics argue that systems analysis favors the status quo and tolerates only modest change in that a primary goal of the system is its own survival. Inputs are

sometimes regarded as "functional" if they contribute to the maintenance of the system and "dysfunctional" if they promote disruption of the system. As such, criticism of the system can be regarded as "bad," and dissension is seen as something that should be avoided (or even suppressed).

Defenders of systems analysis respond that a system can survive by responding effectively to criticism and that systems analysis does not necessarily deny the ability of the system to evolve and change in response to environmental forces.

Despite its limitations, systems analysis is a common framework for analysis, and the systems model can be a useful conceptual tool for organizing political information.

Chapter Two

[1]Thomas Hobbes, *Leviathan,* ed., Joseph A. Melusky, *The Constitution: Our Written Legacy* (Krieger Publishing Company, 1991), pp. 10–11.

[2]See John Locke, *Second Treatise, of Civil Government,* ed., Melusky, pp. 15–19.

[3]Rod Grams, "Dismantle Those Barricades: Return Pennsylvania Avenue to the Way It Was before May 20, 1995," *Washington Post,* May 20, 1996, A21.

[4]*Newsweek,* "Two Societies," Februrary 23, 1998, p. 6.

[5]James Madison, "The Last Day of the Constitutional Convention (September 17, 1787)," as quoted in Melusky, pp. 45–49.

[6]Ibid., p. 49.

[7]Richard B. Morris, "Creating and Ratifying the Constitution," *National Forum* (Fall 1984), p. 12.

[8]Ibid.

[9]In *The Federalist,* Number 1, Hamilton explained that these letters would discuss the inadequacies of the Articles of Confederation, the need for a stronger central government, similarities between the proposed Constitution and existing state constitutions, and the additional security that a new Constitution would provide. *The Federalist Papers,* ed., Clinton Rossiter (New American Library, 1961), pp. 33–37.

[10]Morris.

[11]North Carolina ratified on November 21, 1789, and Rhode Island ratified on May 29, 1790.

[12]James Madison, *The Federalist,* Number 10, ed., Rossiter, p. 77.

[13]Ibid., p. 78.

[14]Ibid.

[15]Ibid.

[16]Ibid.

[17]Ibid., p. 79.

[18]Ibid., p. 81.

[19]Ibid., p. 82.

[20]Ibid.

[21]Ibid., p. 83.

[22]Ibid.

[23]Ibid.

[24]Madison, *The Federalist,* Number 51, ed., Rossiter, p. 321.

[25]Ibid., p. 322.

[26]Ibid.

[27]Ibid.

Chapter Three

[1]Mark W. Cannon, "Why Celebrate the Constitution?" *National Forum: Toward the Bicentennial of the Constitution* 64 (Fall 1984), p. 3.

[2]9 Wheaton 1; 6 L.Ed. 23 (1824).

[3]See, for example, *The Shreveport Case (Houston East & West Texas Ry. Co.* v. *United States)* (234 U.S. 342, 1914); *Stafford* v. *Wallace* (259 U.S. 495, 1922); *NLRB* v. *Jones and Laughlin Steel Corporation* (301 U.S. 1, 1937); *Heart of Atlanta Motel* v. *United States* (379 U.S. 241, 1964); and *Katzenback* v. *McClung* (379 U.S. 294, 1964).

[4]*National Endowment for the Arts* v. *Finely* (524 U.S. 141 L.Ed. 2d 500, 118 S.Ct. 2168, 1988).

[5]For an extended discussion of the War Powers Resolution, see chapter 8 on the presidency.

[6]453 U.S. 57 (1981).

[7]More fully, the Military Selective Service Act authorizes the President to require male citizens and male resident aliens between the ages of eighteen and twenty-six to register for the draft. Registration was discontinued in 1975. In 1980 President Carter recommended that Congress reactivate the registration process and that Congress amend the act to permit the registration and possible conscription of women. Congress considered the president's recommendations at length and decided to reactivate the registration process but declined to permit the registration of women. A three-judge federal district court ruled that the challenged gender-based distinction violated the due process clause of the Fifth Amendment. In a six-to-three vote, the U.S. Supreme Court reversed on direct appeal.

Justice Rehnquist, joined by Chief Justice Burger and Justices Stewart, Blackmun, Powell, and Stevens, wrote the majority opinion. Rehnquist emphasized the Court's traditional deference to Congress in cases involving the national defense and military affairs. Registering women was "extensively considered" by Congress, and its conclusion to register only males was not an "accidental by-product of a traditional way of thinking about females." Rather, Congress's purpose was to prepare a draft of "combat troops," and because women were ineligible for combat, Congress exempted them. Rehnquist noted that the gender classification was "not invidious." He reasoned that Congress was not choosing arbitrarily to burden one of two similarly situated groups, "such as would be the case with an all-black or all-white, or an all-Catholic or all-Lutheran, or an all-Republican or all-Democratic registration." He found that men and women are not "similarly situated" for purposes of a draft or draft registration "because of the combat restrictions on women."

Justice White, joined by Justice Brennan, dissented, noting that not all positions in the military must be filled by combat-ready men and that women could be registered to fill noncombat positions "without sacrificing combat-readiness."

Justices Marshall and Brennan also dissented on grounds that the government had failed to show that registering women would "seriously impede" its efforts to achieve "a concededly important governmental interest in maintaining an effective defense."

[8]See "Hamilton's Opinion on the Constitutionality of a Bank," in Joseph A. Melusky, *The Constitution: Our Written Legacy* (Krieger Publishing Company, 1991), pp. 95–97; "Jefferson's Opinion on the Constitutionality of a Bank," Melusky, pp. 99–101; and *McCulloch* v. *Maryland* (4 Wheaton 316; 4 L.Ed. 579, 1819).

[9]*McCulloch* v. *Maryland.*

[10]See *Myers* v. *United States* (272 U.S. 52, 1926); *Humphrey's Executor* v. *United States* (295 U.S. 602, 1935); and *Wiener* v. *United States* (357 U.S. 349, 1958). The Court has held that presidents can remove purely executive officers on their own authority. Presidents cannot unilaterally remove quasi-legislative and quasi-judicial officers, however.

[11]418 U.S. 683 (1974).

[12]Brutus, "The Anti-Federalists (1787–1788)," Melusky, pp. 87–89.

[13]Hamilton, *The Federalist,* Number 84, *The Federalist Papers,* ed., Clinton Rossiter (New American Library, 1961), pp. 510–20.

[14]249 U.S. 47 (1919).

[15]Ibid.

[16]In *Miller* v. *California* (413 U.S. 15, 1973), the United States Supreme Court reaffirmed the principle that obscene material is not protected by the First Amendment. In the process, however, the Court relaxed *Memoirs* v. *Massachusetts* (383 U.S. 413, 1966) standards and made it relatively easier for local communities to restrict such materials.

In *Memoirs* v. *Massachusetts* a state court had banned the novel, *Fanny Hill,* as obscene, although the court acknowledged that it might have some "minimal literary value." The Supreme Court held that the book could be banned only if (a) the dominant theme of the material taken as a whole appeals to a prurient interest in sex; (b) the material patently offends contemporary community standards; and (c) the material is utterly without redeeming social value. The Supreme Court reversed the state court on the ground that, even though the book was offensive, it was not "**utterly** without redeeming social value."

In *Miller* sexually explicit materials were mailed to persons who had neither requested nor indicated any interest in such mailings. They complained to the police, and following a jury trial, the defendant was convicted of violating a California law making it a misdemeanor to knowingly distribute obscene matter.

Chief Justice Burger, joined by Justices White, Blackmun, Powell, and Rehnquist, wrote the majority opinion. Burger cited the Court's holding in *Roth* v. *United States* (354 U.S. 476, 1957) that obscene materials are not protected by the First Amendment. He claimed that the Court in *Memoirs* "veered sharply away from *Roth*" and produced a "drastically altered test." According to Burger, *Roth* **presumed** that obscene material is, by definition, "utterly without social value," while *Memoirs* required the prosecution to **prove** that challenged material is utterly valueless—a burden "virtually impossible to discharge under our criminal standards of proof." Burger announced that the Court was returning to *Roth* and abandoning as "unworkable" the "utterly without redeeming social value" test of *Memoirs.* Accordingly, Burger concluded that material is "obscene" and can be restricted if (a) the average person applying **local** community standards—rather than uniform national standards—finds that the work appeals to prurient interests, (b) the work is patently offensive, and (c) the work lacks "serious literary, artistic, political, or scientific value." Justice Douglas dissented, as did Justice Brennan, who was joined by Justices Stewart and Marshall.

Although Burger claimed to be returning to the *Roth* test, there the Court held that "ideas having even the **slightest** redeeming social importance . . . have full protection of the (First Amendment)." Burger's more restrictive test extends First Amendment protection only to works of "**serious** value." In sum, this case made it relatively easier to define materials as obscene and to restrict them.

[17]*Chaplinsky* v. *New Hampshire* (315 U.S. 568, 1942).

[18]283 U.S. 359 (1931).

[19]349 U.S. 577 (1969).

[20]393 U.S. 503 (1969).

[21]418 U.S. 405 (1974).

[22]391 U.S. 367 (1968).

[23]491 U.S. 397 (1989).

[24]Burning an American flag arouses strong emotional responses, which makes the action so appealing to political protestors. Flag burning is an ordinary person's way of attracting attention. It is doubtful that many would pay attention if such a protestor called a press conference or issued a position paper. The Supreme Court's decision in *Texas* v. *Johnson* generated a good deal of debate. Politicians, recalling how effectively President Bush had used patriotic themes in his 1988 campaign, rushed to support the flag. The House and Senate overwhelmingly passed resolutions pledging to seek ways to penalize flag burners. President Bush urged that a constitutional amendment be enacted to this end. Others advocated legislation to restrain flag desecration. Both houses approved the Flag Protection Act. President Bush, preferring a constitutional amendment, allowed the bill to become law without his signature.

Demonstrators in Seattle and in the District of Columbia immediately challenged the new law. *United States* v. *Eichman* (496 U.S. 310, 1990) made its way to the Supreme Court. In a five-to-four vote, the Court reaffirmed the premise of *Texas* v. *Johnson*. Once again, Justice Brennan, joined by Justices Marshall, Blackmun, Scalia, and Kennedy, wrote the majority opinion. Brennan held that the defendants' flag burning was expressive conduct and that the act, like the state law in *Texas* v. *Johnson*, improperly suppressed expression out of concern for its communicative impact. Even assuming that a national consensus favoring prohibition of flag burning existed, he said, "any suggestion that the Government's interest in suppressing speech becomes more weighty as popular opposition to that speech grows is foreign to the First Amendment." Further, punishing flag desecration "dilutes the very freedom that makes this emblem so revered."

Justice Stevens, joined by Chief Justice Rehnquist and Justices White and O'Connor, dissented. Stevens conceded that the Government may not prohibit expression simply because it finds the idea itself offensive. However, certain modes of expression can be restricted if such restrictions are supported by legitimate societal interests and if the speaker is free to express his or her ideas by other means.

[25]376 U.S. 254 (1964).

[26]The case arose out of the struggle against racial segregation. On March 29, 1960, the *New York Times* carried an ad charging Montgomery, Alabama, police with conducting a "wave of terror" against Martin Luther King Jr. and others engaged in demonstrations and protests. Alabama courts awarded heavy damages to law enforcement officers. The United States Supreme Court reversed this decision. Writing for the Court, Justice Brennan found that the *State's* interest in limiting defamatory speech is outweighed by the public's interest in "uninhibited, robust, and wide-open debate." Public officials cannot recover for libel unless they can prove actual **malice;** that is, the statements were made with knowledge that they were false or with **reckless disregard** for their truth or falsehood. Public officials and public figures are afforded less protection under libel laws because, unlike common citizens, the former have chosen to enter the public arena after having been forewarned of the risks to their reputations in doing so. Further, they typically have their own means for responding to falsehoods and correcting misinterpretations.

See also, *Gertz* v. *Robert Welch, Inc.* (418 U.S. 323, 1974). See also, Lee C. Bollinger, *Images of a Free Press* (University of Chicago Press, 1991).

[27]408 U.S. 665 (1972).

[28]*Bantam Books, Inc.* v. *Sullivan* (372 U.S. 58, 1963) and *Near* v. *Minnesota* (283 U.S. 697, 1931).

[29]403 U.S. 713 (1971).

[30]Many colonists fled religious persecution in England. Religious intolerance, however, remained common. Some colonies had religious tests for holding certain jobs or offices. The framers prohibited such religious tests for national offices in Article 6 but found it difficult to define the proper place of religion in American public life. Some, like George Washington and Patrick Henry, thought that religion fosters public morality and favored public support for religious activities. Others, like Thomas Jefferson and James Madison, opposed governmental advancement of religion.

The First Amendment provides that "Congress shall make no law respecting an establishment of religion or prohibiting the free exercise thereof." The amendment guarantees *two* things: the freedom to believe what one chooses *and* protection against governmental efforts to establish a national religion. In practice, these twin guarantees can seem to work at cross-purposes. For example, does the free exercise clause entitle the religious majority in a community to conduct prayer services and other religious exercises in public schools? Are they not freely exercising their religious beliefs if they do so? On the other hand, does the establishment clause prohibit such public school prayer as state advancement of religious beliefs through public institutions? Jefferson called for a "wall of separation" between church and state to avoid these kinds of problems. On the other side, some think that the Constitution permits the government to support religion as long as no particular sect is favored over others. That is, the government should be neutral.

In his majority opinion in *Walz* v. *Tax Commission* (397 U.S. 664, 1970), Chief Justice Burger argued that the government's role should be that of "benevolent neutrality." In that case the Court upheld the practice of exempting church property from public taxes.

First Amendment protections were also at issue when a number of states passed laws requiring children in public schools to salute the flag. Children who refused to comply could be expelled. In *Minersville* v. *Gobitis* (310 U.S. 586, 1940), the Court upheld such a law. The child of Jehovah's Witnesses refused to salute the flag on grounds that doing so would violate the family's religious belief that the laws of God are superior to those of government. Writing for the majority, Justice Frankfurter balanced an individual's interest in religious freedom against society's interests in promoting national unity and security. Finding the societal interests weightier, Frankfurter deferred to the board's judgment that compulsory flag salutes would promote national unity. Similar issues were before the Court in *West Virginia* v. *Barnette* (319 U.S. 624, 1943), and the Court overruled *Gobitis*. Writing for the majority, Justice Jackson said that "national unity" is an end that

officials may foster "by persuasion and example," not by "compulsion": "Compulsory unification of opinion achieves only the unanimity of the graveyard." The Bill of Rights, he reasoned, denies those in power the authority to coerce consent. Jackson's words follow.

> To believe that patriotism will not flourish if patriotic ceremonies are voluntary and spontaneous instead of a compulsory routine is to make an unflattering estimate of the appeal of our institutions to free minds. . . . If there is any fixed star in our constitutional constellation, it is that no official, high or petty, can prescribe what shall be orthodox in politics, nationalism, or other matters of opinion or force citizens to confess by word or act their faith therein.

Interest balancing is an inexact science. Congress opens sessions with a prayer. The Supreme Court begins sessions with the words "God save the United States and this honorable court." The Ten Commandments are on display in the Supreme Court. "In God We Trust" appears on our currency. Such official statements acknowledge religious belief. On the other hand, attempts to require impressionable school children to express religious sentiments have usually been disallowed.

Consider the Supreme Court's handling of some released-time programs. At issue in *Illinois ex rel. McCollum* v. *Board of Education* (333 U.S. 203, 1948) was a program under which public school students could attend religious instruction classes during regular school hours if their parents so requested. Participation was voluntary. The school board did not have to pay for the instruction. Classes were held in public school buildings, and attendance was enforced for students who were enrolled in the program. The Court invalidated the program on grounds that it involved the use of tax-supported public schools to spread religious beliefs.

In *Zorach* v. *Clausen* (343 U.S. 306, 1952), however, the Court upheld the constitutionality of another released-time program. A distinctive feature was that religious instruction classes were not held on public school grounds. Writing for a six-to-three majority, Justice Douglas said, "We are a religious people whose institutions presuppose a Supreme Being. . . . [This program] respects the religious nature of our people and accommodates the public service to their spiritual needs."

What about prayer in public schools? The New York State Board of Regents recommended that school districts adopt a denominationally neutral prayer to be said aloud by students in the presence of a teacher at the start of each school day. The prayer read "Almighty God, we acknowledge our dependence on Thee, and we beg Thy blessings upon us, our parents, our teachers, and our country." The parents of ten students argued that the prayer violated their religious beliefs. In *Engel* v. *Vitale* (370 U.S. 421, 1962), the Supreme Court agreed and found the Regents' prayer unconstitutional. Writing for the majority, Justice Black noted that the establishment clause means that "it is no part of the business of government to compose official prayers."

What if the state did not actually compose a prayer for use in public schools? What kind of religious observance might be acceptable? A Pennsylvania law provided for reading from the Bible, without comment, followed by the recitation of the Lord's Prayer and the Pledge of Allegiance at the start of the school day. The Schempps, a Unitarian family, claimed that some of the Bible readings violated their religious beliefs. The Supreme Court combined *Abington School District* v. *Schempp* (374 U.S. 203, 1963) with *Murray* v. *Curlett*. Mrs. Murray and her son, both atheists, thought that a similar Maryland law violated their religious rights on grounds that daily state-sponsored religious exercises put "a premium on belief as against non-belief." In both cases the Supreme Court agreed that the laws amounted to government endorsement of religious practices. Some years later the Alabama state legislature tried to get around the *Engel* decision by authorizing public school teachers to hold a minute of silence "for meditation or voluntary prayer" at the start of the school day. In *Wallace* v. *Jaffree* (472 U.S. 38, 1985), the Court struck down this practice as officially encouraging prayer.

Public schools would face tremendous financial burdens if parochial schools closed for lack of funds. Can the State assist parochial schools without violating the establishment clause? Some general rules emerged from a series of cases in which the Supreme Court allowed the government to "accommodate" religious activities as long as the government did not sponsor them and did not favor one sect over another. Although public funds cannot be used to aid religion, the Court has sometimes permitted public funds to be used to assist parochial school *children* (as opposed to assisting the parochial *schools*).

In *Everson* v. *Board of Education* (330 U.S. 1, 1947), for example, the Court upheld the use of public funds to pay for transporting children to parochial schools as a way of getting children safely to accredited schools "regardless of their religion." In a related case, *Board of Education* v. *Allen* (392 U.S. 236, 1968), the Court upheld a program under which the State was lending textbooks in secular subjects to parochial schools. The books were on secular subjects, so the Court reasoned that they neither inhibited nor advanced religion. Because no public funds actually went to the parochial schools in these cases, the Court held that the *children* were the primary beneficiaries.

In *Lemon* v. *Kurtzman* (403 U.S. 602, 1971), the Court considered a Pennsylvania program that reimbursed parochial schools for the salaries of teachers teaching secular subjects and secular instructional materials.

The Court rejected the program—and a similar one from Rhode Island in a companion case—by a unanimous vote. Chief Justice Burger explained that such aid must have a secular legislative purpose. It must have a primary effect that neither advances nor inhibits religion. And it must not lead to "excessive government entanglement" with religion. In this case the Court concluded that the state could not be sure that parochial school teachers were presenting their subjects to students in a neutral manner unless the state continually monitored teacher performance. Such surveillance would entail "excessive entanglement" between religious institutions and the state.

In *Mueller* v. *Allen* (465 U.S. 388, 1983), the Supreme Court upheld a Minnesota law that gave parents income tax deductions for tuition, textbook, and transportation costs. Unlike similar programs that the Court had previously invalidated, this tax break was available to parents regardless of whether their children attended public or nonpublic schools. As a practical matter, however, Minnesota's public schools were tuition free, so the main beneficiaries were parents whose children attended private—and usually parochial—schools. Nevertheless, the Court concluded that the Minnesota tax plan passed the "*Lemon* test."

In sum, the Court usually upholds aid to parochial schools if it is secular in purpose and effect and does not lead to excessive entanglement between church and state. On the other hand, the Court has disallowed religious exercises in public schools, holding that such religious instruction, prayer services, and so on violate the establishment clause.

The Court has had less difficulty in upholding aid to church-affiliated colleges and universities. In *Tilton* v. *Richardson* (403 U.S. 672, 1971), the Court upheld federal construction grants that went to church-related colleges. The grants stipulated that no federally financed building would be used for religious purposes. Chief Justice Burger's majority opinion argued that there is a difference between aid to colleges and aid to primary and secondary schools: "College students are less impressionable and less susceptible to religious indoctrination."

Finally, consider the case of *Lynch* v. *Donnelly* (465 U.S. 668, 1984). The city of Pawtucket, Rhode Island, had erected a Christmas display that included, among other things, a nativity scene. Did the inclusion of this religious symbol represent a governmental endorsement of religious ideas? By a five-to-four vote, the Supreme Court decided that it did not. In his lead opinion Chief Justice Burger said that when the entire display was viewed within the context of long-established holiday traditions, the creche was permissible. He concluded that the city had a secular purpose, it was not advancing religion, and it had not become excessively entangled with religion. In one dissent Justice Brennan maintained that the inclusion of a nativity scene in the city's Christmas display puts "the government's imprimatur of approval on the particular religious beliefs exemplified by the creche." In a separate dissent Justice Blackmun noted that the majority did an injustice to the message of the creche by stripping it of its religious significance and equating it with all other commercial symbols designed to put shoppers in a money-spending mood.

[31]For example, see *United States* v. *Cruikshank* (1876) where the Court said that the purpose of the Second Amendment was to ensure a well-regulated militia. In *Miller* v. *Texas* (1894) and *Robertson* v. *Baldwin* (1897), the Court held that the Second Amendment is not absolute. As such, laws could be enacted to prohibit carrying concealed weapons or taking weapons into court, schools, polling places, churches, and the like. In *City of Salina* v. *Blaksley* (1905), the Kansas Supreme Court ruled that the Second Amendment protects the collective right of the people to arm their militias, not the right of individuals to carry weapons for their

own purposes. In a 1928 article in the *Marquette Law Review,* legal scholar D. J. McKenna maintained that, at most, the Second Amendment prevents Congress from disarming men so as to prevent them from serving in state militias. In *United States* v. *Miller* (1939), the Supreme Court upheld the National Firearms Act's restrictions on sawed-off shotguns because nothing in the record showed that such weapons had "some reasonable relationship to the preservation, or efficiency, of a well-regulated militia." The Court reasoned that the Second Amendment was designed to render effective the constitutional provision that provides for "calling forth the militia" and it "must be interpreted and applied with that end in view." In *Thompson* v. *Dereta* (549 F.Sup. 297 D Utah, 1982), a court observed that there is not a single case in which a court has upheld the right to bear arms under the Second Amendment outside the context of a militia. In *Quilici* v. *Morton Grove* (1983), the Supreme Court let stand an appellate court decision upholding the authority of a town to **ban** not just the sale but also the **possession** of handguns.

[32]268 U.S. 435, at 441 (1925).

[33]*Johnson* v. *United States* (333 U.S. 10, 1948).

[34]*United States* v. *Matlock* (415 U.S. 164, 1974).

[35]*Terry* v. *Ohio* (392 U.S. 1, 1968).

[36]277 U.S. 438 (1928).

[37]365 U.S. 505 (1961).

[38]389 U.S. 347 (1967).

[39]7 Peters 243 (1833).

[40]Prior to the Civil War, the Constitution provided individuals with little protection against state actions. This situation changed with the postwar ratification of the Thirteenth, Fourteenth, and Fifteenth Amendments. The Fourteenth Amendment provides that no *state* shall "deprive any person of life, liberty, or property, without due process of law." Over the years many rights and liberties deemed essential to due process have been "incorporated" or "absorbed" into the Fourteenth Amendment and protected against state encroachment. Although *Barron* v. *Baltimore* has not been overruled, its practical effect has been limited. Today a case like Barron's could be brought under the Fourteenth Amendment's due process clause. As such, individual rights are now afforded greater national protection against state infringements.

[41]The Seventh Amendment also guarantees the right to a jury trial in civil cases.

[42]391 U.S. 145 (1968).

[43]The right to a jury trial applies at the state level by way of the Fourteenth Amendment's due process clause.

[44]*Duncan* raised several questions. The old common-law standard of **twelve-person juries** applies in federal cases, but would twelve-person juries be required in state cases, too? In *Williams* v. *Florida* (399 U.S. 78, 1970), a defendant had been tried for robbery before a six-person jury. Justice White's majority opinion held that twelve-person juries were **not** required at the state level. What about the matter of **nonunanimous verdicts?** In federal cases the jury verdict must be unanimous. A nonunanimous verdict represents a **hung jury** resulting in a **mistrial.** In *Johnson* v. *Louisiana* (406 U.S. 356, 1972) and *Apodaca* v. *Oregon* (406 U.S. 404, 1972), the Supreme Court ruled that the Constitution does **not** require jury verdicts in state courts to be unanimous. Justice White wrote the opinion for the Court in both cases.

[45]287 U.S. 45 (1932).

[46]For example, in *Betts* v. *Brady* (316 U.S. 455, 1942), the Supreme Court reaffirmed the principle that a state need not necessarily appoint counsel for indigent defendants in all criminal cases.

[47]372 U.S. 335, 1963.

[48]348 U.S. 436 (1966).

[49]In *Weeks* v. *United States* (232 U.S. 383, 1914), the Supreme Court developed the **exclusionary rule** as a way of enforcing

the Fourth Amendment. Evidence gathered by federal agents through unreasonable searches and seizures would not be admissible in federal courts. The exclusionary rule has also been used to bar evidence obtained in violation of the Fifth and Sixth Amendments. But this rule did not apply in state courts. In *Wolf* v. *Colorado* (338 U.S. 25, 1949), the Court ruled that unreasonable searches and seizures conducted by state officials violate the Fourteenth Amendment, but a state could still use this evidence in its own courts if permitted to do so by its own laws.

The Court extended the exclusionary rule to states in *Mapp* v. *Ohio* (367 U.S. 643, 1961). Cleveland police officers were looking for a suspect who was reportedly hiding in a house where they also expected to find gambling materials. They forced their way into the house without a warrant and conducted a search. They found a trunk containing some obscene materials, and this evidence was used to obtain an obscenity conviction against Miss Mapp in state court. Writing for a six-to-three majority, Justice Clark overruled *Wolf* and held that evidence obtained through unreasonable searches and seizures is inadmissible in state, as well as federal, courts.

The exclusionary rule has been very controversial. In 1926 Benjamin Cardozo lamented that "[t]he criminal is free to go because the constable has blundered." Justice Clark replied, "The criminal goes free, if he must, but it is the law that sets him free. Nothing can destroy a government more quickly than its failure to observe its own laws, or worse, its disregard for the charter of its own existence." Chief Justice Burger argued that the rule should be abandoned and replaced with a law authorizing individuals to sue law enforcement officers who violate their rights for monetary damages. Defenders of the exclusionary rule say it is the only effective deterrent to police misconduct.

The Court has created several exceptions to the exclusionary rule. In *United States* v. *Leon* (468 U.S. 897, 1984), the Court created a "defective warrant" exception to the exclusionary rule. In *Nix* v. *Williams* (467 U.S. 431, 1984), the Court created an "inevitable discovery" exception. And in *Maryland* v. *Garrison* (480 U.S. 79, 1987), the Court created an "honest mistakes" exception. As a result, some evidence that would have been excluded previously was admitted in court. These changes illustrate how a "living Constitution" evolves with the times through changing judicial interpretations.

[50]In the 1960s the Supreme Court decided several cases concerning whether juries could decide on the death penalty within legislative guidelines. Then, in *Furman* v. *Georgia* (408 U.S. 238, 1972), the Court *appeared* to strike down the death penalty itself. The decision revealed a severely split Court. The majority could not agree on one single opinion, so five separate concurring opinions were written. Justice Douglas contended that capital punishment is cruel and unusual because it is disproportionately levied against the poor and minorities. Justice Brennan stated that the death penalty is "fatally offensive to human dignity." Justice Marshall agreed that the poor were more likely to end up on death row and found the death penalty to be "excessive and unnecessary punishment." Chief Justice Burger, in dissent, pointed out that the Court had not banned all capital punishment. It simply pointed out that "the present system of discretionary sentencing in capital cases has failed to produce evenhanded justice." His words were an invitation to state legislatures to reform their sentencing procedures, and in *Gregg* v. *Georgia* (428 U.S. 153, 1976), the Court upheld Georgia's modified sentencing procedures over the spirited dissents of Justices Brennan and Marshall. Justice Stewart wrote the Court's majority opinion.

[51]For much of our history, the Ninth Amendment lay "forgotten." In a 1965 concurring

opinion in *Griswold* v. *Connecticut* (381 U.S. 479, 1965), however, Justice Goldberg cited the Ninth Amendment as a source of an unenumerated **right of privacy.** Since then the Amendment has been cited in more than one thousand cases and has received considerable scholarly attention. But the Court has been reluctant to rely upon this amendment. Justice Douglas's majority opinion in *Griswold* maintained that the right of privacy emanated from **penumbras,** which surrounded various provisions in the Bill of Rights and created **zones of privacy.** In other cases the justices have found additional unenumerated rights as part of the **liberty** protected by the due process clauses of the Fifth and Fourteenth Amendments. But what about the Ninth Amendment?

This amendment seems to embody the concept of **natural rights** protected against governmental infringement. Responding to Anti-Federalist calls for the inclusion of a Bill of Rights, Federalists like Alexander Hamilton and James Wilson claimed that a written bill of rights was unnecessary and dangerous. Unnecessary because the national government would possess only powers delegated to it; dangerous because the inadvertent omission of some natural right from a written list might imply that no such right existed. James Madison, author of the Bill of Rights, shared the concerns of Hamilton and Wilson. In a speech to the House of Representatives, Madison explained that the Ninth Amendment was designed to guard against the presumption that unenumerated rights "were intended to be assigned into the hands of the General Government, and were consequently insecure."

[52]166 U.S. 226 (1897).

[53]211 U.S. 78 (1908).

[54]In *Gitlow* v. *New York* (268 U.S. 652, 1925), the Supreme Court upheld Gitlow's conviction for advocating the violent overthrow of the government, but it ruled that freedom of speech and press are among the fundamental liberties protected by the Fourteenth Amendment's due process clause against state infringement. In *Stromberg* v. *California* (283 U.S. 358, 1931), the Court ruled that the Fourteenth Amendment protects freedom of speech. In *Near* v. *Minnesota* (283 U.S. 687, 1931), it held that freedom of the press is likewise protected against state actions. *DeJonge* v. *Oregon* (299 U.S. 253, 1937) nationalized the right of assembly and petition; *Cantwell* v. *Connecticut* (310 U.S. 296, 1940) nationalized the free exercise of religion; and *Everson* v. *Board of Education of Ewing Township, New Jersey* (310 U.S. 296, 1940) nationalized the prohibition against establishment of religion. *Hamilton* v. *Board of Regents* (293 U.S. 245, 1934) also protected freedom of religion through the Fourteenth Amendment.

[55]Some of the rights of the accused have been incorporated into the Fourteenth Amendment and protected at the state level. In *Moore* v. *Dempsey* (261 U.S. 86, 1923), the Supreme Court ruled that due process entitles *state* criminal defendants to fair trials. In *Powell* v. *Alabama* (287 U.S. 45, 1932), the right to counsel was applied in a state capital case. In *Brown* v. *Mississippi* (297 U.S. 278, 1936), a state criminal defendant was protected against coerced confessions. More and more rights were incorporated into the Fourteenth Amendment and protected against state encroachment, including the following: protection against unreasonable searches and seizures (*Mapp* v. *Ohio*, 367 U.S. 643, 1961); prohibition of cruel and unusual punishments (*Robinson* v. *California*, 370 U.S. 660, 1962); the right to counsel in criminal cases (*Gideon* v. *Wainright*, 372 U.S. 335, 1963); protection against compulsory self-incrimination (*Malloy* v. *Hogan*, 378 U.S. 1, 1964); the right to confront hostile witnesses (*Pointer* v. *Texas*, 380 U.S. 400, 1965); the right to a speedy trial (*Klopfer* v. *North Carolina*, 386 U.S. 213, 1967); the right to subpoena favorable witnesses

(*Washington* v. *Texas,* 388 U.S. 14, 1967);
the right to a jury trial (*Duncan* v.
Louisiana, 391 U.S. 145, 1968); the
guarantee of an impartial jury (*Parker* v.
Gladden, 385 U.S. 363, 1966); and the
protection against double jeopardy
(*Benton* v. *Maryland,* 395 U.S. 784, 1969).

Not all of the rights in the Bill of Rights
have been made applicable against to the
states, however. For example, the right to
a grand jury indictment has not been
incorporated into the Fourteenth
Amendment.

[56]163 U.S. 537 (1896).

[57]339 U.S. 629 (1950).

[58]347 U.S. 483 (1954).

Chapter Four

[1]Harold Lasswell, Daniel Lerner, and C. Easton
Rothwell, *The Comparative Study of Elites*
(Stanford University Press, 1952), p. 7.

[2]See Stephen V. Monsma, *American Politics,* 3rd
ed. (Dryden Press, 1976) at pp. 64–65
citing Robert E. Lane and David O. Sears,
Public Opinion (Prentice-Hall, 1964),
chap. 2; Floyd H. Allport, "Toward a
Science of Public Opinion," *Public
Opinion Quarterly* 1 (1937), pp. 7–23;
Bernard C. Hennessy, *Public Opinion,* 2nd
ed. (Wadsworth, 1970), chap. 1; and V. O.
Key Jr., *Public Opinion and American
Democracy* (Knopf, 1951), pp. 216–22.

[3]William H. Flanigan and Nancy Zingale, *Political
Behavior of the American Electorate,* 8th
ed. (Congressional Quarterly, 1994), p. 17.

[4]See *The Public Perspective* 3 (May–June 1992),
pp. 7–9; Center for Political Studies
National Election Studies, 1991, 1992, as
discussed by Flanigan and Zingale at p. 7.

[5]Fred Greenstein, *Children and Politics* (Yale
University Press, 1965).

[6]Flanigan and Zingale, p. 15.

[7]See General Social Survey, 1987, Inter-university
Consortium for Political and Social
Research, as discussed by Flanigan and
Zingale at p. 98.

[8]Jonathan Alter, "Next: 'The Revolt of the
Revolted'," *Newsweek,* November 6, 1995,
pp. 46–47.

[9]As reported by Cindy Simoneau, Thompson
News Service, "Attitudes of Young People
about Rape Are Disturbing," *Altoona
Mirror,* November 22, 1995, B4.

[10]See Paul Lazarsfeld, Bernard Berelson, and
Hazel Gaudet, *The People's Choice*
(Columbia University Press, 1944) and
Bernard Berelson, Paul Lazarsfeld, and
William McPhee, *Voting* (University of
Chicago Press, 1954), as discussed by
Flanigan and Zingale at pp. 106–09.

[11]For a discussion of differences in intensity of
preferences, see Robert Dahl, *A Preface to
Democratic Theory* (University of Chicago
Press, 1956), chap. 4 and George Beam,
*Usual Politics: A Critique and Some
Suggestions for an Alternative* (Holt,
Rinehart, and Winston, 1970).

[12]V. O. Key Jr., *The Responsible Electorate*
(Harvard University Press, 1966).

[13]See, for example, Richard Scammon and
Benjamin Wattenberg, *The Real Majority*
(Coward-McCann, 1970), where they
argue that most voters hold moderate
positions on issues.

Former presidential advisor Dick Morris's
triangulation strategy was an application
of this idea. Following Republican
congressional successes in the 1994 midterm
elections, Morris advised President Clinton
to appeal to moderates by positioning
himself between Newt Gingrich and
conservative Republicans on the right and
liberal congressional Democrats on the left.

[14]See Philip Converse, "The Nature of Belief
Systems in Mass Publics," in *Ideology and
Discontent,* ed., David Apter (Free Press,
1964), pp. 206–61 and Norman Nie and
Kristi Anderson, "Mass Belief Systems
Revisited: Political Change and Attitude
Structure," *Journal of Politics* 36
(September 1974), pp. 541–91.

[15]Morris Fiorina, *Retrospective Voting in American
National Elections* (Yale University Press,
1981).

[16]Michael X. Delli Carpini and Scott Keener, *What Americans Know about Politics and Why It Matters* (Yale University Press, 1996).

[17]David RePass, "Levels of Rationality among the American Electorate," paper delivered at the 1974 meeting of the American Political Science Association, as discussed by Monsma at pp. 75–76.

[18]Arthur Miller et al., "A Majority Party in Disarray: Policy Polarization and the 1972 Election," paper delivered at the 1973 meeting of the American Political Science Association, as discussed by Monsma at pp. 74–75.

[19]Based on data collected by National Election Studies of the University of Michigan and analyzed by Robert S. Erikson, Norman R. Luttbeg, and Kent L. Tedin, as cited in Michael Goldstein, *Guide to the 1992 Presidential Election* (Congressional Quarterly, 1992), p. 49.

These studies presenting a favorable view of voter awareness involve high-visibility presidential elections where information and coverage are abundant. Local-level examples of high voter awareness are also available. In 1978 Philadelphia voters were asked their city charter should be changed to permit a mayor to seek a third consecutive term. Without the charter change, the sitting mayor—Frank Rizzo—would be ineligible to run for reelection in 1979. Rizzo was a very controversial figure. A former police officer and police commissioner, he was a rough-talking law-and-order proponent who at one point left a formal dinner to rush to the scene of a disturbance where he was photographed wearing a nightstick under his tuxedo. He excited strong emotions among supporters and detractors alike. While campaigning for the charter change, Rizzo addressed a group of opponents to a proposed public housing project in the Whitman Park section of the city. Rizzo got carried away by the enthusiastic reception he received and urged those in attendance to "Vote white!" Media coverage was extensive.

Record numbers of blacks registered to vote, and they recorded a 71 percent turnout. Blacks voted in bloc fashion, with 96 percent opposing the charter change. Mayor Rizzo was denied a chance to run for a third consecutive term. Rizzo made an unsuccessful comeback attempt in 1983. He was defeated in the Democratic primary by Wilson Goode, a former city controller who went on to become the city's first black mayor. In 1987 Rizzo ran for mayor as a Republican, and Goode defeated him again. The irony is that Rizzo inspired blacks to register to vote in the first place and Goode was an immediate beneficiary. In this example black voters saw a direct personal stake and acted in accordance with their perceived interests.

[20]Carl Friedrich, *Man and His Government* (McGraw-Hill, 1963). Monsma offers a version of the "watchdog story" at pp. 80–81.

[21]See the discussion in Flanigan and Zingale, p. 35. Angus Campbell distinguished between "high stimulus" and "low stimulus" elections. Angus Campbell et al., eds., *Elections and the Political Order* (John Wiley and Sons, 1966), pp. 40–62.

[22]See Angus Campbell's discussion in "Surge and Decline: A Study of Electoral Change," *Elections and the Political Order.*

[23]From 1906 through 1998, the president's party has lost an average of 32.04 seats in the House in off-year elections.

[24]For historical discussion of suffrage and turnout, see Flanigan and Zingale, chap. 1. Voter turnout rates in the United States are calculated in a potentially misleading fashion. National turnout rates are based on the percentage of eligible adult voters who actually vote. Many "eligible" adults fail to register and are unable to vote as a result. Including unregistered adults in the calculations makes turnout rates artificially low.

[25]Ibid., p. 40.

[26]Ibid., p. 41. See also Stephen Wayne's discussion of class bias in voting behavior in *The Road to the White House, 1996* (St. Martin's Press, 1996), pp. 60–68.

[27]Stephen Ansolabehere and Shanto Iyengar, *Going Negative: How Attack Ads Shrink and Polarize the Electorate* (Free Press, 1995). The authors conclude that political advertising is an important source of information for voters and that it serves a positive function if used responsibly. However, they found that negative ads contribute to voter disillusionment, distrust, and dissatisfaction.

In contrast, a 1996 study conducted by the League of Women Voters found that nonvoters are no more alienated than voters. The study concluded that people do not vote because they do not see the importance of the election on issues that matter to them, they are ill informed about their choices, and they see the process of voting as difficult and cumbersome. See Richard L. Berke,"Nonvoters Are No More Alienated Than Voters, a Study Shows," *New York Times*, May 30, 1996.

[28]Lynne Casper and Loretta Bass coauthored a Census Bureau report on voter turnout in the 1996 presidential election. The report was released on August 17, 1998. The report found that the number of people who said they were too busy to vote (4.6 million) exceeded even voter apathy (3.5 million). "Among Americans who were registered but did not vote, more than one in five told us they didn't go to the polls because they couldn't take time off from work or were too busy," said Casper. That was three times the proportion of nonvoters who gave that reason in 1980. "Time constraints are now the biggest reason Americans who are registered give for not voting," added Bass. "Many people these days are finding their employers are putting so many demands on them, they can't take time off to vote." In addition, 3.2 million cited illness, disability, or emergencies as their reasons for not voting, while 2.8 million said that they didn't like the candidates. See "Americans Too Busy to Vote," *Altoona Mirror*, August 18, 1998.

[29]"Public Has Duty to Vote," *Altoona Mirror*, November 3, 1998, A6.

Chapter Five

[1]See discussion in William H. Flanigan and Nancy H. Zingale, *Political Behavior of the American Electorate*, 8th ed. (Congressional Quarterly, 1994), pp. 111–13 and 131–37.

[2]From 1952 through 1968 an average of 14.8 percent of voters split their tickets by supporting candidates of different parties in presidential and House races. From 1972 through 1996 an average of 24.7 percent of voters split their tickets. Calculated from National Election Studies data (Center for Political Studies, University of Michigan) as reported in Harold W. Stanley and Richard G. Niemi, *Vital Statistics on American Politics*, 1997–1998 (Congressional Quarterly, 1998), p. 129.

[3]Some argue that the increasing importance of television advertising campaigns, direct-mail fund-raising, and media consultants have diminished the importance of parties. Candidates, supported by money and media, rely on personal campaign organizations rather than parties. These developments contribute to the obsolescence of political parties. On the other hand, national party organizations, like the national committees and senatorial and congressional campaign committees, are well organized and well funded. The parties have their own permanent headquarters in Washington, D.C. The national parties provide money and campaign expertise to those who need it. In these ways the parties remain viable organizations. For a discussion of these ideas, see James MacGregor Burns, J. W. Peltason, Thomas E. Cronin, and David B. Magleby, *Government by the People*, 16th ed. (Prentice-Hall, 1995), p. 262.

Different people identify themselves as independents for different reasons. Generalizations are difficult. Some are very interested in politics, and others are apathetic. Some are well-informed, likely to register, and likely to vote. Others are not. Some call themselves independents as a conscious rejection of the positions held by the major parties; others simply have not given the matter much thought. As Flanigan and Zingale put it, "[w]hen we question whether independents are attentive or apathetic toward politics, we must conclude that they are some of both." (Flanigan and Zingale, p. 79.)

[4]Richard Hofstadter, *The Idea of a Political System* (University of California Press, 1969).

[5]See Burns et al. for a brief history of political parties, pp. 246–49.

[6]Party platforms can help illuminate party differences (and similarities). The 1996 Republican platform listed a series of principles. The Republicans called for lower taxes, a simpler tax system, fair and open trade, a balanced federal budget, a balanced budget amendment to the Constitution, reduced government regulation, welfare reform, tough law enforcement, family values, smaller government, state and local control over education and welfare programs, and strong national defense.

The 1996 Democratic platform stressed the values of opportunity, responsibility, and community. The Democrats called for a balanced budget, environmental protection, tax relief for working people, foreign-trade reform, expanded educational opportunities, affordable and high-quality health care, smaller but more efficient government, law and order, welcoming legal immigrants, welfare reform, abortion rights, security through military strength and diplomacy, "putting families first," use of a V-chip to block out television violence, cracking down on illegal sales of tobacco to minors, fighting discrimination, and protecting civil rights.

For a closer look at these platforms, visit the respective parties' web sites at http://www.rnc.org/hq/platform96/plat2.html for the Republicans and http://www.democrats.org/party/convention/convplt.html for the Democrats.

When the Republicans nominated Bob Dole in 1996 instead of Steve Forbes, Lamar Alexander, or Phil Gramm, they emphasized one set of issue positions over another. When the Democrats selected Bill Clinton in 1992 instead of Paul Tsongas, Jerry Brown, Tom Harkin, or Bob Kerry—and when they renominated him in 1996—they did likewise. Similarly, when the parties selected Jack Kemp and Al Gore, respectively, as running mates, they tried to broaden the appeal of their tickets by addressing additional concerns.

[7]James and Sarah Brady addressed the Democratic National Convention in Chicago in August 1996. In his first State of the Union address, President Clinton told Congress that he would sign the Brady Bill if Congress passed it. Congress approved a bill that required a waiting period for the purchase of a handgun to give local authorities time to conduct a background check on the buyer. As promised, Clinton signed it. The law went into effect on February 28, 1994. In 1997 a federal court struck down the background-check provision. The waiting period is to be phased out and replaced by instant computerized background checks. Debate and controversy continue.

[8]For present purposes "power" and "influence" are being used synonymously. Theorists sometimes distinguish between the two, noting that power is accompanied by potential force or coercion. See Robert Dahl, *Modern Political Analysis*, 2nd ed. (Prentice-Hall, 1970).

[9]Newt Gingrich was one of Wright's most vocal critics. When the Republicans gained control of the House in 1994, Gingrich was named the new Speaker of the House. He soon found himself embroiled in controversy and subjected to Ethics

Committee investigations. Ironically, some of his problems centered on a book deal of his own.

[10]*Buckley* v. *Valeo,* 424 U.S. 1 (1976).

[11]In 1992 Perot did not have to limit his spending because he did not receive federal campaign funds. In 1996, however, he did accept federal funds and was required to comply with spending limits.

[12]See John Wright, "Contributions, Lobbying, and Committee Voting in the U.S. House of Representatives," *American Political Science Review* 84 (June 1990), pp. 418–38 and Richard Hall and Frank Wayman, "Buying Time: Moneyed Interests and the Mobilization of Bias in Congressional Committees," *American Political Science Review* 84 (September 1990), pp. 797–820.

[13]Fred Wertheimer, "Campaign Finance Reform: The Unfinished Agenda," *Annals of the American Academy of Political and Social Science* (July 1986), as reprinted in George McKenna and Stanley Feingold, *Taking Sides: Clashing Views on Controversial Political Issues,* 10th ed. (Dushkin, 1997), pp. 44–47.

[14]See Norman J. Ornstein, Thomas E. Mann, and Michael Malbin, *Vital Statistics on Congress, 1991–92* (Congressional Quarterly, 1992), pp. 99–100.

[15]On December 17, 1992, Congress passed NAFTA. Critics worried that Mexican workers would be willing to work for lower wages and that U.S. companies would move their operations to Mexico for lower labor costs. Supporters said NAFTA would remove trade barriers, U.S. exports to Mexico would rise, and additional jobs would be created for American workers. To date the debate over NAFTA's effects continue. Some new jobs have been created, but old manufacturing jobs have been lost. On balance, has NAFTA been good for the U.S. economy? It depends on whom you ask. An analyst focusing on aggregate economic indicators might view NAFTA favorably. A displaced factory worker who lacks the technical skills to compete for one of the new high-tech jobs will see things differently.

[16]Ralph Reed, *Active Faith* (Free Press, 1996), as excerpted in "We Stand at a Crossroads," *Time,* May 13, 1996, pp. 28–29.

[17]For example, various groups successfully cooperated to oppose Robert Bork's appointment to the Supreme Court in 1987. In 1991 group efforts to block Clarence Thomas's appointment to the Court failed.

[18]E. E. Schattschneider, *The Semisovereign People* (Holt, Rinehart, and Winston, 1960). See also, Mancur Olson Jr., *The Logic of Collective Action* (Harvard University Press, 1965). Upper-class groups provide "selective benefits" that go only to group members. Mass-based groups—like the Sierra Club, consumer protection groups, and so on—provide "collective benefits" that go to nongroup members too. You don't have to belong to an environmental group to enjoy nice parks and clean air. A physician *does* have to join the American Medical Association to take advantage of its professional services. This difference in incentive structures contributes to the advantage that upper-class groups have over groups representing the masses.

Chapter Six

[1]AP story by John King, AP political writer, *Altoona Mirror* (September 29, 1996), A11.

[2]He was aided in this effort by a political strategist, Dick Morris, who resigned in August of 1996 amid reports that he had been sharing company and secrets with a prostitute.

[3]See, for example, President Clinton's opening remarks during the second presidential debate, October 16, 1996.

[4]Ellen Goodman, "Attack Ads Have Tonal Change," *Pottsville Republican,* October 19–20, 1996, A4.

[5]In fairness, it should be noted that negative campaigning is nothing new. It has been

around as long as politics. History is full of inventive invective and colorful insults aimed at political foes. But this doesn't make negative campaigns any more appealing.

Sometimes ethical concerns are raised not by personal misconduct, but by manipulative or misleading policy proposals. For example, the day after Jesse Jackson praised Bill Clinton at the 1996 Democratic Convention, Jackson was quoted in newspapers criticizing Clinton's Machiavellian leadership style and "bank shot" political strategies. Jackson argued that Clinton is not a straight shooter. Jackson described Clinton as one who regularly risks disappointing one constituency to posture for another. He can always try to undo the damage later on. Shortly before the convention President Clinton signed a Republican-sponsored welfare-reform bill. Clinton lamented that cuts in the food-stamp program for low-income working families and for single men were too severe and that provisions cutting all assistance to illegal immigrants were also too extreme. But he signed the bill anyway. Applying Jackson's analysis, apparently the president reasoned that he could always fix it later. The Republicans lost what would have been a powerful campaign issue. A politically astute move to be sure, but do moves like this fuel public cynicism?

In *Poison Politics: Are Negative Campaigns Destroying Democracy?* (Insight Books, Plenum, 1997), Victor Kamber contends that negative campaigning is leading to the destruction of democracy by fueling cynicism and distrust.

[6] Think before you answer this loaded question too hastily.

[7] *Newsweek*, October 21, 1996, pp. 34–35.

[8] Jonathan Alter, "The Green Brothers," *Newsweek*, October 14, 1996, p. 39 and Lance Morrow, "Does the Morris Thing Matter?" *Time*, September 9, 1996, p. 78.

[9] Dick Morris served as a political advisor for Republicans and Democrats, for Jesse Helms and for Bill Clinton. Morris worked for whoever paid for his services. Given his ideological "promiscuity," some saw a certain poetic justice to his downfall. As Lance Morrow put it, "A highly paid political prostitute, Dick Morris, comes to grief in the arms of an expensive hooker in Washington—a perfect moral fit." (Morrow, *Time*, September 6, 1996.) Morris is the man who helped Bill Clinton, in the wake of 1994 Republican electoral successes, to imitate the Republican positions that the polls said the public favored. Clinton moved to the center on drugs, kids, education, crime, health, school uniforms, V-chips, and teen smoking. These and other family-friendly initiatives appealed to soccer moms and dads. His poll numbers climbed steadily.

Such developments matter because they fuel public suspicion that "it takes an unwholesome personality—a professional liar or a power fetishist—to go into politics in the first place" (Morrow). When people think about politics, many think about money, manipulation, and phoniness. Such cynicism is dangerous to democracy. Weak participation and low turnout are not surprising when citizens find it difficult to take pride in their electoral processes and their presidents.

[10] Howard Fineman, *Newsweek*, October 21, 1996, p. 33.

[11] King.

[12] Mary Matalin and James Carville, with Peter Knobler, *All's Fair: Love, War, and Running for President* (Random House, 1994).

[13] Significantly, however, many felt anxious about their children's future, which is why the Democrats tried to emphasize children in their 1996 platform. Democrats said they wanted to stop tobacco companies from hurting our children, to shield our children from inappropriate television programs, to provide more educational opportunities for our children, to reduce

the deficit so we do not pass a huge national debt on to our children, to make sure that our children do not live near toxic dumps, to make sure that enemy warheads are not aimed at our children. After all, our children are our future, and we need to build a bridge to that future. This message proved to be powerful.

[14]James David Barber, *The Presidential Character* (Prentice-Hall, 1992).

[15]Ibid.

[16]In 1996 the Iowa caucuses were held on February 12 and the New Hampshire primaries were held on February 20.

[17]For a more detailed discussion, see Stephen J. Wayne, *The Road to the White House 1996: The Politics of Presidential Elections* (St. Martin's Press, 1996) and Michael L. Goldstein, *Guide to the 1996 Presidential Election* (Congressional Quarterly, 1995).

[18]Exceptions to the unit rule include Maine and Nebraska. Here the statewide winner receives two electoral votes, and the remaining electoral votes are awarded to the popular-vote winner in each of Maine's two and Nebraska's three congressional districts, respectively.

[19]For example, in 1968 a Republican elector from North Carolina decided to vote for George Wallace, even though Richard Nixon had won North Carolina's popular vote. In 1976 an elector in Washington state voted for Ronald Reagan instead of for Gerald Ford, who won Washington's popular vote.

[20]What if in 1992 Ross Perot had received 19 percent of the *electoral* vote and not just 19 percent of the popular vote, and what if, as a result, he prevented Bill Clinton and George Bush from reaching 270 electoral votes? The House would then have selected a president from among Clinton, Bush, and Perot. The Senate would have selected either Al Gore or Dan Quayle as vice president. If the Senate selected Gore and the House deadlocked, Vice President Gore would have begun serving as acting president on January 20, 1992. What if Democrats in the House decided that they were happy with preserving that arrangement indefinitely? What if the House eventually selected Bush to be president? President Bush and Vice President Gore?

[21]Andrew Jackson received 155,872 popular votes and 99 electoral votes (he needed 131 electoral votes at the time to win); John Quincy Adams received 105,321 popular votes and 84 electoral votes; Henry Clay received 46,587 popular votes and 37 electoral votes; and William Crawford received 44,282 popular votes and 41 electoral votes.

[22]Rutherford B. Hayes received 4,033,950 popular votes and, eventually, 185 electoral votes. Samuel J. Tilden received 4,284,757 popular votes and 184 electoral votes.

The electoral vote results of South Carolina, Florida, and Louisiana were disputed. After months of controversy, Congress established a special commission to resolve matters. It included five senators, five representatives, and five Supreme Court justices. Eight members were Republicans, and seven were Democrats. They voted along party lines, and all nineteen disputed electoral votes went to the Republican Hayes, giving him the presidency by a single electoral vote!

[23]Grover Cleveland received 5,540,050 popular votes and 168 electoral votes. Benjamin Harrison received 5,444,337 popular votes and 233 electoral votes.

[24]But what if several well-known candidates ran and splintered the popular vote to such a degree that the nationwide winner's share was rather small? Wouldn't this result undermine the winner's ability to govern? Responding to such concerns, an American Bar Association proposal suggests that victory go to the popular-vote winner as long as she or he receives at least 40 percent of the nationwide popular vote. If no candidate reaches this threshold, a runoff election would be held between the top two finishers.

[25]At the time Ohio had twenty-five electoral votes, and Hawaii had four.

[26]For additional discussion, see Joseph Melusky, "An Electoral College Fable: How the Carter-Ford Election Might Have Made Ronald Reagan President in 1976," *Presidential Studies Quarterly* 11, number 3, (Summer 1981), p. 384.

[27]As quoted in Frank Isola, "Knicks Stay the Course," *Daily News*, January 31, 1997, p. 27.

[28]In fact, many presidential and vice-presidential nominees are natives of these states, reflecting the hope that such ties will give them a competitive edge.

[29]It can be argued that the smallest states receive some advantages too in that they are assured of at least three electoral votes no matter how small their population may become.

[30]Supporters of the electoral college sometimes note that its elimination would make states less relevant and that it would be counterintuitive to take such a step when citizens are complaining to pollsters about a big, remote, and unresponsive government in Washington.

[31]From Martin Diamond, *The Electoral College and the American Idea of Democracy* (American Enterprise Institute for Policy Research, 1977), ed., George McKenna and Stanley Feingold, *Taking Sides: Clashing Views on Controversial Political Issues*, 2nd ed. (Dushkin Publishing Group, 1981), pp. 82–83.

[32]Clinton received 370 electoral votes and Bush 168.

[33]Walter Dean Burnham, *Critical Elections and Mainsprings of American Politics* (Norton, 1970).

[34]In 1998 history supported predictions that the Democrats would lose some House seats. Kenneth Starr's investigations and calls for President Clinton's removal complicated the matter. But the Democrats actually *gained* five seats in the House. Accepting blame for this disappointing showing by congressional Republicans, Newt Gingrich announced that he would resign as Speaker and give up his seat in Congress.

See chapter 4, "Linking Public Officials to the Public: Public Opinion and Voting," for more discussion of off-year congressional races and voter turnout.

[35]See chapter 8, "The American Presidency," for more discussion of ways in which presidents can assist congressional candidates and of President Clinton's fund-raising activities.

[36]In mid-June 1997 the House Republicans were suffering from dissension. Some militant sophomores were angry with their leaders for not fighting harder to promote conservative values. The leaders were angry with the sophomores for being too confrontational. A coup against House Speaker, Newt Gingrich, seemed plausible. Gingrich tells a story about how Sonny Bono helped to ease this tension.

Bono asked to be recognized. With a smile and a laid-back demeanor, he said that he had gone from writing and performing gold records to producing one of the most popular television shows of the early 1970s to being a guest performer on *Fantasy Island.* He went from a huge dressing room to a smaller dressing room to a shared dressing room to having to ask permission to use the men's room. Finally, he had a guest role on *Fantasy Island* where he had only one line. He was supposed to say, "It's a nice day, Tatoo," but he blew his line and said, "It's a nice day, Pontoon." Herve Villechize, the late actor who played Tatoo, was irate and blasted Bono. At this point Bono thought to himself, "I've got eight gold records, and I'm taking all this crap from a midget."

The message? Forget the past and move on. In this spirit the Republicans attempted to mend their differences. See Newt Gingrich, *Lessons Learned the Hard Way: A Personal Report* (Harper Collins, 1998), pp. 161–62.

[37]For example, Representative E. G. (Bud) Shuster (R-PA) spent more than $1.2 million on his successful 1996 reelection campaign. His opponent, Monte Kemmler (D), spent $113,294. When Shuster ran unopposed in 1994, he still spent $776,175. The ability to marshall such a

formidable campaign warchest may discourage opponents from challenging the incumbent.

Another example: Representative John P. Murtha (D-PA) spent $785,486 in his successful reelection campaign in 1996. His opponent, Bill Choby (R), spent only $22,867. In 1994 Murtha outspent Choby to the tune of $913,004 to $35,782.

In Senate races incumbents often spend twice as much on their campaigns as do their challengers. In House races incumbents commonly outspend their challengers by three-to-one margins or more.

See chapter 5, "Collective Links to Public Officials: Parties and Interest Groups," for a discussion of campaign-finance laws.

[38]See Barbara Hinckley, *Congressional Elections* (Congressional Quarterly, 1981).

[39]See Thomas E. Patterson, *The American Democracy* (McGraw-Hill, 1997), pp. 328–31.

[40]From the start of 1997 through June 30, 1998, the top four House Republican leaders—Speaker Newt Gingrich, Majority Leader Dick Armey, Majority Whip Tom DeLay, and Conference Chairman John Boehner—raised $3.4 million for their leadership PACs.

During the same time period, the top four Senate Republican leaders—Majority Leader Trent Lott, Assistant Majority Leader Don Nickles, Conference Chairman Connie Mack, and Conference Secretary Paul Coverdell—raised $5.9 million for their leadership PACs.

Only two Democratic leaders have PACs: House Minority Leader Dick Gephardt and Caucus Chairman Vic Fazio. Gephardt raised $686,485 over eighteen months and Fazio raised about $11,000.

See "Leaders Raise Millions for Personal PACs," *USA Today*, August 27, 1998.

[41]The ability to send official mail for free is called the **franking privilege.** In this way members send frequent surveys to constituents, soliciting their views on issues. Member also send newsletters boasting of their accomplishments. Members keep their names before the voters in such ways and send out the message that they care about, and are taking care of, the folks back home.

There are some restrictions. For example, the House and Senate ethics codes prohibit the use of the frank for a mass mailing within sixty days of a primary or general election in which the member is running.

[42]Some years ago Lewis Perdue estimated that a representative's allowances can total more than $1 million over the course of a two-year term (See Perdue, "The Million Dollar Advantage of Incumbency," *Washington Monthly*, 1977). The figure would be considerably higher today.

[43]Term limits have been debated extensively. For a useful introduction to arguments for and against congressional term limits, see Bill Frenzel and Thomas E. Mann, "Term Limits for Congress: Arguments Pro and Con," *Current* (July–August 1992).

[44]*United States Term Limits, Inc., et al.* v. *Thornton* (1995). By a five-to-four vote, the Court ruled that the United States Constitution prohibits states from imposing congressional qualifications in addition to those specifically enumerated in the Constitution's text. State imposition of congressional term limits would effect such a fundamental change in the constitutional framework that it must come through a constitutional amendment.

[45]*The World Almanac and Book of Facts 1994*, "Offbeat News Stories of 1993," p. 975.

[46]Turnover in House elections is generally higher after redistricting occurs. See chapter 7, "Congress," for more discussion of apportionment and districting.

[47]In the 1992 and 1994 congressional elections, turnover in House elections was a combined 188 seats. Although incumbents are hard to beat, substantial turnover does occur.

Races without incumbents are **open-seat elections.** Such elections usually feature strong candidates from both parties and heavy spending. In 1994 Republicans won control of the House and the Senate. Open-seat wins contributed heavily to overall Republican gains. Out of fifty-two open House seats and nine open Senate seats that year, the Republicans won about 80 percent of them. Most Democratic incumbents who sought reelection in 1994 won.

[48]Do the gender, racial, and other demographic characteristics of representatives really matter in more than a symbolic sense? Emerging research suggests that such differences have substantive policy implications. See, for example, Sue Thomas, *How Women Legislate* (Oxford University Press, 1994). Thomas provides evidence that women state legislators express different policy aspirations than their male counterparts do.

Chapter Seven

[1]Congress also performs several **systems maintenance functions.** A law is an agreement struck among competing interests. A consumer group may agree to go along with the insertion of a proposal favored by manufacturers, with the understanding that the group will see one of its own provisions included elsewhere. **Conflict resolution** occurs as legislative coalitions are built. Congress **generates support** for the system when claims are reconciled by giving competing interested parties a chance to speak and be heard. Finally, Congress **creates legitimacy** when affected publics conclude that they should obey a new law—even one that they opposed.

[2]Morris Fiorina, *Congress: Keystone of the Washington Establishment,* 2nd ed. (Yale University Press, 1989).

[3]Madison described the House in *The Federalist,* Number 57, and the Senate in *The Federalist,* Number 62.

[4]As explained in chapter 6, "Elections: Presidential and Congressional," states receive electoral votes equal to the sum total of their Senators and Representatives. A state with seven seats in the House and two seats in the Senate has nine electoral votes. Therefore, as House seats shift, electoral votes shift with them.

[5]A state can choose to have all of its representatives elected in statewide at-large elections, but this arrangement is rare except for states with just one representative.

[6]328 U.S. 549 (1946).

[7]369 U.S. 186 (1962).

[8]*Baker* v. *Carr* involved a dispute about how district lines were drawn for election to the *state* legislature. *Colegrove* involved *congressional* district lines. Strictly speaking, Article 1, Section 4 did not apply in *Baker,* and *Baker* did not squarely overrule *Colegrove.* The Court did overrule *Colegrove* in *Wesberry* v. *Sanders* (376 U.S. 1, 1964). See also *Reynolds* v. *Sims* (377 U.S. 533, 1964); *Kirkpatrick* v. *Preisler* (394 U.S. 526, 1969); and *Mahan* v. *Howell* (410 U.S. 315, 1973).

[9]For example, in 1996 **Senator Rick Santorum** (R-PA), a former representative, bristled at the slower pace of the Senate and hoped that younger senators would replace **Bob Dole** (R-KS) as majority leader. Dole was a defender of stately Senate traditions. His code had three elements: First, keep your word. Second, respect your colleagues. Third, no grandstanding. (See Joe Klein and Thomas Rosenthiel, "Mr. Inside," *Newsweek,* November 27, 1995, pp. 30–31). In contrast, Santorum came to the Senate as an impatient lawmaker, reluctant to hold back his thoughts in deference to his elders.

One month into his term, **Senator Robert Byrd** (D-WV) lectured the thrity-seven-year-old Santorum in connection with a balanced budget amendment. "The Senator will learn, if he's around for a while," said Byrd, who had been in the Senate for thirty-seven years. Later **Senator Robert Kerrey** (D-NE) rebuked Santorum on the Senate floor for referring to President Clinton by his first name while criticizing the president's failure to submit a balanced budget. Santorum next encountered problems with a fellow Republican, **Senator Mark Hatfield** (R-OR), whom Santorum tried to remove as chairman of the Senate Appropriations Committee when Hatfield refused to support a balanced budget amendment. (See Anick Jesdanun, "Senator's Stand," *Altoona Mirror,* June 23, 1996, B4.)

While some senior Republican senators criticized Santorum, his fellow freshman Senator Fred Thompson (R-TN) said, "Santorum's as much a senator as the most senior member, and he has a right to do and say anything he wants." Anything? Whatever the consequences? Time will tell.

For a general discussion of congressional norms, see Herbert Asher, "The Learning of Legislative Norms," *American Political Science Review* 67 (June 1973), pp. 499–513, as reprinted in Glenn R. Parker, *Studies of Congress* (Congressional Quarterly, 1985) at pp. 119–46. See also, F. Lee Bernick and Charles W. Wiggins, "Legislative Norms in Eleven States," *Legislative Studies Quarterly* 7, number 2 (May 1983), pp. 191–201.

[10]Floor leaders ascended to the Speaker's position on the Democratic side when Carl Albert was succeeded by John McCormack, who was succeeded by Thomas ("Tip") O'Neill, who was succeeded by Jim Wright, who was succeeded by Thomas Foley. This string was broken when the Republicans won a majority of House seats in the 1994 elections and Newt Gingrich became Speaker. However, the previous Republican floor leader, Bob Michel, retired. Thus Gingrich, the former Republican whip, became the highest returning party leader on the Republican side. Gingrich's successors, Bob Livingston and Dennis Hastert, however, did not follow the same line of ascension.

[11]For example, in 1965 Gerald Ford, then a little-known congressman from Michigan, upset Charles Halleck for the House Republican floor leader post. In 1971 Robert Byrd of West Virginia unseated Ted Kennedy of Massachusetts as Senate majority whip.

[12]In cases of overlapping jurisdictions, selecting a committee to consider the bill can be important. One committee might be favorably disposed toward the bill while another one opposes it.

[13]There are some parliamentary ways to get around a committee and bring a bill to the floor even if a committee does not want to report it.

In the House an absolute majority (218 representatives) can remove a bill from a committee through a **discharge petition.** Such efforts are rarely successful. By a two-thirds vote, members can enact a **suspension of the rules** and bring a bill to the floor for a vote. The **Rules Committee** can also extract a bill from a committee that is holding it. Further, appropriations and tax bills can bypass the Rules Committee and come to the floor as **privileged business.**

In the Senate the **discharge petition** is difficult to use. By a majority vote, senators can **suspend the rules** and bring a bill from committee to the floor for a vote. Bills passed by the House can also go directly to the Senate floor for a vote without going through Senate committees.

[14]House Democrats required committee chairpersons to share with members the hiring and use of committee staff. Majority party members on the full committee elected subcommittee chairpersons. The number of subcommittees increased as well.

[15]*Seniority* was defined by years of continuous committee service.

[16]In 1975 the House Democrats unseated three chairpersons. Wright Patman (eighty-four years old at the time) was replaced as chairman of the House Banking and Currency Committee. W. R. Poage (then seventy-five years old) was replaced as chair of the House Agriculture Committee. F. Edward Hebert (then seventy-four years old) was replaced as chair of the House Armed Services Committee. (Here is a "bonus" quotable quote from F. Edward

Hebert: "The only way we'll ever get a volunteer army is to draft them.")

Over the years the Democrats unseated several more chairpersons and replaced them with committee members who had less seniority. In 1976 the House Democrats unseated Wayne Hayes (D-OH) as chair of the House Administration Committee after discovering that he had placed a young woman with limited clerical skills on the committee payroll for, shall we say, questionable purposes.

In 1985 the House Democrats removed Melvin Price (then eighty years old) as chairperson of the House Armed Services Committee and replaced him with Les Aspin. Aspin later served as President Clinton's secretary of defense. The irony here was that ten years earlier Melvin Price had been named to replace F. Edward Hebert as the Armed Services Committee chair. The reform that gave Price the position in 1975 was used to take the position from him in 1985.

Following Republican victories in the 1994 congressional elections, Speaker Newt Gingrich exercised relatively more power over the appointment of committee chairpersons than his recent Democratic predecessors did. Nevertheless, it remains accurate to say that members of the majority party continue to chair committees and that seniority no longer guarantees chairs.

[17]*Filibuster* is a translation from the Spanish word for pirate, *filibustero.* In American politics it has been used since the 1850s to describe small bands of senators who use this procedural maneuver to seize control of the Senate like pirates taking control of a ship.

[18]Filibustering is the senatorial equivalent of a professional tag-team wrestling match. Are folding chairs and other foreign objects employed? See the earlier discussion of the congressional civility norm.

[19]Reminiscent of my two-year-old daughter who occasionally says from the backseat, "Stop talking, daddy. Just drive."

[20]Recently, senators have been forgoing the tradition of personally holding the floor to delay a vote. Instead, they can register with their party leader their objections to the Senate's proceeding on some matter. This move is called placing a **hold** on legislation. It signifies the **threat** of a full-fledged filibuster if the Senate takes up the disputed matter.

In spite of this shift to a "gentleman's filibuster," Senator Alphonse D'Amato of New York filibustered against a tax bill in 1992 in an attempt to save jobs in a Cortland, New York, typewriter factory. His filibuster included singing selections from "Deep in the Heart of Texas" (Finance Committee Chairman Lloyd Bentsen of Texas was anxious to finish the tax bill) and "South of the Border" (where D'Amato maintained typewriter jobs were headed).

See discussion in Bill Dauster's, "It's Not Mr. Smith Goes to Washington: The Senate Filibuster Ain't What It Used to Be," *Washington Monthly,* November 1996, pp. 34–36.

[21]Sarah Binder and Steven V. Smith, *Politics or Principle? Filibustering in the United States Senate* (Brookings, 1996). The authors note that no other Senate rule has been the subject of a Hollywood film starring Jimmy Stewart. According to conventional wisdom, the filibuster helps moderate extreme legislation, prevents passage of legislation opposed by popular majorities, and is part of the origins and traditions of the Senate. Binder and Smith dispute these views and conclude that political self-interests, not philosophical commitments to free speech and minority rights, underlie support for the filibuster.

[22]John W. Kingdon, *Congressmen's Voting Decisions* (Harper and Row, 1973).

[23]Party voting has been increasing in the House since the 1970s. Approximately three-quarters of senators and representatives cast party votes, where majorities of both parties take opposing positions. See David Rhode, "Electoral Forces, Political Agendas, and Partisanship in the House

and Senate," in Roger H. Davidson, ed., *The Postreform Congress* (St. Martin's Press, 1992).

[24]Presidents are generally most successful early in their terms (during the so-called honeymoon period), with members of their own party, on foreign policy issues.

[25]See, for example, Roger H. Davidson, *The Role of the Congressman* (Pegasus, 1969).

[26]The following excerpt is from an April 7, 1998, editorial entitled "Stop Labeling Every Project as Being Pork":

> If a highway project is pork, then is a military base pork? Or perhaps a new federal building? Or improvements to an airport? Or what about money going to San Francisco's or some other city's transit system? What about money to fund water projects in the West?
>
> The bottom line is anything can be called pork, when the project isn't in your area or isn't one you support. . . . [I]t's time to stop labeling everything that everyone else gets as pork.

What do you think? Now, when I tell you that this editorial appeared in the *Altoona Mirror*—Altoona is located in Congressman Shuster's district—does your reaction change?

[27]Walter Shapiro, "Two Senators, Two Votes, One Blow against Cynicism," *USA Today*, February 28, 1997, 2A.

[28]Text of the Republican Contract with America:

> As Republican members of the House of Representatives and as citizens seeking to join that body we propose not just to change its policies, but even more important, to restore the bonds of trust between the people and their elected representatives.
>
> That is why, in this era of official evasion and posturing, we offer instead a detailed agenda for national renewal, a written commitment with no fine print.
>
> This year's election offers the chance, after four decades of one-party control, to bring to the House a new majority that will transform the way Congress works.

That historic change would be the end of government that is too big, too intrusive, and too easy with the public's money. It can be the beginning of a Congress that respects the values and shares the faith of the American family.

Like Lincoln, our first Republican president, we intend to act "with firmness in the right, as God gives us to see the right." To restore accountability to Congress. To end its cycle of scandal and disgrace. To make us all proud again of the way free people govern themselves.

On the first day of the 104th Congress, the new Republican majority will immediately pass the following major reforms, aimed at restoring the faith and trust of the American people in their government:

FIRST, require all laws that apply to the rest of the country also apply equally to the Congress;

SECOND, select a major independent auditing firm to conduct a comprehensive audit of Congress for waste, fraud, or abuse;

THIRD, cut the number of House committees, and cut committee staff by one-third;

FOURTH, limit the terms of all committee chairs;

FIFTH, ban the casting of proxy votes in committee;

SIXTH, require committee hearings to be open to the public;

SEVENTH, require a three-fifths majority to pass a tax increase;

EIGHTH, guarantee an honest accounting of our Federal Budget by implementing zero base-line budgeting.

Thereafter, within the first 100 days of the 104th Congress, we shall bring to the House Floor the following bills, each to be given full and open debate, each to be given a clear and fair vote and each to be immediately available this day for public inspection and scrutiny.

1. THE FISCAL RESPONSIBILITY ACT
   A balanced budget/tax limitation amendment and a legislative line-item veto to restore fiscal responsibility to

an out-of-control Congress, requiring them to live under the same budget constraints as families and businesses.

2. THE TAKING BACK OUR
   STREETS ACT
   An anti-crime package including stronger truth-in-sentencing, "good faith" exclusionary rule exemptions, effective death penalty provisions, and cuts in social spending from this summer's "crime" bill to fund prison construction and additional law enforcement to keep people secure in their neighborhoods and kids safe in their schools.

3. THE PERSONAL
   RESPONSIBILITY ACT
   Discourage illegitimacy and teen pregnancy by prohibiting welfare to minor mothers and denying increased AFDC for additional children while on welfare, cut spending for welfare programs, and enact a tough two-years-and-out provision with work requirements to promote individual responsibility.

4. THE FAMILY REINFORCEMENT ACT
   Child support enforcement, tax incentives for adoption, strengthening rights of parents in their children's education, stronger child pornography laws, and an elderly dependent care tax credit to reinforce the central role of families in American society.

5. THE AMERICAN DREAM
   RESTORATION ACT
   A $500 per child tax credit, begin repeal of the marriage tax penalty, and creation of American Dream Savings Accounts to provide middle class tax relief.

6. THE NATIONAL SECURITY
   RESTORATION ACT
   No U.S. troops under U.N. command and restoration of the essential parts of our national security funding to strengthen our national defense and maintain our credibility around the world.

7. THE SENIOR CITIZENS
   FAIRNESS ACT
   Raise the Social Security earnings limit which currently forces seniors out of the work force, repeal the 1993 tax hikes on Social Security benefits and provide tax incentives for private long-term care insurance to let Older Americans keep more of what they have earned over the years.

8. THE JOB CREATION AND WAGE
   ENHANCEMENT ACT
   Small business incentives, capital gains cut and indexation, neutral cost recovery, risk assessment/cost benefit analysis, strengthening the Regulatory Flexibility Act and unfunded mandate reform to create jobs and raise worker wages.

9. THE COMMON SENSE LEGAL
   REFORM ACT
   "Loser pays" laws, reasonable limits on punitive damages and reform of product liability laws to stem the endless tide of litigation.

10. THE CITIZEN LEGISLATURE ACT
    A first-ever vote on term limits to replace career politicians with citizen legislators.
    Further, we will instruct the House Budget Committee to report on the floor and we will work to enact additional budget savings, beyond the budget cuts specifically included in the legislation described above, to ensure that the Federal budget deficit will be less than it would have been without the enactment of these bills.
    Respecting the judgment of our fellow citizens as we seek their mandate for reform, we hereby pledge our names to this Contract with America.

[29]In 1995 the House enacted several reforms. More committee meetings were opened to the public. House committee votes were to be recorded. Three committees and twenty-five subcommittees were eliminated. House committee staffs were

reduced by one-third. House committee chairs were to handle staff hiring. House members were limited to service on two committees and four subcommittees. Proxy voting in House committees was prohibited. The House Speaker was limited to four consecutive two-year terms. House committee and subcommittee chairpersons were limited to three consecutive two-year terms. A three-fifths majority of members voting (a **super majority**) would be needed to increase income tax rates.

As such, Republicans were successful in enacting the procedural agenda spelled out in the contract.

[30]On June 25, 1998, the United States Supreme Court ruled that the presidential line-item veto violates the principle of separation of powers and is unconstitutional. See *Clinton, et al.* v. *New York City, et al.,* 524 U.S.___, 141 L.Ed. 2d 393, 118 S.Ct. ___ (1998).

[31]The Republican freshmen had a substantial impact on congressional rules and procedures, but their zeal for reform ran up against the importance of constituency interests, fund-raising, and the politics of reelection. Some recent studies conclude that such forces stopped them short of their goals. See Linda Killian, *The Freshmen: What Happened to the Republican Revolution?* (Westview, 1998) and Nicol C. Rae, *Conservative Reformers: The Republican Freshmen and the Lessons of the 104th Congress* (M.E. Sharpe, 1998).

[32]See Nolan Walters, "As Nunn Leaves the Senate, an Old Style of Service Goes with Him," *Philadelphia Inquirer,* December 30, 1996, A3.

[33]Ibid.

[34]See Diane Duston, "Senate Exodus Continues," *Altoona Mirror,* December 2, 1995, A1.

[35]Ellen Goodman, "Looking for New Challenges," *Altoona Mirror,* December 10, 1995, B6. See also, Pat Schroeder, *24 Years of Housework . . . and the Place Is Still a Mess: My Life in Politics* (Andrews McMeel, 1998).

Chapter Eight

[1]When locked in a budget dispute with Congress in December 1995, President Clinton vetoed a Republican-backed budget with the same pen that President Lyndon Johnson used thirty years earlier to create Medicare. In an effort to score public relations points, the White House had the pen shipped overnight from the Lyndon Johnson Library in Texas. Photographs portrayed President Clinton vetoing the plan while seated at a desk with busts of Franklin D. Roosevelt and Harry Truman in the foreground!

Similarly, a president might address the nation seated at the desk used by President Lincoln when he signed the Emancipation Proclamation. The unspoken message is clear: "Lincoln was a great president. Lincoln faced grave problems from this desk. I use this desk. Therefore, I am like Lincoln." Obviously, the logic is flawed. If furniture possessed such mystical qualities, you would not have to study political science to pass this course. You would only have to locate the desk or chair of some astute predecessor and take a seat!

[2]George Clinton, "The Letters of Cato," from *The Antifederalists,* ed., Cecilia M. Kenyon (Bobbs-Merrill, 1966), pp. 302–09, excerpted as "To the Citizens of the State of New York," in Harry A. Bailey Jr., ed., *Classics of the American Presidency* (Moore Publishing, 1980), pp. 18–22.

[3]Ibid., p. 19.

[4]Ibid.

[5]Ibid., p. 20.

[6]Ibid.

[7]Ibid., p. 21.

[8]Hamilton, *The Federalist,* Number 69, ed., Clinton Rossiter (New American Library, 1961), pp. 415–23.

[9]Hamilton, *The Federalist,* Number 70, ed., Rossiter, 423–31.

[10]Ibid., p. 423.

[11]Ibid., p. 426.

[12]Ibid., p. 427.

[13]Thomas Cronin, "The Presidential Puzzle," *The State of the Presidency,* 2nd ed. (Little, Brown, 1980), pp. 1–25.

Such expectations tempt candidates to overpromise and presidents to overextend themselves in an effort to satisfy unrealistic demands.

[14]Ibid., pp. 6–7.

[15]Ibid., p. 7.

[16]Ibid., p. 11.

[17]As our expectations are extreme, our reactions are extreme, too. Perhaps we give presidents too much credit when things go well and too much blame when things go badly. We talk about President Roosevelt's New Deal and President Johnson's War on Poverty, but we also speak of President Hoover's Depression and President Johnson's War. As President Kennedy observed, "I know that when things don't go well, they like to blame the president, and that is one of the things presidents are paid for."

The president is powerful but not the sole cause of our national condition. The president reacts to international developments, foreign leaders, domestic pressures, congressional opponents, and a climate of public expectations. It is a tough job. Demands are varied. In a single day a president may be called on to decide whether or not to extend diplomatic recognition to the Palestine Liberation Organization, send American troops to Bosnia or some other world trouble spot, exhort the nation (and Congress) on television to support his new economic proposals, preside over a ceremony on the south lawn, and meet with reporters. It has been said that a president wears many hats.

[18]Ibid., p. 13.

Jimmy Carter had been a peanut farmer. He continued to use the name Jimmy while president. He walked down Pennsylvania Avenue during his inaugural parade. He carried his own luggage. He wore a sweater while giving a televised fireside address. He was down to earth. But critics maintained that he would have

been a more effective president if he had acted more "presidential." In contrast, Ronald Reagan's inaugural events featured limousines, champagne, glamorous parties, and Hollywood celebrities. Public reaction? Complaints about arrogance and elitism were common.

[19]Clinton Rossiter, *The American Presidency* (Harcourt Brace Jovanovich, 1960), excerpted as "The Powers of the Presidency," in Bailey, pp. 70–83.

[20]See, for example, Cronin, "The Textbook and the Prime-Time Presidency," pp. 75–118, where he maintains that many observers tend to exaggerate the promise of the presidency.

[21]William Howard Taft, *Our Chief Magistrate and His Powers* (Columbia University Press, 1916), excerpted as "A Restricted View of the Office," in Bailey, pp. 37–39.

[22]*The Autobiography of Theodore Roosevelt,* Centennial Edition (Charles Scribner's Sons, 1913, 1941, 1958), excerpted as "The Stewardship Doctrine," in Bailey, pp. 35–36.

[23]John Nicolay and John Hays, eds., *The Complete Works of Abraham Lincoln,* vol. 10 (Francis D. Tandy Co., 1894), excerpted as "The Prerogative Theory of the Presidency," in Bailey, pp. 33–34. Lincoln's view resembled John Locke's ideas in his *Second Treatise of Government,* where he argued that the law cannot provide for many things and such things must be left to the discretion of the executive.

[24]Presidents should be careful when they preempt television programs to address the nation. On August 17, 1998, President Clinton testified about his relationship with former White House intern, Monica Lewinsky. That night he went on television and temporarily knocked the Miss Teen USA pageant off CBS. Disappointed audience members complained that the president should have checked the TV schedule before going through with his speech!

[25]It is worth noting that the Constitution's failure to specify how some of these appointees will be removed has given rise to controversy and litigation over the years.

[26]Robert Spitzer, "Regular Veto" in *Encyclopedia of the American Presidency,* eds., Leonard Levy and Louis Fisher (Simon and Schuster, 1994), p. 1555.

[27]In 1988 President Reagan considered a bill that required plants to give sixty-days advance notice to surrounding communities before they closed. Reagan did not support the bill, but he reasoned that Congress would be able to override a veto and such a veto would give the Democrats a potent campaign weapon against George Bush. He decided to allow the bill to become law without his signature.

In 1989 the Supreme Court ruled that the First Amendment permits flag burning as a symbolic form of expression (*Texas* v. *Johnson,* 491 U.S. 397). In October 1989 Congress approved a bill outlawing flag burning. President Bush wanted a constitutional amendment to this effect. He believed that a law could not overturn a Supreme Court decision, a prediction that proved accurate when the Supreme Court later invalidated the law in question (*United States* v. *Eichman,* 496 U.S. 210, 1990). On the other hand, it was politically difficult to veto such a "patriotic" measure. Bush himself had capitalized upon such issues during his successful campaign against Michael Dukakis in 1988. Bush's solution? He decided to let the bill become a law without his signature.

[28]The pocket veto can be manipulated for political purposes. Imagine several congresspeople who are under pressure from constituent groups demanding an end to medical and scientific experiments on animals. In fact, the congresspeople accept the need for such experimentation, but they face tough reelection battles. They wait until the closing days of a congressional session, ask their colleagues to support the bill banning such experiments, and send it to the president. When the president neither signs nor vetoes the bill and Congress adjourns, the bill is killed. The sponsoring representatives can posture for their constituents and claim credit for a "good try"; the president can deflect criticism by complaining that Congress should not have waited until the last minute to send him such important legislation.

Recent presidents have asked for an **item veto,** similar to a power enjoyed by forty-three state governors. An item veto gives a chief executive the power to veto specific appropriations items while approving the rest of the bill. Proponents of the item veto argue that it permits presidents to eliminate wasteful spending riders attached by lawmakers seeking money for pork barrel projects in their home districts. In this way presidents can combat deficit spending more effectively. Critics complain that the framers did not intend the president to exercise such "editor in chief" powers over Congress. A president needing a few votes to pass a pet bill could extort those votes from isolated congresspeople by threatening to remove projects benefiting their districts from an upcoming appropriations bill. Regarding deficit reduction, if presidents want balanced budgets, they should *propose* them in the first place. Further, the item veto encourages congressional irresponsibility. Legislators can pack a bill with expensive projects to benefit their own constituents and leave it to the president to make the politically difficult cuts needed to restore fiscal sanity.

In 1996 President Clinton signed a line-item veto bill and promised to scrutinize "the darkest corners of the federal budget." The line-item veto took effect in January 1997. The legislation provided that after the president signs an appropriations bill, he would have five days to send a message to Congress rescinding specific items. The president could also cancel tax breaks that benefit one hundred or fewer taxpayers and could delete new entitlement programs or changes that expand existing benefits. Congress could then pass a **disapproval**

bill to overturn the president's rescissions, but a president could veto this bill. It would then take a two-thirds vote of the House and the Senate to override this veto.

Acknowledging the efforts of his Republican and Democratic predecessors, President Clinton kept the four pens he used to sign the line-item veto bill and sent them to former Presidents Carter, Ford, Reagan, and Bush—all of whom had sought this power.

In April 1997 a federal judge declared the line-item veto unconstitutional. United States District Judge Thomas Penfield Jackson ruled that the power to "make" laws is the "exclusive, nondelegable power of Congress." The line-item veto transforms the president into "a co-maker of the nation's laws." President Clinton exercised his new line-item veto for the first time on August 12, 1997. Legal challenges ensued. On June 25, 1998, the United States Supreme Court agreed with Judge Penfield. Writing for a six-to-three majority in *Clinton, et al.* v. *New York City, et al.*, Justice Stevens held that the line-item veto violates the principle of separation of powers.

[29]Richard E. Neustadt, *Presidential Power and the Modern Presidents: The Politics of Leadership from Roosevelt to Reagan* (Free Press, 1990), p. 11.

[30]Ibid., p. 10.

[31]Jonathan Daniels, *Frontier on the Potomac* (Macmillan, 1946), as quoted in Bailey, p. 89.

[32]For an extended discussion of President Clinton's efforts to persuade Congress to support his budget proposals, see Bob Woodward, *The Agenda: Inside the Clinton White House* (Simon and Schuster, 1994). See especially the discussion of Clinton's call to first-term Representative Marjorie Margolies-Mezvinsky of Pennsylvania at pp. 300–02. Her yes vote was political suicide in her home district, but she gave Clinton her vote when he needed it to put his budget over the top. As she cast her vote, Republicans in the House chamber chanted, "Bye-bye Marjorie!" She was defeated when she sought reelection. See also Tip O'Neill with William Novak, *Man of the House* (St. Martin's Press, 1987), where O'Neill contrasted Ronald Reagan's energetic personal lobbying on behalf of his legislative agenda with Jimmy Carter's reluctance to engage in such activities.

[33]This anecdote about President Kennedy appeared in Nicholas Henry, *Public Administration and Public Affairs*, 6th ed. (Prentice-Hall, 1995) at p. 2. It was previously reported in Peter Goldman et al., "The Presidency: Can Anyone Do the Job?" *Newsweek*, January 26, 1981, p. 41.

[34]As quoted in Hugh Sidey, *A Very Personal Presidency* (Atheneum, 1978), p. 260 and repeated in Cronin at p. 145.

[35]As quoted in Cronin at pp. 150–01 and in Henry at p. 7.

[36]This anecdote about Amy Carter appeared in Henry at p. 2. It was previously reported in "Amy's Homework Aid Costs Thousands," *Arizona Republic*, February 9, 1981.

[37]*Clinton* v. *Jones*, 117 S.Ct. 1636, 137 L.Ed. 2d 945 (1997). Justice Breyer filed a separate concurring opinion.

[38]President Clinton used a very specific definition of "sexual relations" and claimed that he did not commit perjury, in a technical sense, because oral sex was not included in the definition. Does oral sex count as sexual relations? Such semantic distinctions took on great legal and political significance.

The debate is reminiscent of a scene from the movie, *Clerks*, where one of the male leads, Dante, and his girlfriend, Veronica, discuss her sexual history. Dante wants to know how many guys she has had sex with. The answer is either three or thirty-seven, depending on what counts.

[39]Congress censured Andrew Jackson in 1834 after he removed government funds from the Bank of the United States and fired some cabinet members who disagreed with him. Jackson's Democrats, however, won control of Congress in 1836, and the Senate voted to expunge the censure.

[40]Irving L. Janis, *Victims of Groupthink: A Psychological Study of Foreign-Policy Decisions and Fiascoes* (Houghton-Mifflin, 1972).

[41]George Reedy, *The Twilight of the Presidency* (New American Library, 1970).

[42]"President Clinton in Contempt," *Washington Post*, April 14, 1999, p. A26. On July 29 Judge Wright ordered President Clinton to pay $90,686 to cover extra legal costs for the Paula Jones team. This action resulted from the President lying under oath.

[43]President's Committee on Administrative Management, *Administrative Management in the Government of the United States, January 8, 1937* (U.S. Government Printing Office, 1937), pp. 1–6, excerpted as Louis Brownlow, Charles E. Merriam, and Luther Gulick, "Report of the President's Committee on Administrative Management," Bailey, pp. 128–31.

[44]Cronin, p. 243.

[45]Ibid.

[46]Louis W. Koenig, *The Invisible Presidency* (Holt, Rinehart, and Winston, 1960). Stephen V. Monsma also used the idea of concentric circles to describe the presidential structure in *American Politics,* 3rd ed. (Dryden Press, 1976), pp. 187–94.

[47]The inner circle is an informal concept. One does not take a civil service test or send a resume to the White House asking for a job as a member of the president's inner circle.

[48]During Clinton's first term economic advisors who wanted him to emphasize deficit reduction repeatedly clashed with political advisors who wanted him to follow through on social programs he championed during the 1992 campaign. See Woodward for an extended discussion of such debates inside the Clinton administration.

[49]From Jerald F. terHorst, *Gerald Ford and the Future of the Presidency* (Third Press, 1974), p. 171 as quoted in Monsma at p. 192.

[50]Recall that Vice President Gore had to cast the deciding vote to secure Senate approval of President Clinton's first budget.

[51]"Running Mates," PBS telecast, October 2, 1996.

[52]Ibid.

[53]Ibid.

[54]Walter Mondale was the first vice president to have an office in the White House. President Carter insisted that Mondale receive all of the same reports he received and be invited to all of the same meetings as the president. The Mondale vice presidency represented a major role shift. Since Mondale, vice presidents have functioned as real presidential advisors. Vice President Gore is widely regarded as the most involved vice president in history. When Bob Dole selected Jack Kemp as his running mate in 1996, Kemp told reporters that his model for the role he hoped to play in a Dole administration was Al Gore. Clinton and Gore are seen together on television more frequently than any previous tandem, with the possible exception of Carter and Mondale (as discussed in "Running Mates").

[55]Unfortunately for Bush, Quayle's youthful enthusiasm and frequent misstatements made him a favorite of comedians. A media "gaffe watch" went into effect, resulting in widespread reports when Vice President Quayle inadvertently urged a school boy to misspell "potato." President Bush consistently supported Quayle in public and resisted pressure to remove him from the ticket in 1992. According to Bush biographer Herbert Parmet, however, days after naming Quayle as his running mate, Bush made the following entry in his diary: "It was my decision, and I blew it."

Bill Clinton and Al Gore's ticket balancing was subtle. While they resembled each other in terms of age, ideology, and region, Gore was a United States senator, a Vietnam War veteran, and a "family man." Gore helped to strengthen the ticket in light of Clinton's perceived deficiencies in these areas.

[56]Reedy, p. 77.

[57]Another was President Reagan's National Commission on Excellence in Education, which produced a highly critical report of

the American educational system entitled "A Nation at Risk."

[58]Aaron Wildavsky, "The Two Presidencies," *Transaction* (December 1966). Wildavsky's central argument that presidents are relatively more powerful in foreign affairs than in domestic affairs remains convincing. Wildavsky and Duane Oldfield reexamined the original argument in a later article entitled "Reconsidering the Two Presidencies," *Society* (July–August 1989). The latter article appears in Mitchel Gerber's, *Sources: Notable Selections in American Government* (Dushkin, 1996), pp. 252–58. Wildavsky and Oldfield contend that the Vietnam War, nuclear proliferation, increased ideological and partisan divisions between the president and Congress, and other recent developments have made consensus difficult and have diminished presidential control over foreign policy. While the original article may have exaggerated the degree of presidential control over foreign policy, the president's foreign affairs powers must not be understated. After all, the president remains commander in chief and this role matters.

[59]Constitutionally, the president makes **treaties** with the advise and consent of the Senate. Presidents can also make **executive agreements** with chief executives of other nations. Such executive agreements require no Senate ratification and hold a great potential for conflict and confusion. As Article 6 of the Constitution has been interpreted by courts, the Constitution—plus any federal laws, treaties, executive agreements, or other national enactments that are consistent with the Constitution—are the "supreme law" of the land. If there is a conflict between a national action and a state law, the state law must give way.

A **congressional statute** requires action by two branches to pass. Likewise, a **treaty** requires action by two branches to take effect. The two are essentially *equivalent.* Either one prevails over a state law to the contrary. But if there is a

conflict between a congressional statute and a federal treaty, what happens? Courts have held that as equivalent enactments, the *more recent* of the two takes precedence.

Unlike a treaty, an **executive agreement** requires action by a single branch. If an executive agreement conflicts with a state law, the executive agreement "wins." But what if there is a conflict between a treaty (two branches were involved) and an executive agreement (only one branch was involved)? The Supreme Court faced this question in *Goldwater* v. *Carter* (100 S.Ct. 533, 1979).

In 1954 the United States entered into a mutual defense treaty with the Republic of China. The treaty was ratified by the Senate. In 1978, in an effort to improve relations, President Carter made an executive agreement with the People's Republic of China. In the process Carter terminated the 1954 treaty. Senator Barry Goldwater, acting on behalf of the Senate, challenged Carter's authority to act unilaterally in this fashion. Because the Senate was involved in making the treaty, he reasoned, the Senate should be involved in its termination. A United States district court agreed with Goldwater. President Carter complained that a president needs discretion when conducting delicate international negotiations and that it was not feasible to expect him to tell the People's Republic of China that the deal was off. A United States court of appeals agreed with the president. Senator Goldwater appealed to the United States Supreme Court. The Court vacated the appellate court's decision (out went Carter's victory). The Court then remanded the case to a United States district court with instructions to dismiss the complaint (out went Goldwater's victory). What did this mean? President Carter's executive agreement with the People's Republic of China remained in force. However, the Court refused to address the merits and refused to establish a *general* rule permitting future presidents to terminate treaties on their own whenever they wanted to do so. The area remains unsettled legally. Politically, however, the case illustrates how the Court can assist a president in a difficult international situation.

[60]299 U.S. 304; 57 S.Ct. 216; 81 L.Ed. 255 (1936).

[61]See John E. Mueller, "Trends in Popular Support for Wars in Korea and Vietnam," *American Political Science Review*, 65 (1971) pp. 369, 370. Mueller notes that in 1966 people were asked, Do you support bombing North Viet Nam? In May—just before bombing began—50 percent of respondents indicated their support. In July—just after President Johnson announced the start of bombing—85 percent supported the action. In 1968 people were asked, Do you support a bombing halt? In March—before a limited bombing halt—49 percent of respondents wanted to stop the bombing. In April—just after Johnson announced a limited bombing halt—74 percent supported the decision. Mueller also explains that as the number of American casualties mounts, public support for military action drops. In Vietnam and Korea opposition grew by 15 percent when casualties hit one thousand and by another 15 percent when casualties totaled ten thousand. American casualties in fighting against Iraq numbered fewer than one hundred killed in combat (251 killed including the initial "Desert Shield" portion of the operation and accidental deaths).

[62]Some United Nations Security Council members—China, Russia, and France—opposed the U.S. and British strikes against Iraq. Russian legislators had a most unusual response. On December 17, 1998, Russia's lower chamber of parliament considered a motion appealing to Monica Lewinsky to help halt the military strikes. "The State Duma appeals to Monica Lewinsky to undertake corresponding measures to restrain the emotions of Bill Clinton," said Alexander Filatov's motion.

[63]On March 1, 1991, following victory in the Gulf War, President Bush's approval rating stood at an astonishing 91 percent! Polls revealed that 72 percent of those surveyed said they would vote to reelect Bush no matter who ran against him.

[64]By March 1992 President Bush's popularity had fallen to 32 percent. In the November election later that year, he lost to Bill Clinton. As Bush learned, public support "boosts" from foreign affairs are only temporary.

[65]From text of the *War Powers Resolution*, Section 2(a), Purpose and Policy.

[66]This section seems to fall within the Supreme Court's definition of an unconstitutional "legislative veto." See *Immigration and Naturalization Service* v. *Chadha*, 462 U.S. 919; 103 S.Ct. 2764; 77 L.Ed. 2d 317 (1983). The Court held that such congressional orders should themselves be presented to the president for a signature or veto.

[67]The sixty-day period can be extended for another thirty days if the president certifies to Congress that unavoidable military necessities respecting the safety of United States armed forces require a more gradual removal.

The above-mentioned legislative veto authorized Congress to order the president to withdraw troops. In contrast, this second provision requires a president to obtain congressional approval for an extension on troop deployment. The latter provision stands on firmer constitutional ground.

[68]President Nixon's successors have had their own problems with the War Powers Resolution. In May 1975 Cambodia captured a United States merchant ship, the *Mayaguez*. Instead of resorting to diplomatic channels, President Ford sent in the marines to secure the release of the crew. American casualties were heavy—some forty United States Marines were killed. Critics argued that Ford should have consulted with Congress before engaging in hostilities.

Some said that President Carter violated the War Powers Resolution when he authorized the secret attempt to rescue United States hostages being held in Iran. Operation Eagle Claw, as it was known, failed when a transport plane and a helicopter collided and exploded in a desert sand storm. Carter explained that he had not consulted with Congress in advance because he wanted to ensure the secrecy of the mission. Offended congressional leaders pointed out that Congress knew about the Manhattan Project that produced the atomic bomb and secrecy was not breached. Besides, leaks can just as easily come from the executive branch.

Critics said that President Reagan violated the War Powers Resolution when he sent United States troops to Beirut in 1982 without specifying how long they would remain. Reagan replied that they would remain as long as they were needed. He received additional criticism after the sixty-day deadline expired and the troops remained in Beirut. He explained that, in his opinion, the War Powers Resolution did not apply in this case. The troops were not in a combat. They were not in a situation of "imminent hostilities." Rather, they were part of a multinational peacekeeping force. Underscoring their noncombat status, many carried unloaded weapons. On October 12, 1983, the president and Congress finally reached an agreement authorizing United States Marines to stay in Lebanon for an additional eighteen months. Speaker of the House, Thomas ("Tip") O'Neill claimed victory for Congress, saying that Reagan had acknowledged his need to obtain congressional authorization. Reagan contended that his action should in no way be viewed as any acknowledgment that his constitutional powers can be "impermissibly infringed by congressional action." This battle of wills became moot when, eleven days later, a United States Marine barracks in Beirut was hit by a truck loaded with explosives. Guards, carrying unloaded weapons, were unable

to fire upon the approaching truck bomb. American deaths totaled 241. Four months later, President Reagan announced that the marines were being withdrawn.

On October 25, 1983, just two days after the tragedy in Beirut, President Reagan called congressional leaders to the White House to tell them that United States troops were currently en route to Grenada. A number of American citizens, many of them medical students, were on the island. The president observed that a Communist uprising threatened their safety. He considered himself to be in full compliance with the War Powers Resolution. Critics objected that he should have consulted with Congress *before* sending the troops. They were about to land on the island when Reagan informed lawmakers, making his "consultation" a mere formality.

It is interesting to note that the United States Army awarded 8,612 medals as a result of the brief 1983 Grenada campaign even though it never had more than seven thousand officers and enlisted soldiers on the island. Army officials explained that many medals were given to staff and rear-area support troops at several bases in the United States. The army defended its awards system as a "valuable and effective leadership tool to build morale and esprit." (From "Off-Beat News Stories of 1984," *The World Almanac and Book of Facts*, Funk and Wagnalls, 1985, p. 716.)

Former Reagan Administration official Alvin Snyder wrote a book called *Warriors of Disinformation*. Snyder headed the television arm of the United States Information Agency. He claims that President Reagan did not have to invade Grenada to rescue five hundred American medical students. The Cuban-backed government offered to let the United States fly them out days before the invasion, but the president went ahead with the invasion to show that United States armed forces could fight and win (as reported in *Newsweek*, October 30, 1995, p. 6).

In 1990 President Bush sent United States troops to Saudi Arabia as part of a multinational force trying to deter Iraqi expansionism. The operation was called Desert Shield. Secretary of State James Baker told Congress that the War Powers Resolution did not apply. But President Bush did get congressional approval shortly before Operation Desert Storm commenced. The aim of this operation was to enforce United Nations Resolution 660, which required Iraq to withdraw from Kuwait.

In 1993 Senator Robert Dole sponsored legislation to prevent President Clinton from sending United States troops to Haiti or Bosnia without congressional authorization. Senator Don Nickles tried to prevent United States forces from operating under United Nations command. Both efforts failed, but they served notice that the president should seek congressional support for military interventions. President Clinton did get congressional approval for the use of United States troops in Somalia. In 1998 he provided advance notice to congressional leaders concerning his plans to order military strikes against a terrorist camp in Afghanistan and a chemical warfare plant in the Sudan.

[69] As quoted in Cronin at p. 146.

Chapter Nine

[1] Nicholas Henry, *Public Administration and Public Affairs,* 6th ed. (Prentice-Hall, 1995), pp. 6–7.

[2] Are powerful, unelected civil servants accountable to the public? Various arguments are advanced in this regard. Some note that agency bureaucrats report to supervisors who are appointed by the president. Agency budgets are coordinated through the president's Office of Management and Budget. Congress makes appropriations decisions and has oversight committees to monitor agency operations. Reorganizations can eliminate agencies or can produce new rival agencies. In these ways unelected civil servants answer to elected officials.

It is sometimes noted that bureaucrats are products of the same political socialization processes as the rest of us. As such, we can count on them to restrain themselves from exercising too much discretionary power. (Are you reassured by this claim?) Further, bureaucrats come from all walks of life and represent broad cross sections of American society. Bureaucratic agencies are much less elitist than other branches are. The problem with this "representative bureaucracy" argument is that once citizens begin working for agencies, they may see the world through agency eyes and seek to advance agency, rather than general, interests.

Another argument is premised on agency self-interest. Bureaucrats fear adverse publicity. They fear that inappropriate actions may awaken public opposition, leading to budget cuts and reductions in force. As such, unelected bureaucrats anticipate how the public would react if the public found out what they did and take steps to prevent a public backlash.

Do unelected civil servants exercise discretionary power? Yes. Are they sufficiently accountable? They are somewhat accountable. "Sufficiency" is in the eye of the beholder.

[3] Al Gore, *Creating a Government That Works Better and Costs Less: The Report of the National Performance Review* (Plume-Penguin, 1993). See also, Martin A. Levin and Mary Bryna Sanger, *Making Government Work: How Entrepreneurial Executives Turn Bright Ideas into Real Results* (Jossey-Bass, 1994).

[4] "Politics: Fable vs. Fact," *Time,* April 1, 1996, p. 62.

[5] See Michael Lipsky, *Street-Level Bureaucracy: Dilemmas of Individuals in the Public Sector* (Russel Sage Foundation, 1980).

[6] See H. Gerth and C. Wright Mills, *From Max Weber: Essays in Sociology* (Oxford University Press, 1946).

[7]Weber believed that certain **patterns of authority** can be observed in any organization. Some organizations are characterized by **charismatic authority.** In such a setting members are devoted to a certain individual on the basis of his or her personal heroism, sanctity, or exemplary character. Obedience is owed to a particular person who, for some reason, deserves it. Other organizations are characterized by **traditional authority.** Once again, obedience is owed to an individual leader or "chief" who occupies a leadership position. Such leaders occupy such positions, however, because of tradition, and the leaders are bound by tradition as they exercise their powers. Still other organizations are characterized by **rational or legal authority.** Here obedience is owed to formally established patterns and rules. The leader assumes an office on the basis of such formal rules. Authority inheres in the *office*, not in the person. When one leader leaves, a successor will be named in accordance with the rules and obedience will be owed to the new officeholder. Obedience is owed to the office, not to the individual who holds it. While Weber conceded that mixed types could exist (for example, a charismatic individual in a position of formal authority), he maintained that rational, legal authority best characterized bureaucratic organizations. (See Weber, *The Theory of Social and Economic Organization*, Free Press, 1947, translated and edited by A. M. Henderson and T. Parsons, pp. 328–40, excerpted as "Legitimate Authority and Bureaucracy," in D. S. Pugh, ed., *Organization Theory*, 2nd ed., Penguin Books, 1984, pp. 15–27.)

[8]Gerth and Mills.

[9]Speaking of Social Security numbers, in 1998 the Selective Service sent Sam Garmize a letter, ordering him to register for the draft or face prosecution. Sam is a *parrot!* Sharon Garmize of Luzerne County, Pennsylvania, informed the government that Sam is a blue crown mealy Amazon parrot. Seeking proof, the Selective Sevice asked for Sam's Social Security number.

[10]In their book, *Organizations* (Wiley, 1958), J. G. March and H. A. Simon describe some of these dysfunctional consequences. See an excerpt from their book, entitled "Dysfunctions of Bureaucracy," in Pugh at pp. 28–39. They cite research by R. K. Merton ("Bureaucratic Structure and Personality," *Social Forces*, 18, pp. 560–68); P. Selznick (*TVA and the Grass Roots*, Berkeley, 1949); and A. W. Gouldner (*Patterns of Industrial Bureaucracy*, Free Press, 1954). Merton found that organization members generalize responses from situations where the response is appropriate to situations where it is inappropriate. Rules, routines, and procedures assume an importance of their own, and decisions are made according to existing categories whether they fit or not. Selznick found that delegation of authority and division of labor produce specialized subgroups that eventually put their own interests ahead of the interests of the organization at large. He termed this phenomenon, "bifurcation of interests." Gouldner found that when organizational members know formal rules and expectations, they work to meet those minimum standards. In sum, unintended learning takes place within bureaucratic organization, and the lessons learned can undermine organizational efficiency.

[11]Woodrow Wilson, "The Study of Administration, *Political Science Quarterly* 2 (June 1887).

[12]Ibid.

[13]Ibid. Frank Goodnau also discussed the politics-administration dichotomy in *Politics and Administration: A Study in Government* (Russell and Russell, 1900).

The distinction between government and business is also of interest. Some argue that governmental administrators should act more like their business counterparts. Efficiency and economy should be stressed. While this idea has appeal, Paul Appleby pointed to some major differences between the public and private sectors in *Big Democracy* (Alfred A. Knopf, 1945).

[14]Frederick Taylor, *Principles of Scientific Management* (Harper & Row, 1911). See also, testimony before the U.S. House of Representatives, January 25, 1911, excerpted as "Scientific Management," in Jay M. Shafritz and Albert C. Hyde, eds., *Classics of Public Administration,* 4th ed. (Harcourt Brace, 1997), pp. 30–32. A more extended excerpt of the same testimony appears in Pugh at pp. 157–76. See also *Bulletin of the Taylor Society* (December 1916), an abstract of an address given by Taylor before the Cleveland Advertising Club, March 3, 1915, two weeks prior to his death. The abstract appears in Jay M. Shafritz and Philip H. Whitbeck, eds., *Classics of Organization Theory* (Moore Publishing, 1978), pp. 9–23.

[15]Another prominent classical theorist was **Henri Fayol.** Fayol, a French executive engineer, developed a general set of **management principles.** His work was originally published in 1916, but it became influential in the United States following the publication of an English translation in 1949. (See Fayol, *General and Industrial Management,* trans. by Constance Storrs, Pitman Publishing, 1949, excerpted as "General Principles of Management," Shafritz and Whitbeck, pp. 23–37.) **Division of work** is one of his key principles. Another is **unity of command.** That is, employees should get orders from one source only. Otherwise, conflicting orders result, causing confusion and damaging morale. Another of Fayol's key principles is **unity of direction.** All employees should work towards the same objective; their efforts should be coordinated. A **scalar chain** is important so communications can flow consistently from superiors, through every link in the chain, to subordinates. Recognizing that undesirable delays might

result, he suggested that temporary **gang planks** be laid down, on occasion, to facilitate more direct communications between parties. Fayol's other principles include **authority, discipline, subordination of the individual to the general interest, remuneration, centralization, order, equity, stability of tenure of personnel, initiative,** and **esprit de corps.** He stressed that these principles were "flexible" and needed to be applied with a sense of "proportion."

Luther Gulick also discussed administrative "principles." (See Luther Gulick and Lyndall Urwick, eds., *Papers on the Science of Administration,* Institute of Public Administration, 1937, excerpted as "Notes on the Theory of Organization," in Shafritz and Hyde, pp. 81–89.) Like Fayol, Gulick stressed the importance of **division of work,** but Gulick described limits on coordination. The first involved the supervisor's limited **span of control.** As a practical matter, one supervisor can supervise only so many subordinates. How many depends on the task. Where work is repetitive and routine, one supervisor can supervise more subordinates than where the work is more diversified. The second limit is related to **unity of command.** Gulick believed that confusion results when an individual takes orders from more than one supervisor.

Gulick is also known for summarizing the duties of chief executives with the acronym **POSDCORB.** The initials stand for **planning** what is to be done, **organizing** the formal structure, **staffing** the organization, **directing** the enterprise, **coordinating** the various parts of the work, **reporting** on what is being done, and **budgeting.** These seven elements could be used to organize subdivisions of the executive office.

Herbert Simon criticized these administrative principles, calling them the **proverbs of administration.** (See Simon, "Proverbs of Administration," *Public Administration Review* 6, Winter 1946, pp. 53–67, reprinted in Shafritz and Hyde, pp. 127–41.) He questioned the utility of these so-called principles on grounds that they were inconsistent, conflicting, and inapplicable to many real-world administrative problems. Proverbs, he noted, occur in mutually contradictory pairs. "Look before you leap," yet "He who hesitates is lost." "The early bird catches the worm," but "Haste makes waste." "The pen is mightier than the sword," still "Might makes right." Regardless of one's circumstances, it is always possible to find a proverb whose rhetoric covers the situation. Similarly, Simon reasoned, that "[f]or almost every principle, one can find an equally plausible and acceptable contradictory principle." (Ibid., p. 127.)

Simon examined several accepted administrative principles. The first is that **specialization** increases administrative efficiency. But there are different ways to specialize. Let's say a school district with three buildings is about to hire three new teachers. Plan A is to assign one new teacher to each building and have the teacher teach all subject areas. Plan B is to let teacher A teach math at all three schools while teacher B teaches social studies at all three schools and teacher C teaches English at all three schools. Which plan is better? The principle does not indicate which kind of specialization will be most efficient. Empirical research is needed to determine what works best where. Until then, the principles are merely proverbs.

The principle of **unity of command** holds that it is unwise to place subordinates in positions where they receive orders from more than one superior. But sometimes, Simon noted, specialized instructions are needed. If an accountant in a school department is subordinate to an educator, does it mean that the head of the finance department should not communicate directly with the accountant regarding the technical accounting aspects of the work?

Another principle is that limiting a supervisor's span of control increases efficiency. The dilemma is that limiting span of control in large organizations produces numerous bureaucratic layers and much red tape. Simon offered an equally plausible alternative: Administrative efficiency is enhanced by minimizing the number of organizational levels through which a matter must pass before it is acted upon. Once again, he called for empirical research to determine the best course of action in particular circumstances. In this way a **science** of administration could be developed.

[16]**Mary Parker Follett** criticized the classical approach. She wrote in the 1920s and anticipated many of the ideas of the later human relations theorists. She advocated **participatory management** as a means for securing worker cooperation. She observed that supervisors cannot simply give orders and expect obedience. Sometimes the subordinate does not understand the order or disagrees with it. Even reasoning with workers may not help if their earlier experiences have instilled resistant **habit patterns.** Orders will be ineffective if they are given in an abusive fashion. People resent **menial treatment.** They resent the expectation that they should follow orders blindly without exercising any judgment. Follett suggested that "orders" should come from **the law of the situation.** Supervisors and subordinates should jointly examine the situation and determine what needs to be done. The situation determines what needs to be done, not the supervisor. Subordinates who participate in this examination will more readily cooperate in doing what needs to be done. The following anecdote is illustrative:

> I think it is told in the life of some famous American that when he was a boy and his mother said, "Go get a pail of water," he always replied, "I won't," before taking up the pail and fetching the water. This is significant; he

resented the command, the command of a person; but he went and got the water, not, I believe, because he had to but because he recognized the demand of the situation.

(See Follett, "The Giving of Orders," Shafritz and Hyde, pp. 53–60, quote at p. 57.)

[17] Follett's observation that how an order is given affects its execution was an early acknowledgment that human workers cannot be handled as if they were machine cogs.

[18] For example, **Edgar Schein** discussed the importance of formal and informal groups. (Schein, *Organizational Psychology*, 2nd ed., Prentice-Hall, 1970, pp. 80–89, excerpted as "Groups and Intergroup Relationships," in Walter E. Natemeyer, *Classics of Organizational Behavior*, Moore Publishing, 1978, pp. 149–56.) **Formal groups** carry out specific tasks for an organization. **Informal groups** form because employees seek ways to satisfy their social needs for friendship and association. Further, informal groups help workers to enhance their self-esteem, increase their power, and help get the job done by picking up the slack for a sick coworker. They also give workers a way to establish and test reality, as when several workers agree that their supervisor's demands seem excessive. Individuals who find a place in a group feel more secure. Schein believed that workers who are able to fulfill such social needs will be more productive.

Rensis Likert also stressed the importance of group relations. (Likert, *New Patterns of Management*, McGraw-Hill, 1961, excerpted as "The Principle of Supportive Relationships," Shafritz and Whitbeck, pp. 149–61.) individuals are most productive when they think their organization's mission is genuinely important and that they are personally contributing to the attainment of that mission. Likert contended that group relationships could help bring about this state of affairs. The response we get from people we are close to, whose approval and support we seek, contributes to our sense of personal worth. If we belong to effective work groups with high performance goals, we will try to satisfy these group expectations. Management should try to build such effective groups, **linking** them to the overall organization by means of people who hold **overlapping group memberships.** Assume that you have influence with your supervisor and that your supervisor has influence with his or her supervisors. In this way your supervisor carries your views upwards to the next level, linking you to the next group and giving you a reason to support decisions made higher up in the organization. Groups, representation, participation, and other familiar political concepts have direct workplace applications. "Industrial democracy" is based upon such ideas.

[19] For example, **Chris Argyris** thought that adult workers have psychological needs to express their capabilities in a setting free from direct control, direction, and supervision. A certain degree of independence is needed to accomplish meaningful tasks. Argyris maintained that traditional organizations treated employees as infants and tried to control all behavior through close supervision. Frustrated adults would cope by withdrawing, daydreaming, loafing, and engaging in "adaptive behavior" that undermined organizational objectives. Argyris recommended enlarging worker responsibilities to provide them with the kind of meaningful challenges needed to motivate them. (See Argyris, *Personality and Organization*, Harper & Row, 1957, pp. 229–37.)

Douglas McGregor said that traditional managers make certain negative assumptions about their workers. (McGregor, "The Human Side of Enterprise," *Management Review*, November 1957, reprinted in Shafritz and Hyde, pp. 192–97.) According to McGregor, managers assume that the average worker is lazy by **nature,** works as little as possible, lacks ambition, dislikes responsibility, prefers to be led, resists change, and is not very bright. McGregor labeled this set of propositions **Theory X.** He did not deny that such behavior occurred, but he did not agree that it was attributable to human nature. Rather, if workers were lazy, McGregor believed, they were that way because traditionally run organizations failed to provide workers with opportunities to satisfy their psychological needs on the job. McGregor offered **Theory Y** as a more optimistic alternative. Theory Y assumed that people are not naturally passive or lazy, they are not naturally resistant to organizational needs, and they are willing to accept responsibility. (See also, William Ouchi, *Theory Z: How American Business Can Meet the Japanese Challenge,* Avon, 1981.)

Borrowing heavily from **Abraham Maslow** (see Maslow, "A Theory of Human Motivation," *Psychological Review* 50, July 1943, pp. 370–96, reprinted in Shafritz and Hyde, pp. 114–21), McGregor explained that human needs are arranged in a hierarchy of importance. The most basic needs are **physiological needs** for food, shelter, clothing, and so on. A hungry person can be motivated by food. A person whose basic needs are unmet can be motivated by wages. But once such needs are relatively satisfied, they no longer motivate behavior. You need air to breathe. If you have air, you are not concerned about it. If you are scuba diving and your air tank malfunctions, you will care about nothing else. When physiological needs are relatively satisfied, **safety needs** emerge. Next come the **social needs,** followed by **ego needs** and, finally, the **need for self-fulfillment** or **self-actualization.** This is the need to realize or actualize one's potential. These ideas are central to motivation theory. They are relevant in the sense that supervisors who want to motivate their subordinates must give them the opportunity to satisfy their higher-level needs at work. Without such opportunities workers will be frustrated, unproductive, and inefficient. To this end McGregor recommended decentralization, delegation of authority, job enlargement, and participative and consultative management techniques.

Frederick Herzberg was convinced that factors related to worker **satisfaction** are separate from factors related to **dissatisfaction.** (Herzberg, *Work and the Nature of Man,* World Publishing, 1966, pp. 71–91, reprinted in Pugh, pp. 334–51.) Dissatisfaction centers on questions concerning company policies and administrative practices, supervision, salary, and working conditions. Worker satisfaction, on the other hand, relates to achievement, recognition, responsibility, and advancement. Dissatisfaction involves the *environment* in which the work is done; satisfaction involves the *work itself.* Herzberg termed the dissatisfiers **hygiene factors** and the satisfiers **motivators.** Supervisors and managers can manipulate the workplace in an attempt to ease dissatisfaction, but hygiene success does not automatically produce motivated workers. Instead, a motivated individual is one who is satisfied that his or her job provides a sense of worth, pride, growth, achievement, and accomplishment. In short, supervisors can "give" dissatisfaction and can eliminate it; they cannot directly "give" workers satisfaction. Workers must achieve satisfaction for themselves by accomplishing something meaningful.

[20]Warren Bennis, "Organizations of the Future," *Personnel Administration* (September–October 1967), reprinted in Shafritz and Hyde, pp. 242–53.

[21]Ibid., p. 248.

[22]Ibid., p. 250.

[23]C. Northcote Parkinson, *Parkinson's Law and Other Studies in Administration* (Houghton Mifflin, 1957), as excerpted in Shafritz and Hyde, *Classics of Public Administration* (Moore Publishing, 1978), pp. 194–98.

[24]Ibid.

[25]**Anthony Downs** noted that the resources necessary for expansion are limited. Wanting more subordinates does not mean that you are going to get them. (Downs, *Inside Bureaucracy*, RAND Corporation, 1967, as excerpted in Shafritz and Hyde, 1997, pp. 262–74.)

Bruce Porter argued that the growth of American bureaucracy was caused by the nation's involvement in four major wars during the twentieth century: World War I, World War II, the Korean War, and the Vietnam War. From 1916 to 1976, almost 2.5 million permanent positions were added to the executive branch payroll. Approximately 80 percent of the total—1.95 million slots—were added during wartime. (Porter, "Parkinson's Law Revisited: War and the Growth of American Government," *The Public Interest* 60, Summer 1980.) During each war hundreds of thousands of new civil servants were hired to deal with wartime needs. During postwar demobilization periods, however, the number of civilian employees laid off was substantially less than the number hired to assist in the war effort. Porter described this pattern of growth as a **ratchet phenomenon.** He reasoned that Congress did not seek more drastic layoffs following the wars for three reasons. First, with soldiers returning home to the labor market, Congress was hesitant to order massive layoffs that would increase unemployment. Second, there was little public demand for layoffs because postwar tax cuts were possible. Third, in the absence of a crisis, Congress acts slowly. In short, the longer deep cutbacks are avoided, the more accepted the enlarged agency becomes. As Parkinson put it in a newspaper interview, in wartime "you can build in two weeks a bureaucracy which would take years to accumulate in peacetime, so you can actually watch the plants grow and proliferate." (Porter citing Parkinson's June 19, 1978, *New York Times* interview.)

[26]Lawrence J. Peter and Raymond Hull, *The Peter Principle* (William Morrow and Company, 1969), as excerpted in Shafritz and Hyde (1978), pp. 347–50, quote at p. 350.

[27]Ibid.

[28]Scott Adams, *The Dilbert Principle: A Cubicle's-Eye View of Bosses, Meetings, Management Fads & Other Workplace Afflictions* (HarperBusiness, 1997), pp. 11–17. People lower on the organizational chart probably find Dilbert more amusing than their supervisors do.

[29]Ibid., quote at p. 14.

[30]The head of the Justice Department is called the attorney general.

[31]In *Myers* v. *United States* (272 U.S. 52, 1926), the Supreme Court upheld President Wilson's removal of a federal postmaster. An 1876 statute specified that with the advice and consent of the Senate, the president could remove postmasters. In this case President Wilson acted without congressional support. The Supreme Court ruled that a president's constitutional power to execute laws in faithful fashion included the power to appoint and remove executive subordinates.

In *Humphrey's Executor (Rathbun)* v. *United States* (295 U.S. 602, 1935), the Court restricted the president's power to remove members of independent commissions like the Interstate Commerce Commission and the Federal Trade Commission. Congress specified the causes for which such appointees could be removed to preserve their independence from political pressure or control. In this case President Franklin Roosevelt removed a Federal Trade Commission officer without demonstrating "inefficiency, neglect of duty, or malfeasance in office." A president can remove purely executive officers, but cannot remove officers who are not essentially executive, who perform quasi-legislative and quasi-judicial duties, and whose removal has been restricted by Congress.

Postmasters are executive officers, subject to presidential removal. Federal Trade Commission officers are not merely arms of the executive, so Congress can restrict their removal. What about the removal of quasi-judicial officers when Congress has said nothing? In *Wiener* v. *United States* (357 U.S. 349, 1958), the Court ruled against President Eisenhower's removal of a War Claims Commission officer under such circumstances. The Court concluded that presidents lack power to remove quasi-legislative and quasi-judicial officers on their own authority.

[32]Hugh Heclo, *A Government of Strangers: Executive Politics in Washington* (Brookings Institution, 1977).

[33]C. Brauer, "Tenure, Turnover, and Postgovernment Employment Trends of Presidential Appointees," in G. Calvin MacKenzie, ed., *The In-and-Outers* (Johns Hopkins University Press, 1987), pp. 1–29, as cited in Henry, p. 238, note 16.

[34]For a general discussion, see Henry, "Managing Human Resources in the Public Sector," pp. 236–90. If you think you might want a civil service job, you should talk with the people in your career planning and placement office.

[35]Ibid., p. 258.

[36]In federal parlance a reduction in force is called a "rif."

[37]"Federal Politics Personnel Manual: The 'Malek Manual,'" *The Bureaucrat* 4 (January 1976), pp. 429–508.

[38]See *Congressional Quarterly* (November 13, 1993), p. 3146.

Chapter Ten

[1]Benjamin Cardozo, *The Nature of the Judicial Process* (Yale University Press, 1921), p. 166.

[2]Alexander Hamilton, *The Federalist*, Number 78, *The Federalist Papers*, ed., Clinton Rossiter (New American Library, 1961), pp. 465–66.

[3]2 Dallas 419 (1793).

[4]Henry J. Abraham, *The Judicial Process*, 6th ed. (Oxford University Press, 1993), p. 171.

[5]Ibid., p. 329.

[6]6 Peters 515 (1832).

[7]Albert J. Beveridge, *The Life of John Marshall*, vol. 4 (Houghton Mifflin Company, 1919), p. 551 (italics supplied), as quoted in Abraham, p. 333, note 106.

[8]417 U.S. 683 (1974).

[9]The vote was eight to zero, and the opinion was issued under Chief Justice Burger's name. Justice Rehnquist recused himself, since he had served in the Justice Department while some of the events at issue occurred.

But what if the president *had* refused to comply? Would nine robed justices have come charging down Pennsylvania Avenue, brandishing law books, shouting at the president that he better comply "or else"? Of course not. And in this case President Nixon would have been under tremendous political pressure to comply. Nevertheless, it is instructive to note that, technically, the courts cannot enforce their own decisions.

[10]See, for example, Robert Bork, "The Case against Political Judging," *National Review*, December 8, 1989.

[11]See, for example, Leonard W. Levy, *Original Intent and the Framers' Constitution* (Macmillan, 1988).

[12]From an 1897 address, reprinted in his *Collected Legal Papers* (A. Harcourt, 1920), p. 187, as quoted in Abraham, p. 11, note 23.

[13]For a brief discussion of *Korematsu* v. *United States* (323 U.S. 2214, 1944); *Hirabayashi* v. *United States* (320 U.S. 81, 1943); and *Ex Parte Endo* (323 U.S. 283, 1944), see Joseph A. Melusky, *The Constitution: Our Written Legacy* (Krieger, 1991), pp. 179–83.

[14]The Court appoints the clerk, the reporter of decisions, the librarian, and the marshal. The chief justice appoints the administrative assistant, the court counsel, the curator, the director of data

systems, and the public information officer to assist with administrative responsibilities. Each justice hires several recent law school graduates to serve as law clerks. The clerk works for a justice for one year, sometimes two. Clerks help justices by reviewing petitions, performing research tasks, and serving as sounding boards.

Congress sometimes authorizes the Court to establish procedural rules for lower federal courts. Such rules now govern civil and criminal cases in district courts, bankruptcy proceedings, admiralty cases, appellate proceedings, and misdemeanor trials before U.S. magistrates.

[15]These courts hear appeals from district courts, territorial courts, tax court, or independent regulatory commissions. The U.S. Court of Appeals for the Federal Circuit has twelve members, and it hears appeals from the Court of International Trade, the U.S. Court of Federal Claims, the U.S. Court of Veterans Appeals, the tariff commission, and the patent office. Appellate courts can affirm a lower court or commission decision, reverse a decision, or remand the case back to the lower court for further review.

[16]District judges appoint U.S. magistrates, law clerks, bailiffs, court reporters, stenographers, clerks, probation officers, and professional administrators to assist them. U.S. magistrates issue arrest warrants; hear evidence to determine whether or not to hold the accused for grand jury action; set bail; conduct pretrial discovery proceedings; review preliminary petitions; appoint counsel for indigent defendants; and, with the consent of parties, try civil cases, misdemeanors, and cases involving minor federal offenses. District judges appoint magistrates for eight- and four-year terms; magistrates must have been members of the bar for at least five years at the time of their selection and are often former law clerks or close associates of the appointing

judge. The president, with the advice and consent of the Senate, appoints a U.S. marshal and a U.S. attorney for each district. The former makes arrests, guards prisoners, and serves court orders. The latter prosecutes for the government in criminal cases. The attorney general of the United States appoints additional assistant U.S. attorneys. The courts of appeals appoint bankruptcy judges, who serve fourteen-year terms as judicial officers of the district courts.

[17]In cases involving citizens of different states, however, state courts can handle disputes exceeding $75,000 if the litigants agree.

[18]**The United States Court of International Trade** was established as the Board of United States General Appraisers in 1890. In 1926 it became the United States Customs Court. Congress changed it from a legislative to a special constitutional court in 1956. In 1980 Congress named it the United States Court of International Trade. It has nine judges, no more than five of whom can be from the same political party. The court has a clerk and deputy clerks, a librarian, court reporters, and other supporting personnel. Cases may be tried before a jury. The judges sit in panels of three at various ports of entry. Its main offices are in New York City.

The court has jurisdiction over civil actions against the United States in which rulings and appraisals made by customs officials are disputed. Appeals from its decisions are taken to the U.S. Court of Appeals for the Federal Circuit. Ultimately, review may be sought by the U.S. Supreme Court.

Special legislative courts include the **United States Court of Federal Claims.** The court of claims was established as a constitutional court in 1855. In 1982 it was replaced by the claims court, an Article 1 legislative court. Its name was changed to the United States Court of Federal Claims in 1992. The court has one chief judge, designated by the president, and fifteen associate judges. The judges are appointed for fifteen-year terms by the president with the advice and consent of the Senate. The court handles suits for damages by citizens against the government. It has nationwide jurisdiction. Trials are conducted before individual judges at locations most convenient to citizens.

The court has jurisdiction over claims seeking monetary judgments against the government. Such claims must be based on the U.S. Constitution, a federal law, an executive department regulation, or a contract with the United States. Congress sometimes gives the court jurisdiction over specific types of claims. Judgments can be appealed to the U.S. Court of Appeals for the Federal Circuit.

The **United States Court of Appleals for the Armed Forces** (formerly the U.S. court of Military Appeals) was established as an Article 1 legislative court in 1950. Subject to *certiorari* review by the U.S. Supreme Court, it is the final appellate tribunal in court-martial cases. It has five civilian judges, though they may hold reserve commissions in "any armed force." They are appointed by the president, with the advice and consent of the Senate, for staggered fifteen-year terms. They are eligible for reappointment. The president can designate the chief judge and may also, following notice and a hearing, remove a judge for neglect of duty, for malfeasance, or because of a mental or physical disability. Judges must be members of the bar of a federal court or of the highest state court. Since the 1950s military defendants have found that most provisions of the Bill of Rights and standards used in other federal courts have been applied to military hearings.

At its discretion the U.S. Court of Appeals for the Armed Forces reviews decisions of courts-martial involving prison sentences of more than one year and/or punitive discharges. The court must review cases certified for its review by the judge advocate general, decisions involving admirals or generals, and cases involving the imposition of the death penalty, regardless of the rank of the accused. Prior to 1983 there was no direct appeal from the Court of Appeals for the Armed Forces. The U.S. Supreme Court sometimes used habeas corpus proceedings to reach cases. 1983 amendments authorize the U.S. Supreme Court to review decisions of the U.S. Court of Appeals for the Armed Forces through discretionary writs of *certiorari*.

The **United States Tax Court** was established in 1924 as the United States Board of Tax Appeals, an independent agency in the executive branch. In 1942 its name was changed to the Tax Court of the United States. In 1969 it became an Article 1 legislative court, and its name was changed to the United States Tax Court. It has nineteen judges who are appointed to fifteen-year terms by the president with the advice and consent of the Senate. The chief judge is elected by his or her colleagues to a two-year term. The chief judge can call into service additional senior judges. The chief judge also appoints fourteen special trial judges who serve at the pleasure of the court. The court conducts trials at various locations within the United States, but the office of the court is in Washington, D.C. A single judge or a special trial judge conducts each trial session. The court deals with claims that the Internal Revenue Service misinterpreted the tax code as it specifically applied to the plaintiff. As such the commissioner of the Internal Revenue Service is always the respondent party.

The taxpayer may opt to use simplified procedures in small tax cases, provided that the court's decision is accepted as final and not subject to review by another court. The maximum for such cases is $10,000 for any disputed year. All other decisions are subject to review by the courts of appeals and, subsequently, by the U.S. Supreme Court through *certiorari* appeal.

The **United States Court of Veterans Appeals** was established as an Article 1 legislative court in 1988. It consists of a chief judge and at least two, but not more than six, associate judges. Judges are appointed to fifteen-year terms by the president with the advice and consent of the Senate.

The court has exclusive jurisdiction to review decisions of the Board of Veterans Appeals. The court may not review the schedule of ratings for disabilities. The court's decisions can be appealed to the U.S. court of appeals for the Federal Circuit.

Territorial courts are also in operation. Congress established Article 1 legislative courts for Guam in 1900, the Virgin Islands in 1917, and the Northern Mariana Islands (administered by the United States under a United Nations trusteeship agreement) in 1978. The Canal Zone had such a court from 1912 to 1982, but it was abolished pursuant to the Panama Canal Act of 1979. There is one judge each in Guam and the Northern Mariana Islands and two in the Virgin Islands. The judges are appointed to ten-year terms by the president with the advice and consent of the Senate.

These courts have jurisdiction over questions of national law as well as over many local matters that, within the states, are decided in state courts. Decisions can be appealed to a U.S. court of appeals.

Congress established a district court for Puerto Rico in 1900. Since Puerto Rico has separate local courts, its territorial court has jurisdiction only over cases involving national law. This court was established under Article 3 and, like other district courts, is classified as a constitutional court. Its judges are appointed to life (or "good behavior") terms.

Additional judicial bodies include the **Judicial Panel on Multidistrict Litigation.** This panel was created in 1968. It consists of seven federal judges chosen by the chief justice from appellate and district courts. It coordinates and consolidates proceedings by temporarily transferring to a single district pending actions in different districts that involve one or more common questions of fact.

The **Judicial Conference of the United States** was established in 1922. The chief justice is required to submit to Congress an annual report of the Judicial Conference and its recommendations for legislation. The chief justice heads this group, which also includes the chief judges from the thirteen federal circuits, twelve district court judges, and two bankruptcy judges. The Judicial Conference meets at least twice a year to make a "comprehensive survey of the conditions of business in the courts of the United States," to plan for the assignment of judges to or from circuits or districts, and to submit suggestions to courts "in the interest of uniformity and expedition of business." It also sets policy for the Administrative Office of the U.S. Courts.

The **Administrative Office of the United States Courts** was created in 1939. After consultation with the Judicial Conference, the chief justice appoints its director and deputy director. It handles the nonjudicial administrative business of federal courts, including maintenance of workload statistics and disbursement of funds.

The **Federal Judicial Center** was created in 1967 to improve judicial administration in U.S. courts. The center is the judicial branch's agency for planning and policy research, systems development, and continuing education.

The **United States Sentencing Commission** was instituted in 1984 to establish sentencing policies and practices for federal courts, including guidelines concerning the appropriate form and severity of punishment for persons convicted of federal crimes. For more information, see Henry J. Abraham, *The Judicial Process* (Oxford University Press, 1993); Harold W. Stanley and Richard G. Niemi, *Vital Statistics on American Politics* (Congressional Quarterly, 1994); *The United States Government Manual*

1998/1999 (Office of Federal Register, National Archives and Records Administration, 1998).

[19]416 U.S. 312 (1974).

[20]Generally, the Court hears oral argument for the first three days of these weeks, meeting from 10:00 a.m. until 12:00 noon and again from 1:00 p.m. until 3:00 p.m. The justices spend remaining days considering petitions and writing opinions. Seating is limited. Some seats are reserved for the press, family members, and members of the bar. Fewer than two hundred seats are available for the public on a first-come, first-served basis. There are usually two public lines for these seats—one is a three-minute-stay line and the other is a stay-as-long-as-you-wish line.

[21]Joan Biskupic, "Rehnquist Blasts Poor Preparation for Arguing Cases," *Washington Post*, May 20, 1996, A19.

[22]Ibid.

[23]As quoted by Abraham, p. 192, note 105, citing "Memorial for Stanley Silverberg," *Of Law and Men*, ed., Philip Elman (Harcourt, Brace, 1956), pp. 320–21.

[24]Abraham, p. 192, citing Edwin McElwain, "The Business of the Supreme Court as Conducted by Chief Justice Hughes," 63 *Harvard Law Review* 6 (1949).

[25]Nine chairs surround a rectangular conference table. Each chair bears a justice's nameplate. The chief justice sits at the south end of the table, and the senior associate justice sits at the north end. Three associate justices sit on one side, and four sit on the other. Chief Justice John Marshall's portrait observes the scene. See Abraham, pp. 195–96.

[26]Bob Woodward and Scott Armstrong, *The Brethren: Inside the Supreme Court* (Simon and Schuster, 1979).

[27]Rehnquist noted that the justices do not always adhere to this tradition. In the interest of saving time, they sometimes vote immediately after they offer their views (remarks to participants in a Washington Center sponsored academic seminar on "The Legal System and Legal Careers," January 1984).

[28]Abraham, p. 125. For a general discussion, see Abraham, pp. 199–217.

[29]Justice Harlan's dissent in *Plessy* v. *Ferguson* (163 U.S. 537, 1896) influenced the Court when it overruled *Plessy* years later in *Brown* v. *Board of Education of Topeka* (347 U.S. 483, 1954).

[30]Abraham, pp. 218–19.

[31]Michael Kramer, "Cheap Shots at Judges," *Time*, April 22, 1996, p. 57.

[32]Anthony Lewis, "Destroy the Guardians," *New York Times*, April 11, 1997.

[33]The ratings have been controversial, however, and in 1997 Senator Orrin Hatch (R-UT), chairman of the Senate Judiciary Committee, announced that these ratings would no longer be used.

[34]As quoted in Abraham at p. 65.

[35]News conference at Kennebunkport, Maine, July 1, 1991 (C-SPAN, "Supreme Court Justice Nominated," Kennebunkport, Maine, July 1, 1991, ID: 18649).

[36]Displeasure with Stevens's gender contributed to particularly careful scrutiny of his appellate court record in sex discrimination cases. See Joseph Melusky, *Justice John Paul Stevens' Equal Protection Analysis* (University Microfilms International, 1983).

[37]For a discussion of the Haynsworth and Carswell nominations, see Abraham, pp. 77–80.

[38]As a point of information, Sandra Day O'Connor and William Rehnquist were classmates at the Stanford University School of Law. Rehnquist was first in the class; O'Connor was third. How would you like to be the person who was second? You are attending a class reunion, and the conversation might go something like this: "Well, Bill and Sandy here seem to have done pretty well for themselves. Tell us, what have you been up to?"

[39]Ibid., pp. 71–72.

[40]*Northern Securities* v. *United States* (193 U.S. 197, 1904). The case went Roosevelt's way by a five-to-four vote, but Justice Holmes voted with the minority.

[41]As quoted by Abraham at p. 74, citing James E. Clayton, *The Making of Justice: The Supreme Court in Action* (E. P. Dutton, 1964), note 71, p. 47.

Chief Justice Earl Warren was appointed to the Court in 1953. The Warren Court years were marked by judicial activism and generally liberal decisions. The Warren Court oversaw an expansion in the rights and liberties of individuals, including the rights of persons accused of crimes. It might be surprising to note that a moderate, Republican president, Dwight D. Eisenhower, was appointed to the Warren Court. Here is the rest of the story. When Eisenhower was campaigning for the presidency, he was concerned about carrying California. He approached Warren, a prominent politician and governor of California, and asked for his help. Eisenhower promised to appoint Warren to the Supreme Court in return. When Chief Justice Vinson died in 1953, Eisenhower kept his promise and nominated Warren. Some rank Warren with John Marshall as one of the two greatest chief justices in history. Eisenhower did not agree. Looking back on the Warren appointment in later years, Eisenhower reputedly called it, "the biggest damn fool mistake I ever made." See Daniel B. Rodriguez, "Earl Warren," *The Supreme Court Justices: A Biographical Dictionary,* ed. Melvin I. Urofsky (Garland, 1994), pp. 500–09.

[42]At the time only six justices served on the Supreme Court. Congress later increased the number to nine. Robert Harrison declined his appointment in the apparent belief that his post as chancellor of Maryland was more important. John Rutledge was officially listed as a member of the Court for three terms, but he never attended sessions. Eventually, he resigned formally so he could accept the chief judgeship in South Carolina.

[43]1 Cranch 137; 2 L.Ed. 60 (1803).

[44]Presidents are now inaugurated on January 20.

[45]Such a writ is a judicial order requiring an official to perform his mandated duty. Marbury's argument was that Madison lacked discretion to decide whether or not he should deliver Marbury's commission. The *discretionary* decision was made by President Adams. A secretary of state's job is simply to deliver the envelope in much the same way that a mail carrier delivers the mail.

[46]Some critics argue that all public officials take an oath to uphold the Constitution, so all must interpret the Constitution in order to uphold it. If the Supreme Court decides that a law is constitutionally defective, it should be the lawmakers' responsibility to effect a remedy. Others contend that once Marshall concluded that the Supreme Court lacked jurisdiction, he should not have proceeded to address the merits. Still others maintain that, in light of his own failure to deliver Marbury's commission, he should have recused himself.

[47]As discussed previously, President Nixon indicated that he was looking for a definitive decision from the Supreme Court. Commentators speculated that he might refuse to comply with a decision that he perceived as less than definitive. Such speculations were never tested, as the Supreme Court reached a unanimous decision in an opinion issued under Chief Justice Burger's name.

[48]*United States* v. *Nixon,* 418 U.S. 683 (1974).

[49]Recall that Nixon had appointed Ford to the vice presidency following Spiro Agnew's earlier resignation.

[50]See, for example, Phyllis Schlafly, "It's Time to Reform the Imperial Judiciary," from *The Phyllis Schlafly Report* (September 1981); William A. Stanmeyer, "Judicial Supremacy," in ed., Robert W. Whitaker, *The New Right Papers* (New York, 1982); and Joseph Sobran, ""Minority Rule," *National Review,* December 31, 1985.

[51]William J. Brennan Jr. "The Constitution of the United States: Contemporary Ratification,"

presented at a symposium at Georgetown University, Washington, DC, October 12, 1985. As quoted in George McKenna and Stanley Feingold, *Taking Sides: Clashing Views on Controversial Political Issues,* 6th ed. (Dushkin, 1989), pp. 143–49.

Conclusions

[1]An ironic personal note: As I write, my car is at a service station. I had it towed in yesterday after my brakes broke. Now I know what those yellow and red warning lights meant.

[2]Is something wrong with politicians? Again, *probably.* Is something wrong with *all* politicians? *No.* Resist the easy temptation to dismiss politics with a cynical wave of your hand. Many officials are dedicated public servants doing the best they can.

But then a president attempts to evade legal problems by torturing the English language. He attempts to survive politically by offering semiapologies and attacking the tactics of his critics. Members of Congress conduct impeachment inquiries amid charges of partisan gamesmanship. The search for heroic figures proves daunting and threatens to turn democracy into "de*mock*racy."

It is important to keep perspective, however. Clinton's crisis was not a constitutional crisis. The Constitution provides the impeachment tool for use in extreme circumstances. It permits the removal of public officials unfit for office. Two questions are most relevant: First, do circumstances really warrant impeachment? Second, if so, do we have the will to proceed?

[3]"Fallows Blames Media for Democracy's Decay," *Brown Daily Herald,* March 1, 1996.

[4]Ibid.

[5]Ibid.

[6]Ibid.

[7]Ibid.

[8]Senator Bill Bradley, "Freeing Democracy from the Power of Money," January 16, 1996, address at the John F. Kennedy School of Government at Harvard University. The text of Bradley's speech can be found at http://ksgwww.harvard.edu/~ksgpress/bradley.htm.

[9]Bradley summary can be found at http://ksgwww.harvard.edu/~ksgpress/bradsum.htm.

[10]Robert W. Merry, "A Shay or a Scow? America's Democracy Could Go to Pieces All at Once—Or It May Be Unsinkable," *American Caucus,* October 10–12, 1992, p. 10.

[11]The nationwide telephone survey contacted six hundred teenagers between the ages of thirteen and seventeen. The survey's margin of error is plus or minus 4 percent. The complete survey—including questions, answers, and results—can be accessed at http://www.constitutioncenter.org.

[12]As quoted in "More Teens Can Name Three Stooges Than Can Name Three Branches of Government," September 2, 1998, http://www.constitutioncenter.org/QuestionnairePress.htm.

[13]*The American Freshman: National Norms for Fall 1998,* Higher Education Research Institute, 3005 Moore Hall, UCLA Graduate School of Education and Information Studies, Box 951521, Los Angeles, California 90095-1521.

[14]The Constitution's basic premise is popular sovereignty or rule by the people, not rule by the government. Akhil Reed Amar and Alan Hirsch elaborate on this principle in *For the People: What the Constitution Really Says about Your Rights* (Free Press, 1998). They discuss the people's right to amend the Constitution, jury service, and the right to use courts to curb excesses of government power.

Also of interest is *The Public Voice in a Democracy at Risk,* edited by Michael Salvador and Patricia M. Sias (Praeger, 1998). The book discusses obstacles that inhibit citizen participation and the need to better prepare citizens for contemporary political life.

[15]For detailed suggestions on steps an individual can take, see Katherine Isaac, *Practicing*

Democracy: A Guide to Student Action (St. Martin's Press, 1998). In the preface Isaac states that "a healthy democracy requires not only the *right* to participate in the political system, but that its citizens constantly exercise and expand those rights and opportunities" (p. viii). Individuals can take action by distributing pamphlets, attending and speaking at public meetings, gathering or signing petitions, writing letters or making phone calls, boycotting products, blowing the whistle on unethical practices, or joining groups. The book contains practical advice for how to effectively engage in such activities.

Minichapter

[1]H. Hugh Heclo, "Review Article: Policy Analysis," British Journal of Political Science 2 (January 1972), pp. 84–85, as cited in Charles O. Jones, An Introduction to the Study of Public Policy, 2nd ed. (Duxbury Press, 1977), at p. 4, note 3.

[2]Jones, p. 4.

[3]Theodore J. Lowi and Benjamin Ginsberg, American Government: Freedom and Power, brief 4th ed. (W. W. Norton & Company, 1996), p. 335.

[4]See David Easton, A Framework for Political Analysis (Prentice-Hall, 1965). See also, Thomas R. Dye, Understanding Public Policy (Prentice-Hall, 1972), pp. 18–20.

[5]In the interests of brevity, an in-depth look at a policy case study is not included in this book. Such case studies can be illuminating, but they can become dated rather quickly. If you want to examine specific policy developments in more detail, see Bob Woodward, The Agenda: Inside the Clinton White House (Simon and Schuster, 1994) for a discussion of President Clinton's efforts to enact his first budget. See also Steven Waldman, The Bill—How Legislation Really Becomes Law: A Case Study of the National Service Bill (Penguin Books, 1995).

Many fine case studies are available, and I encourage interested instructors to select one that is especially relevant to your own students. This brief introduction to policy-making processes and categories is designed to help frame your discussions.

[6]Theodore J. Lowi, "Distribution, Regulation, and Redistribution: The Functions of Government," in Randall B. Ripley, ed., Public Policies and Their Politics (Norton, 1966), as cited in Steven V. Monsma, American Politics, 3rd ed. (Dryden Press, 1976), at p. 322–23, note 1.

[7]See Monsma, p. 342.

[8]Ibid., p. 324.

[9]See Lowi and Ginsberg, pp. 336–38.

[10]See Monsma, pp. 323–44. Pork barrel legislation, discussed in the chapter on Congress, is an example of distributive or promotional policy. As an example, see the 1998 transportation bill ("Congress Clears Huge Transportation Bill," CQ Weekly, May 23, 1998, pp. 98–100).

[11]See Monsma, p. 324.

[12]There are crises and there are crises! It is one thing to learn that a foreign power has placed missiles in a threatening location. It is quite another to learn that those missiles have been launched and are heading this way.

[13]See Monsma, pp. 342–43 and 355–59.

[14]Ibid., pp. 342–55.

Index

Page numbers followed by *f* and *t* refer to figures and tables, respectively.

A

access
   to ballot, 103
   by PACs, 109–110
accountability, and democracy, 69. *See also* anticipated reactions
activity-passivity, as baseline for presidential character types, 125
Administrative Careers with America exam, 228
administrative courts, federal, 237
administrative theory, 220–222
advisors, presidential, 203
advisory opinions, 234
affirmative action, 29–30
agencies, independent, 205, 226
American Bar Association, 246–248
American Presidency, The, (Rossiter), 188
amicus curiae brief, 113, 243
Annapolis, and Articles of Confederation, 26
anticipated reactions, 7, 78–79
Anti-Federalists, 32–33, 97
appellate courts, intermediate, 236, 239
appellate jurisdiction, 237, 239
appointive positions, in bureaucracy, 227
appointments
   interest group influence and, 111, 113
   judicial, 113, 246–251
   presidential, 227–228
apportionment, 155–157
apprenticeship periods, in Congress, 158
army, constitutional provision for, 44
Article 1 of US Constitution, 36, 43, 237

Clause 8, 43–44
Clause 11, 44
Clause 12–16, 44–45
Clause 18, 45
Section 7, 163
Section 8, 45
Article 2 of US Constitution, 36, 45
Article 3 of US Constitution, 36, 46, 237, 252
Article 4 of US Constitution, 46
Article 5 of US Constitution, 46
Article 6 of US Constitution, 46, 252
Articles of Confederation, 25–26
arts, constitutional provision for, 43–44
attitude, 69

B

bail, excessive, 59
Baker v. *Carr,* 157
ballot, access to, 103
Barber, James David, 125–126
bargaining
   by members of Congress, 172
   by president, 195
Barron v. *Baltimore,* 57, 62
beltway issues, and members of Congress, 151
Bennis, Warren, 222
bicameralism, 154
   as constitutional compromise, 27
Bill of Rights, 46–65
bill of rights, written, 46
Bork, Robert, 62
Boston Tea Party (1773), 24
boundaries, of systems, 11–12
Bradley, Bill, proposal to restore democracy, 260–261

D